My Dearest Angel

LETCHER AND PAUL FAMILY TREES

LETCHER FAMILY
Governor John L. and Susan Holt L.
(1813–1884) | (1823–1899)

1 William Holt L. (1844) died in infancy
2 Elizabeth Stuart L. (1846–1914) Harrison
   one son, John Letcher Harrison, d. 1950
3 Samuel Houston L. (1848–1914)
   never married
4 Andrew Holt L. (1850–1860)
5 John Davidson L. (1853–1938)
   married late, no offspring
6 Susan Holt L. (1855) died at birth
7 Margaret Kinney L. (1857–1938) Showell
   *four children, their descendants now living in
   Delaware*
8 Mary Davidson L. (1859) died at birth
9 Virginia Lee L. (1862–1941) Stevens
   two stillborn children
10 Fannie Wilson L. (1864–1928)
   never married
11 **Greenlee Davidson L.** (1867–1954),
   m. Katherine Seymour Paul
   *three children, one of whom lived to
   perpetuate the Letcher name*

PAUL FAMILY
Judge John P. and Kate S. Green P.
(1839–1901) | (1847–1927)

1 **Katherine Seymour P.** (1876–1947),
   m. Greenlee Davidson Letcher
2 John Rockingham P.(1877–1879) died young
3 Virginia Maria P. (1880–1933) *never married*
4 Lilian C. P. (1882–1953) Flynn
   married late, no children
5 John P. (1883–1964)
   married twice, no children
6 Charles Green P. (1886–1943)
   never married
7 Garrett Seymour P. (1888–1960)
   *married twice, three children to
   perpetuate the Paul name*

JOHN SEYMOUR LETCHER, M. ELIZABETH MARSTON

1 Katie Paul Letcher Lyle
   a son and a daughter
2 John S. Letcher, Jr.
   three daughters
3 Elizabeth Letcher Greenlee
   a son and a daughter
4 Peter M. Letcher
   two daughters

My Dearest Angel

A Virginia Family Chronicle, 1895–1947

KATIE LETCHER LYLE

Foreword by Elizabeth Forsythe Hailey

OHIO UNIVERSITY PRESS

Athens

OHIO UNIVERSITY PRESS, ATHENS, OHIO 45701

© 2002 by Katie Letcher Lyle

Printed in the United States of America

All rights reserved

Ohio University Press books are printed on acid-free paper ∞ ™

10 09 08 07 06 05 04 03 02   5 4 3 2 1

Library of Congress Cataloging-in-Publication Data

Lyle, Katie Letcher, 1938–

My dearest angel : a Virginia family chronicle, 1895–1947 / Katie Letcher Lyle.

   p. cm.

Includes bibliographical references and index.

ISBN 0-8214-1410-0 (acid-free paper) — ISBN 0-8214-1411-9 (pbk. : acid-free paper)

   1. Letcher, Greenlee D. (Greenlee Davidson), b. 1867. 2. Letcher, Katherine Seymour P. (Katherine Seymour Paul), 1876–1947. 3. Legislators—Virginia—Biography. 4. Virginia—Social life and customs. 5. Virginia—Biography. I. Title.

CT275.L3727 L94 2002

975.5'042'0922—dc21

[B]

2001036348

THIS BOOK IS DEDICATED THE MEMORY OF MY PRECIOUS GRANDPARENTS, who of course gave me life, but who also gave me love, fun, and self-confidence in our years together, and the subject matter for *My Dearest Angel, When the Fighting Is All Over,* and *Good-bye to Old Peking*. And to the memory of all the others in this book who have gone on. And lastly, to all my living cousins, descendants of the people this book is about.

Contents

Illustrations

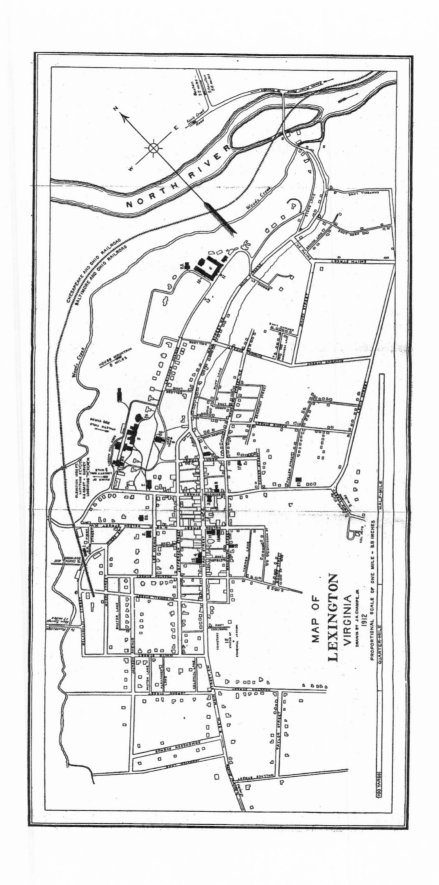

MAP OF
LEXINGTON
VIRGINIA

DRAWN BY J.A.CHAMPLIN,JR.
1912

PROPORTIONAL SCALE OF ONE MILE = 8.8 INCHES

NORTH RIVER

Foreword

As a novelist, I am fascinated by the subject of marriage—especially the often dramatic conflicts and accommodations that are inevitable in a lasting marriage. When the participants are playing for keeps, the stakes are immediately higher and the game more compelling.

In the lifelong correspondence between her much-loved paternal grandparents, whose marriage vows were pledged in Victorian times and tested through two world wars, and the private battles that often inflict the greater scars, Katie Letcher Lyle has constructed a saga that compels our attention and our sympathy. What makes these letters unique and transforms them from a record whose interest is primarily social and historical is the guiding eye of a loving granddaughter whose own memories enrich, inform, and frame this correspondence, adding richness and resonance to the narrative.

Letters are an inherently dramatic device, as I discovered in my first attempt at fiction. They span time, eliminate the need for physical description, allow each character a distinctive voice, and challenge the reader to look between the lines and hear what is being said in the silences.

These letters speak volumes. The torrent of words exchanged in the fevered first encounters between the ardent young suitor and the beautiful object of his affection reflect emotions raging unchecked. We know the passionate tone will be tempered by time, but what a delight it is all the same to allow ourselves to be carried along by the unchecked currents of emotion.

Who could not wish for a lover who would write: "Your letters so full of the love my life and heart crave alone enable me to possess my soul in patience until I can return to my heart's home, to you, Sweet Angel, My Own, My Love, My Life."

And, in the beginning, the response is equal in passion: "Dear heart, my great love for you has made a woman of me and it is no girl's fancy for a man older than herself and bright and strong but the love of a woman's life that I give my heart's beloved now."

Young love is always heated and headstrong, and full and flowery expression was encouraged at the turn of the century, so the beginning of this courtship is described in the kind of effusive, overwrought language that seems appropriate for the emotional state of the correspondents.

The heart of drama is conflict—and conflict is inevitable when the male and female leads are as opposite in temperament as Katie and Greenlee. She was shy, private, sharp, and suspicious but fiercely loyal to family. He was warm, generous, trusting, at times almost indiscriminate in his affections although unwavering in his devotion to his "beautiful angel." However, the conflicts in this marriage were more subterranean than overt, and the protagonists tended to deal with them in an indirect manner more befitting the times than the confrontation demanded in a contemporary relationship. Greenlee traveled and found comfort and diversion in hard work and congenial company while Katie went back home to Harrisonburg to take refuge in the less demanding roles of daughter and sister.

Much is left to the reader to imagine. The number of words devoted to a topic is in no proportionate relation to the importance of the subject described—or its impact on the life of the participant. The reader must surmise what is truly being felt from what is being said—or not being said.

There are at least twice as many words from Greenlee as there are from Katie. Like a twentieth-century Pepys, he is interested in all the details of the daily pageant—the stories he hears, the people he meets. Early in their marriage Katie writes affectionately: "My Dear, Dear Love—If you were shipwrecked on the coast of Patagonia, I believe you'd run across old acquaintances or make new ones and be invited to supper with the chief of the tribe that very night."

Greenlee chooses to live in the larger arena, and his letters provide a vivid picture of a specific time and place—a small but intellectually and historically prominent town in Virginia in the first half of the twentieth century. His correspondence is rich with social and historical significance. With Katie, on the other hand, the drama is confined to the timeless conflicts within the family that provide the stuff of literature. Her retreat into silence following the death of first one son and then another is as heartrending as the loudest lamentation from a bereaved mother.

A gifted southern storyteller who has lived much of the story being told through these letters, Katie Letcher Lyle brings a sensitive eye and ear to the shaping of this massive correspondence. She combines a strong narrative sensibility with a historian's appreciation of context and vivid detail. The cardinal rule of writing is, "The more specific you are, the more universal," and these letters are full of wonderfully original images and turns of phrase that a writer of fiction can only envy.

Like any drama, a lasting marriage falls into scenes and acts, and the author, attuned to these natural divisions, has created a clear and coherent structure for the book. Her introductions to each segment are scrupulously researched and supported by additional correspondence and insightful references and at the same time infused with a granddaughter's affection for her subjects and the convergence of her own history with the story she is telling.

This history of a marriage through letters is of particular interest now, at the end of the century—and the millennium. The time when people put their personal histories into permanent written form is ending. A contemporary relationship relies on the telephone and cyberspace for communication, leaving no paper trail for succeeding generations to follow.

My Dearest Angel presents us with two lives in their entirety, beginning with the family histories and early childhoods of the two protagonists. From the beginning the reader is caught up in the compelling drama of watching two lives unfold, come together, bear children, and then finally and inevitably part.

However, beyond the story of Katie and Greenlee and their life together, these letters provide a richly human history of life in America in the first half of the twentieth century, and I, for one, came away from reading this intimate correspondence with a very personal sense of how much we have lost.

A hundred years ago a marriage was much more than a two-character play. A husband and wife starting life together could count on a large and colorful cast of supporting characters, usually blood related, to complicate at times but more often than not, as in the case of Katie and Greenlee, to aid and abet their evolving life as a family. Although Katie seems to have found little comfort in the physical proximity of Greenlee's family, they were clearly a consolation to him during Katie's many absences, and the closeness and deep affection between Katie and her family served to strengthen and buttress the marriage in times of illness and stress. Greenlee, whether because of his open and loving nature or an instinctive understanding of his wife's physical and emotional frailty, welcomed the presence of Katie's mother and sisters into their lives. He visited them at their home in Harrisonburg when Katie was in residence and often when she was not.

His mother-in-law, still young and vibrant when her husband died, comes across in her letters as a playful, loving, and loyal figure whose pride and pleasure in her family remained constant till the end of her life. When Katie's many (and often unexplained) illnesses took her away from home, the affectionately named "Nuzzer Mudder" moved into place to look after her daughter's house, husband, and children. And Nuzzer Mudder was often accompanied by her unmarried daughter, Lilian, called "Idge." Greenlee was so grateful for their help he invited them to move in. If these two young people had been forced to face the challenges of married life alone as young couples in this age of nuclear families often do, one wonders whether the marriage would have survived.

Marriages in the first half of the twentieth century were subjected to severe historical challenges—two world wars and the Great Depression—that put their protagonists to the test in ways previously unimagined but strengthened and enriched the rest of their lives. For many Americans, World War I was their bridge to countries and cultures they never expected to experience firsthand. Greenlee was invigorated by his wartime adventures and Katie was equally recharged and newly empowered by the growing independence he experienced as a result of his absence from the home front. Knowing that he was away in the service of a larger cause, she saw him for the first time in their marriage as more hero than husband. And, like many women of her time, she was emboldened by the discovery of how much she was capable of doing on her own.

I am writing this foreword in Dallas, Texas, where I am visiting my parents who are celebrating their sixty-second anniversary. They still live in the home where I spent my high school years, and when I visit I stay in the garage apartment where my husband and I spent our first summer of married life. So my reading of *My Dearest Angel* is resonant with the memory of other marriages. My parents have seldom spent a night apart—and I can only regret that when they die and this house is sold, no letters will be found to show the ebb and flow of their relationship from 1937 into the new millennium. For a novelist there is only one way to confront this silence, and their unwritten correspondence is already taking shape inside my head.

Katie Letcher Lyle is more fortunate, and as readers we can only be grateful that she has chosen to share her good fortune—and this legacy of illuminating correspondence—with us.

—ELIZABETH FORSYTHE HAILEY

Preface

The source of this book are the letters of Greenlee D. Letcher and Katie Paul Letcher. I happen to be a writer, they happened to be my paternal grandparents. To explain how the letters fell into my keeping, and why I found them worthy of a book, I must start with the Civil War.

Near the end of the war, my great-grandfather, ex-governor of Virginia (1860–64) John Letcher, was living back in his hometown of Lexington when the Union forces, under the unpredictable General David Hunter, occupied Lexington in June of 1864, six months after his term had expired. The small, hilly town in the Shenandoah Valley, built along the north fork of the James, later called the Maury, River, was home to the Virginia Military Institute, which had trained hundreds of Confederate warriors. Letcher expected he'd be hanged as a traitor if caught by the Yankee troops and so removed to a location in the mountains nearby. When they couldn't catch Letcher, the Northern forces spitefully burned his house down, giving Mrs. Letcher ten minutes (some sources say *three*) to get her six resident children up, dressed, and away from the house. Everything they owned was destroyed or stolen, and the family for a time after that lived wherever they could find lodgings, aided by the charity of cousins, friends, and neighbors, accepting gifts of furniture later from their friend, Robert E. Lee. So almost none of the Letcher letters and papers predate the Civil War. Eventually, the governor's grown children built houses nearby on Letcher Avenue, between VMI and Washington and Lee, only one of them leaving Lexington. The governor died in 1884, and Mrs. Letcher and her unmarried sister died in 1899 and 1900. As the governor's eleven children aged and died, paper memorabilia passed from attic to attic, obviously with losses at every step.

My grandfather, born in 1867, was the youngest of the governor's eleven children, and my father was the only surviving child in the next generation. Thus, much family memorabilia ended up in his garage, whence I rescued after his death three huge cartons of letters, postcards, papers, documents, check registers, Confederate bills, files, receipts, old photographs, notebooks, envelopes of stamps, deeds, bills, depositions, certificates, proclamations, diplomas, and market lists belonging to four generations of my family.

VMI was burned down by General David Hunter's troops in June of 1864.

Prior to my discovery of the letters between my grandparents, I had been reading diaries of nineteenth-century women for ten years, looking for one to edit, or at least hoping to be able to write a book about the diaries. I had many questions to ask of these dignified and private diarists: were you happy? did you have a concept of happiness? did you expect love in your marriage? what did you feel about the crowding in of unmarried relatives? were you bored? did you resent the children who kept coming? did you withhold affection from infants because so many of them would die? These questions were not really answered in any of the 144 diaries I eventually read or skimmed. Those diaries were fascinating, but in the end, I found no book there.

But what I was doing turned out to be background reading for this project that I had no idea was in my future. The *stuff* in the boxes finally, with the help of a secretary, amounted to roughly seventeen file feet of papers. Among them were hundreds of hastily penned postals and letters from my grandfather home to his wife, my grandmother, written as he traveled throughout the country working as a lawyer or training soldiers to fight in World War I. Fortunately, he dated them all. He was a genial, chatty man, eager to share what he saw and learned of the world. I glanced at some, but his handwriting was nearly impossible to read.

At first there seemed to be only a few postcards and almost no letters from my

*While Federal troops occupied Lexington in June of 1864, some of
the Yankee soldiers tented on the campus of Washington College.*

grandmother. But then she was much quieter, less communicative. I knew them
well, having lived with them as a child. After my grandmother died, my grandfather lived with us until his death in 1954.

When I finally broke open a small, locked, wooden box that sounded as if it
contained more papers, I discovered my grandmother's letters to my grandfather,
carefully stacked and preserved, undated, but fortunately returned to their postmarked envelopes. Her handwriting too was dreadful.

Realizing the rarity of finding both sides of a correspondence, I *had* to read
them. I arranged Greenlee's letters and postals chronologically, then dropped
Katie's in where they belonged, all strung out across the floor in six plastic dish-
pans, and started to work on their lifelong epistolary conversation. As we catch on
easily to our own babies' babble, I quickly got fairly proficient at reading their
scripts. Although for some years there were no letters, which means either that
they'd been lost, or that neither of the Letchers left home in those years, in general I felt I had most of their correspondence. My grandfather's letters and cards
usually began, "My Beautiful beautiful Angel," or at least "Dearest Katie," while
her cool postals, open for all the world to read, usually began abruptly, often with
no greeting at all. His were long and chatty, often passionate, scribbled urgently,
while hers were brief, restrained, and often peremptory, written in her severely

right-slanted, very tall scrawl. She sometimes wrote palimpsest, or back over top of what she had already written, the paper turned sideways.[1] The letters are not formal, but they are decorous. Both writers were educated, literate, even eloquent at times, yet very different. Katie's letters are dry, witty, sardonic, matter-of-fact, and Greenlee's are full of the love of life and of her. He found absolutely everything interesting and was constant in his adoration of "My Beautiful Angel."

Soon I was taking the correspondence in small batches to a typist, still with no idea of doing anything more than making them more accessible to anyone who might want to read them. Then I began to feel that their lives deserved a book. I applied for, and won, a three-month fellowship to the Virginia Foundation for Humanities and Public Policy in Charlottesville, where I did the first draft of the book—it consisted of the letters themselves, which, when finally all typed, amounted to 3,000 double-spaced pages. There was much supporting information among the other papers, and local newspapers are available on microfilm, so it took another two years to cut and edit the letters, explain things, and round out the story of their lives.[2] My grandparents apparently discarded nothing. In this correspondence, most gratifyingly, are the answers to all the questions I had had for the diary-writing women. This book tells the story of my grandparents' lives and their world, as told through their writing, and with additional narrative.

Katie Paul was the oldest child of a staunchly Republican circuit judge and state senator from Harrisonburg, Virginia, a pleasant Shenandoah Valley city surrounded by mostly German and Amish farmers. Greenlee Letcher was the youngest son of Virginia's Jacksonian Democrat Civil War governor, from the small college town of Lexington, sixty-five miles from Harrisonburg.[3] He became the youngest state legislator in Virginia, ever. His work as a lawyer took him all over Virginia and West Virginia, and as far afield as Oklahoma, Alabama, Niagara Falls, once to Montana—and to France during World War I. Here is a typical paragraph from him: "Thursday night we went over about a mile into the trenches and a gas attack was simulated. The trenches being flooded as in Europe, some men even lost their boots in the mud which was almost to the waist in places. That afternoon we all went through a gas house being in the gas a considerable time with masks on. We became able to adjust the masks to get full protection. It was all wonderfully interesting."

Greenlee had political aspirations before marriage; but it must quickly have become apparent that Katie was not the kind of wife a politician needed. Typically, he accommodated gracefully and deflected for the rest of his life flattering invitations and urgings that he run for office, giving no explanation except that he preferred private life.

My grandmother before marriage wrote ardently and enthusiastically, as young lovers do; but later, she was frequently angry at my grandfather, obviously preferring to go home to Harrisonburg and stay with her family, which included her parents, a grandmother, and five younger siblings. My grandmother, raised like other well-bred women of her time, never lifted a hand to a household task, yet of course she had no profession to call her own. Helpless about cooking and housekeeping, she was enslaved by the whims of the black servants she hired and fired. A letter to her mother reads: "We have a new cook and are holding our breaths for fear that we may do something to displease her and cause her to wing her flight to other spheres."

Katie and Greenlee married in 1898. Their story is a study of the time and the manners of the first half of the twentieth century. One sees these two complex personalities struggle against the vicissitudes of a world equally as beautiful and as terrible as ours. Greenlee was shored up, changed forever, by love. He functioned optimally when he believed he was loved, wilted when he felt rebuffed. He was blessed with abundant energy, an even temper, and an irenic and gregarious disposition. For him, love was his keel, which allowed him to steer his ship through the many shoals upon which Katie's ship jammed and cracked. He was honest and more direct about his needs than I imagine most men were at the time, and his needs scared and repelled her. Being adored was to Katie, in the end, intolerable. She functioned better when he was away and functioned best when she knew he wasn't coming back for a long time.

"Andaddy" (my childish effort at Granddaddy) was a slight man, slender and physically tireless. His hair was wispy and white and shaggy, for he mostly cut it himself rather than waste money and time on barbers. His face was usually red, wind-chapped, and wreathed with pleasure. He had no attachment to material things. His clothes were shabby, wrinkled, and dirty. I suppose I noticed because my mother talked about them. Andaddy patched his clothes himself, with thick, greasy, black thread and a great big needle that left puckery darned lumps. If his ancient belt broke, he used a piece of rope to hold up his trousers—once, for two years, according to his old friend, Nell Paxton—before he got around to replacing the belt. Whether this was because Katie couldn't or wouldn't mend, or because he was resourceful and thrifty, and because to him clothes and haircuts were unimportant, is not clear—although it seems to me that both were true. Greenlee enjoyed food as he enjoyed life, without preference or prejudice. Fit and optimistic, he took on the world cheerfully, excelling at everything he put his hand to. In his late thirties, after scorning golf as a waste of time, he became a golfing champion. He trekked each morning to his downtown law office, trudging home up the long hill of Letcher Avenue each night with funny stories from the day, good-natured tears in his eyes from laughing about the foibles of his fellow men, and an embracing sense of goodwill about the world. He could be playful, and he could be preachy. His voice was loud and enthusiastic, with lots of inflection, and he was an extremely popular speaker and master of ceremonies all his life. He knew and loved everybody, and apparently everybody knew and loved him. He belonged to a myriad of men's clubs and service clubs, so even when he was not traveling, he was gone from home several nights a week, leaving Katie, whom I called "Nainai," alone.[4] Although he took cold sponge baths each morning, I never knew him to take a full bath in the tub. He used to say the Romans went to pot from too much bathing, which he believed would weaken a person. He slept with his windows open year-round and never wanted to heat the house enough to suit my mother when we lived with them, saying too much heat would make us all "sick." When I hugged him, he smelled musty and oniony.

Andaddy was known as a joker, as were many of his lifelong friends. His humor was jolly, corny, and unsubtle. Practical jokes were stylish then, the products of slower times and fairly benign intents. One story had to do with riding the twenty miles out to the resort hotel at Wilson Springs one winter for a party to usher in the new year. He was too young to attend the dance, but one of his older brothers was dressed formally for the occasion. The team of horses pulling their carriage balked at crossing a stream swollen beyond its usual meander by melting snow. The elegantly attired older brother got out to try to coax the horses through the raging creek—at which point Andaddy applied the whip to the horses' backs. They leapt forward, plunged into the water, upsetting the carriage, and drenching Andaddy's brother—thus (appropriately, Andaddy thought) pricking his vanity. He found it so funny he could hardly get through the telling of it.

Katie was a large, soft woman with serious black eyes, nearly as tall as her husband when I knew them, and probably a score of pounds heavier. She'd been slender and honey-blonde as a young woman, but when I knew her she had straight, soft, white hair that she wore softly twisted into a bun, and she smelled of 4711 Cologne. Her voice had a flat, ironic tone: "Don't fight nobody; don't call nobody Fool," she'd warn me, as I sailed out the door on some adventure, echoing a childhood story about my father, who'd come home from somewhere, and when asked if he'd been a good boy, nodded, saying, "Di'n't fight nobody, di'n't call nobody Fool." She could be sharp, especially about money. She perceived that there wasn't enough of it. My grandfather refused to worry about such things and fluffed her off when she did. She disliked practical jokes but had a subtle, dry wit. Her great, if vague, admonition was, "Don't let down," a rule with a wide range of applications. Someone who had "let down" might have been getting into the sherry too early in the day. It might label someone whose slip showed when she came to call or refer to an old acquaintance who had put on too much weight too fast. I was "letting down" if I forgot and asked for a chicken leg, or, Heaven forbid, a chicken *breast.* You asked for *dark meat* or *white meat.* But her attitude towards *me* generally was one of tolerant amusement, while she scolded Andaddy when he forgot to send out the bills, or wouldn't dun the renter living above his downtown office who was constantly in arrears. Nainai had distinct food preferences — creamed celery, deep-dish cherry pie, oysters in any form but especially deep-fried, cheese sandwiches fried in excessive amounts of butter, grapefruit broiled with sherry and brown sugar, and caramel (butterscotch) ice cream — and she *hated* other things, raw onions for instance. She could not manage to get thin, although she detested her fat body.

Together my grandparents were the same as they appear in these letters. Katie was slow, stubborn, broody. She took no exercise, and her furies were slow to dissipate. She told me often, "You have to be a good hater!" When scolded, Andaddy responded by "Aw-shucking" her, saying things like, "Ah, Angel, it's not so bad . . . ," chuckling and growing red-faced. It was clear, even to a child, that he was philosophical about Katie's snits and rages, shrugging them off like water from his big, black umbrella when he came home wet and shook it out in the hall. As an adult, I once asked my father if he thought his parents' marriage was happy, and he replied, "Oh, I reckon as happy as any." Then he added: "Pop was happy."

Katie wrote letters because she spent so much time home in Harrisonburg visiting her family, and because she spent considerable time in hospitals. Frail in health, she cultivated virtually no friends beyond her own kin. She was practically blind by the time I knew them, so the world was difficult to maneuver, and her house must have seemed at least safer than the outside world. In those days, as now, Lexington had a genial tolerance for people regarded as different or odd; Katie was thought of as an invalid, and people always inquired kindly about her health. It is my impression that, for all her withdrawal from public life, she was much loved. Life was cruel to her: she did not feel well, she suffered the deaths of two children, and her degenerating eyesight prevented reading, her only hobby, increasingly from her twenties on. I remember her slowly perusing line after line of a large-print book, left to right, with a huge magnifier, the page right up in her face.

Life then was easier for men in general, and it certainly was for Greenlee, who enjoyed abundant health, plenty of adulation, and good fellowship in the world beyond their union. He wrote Katie once: "I wish you could see the world as I can: interesting every minute no matter what happens."

Greenlee, a social creature if ever there was one, went out alone, to dinners, to meetings, to business, to conventions. When he wasn't going out, Greenlee invited people home to dinner, and Katie was reluctant hostess to his childhood school-mates, his "brother rats" (classmates) from VMI, *their* children and friends, his political cronies, clients, anyone remotely French after his two-year sojourn in that country, and even strangers he met on the train. As a son of Virginia's Civil War governor, he knew *everyone*. President McKinley, though a Republican, sojourned with them. Greenlee was friends with George Catlett Marshall. He was thick with William Jennings Bryan, a Democrat; however, Bryan alienated my grandmother permanently while visiting in 1908 by refusing her sherried grapefruit with brown sugar, and delivering a tirade at the dinner table on the evils of alcohol. Typically, my grandfather was always amused to tell that story, and typically, my grandmother always snorted and ruffled her feathers.

It was much harder for Katie to maintain a sense of self because she was, whether she imposed it on herself or not, a prisoner. Her dissatisfactions were expressed in almost continual bodily illness.[5] Not corporately religious, Katie was denied the comfort and camaraderie that belonging to a church can afford. Greenlee probably is best described as a deist, yet I think he mostly went to church to "catch up" with everyone. Andaddy collected and disseminated an amazing amount of benign gossip, and he never forgot a name or a face. People were his lifelong passion, and he put service to others above personal gratification.

Katie was his near-opposite, not caring much for anyone except her family. She wouldn't play docile wife: when he wrote her to send some flowers to Lexington for Decoration Day from the bigger city of Harrisonburg, she apparently declined, for the next letter from him says, "Oh, you're right, of course, I'm perfectly capable of getting them myself." When I knew her, she never left her house—not for shopping, not for church, not for social functions. She did not attend her only son's wedding.

It had to have been frustrating that Greenlee refused to acknowledge her piques, her rages, her "unladylike" aspects. He adored her, and she simply (in his mind) could *not*, in feminist Nancy Miller's words, "mean or want what [men] have always been assured [women] could not possibly mean or want." Not surprisingly, in the teens of the century, Katie took up the cause of women's suffrage, becoming chairman of the local suffrage organization for a time, prefiguring the women's liberation movement a half-century later. The only other organizations Katie belonged to were the Daughters of the American Revolution and the United Daughters of the Confederacy. Although motives are always difficult territory, perhaps she aligned herself with female suffrage in part to *get even* with her husband, whose power was all the more maddening for being so *pleasant*. Nearly always, Greenlee ignored her anger, probably not admitting it even to himself. When forced to respond, he reacted with hurt and sadness, panic, and, once, with a veiled threat. I can't imagine, however, that he would not have been in favor of women having a vote.

There is of course a vast difference between life a century ago and life today. The circumscription of a woman's life then is difficult to appreciate (her doctors and her husband corresponded *about* her!). Medicine was almost medieval and probably almost killed my grandmother more than once. It was a man's world.

At the same time, so very much in these letters is *familiar;* the emotional minefields of marriage have not changed in a century. A recent PBS special on the twentieth century argued that the end of that century was similar in many respects to the end of the nineteenth: people then and now felt overwhelmed by burgeoning technology, racial issues, the vexing problems of wars elsewhere in the world, the breakdown of familiar institutions, the passion of early marriage fading into domesticity. So there is universality in my grandparents' story, as well as particularity.

A drawback in reading any letters is that, because there was no sense of a larger audience, there was no need to explain things—idioms, nicknames, references, and so on—so that there are many unsolved remarks such as "Tell Ed G. if he doesn't keep his mules up, the same thing will happen again." Greenlee omits all but the slightest references to business details, for Katie already knew what he was talking about. Sometimes other letters, from her family or his colleagues, would enlighten, and sometimes local newspapers could shed light on some puzzle. Because the papers from his "uptown" office were destroyed after his death, as most lawyers' are, I can only refer generally to the kinds of legal work Greenlee did. I've filled in the story of their lives with speeches, newspaper articles, others' letters, and letters Katie and Greenlee wrote to people other than each other, Virginia Military Institute records, and local history sources, both written and oral, and, of course, with my own memories. Unless otherwise indicated, all quotations throughout this book are culled from my grandparents' letters, still in my possession.

The rapidity of the mail between them will astonish readers who have grown accustomed to long delays and lost mail. Letters traveled the sixty-five miles between Lexington and Harrisonburg overnight, with several deliveries every day. These days, it takes a letter a week to make the journey, as it must be first routed to a central sorting spot farther then sixty-five miles from either location.

In the text I have used brackets for brief explanations, endnotes for longer ones. Often I've felt torn in regard to these aids: shall I help the reader by noting (again) who a person is, or can I assume that the reader remembers someone mentioned fifty pages before? I hope the reader will forgive where I have erred either way. I have corrected a few spelling errors without notice, but if a word was clearly misspelled on purpose, I've let it stand. I've left punctuation pretty much as it is in the letters, on the theory that unless it's confusing, I ought not to "fix" it.

I have consulted sources on manners and morals of the nineteenth century, on early feminism, on American marriage, and so forth. They are listed in the selected bibliography and are occasionally quoted or referred to directly within the text. These sources have informed to some extent the ways I have read these letters and understood my grandparents' relationship.

I have allowed the few cases of "political incorrectness" to stand. I don't see as relevant judging my Celtic ancestors for practicing human sacrifice, or my Southern ones for owning slaves—or my grandparents for being insensitive about Negroes; these facts just are, products of another time. I can only hope that future historians will not judge me for whatever in my life and behavior they will undoubtedly find egregious. We never know when society as a whole will decide it is barbaric being a meat-eater, or drinking alcohol, or euthanizing an old, sick animal.

These letters allow us as intimate a view as I think anyone could have of one marriage. Katie and Greenlee's relationship lasted from Christmas night of 1895 when they met until her death on Christmas Eve in 1947 with all her family around her for the first and only time (husband, son, daughter-in-law, and four grandchildren). Carolyn G. Heilbrun, in *Writing a Woman's Life,* comments on how rare is the whole story of a marriage, with both voices speaking their truths.[6] Although Katie and Greenlee's marriage may not be unusual for the time, the fact that this relationship can be so fully documented is certainly unusual.

Since beginning this project, I have been determined to let my grandparents speak for themselves as much as possible, so although this book is a biography *of them,* I wanted readers to see and hear these two remarkable people—in their own words.[7]

Acknowledgments

HEARTFELT THANKS

—to Cynthia LaRue for bringing order out of chaos, for it is she who tackled the disheveled and filthy boxes of papers and worked many months putting them in order.

—to the Virginia Foundation for Humanities and Public Policy, for affording me a heretofore unknown luxury, uninterrupted time from September to December 1998 to complete a draft of this book, and for the pleasant and useful companionship of Rob Vaughan and my fellow Fellows there.

—to Janet Cummings, typist *extraordinaire* and marvelous reader of impossible antique handwritings.

—to Royster, for care and feeding of the bestial members of our household while I worked/played in Charlottesville, and for his selfless and endless support of everything I do.

—to Carter Drake and Mario Pellicciaro for trying to help me translate the Letcher motto, bad Latin at best: *Imago Animi vultus vitae nomen est.* They gave up. My own poor rendering goes something like this: "Our name is the image of spirit, the face of life!" (The name probably derives from the French *leche,* for milk. The motto's originator was an outrageous metaphorist.)

—to Louis Rubin and Joyce Davis for recommendations that helped me obtain the grant from the Virginia Foundation, and for their outstanding support through the years.

—to Doug Schneider, M.D., Bruce T. Carter, M.D., Malcolm Cothran, M.D., Joan Robins, R.N., and John D. Harralson, M.D. for consultations on the medical aspects of these letters.

—to Lisa McCown, of Washington and Lee, without whom no local historical research at all could be accomplished.

—to Henry Foresman and Louise Johenning, who remembered Greenlee and Katie and could tell me about them.

—and gratitude goes to Nell Owen Paxton, 1903–1999, for her diamond-sharp memory of nearly everyone I asked her about—but mostly for her ready wit and young heart to the end.

—to Dr. Barry Machado, for his helpful insights into World War II.

—to Sally Hill McMillan, my faithful agent and friend.

—to Gillian Berchowitz, my editor at Ohio University Press, who has believed in this book since the beginning, and to all the staff who eased my way.

My Dearest Angel

The Letchers in August 1899. This photo was taken by Michael Miley, the famous photographer of Robert E. Lee. Note the century plant in the foreground, surely a symbol of the turning of the century. Greenlee is the young man standing casually and confidently at the left; Katie is the young woman in black on his left, at the time eight months pregnant. Seated to the right of Greenlee is Sam Houston Letcher. The governor's widow is the elderly woman with the head covering, and her sister Mag is the other elderly woman. Between them is Letcher Harrison, sitting in front of his mother, Lizzie Letcher Harrison. The lady with the lampshade hat is Jennie Letcher, who in another year would become Jennie L. Stevens. James Albertus Harrison is on her right. The plump woman in the corner is Fannie. The tall man to the left of Lizzie is John D. Letcher, bachelor, on a rare visit home. Maggie Letcher Showell sits in front of Fannie Letcher, and the young girl in front and the little boy leaning on Uncle Houty are her children.

1 *Background and Beginnings (1867–1898)*

"It is the night of the Winterfest, a night on which a peal of thunder is an omen of dreadful significance." From the Winterfest, play of Mr. Kennedy laid in the 11th century in Iceland.

    Nota Bene *I met Mrs. Letcher one night in Xmas week just after a terrible storm with thunder and lightning, Dec. 26, 1895, at a Ball at Wilton's Hotel, Harrisonburg, and I read her the above soon after and told her there was something in it.*

—FROM THE NOTEBOOKS OF GDL, 1912

Greenlee Davidson Letcher was the youngest of the eleven children of Virginia's Civil War governor, John Letcher. He was named for his father's cousin and aide during the war, Captain Greenlee Davidson, killed at Chancellorsville, where Stonewall Jackson fell at the hands of his own men. Although Greenlee was not born until two years after the war ended, stories of the "late unpleasantness" were ever-present in his young life. Their hometown of Lexington, founded in 1778, was, like nineteen other towns in the United States, named for the Massachusetts Lexington that stood for freedom; its first street was named for George Washington, a Virginian who once surveyed the nearby Natural Bridge, which gave Rockbridge County its name. Lexington grew up at the crossroads of two ancient native trails in the hilly, southern end of the Shenandoah Valley, twelve miles north of the famous Natural Bridge. The area was settled mainly by hardworking Scotch-Irish Calvinist farmers, and soon boasted two colleges. Cyrus McCormick invented the reaper near here, and James Gibbs invented the sewing machine nearby.

Susan Holt Letcher was forty-four at the time of her last child's birth. Ex-Governor John Letcher at fifty-four was nearing the end of an impressive, anguishing career.

Young Greenlee willingly accepted the heavy mantle of having as a father someone famous almost to reverence in the state, someone closely linked with Robert E. Lee and Stonewall Jackson. His oldest brother, Sam Houston Letcher,[1] had been a VMI cadet at fifteen and part of the New Market charge in which ten cadets were killed and scores more young men—boys, really—were wounded. One of his sisters, Jennie (Virginia Lee Letcher), was Robert E. Lee's only goddaughter, Lee being one of their father's closest friends.

The governor's father, William Houston Letcher, a carpenter and businessman, lived in a big house next to the one the Yankees burned, but John Letcher—fearing that if he took his family there, and the Yankees returned, they would burn that house also—instead rented a house half a mile away, in the middle of town. There, Greenlee, their last child, was born, in 1867, into a family reduced to poverty, forced to live on the charity of cousins, friends, and neighbors, including Robert E. Lee, who had come to Lexington to take the presidency of Washington College after the war. Chosen as Greenlee's godmother was Robert E. Lee's oldest daughter, Mary Custis Lee (1835–1918), who trusted him so entirely that she named him the executor of her will.

The household was at this time overflowing: Greenlee's aged grandmother lived there, Susan Holt Letcher's twice-widowed mother, Elizabeth Holt Yount. Susan's younger sister, Margaret, Greenlee's adored "Aunt Mag," had lived with Governor and Mrs. Letcher since their wedding in 1843.

In addition to the four adults, Greenlee had six older siblings (three had died as infants, another at age ten). John Letcher as governor had earned the moniker, "Honest John Letcher, Watchdog of the Treasury." After the war, the Letchers were slowly able to recoup their personal losses to some extent with money from the ex-governor's law practice and from his newspaper, the *Valley Star,* started in 1839 to air his liberal views—but they were never again to be far from poverty.

Greenlee Letcher's personal history in some ways begins with that fire that destroyed everything three years before he was born. Hardly any personal letters from before the fire survive, no scrapbooks or diaries, and only a handful of the governor's papers, which had been stored in an office away from the house. Somehow an 1824 letter from their cousin Sam Houston survived, and several letters from Lee, Jackson, Mosby, and J.E.B. Stuart, whose mother was a Letcher.

Greenlee was born, then, after the pain of the war was at least beginning to disperse, and the Letchers had begun to rebuild from devastating loss. Thereafter, as for many Southern families, money was scarce, and there was in the family a recurring theme to save, to be frugal. Young Greenlee believed in the "lost cause" of the South, and all his life revered Lee and Jackson and his father. When he was two, the railroads met at Promontory Point, Utah, linking up for the first time the east and west coasts of this vast continent. When Greenlee was nine, George Arm-

Main Street of Lexington, Virginia, around the turn of the twentieth century

strong Custer died at Little Bighorn trying to wipe out the Sioux Indians. Greenlee grew up longing to be a soldier, to relive the glory of his forebears.

He was a natural student, an optimist, a peacemaker, and the only one of the governor's sons ever to be dubbed "Gov" or "Guv," which he seems to have been called by his chums from childhood. When he was eight, in 1875, Greenlee received a letter from a Baltimore lawyer, surely a friend of his father's, promising him a copy of "Mother Goose," and thanking him for the "correction of my misspelling . . . .[T]he name of the newspaper is spelled 'Sun' and not 'Son' so you were right."

Victorian parents were a didactic lot. Greenlee's mother wrote to him when he was age six from Richmond, on December 31, 1873, news of the family and many cautions:

> Your time has come at last for a letter. I hope it will give you as much pleasure to read as it does me to write it. . . . The fire bells are ringing, if you were here I suppose you would run out to see where it is, but you would have to look about a great while in a big city like this before you could find it. . . . Your Pa talks a great deal about you—There is a little man who sits in front of me at the table who behaves so nicely—He

allows a napkin to be pinned on him every time & whatever his Mother gives him to eat he eats without saying a word—he eats everything with his fork after it is cut up for him . . . .You must not forget to say your prayers & remind Fannie and Jennie about theirs—and how about *the teeth*—Your devoted Mother.

And on December 5, 1875, Governor Letcher, serious in his role of *paterfamilias,* wrote to his son from Richmond: "I am greatly pleased to hear from Aunt Mag that you are trying to be a good boy. I am sure if you will do all she and Grandma tell you, you will be, always, well-behaved, and a first rate Boy. You must do all brother Houston tells you to do, as he wishes you to be a first rate Boy as much as we do. . . . Be obedient to Grandma, Auntie, and Brother Houston, and always kind to your sisters." "Grandma" was Elizabeth Yount. Aunt Mag, younger than Mrs. Letcher, appears to have accepted her lot as a maiden aunt without complaint.

Greenlee wrote at age nine to his absent parents, who were in Richmond for treatment following the first of three strokes that paralyzed and eventually killed his father. He outlined his hand on the page, and on March 4, 1876, wrote carefully,

My dear Papa, I have not heard from you for a long time. Sister Lizzie is just done hearing my lesson for tonight. Fannie is writing a letter too. We went to church Sunday night and got caught in the rain and we went in Professor Nelson's porch. I am very glad that you are better when I heard from you. Brother went down to Dr. Jonston's this evening. Sister is just coming home from church to night. Sister has caught a new beau and who do you think it is? I will tell you who it is, Captain Williamson. Shake my hand both Papa and Mama. Greenlee D. Letcher.

[and, on the reverse side]

My dear Mama. How are you now? I forgot to write on the other side about Papa. Is he better now? Have you asked Miss Sue Taiylor [*sic*] for those stamps she promised me. You have not written to me for a long time. How are you now. Sister Lizzie is a very good housekeeper. Jennie is writing to brother John tonight. Aunt Mag has gone to church tonight. We churn twice a week since you have been away. Frank [a servant] was sick but now is quite better. Your affectionate little Greenlee L.[2]

John Letcher, Civil War governor of Virginia, 1860–64

Lizzie, twenty-eight, the oldest child, was still living at home.[3] Fannie, born in 1864, was twelve at the time of Greenlee's letter. Timid and quiet, perhaps mildly retarded according to my father, she would live at home all her life. "Brother" was Sam Houston Letcher, then twenty-seven, the New Market cadet at fifteen, now a Lexington lawyer, living at home.[4] "Sister" was undoubtedly Margaret Kinney Letcher, called Maggie, nineteen at the time of this letter.[5] The Jennie in Greenlee's letter was Virginia Lee Letcher, born in the governor's mansion in Richmond in 1862; thus she was fourteen.[6] The brother John *she* was writing to was twenty-two and had already gone west to make his fortune. In fact, a frantic 1895 letter from him in Oregon back to Greenlee in Lexington, urges Greenlee to "get me a PhD, and send it out here. Unless it arrives, a Harvard man will win." The position he sought was president of the University of Oregon at Eugene. (Greenlee declined to comply with the request.)[7]

The rest of the family were nominally Christian, Episcopalian by denomination, but they considered John D. something of a fanatic. When "Aunt Loulie" died in 1920, John came home to Lexington to spend the rest of his days. From time to time, he took out ads in the *Lexington Gazette,* offering his services as a surveyor and civil engineer.

Frank may have been a servant; he was not mentioned again. The servants were considered part of the family; in one letter to his children, Governor Letcher sends "Love to all, Black and White, and kisses to the babies."

In August 1882, the teenaged Greenlee wrote his mother a silly, cheery note from a summer job. Rawley Springs was a resort seventy miles from Lexington. VMI chemistry professor Hunter Pendleton and his family were neighbors.

> Dear Mother, I hear the most flattering accounts of your improvement and health since you have been at Rawley. Our household was thrown into the greatest state of excitement the other evening by Sister coming home and telling that the Pendletons had received a letter from Miss Rose announcing the startling fact that the iron water was agreeing with you so well that you were fattening rapidly. I immediately set out to the nearest carpenter and gave him the order to widen every door in the house and yard. But as the carpenters are very busy . . . I fear you will have to stay in the porch a night or two. We also had your new bed traded for one three times its width thinking that the immense corpulency which you have acquired would take the shape of a pancake when you lay down.
>
> Maggie is now quite well but Brother John is suffering with boils— a very undignified complaint—one is on his knee and the other is—I do not like to say, but it is always between him and the thing he sits on. The first adds much grace to his carriage and the second gives ease and beauty to his figure when he is at rest. Papa is very well, has been since you left. He seems to miss you ever so much. . . .
>
> I am going to the hop tonight. You must excuse this hastily scribbled mass of foolishness from Yr. aff. Son, G. D. Letcher

Greenlee prospered in that crowded but loving environment. From early on, the boy excelled at everything he tried and titled an essay in 1880, when he was thirteen, "Duty, the Sublimest Word of the English Language." In 1882, at age fifteen, Greenlee, according to a local newspaper, had "completed with distinction the entire course of Algebra and Trigonometry." Later the same year he was named Distinguished Scholar of the Lexington Public Schools. He entered VMI in 1883, when he was sixteen. While there, he wrote, in a rhetoric paper entitled "Should a Lawyer Defend a Case Which He Believes to Be Bad?": "After a minister of the Gospel, the highest calling on earth is the Lawyer." He answered the rhetorical question of the paper's title resoundingly in the affirmative, asserting that there were no bad cases, and citing "hallucinatory confessions which later proved to be false," reverses in what is or is not legal, and judgements overturned again and again in other tribunals."

While he was at VMI, in February of 1884, his father died.[8] Sister Lizzie married J. A. Harrison in 1885, and their son, Letcher Harrison, was born safely in 1890 after two other male children died in infancy.

Before Greenlee had even graduated from VMI, he had founded the influential VMI Alumni Association and was its president for the next six years. In addition to excelling academically, he played on VMI's baseball and football teams. In 1886, Greenlee finished first in his graduating class of thirty, winning the first Jackson-Hope Medal for all-round excellence, as well as the medal for excellence in oratory. After graduation, he was invited to stay on as a professor, but a full scholarship to the nearby Washington and Lee Law School turned his head in that direction, and he graduated first in his law class two years later.

Greenlee began to think early about a career in politics. Harboring an ardent affection for General Lee, General Jackson, and his father, he wrote about them and their accomplishments (always varying the texts and always linking them to current issues) in speeches throughout his life. His mentor, James A. Quarles, a philosophy professor at Washington and Lee, was elected with his help to the state legislature in 1886 to represent the district which includes Rockbridge County.

The summer of 1887 Greenlee went to Winchester, Ohio, with a Lexington chum, Bill Anderson, to work, and although it is not clear what the nature of his job was, it is clear that it was strenuous.[9] He wrote his mother:

> I am leading a life of painful activity. I am no bird but if I was I would stand a good chance of catching the worm. I think the sun looks a little mift [sic] when he crawls up and finds me waiting for him, and his hurt expression makes me feel a little badly all day. I arise and have breakfast at half past four in the morning, get on the train, and go from 20 to 40 miles to work—eat a cold snatch at 12 o'clock—enjoy the glowing climate all day and return at 7 and ½ o'clock in the evening. Yesterday was the hottest day I ever felt, and I am certain I perspired about a half

gallon. . . . We are fed quite well but that would make very little difference, our appetites would supply any deficiency. . . .

Tell Mrs. Anderson that Bill is looking finely, his complexion being a
bright vermilion. Kiss Grandma for me. Aff., Greenlee

When he was not yet twenty-one, Greenlee wrote an astonishing essay, "How to
Be Happy," focusing on what he felt were the three components of happiness: love,
work, and hope. Printed in the *Southern Collegian* in 1888, it was retitled "The
Sum of Human Happiness." He concluded that happiness comes from within and
that all a man need strive for was something rewarding to do, something to love
(defined strictly as a good marriage), and something to hope for, which, not un-
surprisingly, he defined, in religious terms vague enough to offend no one, as
"eternal glory." He believed, at that young age, keeping hope alive would guide the
soul, at the time of death, "not plunging into the blackening darkness, but glid-
ing into the blushing dawn." Sigmund Freud and Alfred Adler have both been
credited with concluding that "To be happy, we all need someone to love, something to do, and something to hope for," but Greenlee Letcher wrote it down at
least twenty years before either of those contenders.

The year 1888 was a busy one for the young lawyer. C. A. Graves wrote from
the Washington and Lee Law Department, in a general letter of recommendation:

> In June 1887, Mr. Letcher received the Hamilton Law Scholarship,
> which is awarded to the student attaining the highest proficiency in the
> Junior Class in Law. . . . At the last Commencement of the University,
> Mr. Letcher . . . received the prize awarded for the best essay on a legal
> subject. . . .
>
> The above will show that so far as academic honors are concerned,
> Mr. Letcher's record has rarely been surpassed. But aside from these,
> Mr. Letcher possesses qualities which ensure success in life, and which
> should make him an ornament to his chosen profession, the Law. . . .
>
> It only remains to say that Mr. Letcher is a gentleman of high char-
> acter and blameless life. I heartily commend him as worthy of the
> confidences and esteem of all with whom he may come in contact.

Greenlee considered following his brother John west toward greater opportunities than Lexington could afford (his father before him had also considered going
west), and John urged him to come. His former professor and admirer, Hugh
Sheffey, now a lawyer for the B&O Railroad, wrote:

I am informed that my young friend and former Law pupil, Greenlee D. Letcher, . . . proposes removing to the West. . . . He has been well trained in the principles of his profession, has a remarkably clear and vigorous intellect, speaks with the earnestness of youth and the self possession of mature years; and has inherited much of the capacity of his father for ready speech and impressive oratory. . . . I believe the son will prove himself worthy of his honored Sire; and I commend him to the confidence of all within the range of my influence.

"The West" was at the turn of the twentieth century an idea fraught with excitement and possibility: it had only been fifty years since the gold rush, only twenty since the railroad had first linked the two coasts of the United States, and Horace Greeley's well-known injunction, "Go West, young man," still rang in the ears of ambitious eastern boys growing to manhood. It is easy to understand the romantic lure of those unlimited horizons beyond the crowded and perhaps over-civilized eastern seaboard. On the other hand, the fame of his father and his good name would be a tremendous help to an ambitious young fellow seeking public office and fame in the Old Dominion, and it might have seemed rash to turn his back on the privilege his birth had given him.

While making up his mind what to do, Greenlee practiced law with his older brother, Samuel Houston Letcher. He seems to have considered moving to Richmond, for "Houty" (as his brother was called; on occasion he is also Houtie, Houty, Uncle Hooty, and Hous) wrote him a week before Christmas of 1888 from Richmond of a gay social round, the weather, and future job opportunities:

> Dear Guy, . . . There are a wonderful sight of things for me to buy in the stores. I have gotten some things which I hope will be all right for Miss McBride and Miss Carmichael. . . .
>
> I dined yesterday with the Purcells and spent the evening at Cadet Bowie's today I dined with Stokes, who has one of the most beautiful houses on West Franklin. I called at Col Buford's, but your sweetheart had retired. The old Colonel and I had it all to ourselves. It has been unusually cold, but good weather for walking around. Col Maury seems to think there will be no difficulty in getting you in one of the offices of an old lawyer here. He and Purcell will manage it, I think. Love to all. Affectionately, Hous

Houty, a ladies' man with the good sense to avoid matrimony, here played it safe, buying gifts for *two* girls!

In the end, Greenlee stayed in Lexington. In 1891 he ran for state legislature and won, becoming, at twenty-four, the youngest lawmaker in Virginia's history. Early predictions had him following in his father's footsteps.

In those days, legislators had free train passes on Virginia trains, but my grandfather laughed in later years about the difficulty he had persuading conductors on trains that he was old enough to be a state senator, so more often than not, they would not believe him and he was forced to pay. The local paper, even without any news, wrote about him, upon his return from a legislative session: "ONE OF THE YOUNGEST.—Mr. Greenlee D. Letcher of Rockbridge, a son of the beloved ex-governor, is a young lawyer of great prominence. He is an excellent speaker and full of vehemence and energy" (from the *Lexington Gazette and Citizen,* 10 Dec. 1891).

Lexington was an unusual small town, as it still is. People who live in the rural United States generally are willing to forego the cultural offerings and variety of city life, for the slower-paced, safer lives, and healthier air and water that country living affords. City dwellers, on the other hand, shudder at the claustrophobic smallness of rural places: everyone in town knows everyone else's business, while small-town dwellers have the comfort of knowing they will probably not die among strangers, because neighbors check up on one another. People who prefer cities will give up the small-town benefits for more excitement and stimulation, a greater variety of people, restaurants and shopping, and career opportunities. Looking at it negatively, the choices seem to be to die of stress or of boredom. But Lexington, although still today under seven thousand, is home to a college and a university, both of which have excellent libraries, full sports schedules, theatrical and musical departments, speakers of major importance, and students from everywhere. The colleges draw culturally sophisticated people to the faculties, the town, and surrounding countryside; upgrade local public education; and bring excitement and stimulation as well as famous visitors who would rarely be found in so small a town. Yet its smallness discourages rampant crime, traffic jams, heavy drug traffic, and other big-city headaches. Lexington to its admirers boasts the best of both kinds of American living, rural and urban, relatively devoid of the problems of either.

As he entered politics and the law, Guv became Greenlee's universal nickname, obviously because, at least in character, he was like his father. An invitation to join an Oregon firm is one of eleven tendered to Greenlee, the others from Virginia lawyers. Greenlee's prominence locally was such that the *Lexington Gazette and Citizen* reported:

Greenlee Letcher, standing third from left, *on the opening night of the Rockbridge Hotel, 1885*

Mr. Greenlee D. Letcher has received a flattering offer of a law partnership from a leading law firm in Pendleton, Oregon. He is considering the proposition. We hope he will conclude it to be in his interest to remain here. No section of our land holds forth greater promise to deserving young men than the Valley of Virginia, and there is no young man the people of Rockbridge would be more pleased to advance and honor than the son of "Honest John" Letcher. Mr. Letcher has already given promise that he will tread worthily in the steps of his distinguished father.

He decided eventually to continue to practice law with his brother. This arrangement continued until 1898, when Houston was appointed to a judgeship. From then on, Greenlee had associates from time to time but no partners in his civil law practice. On January 1, 1899, Greenlee began stamping his letters, "G.D. Letcher, Atty. at Law, Lexington, Va., Successor to Letcher and Letcher, Attys at Law."

Greenlee loved his homosocial world and was eager to be of service, joining the Lexington Volunteer Fire Department and the Chamber of Commerce. Through the years he was active in the Masons, Shriners, Odd Fellows, and Knights of Pythias. Throughout his life he was also in the Sons of Confederate Veterans, the

Fortnightly Club of Lexington, the Lexington Golf Club, the Kappa Alpha fraternity, the Virginia Democratic Committee, the VMI Alumni Association, and the Blue Grass Trail Association, committed to building a modern highway system throughout Appalachia.

Greenlee's letter in January of 1890 to brother Houston reveals his driving energy, and it sounds from the tone that Greenlee had already taken the reins, which Houty, of a more relaxed inclination, readily gave over.

> Dear Brother, . . . Stir up Weatherford—there is little time. . . . I rec'd Jennie's letter last evening and will answer it soon—very busy now. When will you be down I ask because I want full instructions as to protecting V.M.I. interests in the Appropriation Bill—we have begun work on it. I objected to the Prohibition feature in the Buena Vista Municipal Charter, so Glasgow took it back for further consultation. *Say nothing* about this however as I am afraid a row is going to be kicked up about it anyway.[10] Collect $2.50 for me from S. B. Zollman and $2.50 from Mary Edmondson.

One early example from Greenlee's active life indicates the extent of his energy. In the summer of 1890, he went to Charlottesville to take a summer law course. He was at the same time president of a speculative organization called the West End Glasgow Land Company, 385 acres of developable land in that riverside town, fifteen miles from Lexington, at the confluence of the N&W and C&O railway lines. His letters throughout the summer to his manager, John Varner, are emphatic and directive, and extremely confident for one so young.[11] Some excerpts: "Write me the exact amount we have in the bank. . . . Go to Glasgow every day and canvass actively so as to get ahead of the Glasgow agents. . . . Keep the accounts straight. . . . Jog Leech about prompt collecting. . . . What has happened to your circular letter? Send maps to all who inquire. . . . Prepare a business circular letter to be sent to each member of our Board of Directors. Get signs ready to put up quickly. . . . Scott complains that you never go up to West End to encourage him. . . . The signs are to read 'Industrial Sites Free; Lots for Business Houses and Homes Cheap.'" The plan involved a successful attempt by Greenlee to lure the governor of Virginia, General Fitzhugh Lee, a nephew of Robert E. Lee, to buy property there, to enhance the West End image—although he warned Mr. Varner to keep the matter under wraps. Fitz Lee actually became the president of the project, drawing in the duke and dutchess of Marlboro. Greenlee successfully petitioned the legislature for a post office to be built at West End.

The Rockbridge Hotel was the flower of the project, with two hundred rooms and suites and a roof garden. Costing hundreds of thousands of borrowed dollars, its opening was on September 17, 1892, an enormous affair with bands, champagne fountains, and guests from across the country and from Europe. Sadly, the night of the opening, the company, together with the fabulous hotel of cut stone, towers, and wide bay windows, went into receivership, a direct result of the failure of Baring Brothers, international bankers, "sending a wave of alarm across the Atlantic," the papers said. The United States Treasury felt a drain on its gold reserves, and a full-fledged panic developed early in 1893. General Fitzhugh Lee resigned, and for fourteen years rescue attempts were made. In the end the deserted hotel, the company's only tangible asset, then falling into ruin, was sold for $10,500.

Greenlee invested five thousand dollars in the company, which he must have borrowed. Had the boom developed, he would have been a wealthy man. Reading through Greenlee's urgent letters on the company's behalf shows his superhuman drive, especially given that he was also in summer school, and only twenty-three years old. As it was, he probably remained poor a long time paying back the loan.

In 1893 he paid fifty dollars for five shares in the new Lexington Telephone Company, which prospered. Before he met Katie, who put an end to it, he bought into every venture that came along, losing money in nearly all of them: they included the Irish Creek Mineral and Development Company, the Lexington Manufacturing Company, the Railway Electric Signal Company, the Lexington Development Company, the Bank of Lexington, the National Bank of Virginia, and of course the West End Glasgow Land Company. Only the Lexington Telephone Company and the Mutual Fire Insurance Company paid off, bringing income for the rest of his life.

Often the youngest in a long line of children outshines the rest, having had opportunities to study many role models and to learn by example what pleases, what works, and what doesn't. In addition, younger children often strive to match or excel what older siblings can do. His father had been a legislator at thirty-two; Greenlee was a legislator at twenty-four. In July of 1896 he attended the National Democratic Convention where he met and heard William Jennings Bryan, was deeply impressed, and promptly invited him to Lexington to visit.[12]

It was said of Letcher that when he addressed a jury, you could "hear him all the way down to the river." The late Lexington lawyer, Henry Foresman, recalled that he "had a huge voice for such a little man."

In addressing the Democratic Party of Virginia in 1897, he stated emphatically that "the Democratic platform is the greatest exposition of the true principles of government underlying the Constitution ever promulgated by any Party," and he referred to William Jennings Bryan as "the next President of the United States." He explained that the platform "stands for local self-government, state Rights [*sic*], the rehabilitation of silver, and a return of their money to an impoverished people." A local woman, Margaret Freeland, a great fan of Greenlee's, managed his successful campaign for chair of the local Democratic Party in 1897.[13]

Greenlee Letcher, youthful as he was, was chosen to preside at the opening ceremonies of the Lexington Courthouse on June 2, 1897; it appears he was already renowned as an orator and was a popular speaker. At the beginning of one undated speech, according to the *Lexington Gazette ("The Oldest Weekly in the South")*, he explained that he knew why Daniel went so complacently into the lions' den: he knew he wouldn't be required to make a speech after the banquet. In 1898, local papers reported that during a trial, Greenlee Letcher "made a speech for the prosecution in which he showed decided talent; the fire of eloquence inherited from his distinguished father, 'Honest John Letcher,' Virginia's beloved governor during the war, who before a jury was one of the most powerful men the old Mother Commonwealth has produced."

This slender, popular, pleasant-faced young man, poised on the brink of his career, knew who he was. He must have appeared shining and princelike to young women. Ruth Floyd Anderson McCulloch, a local schoolteacher and historian, related in a memoir that Greenlee, along with others, "graced the dances at the Natural Bridge Hotel" around 1890. If he entertained thoughts about any of the girls, they were light thoughts. He must have been too busy working—that is, until Christmas night of 1895.

While Greenlee was growing up in Lexington, sixty-five miles down the Valley[14] in Harrisonburg his future bride's life unfolded. Although at first appearance it would seem they shared a generally common background, in fact Greenlee and Katie's lives could not have been more different. The Letchers were hardworking Jacksonian Democrats, plain folk who did not mind living in each others' pockets, not far above poverty, and although nominally Christian—the governor's wife was active in building Grace Church in Lexington, which later became the Robert E. Lee Memorial Episcopal Church—the evidence is that the Letchers were not nearly as religious as most of their neighbors. There is far less religiosity in their letters than in the letters of many other folks of that period. They exhibit, as a group, physical stamina, pragmatism, steadiness of disposition, a serious attitude toward work,

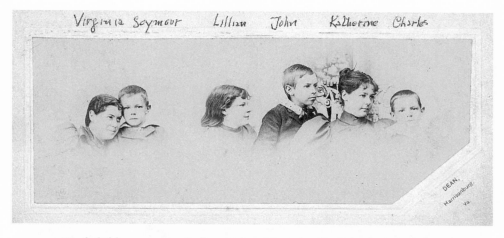

Virginia Seymour   Lillian   John   Katherine   Charles

Paul children, c. 1893. Left to right: *Virginia, Seymour, Lilian, John, Katie, and Charlie*

a distaste for affectation, and compassion for the less fortunate. Politically, today we would call them liberals.

Katie Seymour Paul was a bird of another plumage. Her family claimed descent from both Robert Bruce of Scotland and the ill-fated Jane Seymour, third wife of Henry VIII, who died in childbirth in 1537 bearing the child who would become Edward VI—and beyond that, to one Guy de St. Maur, who reportedly entered England with William the Conqueror in 1066! John Paul, Katie's father, was a Confederate veteran and a judge for the western circuit of Virginia, living in the prosperous city of Harrisonburg, which then boasted several thousand inhabitants, generally of German extraction. The Pauls had come a generation before from Pennsylvania to the rich, rolling hills of the Shenandoah Valley. In an Amish area, they were proudly Episcopalian. They educated their children privately. We first meet eldest daughter Katie at age six, on May 22, 1884, cadging for the favor of her "Dear teaker."

> I have benn very happy for this last week. I am so glad that we have goten into long devision I like all of my lessons we have a very nice spelling lesson for tomorrow: Pappa did not hear and Of cours he will not be hear today. But Mamma is coming I hope we will have a good spelling lesson today. perhaps a good reading lesson. My copy book is almost finished I do not think I have more than three more pages. good bye. Yours Truly. Katie Paul

Kate Green Paul in the living room of the Pauls' Harrisonburg home, late in her life

The Pauls were, from the tone of their letters, social, fun-loving, and lively. The family has produced three generations in a row of lawyers and judges. Yet many of them suffered regularly from nervousness and depression, some apparently from more severe forms of mental illness. They kept a notebook in their Harrisonburg living room in which family members were invited to write, and they jotted down everything from religious sentiments and practical aphorisms to a poem entitled "Charlie's Spotted Cat." They were affluent, socially prominent, capable of snobbery, and clannish. Politically, they were what we would today call conservative.

Judge John Paul and his wife, Kate Green Paul, had six children. Katie seems always to have been quite serious, a typical eldest child. Both her younger sisters were more frivolous. Their father, a Republican, was elected as a readjuster to the Forty-seventh Congress (1881–1883), which means he was in charge of readjusting the state debts.[15] Paul was also elected a senator to the Forty-eighth Congress.[16]

Katie's next sister was Virginia (called Bun and Bunch), born four years after Katie. She lived mostly at home and would die in 1933, unmarried. In between, a

Katie, c. 1881

boy named John Rockingham died at two. So Katie, as oldest, had little chance to be the baby; she was crowded out early from that happy position. Two years after Virginia came Lilian (Idge),[17] then followed the boys: serious-minded John was born in 1883,[18] elusive Charlie in 1886,[19] and sweet baby Seymour, whom everyone adored, in 1888.[20] All three boys would come to Lexington to go to VMI, and two would graduate, but Charles, who did not, was still elected president of his class.

Katie was educated at Mrs. Conway's school in Memphis, Tennessee, and at Stuart Hall in Staunton. Perhaps she was attending Stuart Hall when she met Greenlee, for a letter from her mother is addressed to her at a Frederick Street address in Staunton, when she was having her teeth worked on, a month or so before the wedding.

As she grew up in that young household, Katie was the object of much male attention. She saved letters from at least four men.

During the Christmas season of 1895, Mrs. Paul and other women of Harrisonburg sponsored a cotillion. The local newspaper (December 26, 1895) described, next to her name, what every girl wore. The headline reads: "The Flower of Harrisonburg's Beauty and Gallantry Were There." Both Katie and Virginia were "presented," along with friends Claire Amiss and Maggie Ott (whose name appears as a bride many years later in this correspondence). Virginia wore "blue silk and rubies," while others wore "cardinal cashmere and white lace," "yellow chiffon and diamonds," "black lace and jet." Miss Katherine Paul, however, wore *"white silk and pearls."* Among the out-of-town guests was listed Greenlee D. Letcher of Lexington.

For the rest of their lives, Greenlee would address Katie in letters as "My Beautiful Beautiful Angel" or some similar endearment. It is hard to know how much of Greenlee's oft-repeated adoration was genuine, and how much mere flowery Victorian convention, but at least one letter (January 11, 1900) gives solid evidence of Katie's being Greenlee's one and only love. The evidence is that he saw her pure and angelic, all in white amid that flash and glitter, for the first time that night, fell in love, and never for an instant thereafter faltered. Among Greenlee's papers is not one single letter from another girl.

For Katie, it was obviously not love at first sight. She kept her letters from other beaux and took three years to make up her mind. An undated note from Herbert S. Thomas reads: "Dear Miss Katherine, I shall be glad to have you go with me to Dr. Amiss Friday evening. If agreeable please let me know at what hour to call for you. Don't forget the two-steps you promised, and our night of the roses."

In August 1896, according to the Harrisonburg papers, Kate, Katie, and Virginia gave a dance at their home in Harrisonburg. Life at the Pauls' with three eligible daughters was endlessly urbane and convivial. From a Staunton restaurant, William D. Coleman wrote to Katie: "An hour's detention in Staunton presents the problem of how to dispose of the time. I have solved it in a way most delightful to myself, by using it to procure the flowers herewith sent to you. The fragrance of these roses leaves me for you like the echo of the happy day we spent yesterday at Rawley. (Please don't criticize the metaphor.)"

In September 1896, W. H. Keester related an amusing story from Charlottesville, where he taught at the university,

> Morgan and his bonny bride—notice I did not say "bony"—came in
> upon me while I was at supper, and as soon as I saw him coming, I

thought how it used to be, but Now! but Now! thought I, what Now? Before I could think up that set speech he was upon me, and said, "Professor Keester, this is my Wife!" I pushed my chair back and jumped up, and I said Morgan, I am glad to see you back and I want to congratulate you on the success of your trip. I see you have brought another to our table. . . . Just then Carter came in, and I remarked: a popular place this for newly married couples, and he says, Yes, but we're the youngest. . . . I enjoyed the affair immensely and told him that considerable lamentation had been made from the girls in town at his going off so unexpectedly.

Days and nights were lively, with visits from Kentucky cousins and school chums, dances, corn roasts, watermelon parties, picnics, and hayrides. The same Mr. Coleman (a Republican like Katie) wrote from Abingdon, Virginia, on November 1, 1896, in part,

> My Dear Miss Katherine, Instead of attending church tonight, I am indulging myself in the pleasure of writing to you. . . . It is "All Saints Day," anyhow, and there is a Saint Katherine. This morning I wrote you a brief note, whose brevity, I fear, was its only merit. Tonight I have a great desire to write you "a real long letter," but if I do so, I fear you will think its length is its greatest, though not its only, fault. . . . Your highly valued letter, addressed to me at Danville, I received an hour or so before taking the train for Abingdon. . . . My conclusion was that it would please you best for me to write you about occurrences here rather than a dull essay about what was going on in the limited sphere of my own thoughts . . . .I am going home tomorrow morning and will get there in full time to cast my vote for McKinley. He will certainly be elected.

Although Katie went on seeing other fellows, from Centreville, Alabama, Elmer Zarbell wrote on April 18, 1897, suggesting that the gossip mill had reached even to that distance and was pairing off Katie and Greenlee:

> Dear Miss Katherine, . . . [W]ho keeps the Harrisonburgers straight now? Of course you will be surprised to learn that I have located my future in a new country. It's Guatemala now. Did I ever have it there before? It is the only place to get the necessary "million." . . . I have been making great progress in Spanish, so that now I can ask for something

to eat. I think that will do to start on. . . . Has any one appeared to take the "Guvnor's" place in *society?* Is "Leech" very despondent? Please carry "my respects" to the next meeting of the Paradise Club.[21]

Further describing the gay life in Harrisonburg, while Katie attended Stuart Hall in Staunton, twenty-two miles from her home, her mother wrote, on May 10, 1897:

> Dear Katie, I have just finished hearing the urchins Sunday-School lesson [urchins were the two littlest boys, Charlie and Seymour]. Idge has pottered off down to Quita's to take her some of our Sunday pudding and John has gone to the Y.M.C.A. Idge and I went to Church this morning and heard an unusually good sermon, even for Mr. Yerger. Mrs. Bear and Miss Alice Cowan besought me to tell you that they *must* have one more girl for the Greek drill and wouldn't you be that one. The drill will come off on the 22nd. If you want to escape you'll have to go to Abingdon with Papa. I suppose you got the hat and the box of handkerchiefs.
>
> They are still talking of the dance here next Thursday night, but I don't know anything positively. Mr. Keester was here asking about you. . . . The urchins send love. John rode up to Mt. Crawford on his wheel Saturday and helped the school team beat the Mt. Crawford Nine at base-ball. . . . Mamma.

In both 1896 (at Old Point Comfort) and in 1897 (at Hot Springs) Katie attended the state bar association meeting with her parents—and possibly with an ulterior motive. She wasn't interested in the law, but if she'd been paying attention, she *knew* that up-and-coming Greenlee Letcher would be there, so by that time perhaps he was standing out as a possible mate.

Meanwhile, Greenlee, up the Valley, entered enthusiastically into the life of Lexington and Rockbridge. A letter dated July 12, 1900, indicates that Katie and Greenlee had had a courtship of nine months, although the first extant letters between them date from only a month before the wedding. Greenlee's are in remarkable contrast to the silly letters from Katie's other suitors. On November 4, 1897, he wrote of a mysterious decree, surely about their marriage, while he was still a state senator:

> My Lovely Katie, I was suddenly called to Buena Vista yesterday on a legal matter too late to catch the train. Went on horseback, returning

last night by moonlight and with a yearning *hope,* but not an *expectation,* I went to the Library to see if there was a letter from you, but found none, ate my supper, went to the office, and still hoping asked Brother in a nonchalant way, if there was any mail for me, when he suddenly recalled that in his pocket he had a letter for me and brought to light your letter, which brought light to me—My angel your letters are always bearers of light and joy to me, and every one adds to the conflagration in my heart. . . . We carried Rockbridge by about 110 for the Legislature—you can imagine how close this was, when a change of 2 ½ votes at each precinct would have changed the result. My Brother is elected by over 400, and the Senator [that is, Greenlee] correspondingly feels good, and sometimes smiles. Will your father be at home on the 13th? I want his autograph in the book he gave me, and will make a report in the Bridge Case and have a decree. . . .

We will try not to interfere with Mr. Keester's trip to the Boat Race next year, and don't discourage him from being there, but don't let him get into such a condition that his heart would be broken if you should happen not to be with him, for I would like to have the engagement myself under all the circumstances.

Another letter later that day expresses his yearning: "Katie, My Love and My Angel, I wish you were with me *now,* and in my yearning and impatience I would marry at once with all the risks of boarding and everything else, but in the light of every reason of expediency it is unwise—I must wait until May. My impatience, with my love, increases every day."

Most of us enter adulthood, as Carolyn G. Heilbrun has noted, encouraged by almost every aspect of our society to expect a perfect marriage. She goes on to observe that we marry in our culture on the basis of sexual attraction, although that overwhelming emotion proves over and over to be a specious clue to future happiness.[22] Katie by now was clearly in love with Greenlee, although she admitted to being at times terrified. His letters from the late courtship period have disappeared, but he kept hers locked in the wooden box. The first extant letter to Greenlee from Katie seems to allude to a long-ago meeting when he was a VMI cadet. Greenlee graduated in 1888, and she would have been about eleven. Here, Katie's voice, strongly ardent, is heard, however briefly. As for Greenlee, once he tasted love, he never stumbled from the path of perfect devotion. The reference to hypnotism may not be so strange as it appears, for he was endlessly curious.

New ideas grabbed his imagination all his life. On November 18, 1897, Katie wrote him:

> My dear dear love, Each day I think I could love you no harder and each day I find my love still growing—and you know that I love you with all my heart and that all my questioning and worrying is over now and my soul is filled with light and joy. The happiness and peace of your last visit still lingers in my heart, the sweet realization that we are absolutely each others' without a shadow of doubt or restraint. Heart of my heart, soul of my soul, I love you. I met Mr. Stephenson on the street yesterday and he told me he had an apology to make. I knew it was some variation of his political joke, but I looked ignorant and innocent though I could feel the color flaming in my cheeks and asked what for, and then he chuckled and said, "Well you know I've been accusing you and Greenlee Letcher of trying to break up the Democratic party, but I want to retract it all now, since Mr. Letcher was here the other day trying to keep the Republicans from even having a candidate. *You* may have design in my party, but he's a Democrat after my own heart.". . .
>
> I am amused at the way people seem to think they must tell *me* that they "saw Mr. Letcher in town a few days ago." I wonder what interest they think *I* have in it. But they all like you and say lovely things about you and I'm so proud of you, and so happy because you are mine. Darling, you won't undertake to investigate hypnotism will you? Please don't, dear. Not only because it is so uncanny and disagreeable and such bad form, but because I ask you not to—and if you, Mr. Letcher, asked *me* not to do a thing I would be glad to yield. Poor Mr. Barksdale! Are you going to the rescue? I'm sorry for him but I can't say that I blame the girl if he will insist upon drinking. Don't bother with him, Dear, and let your brother take charge of the case with Mr. Sipes next week. . . .
>
> I'm afraid we are not going to have Mary Morton [a school friend] this Christmas. She begins her letter by saying how anxious she is to come but can't let us know positively yet, and then at the end remarks in a most non-chalant way, "By the way I hope for a visit from Will during the holidays." Will! If it was my friend Mr. Letcher I'd understand. *My friend Mr. Letcher* how dear and sweet he is and how I do

love him. . . . Dear heart, my great love for you has made a woman of me and it is no girl's fancy for a man older than herself [by nine years] but the love of a woman's life that I give my heart's beloved now. With a kiss to the cadet who was mine then even as I was his, though we knew it not.

On Christmas Day of 1897 came an invitation from Greenlee's old professor, J. Hoge Tyler, to accept a position on his staff in Radford, Virginia.[23] By the time he was invited, however, Greenlee was committed to staying in Lexington, and contemplated being married the following May. On March 15, 1898, he wrote to Katie:

Circuit Court is drawing to a close & will perhaps adjourn tomorrow and I anticipate nothing which will prevent my seeing the most Beautiful Thing on earth, next Saturday, and spending Sunday at the Shrine of my heart's worship, and should anything unforeseen prevent me I would be the most desolately heartbroken thing that ever lived—but banish the unhappy thought. I *will* see My Angel, as fate will not be so unkind as to disappoint me . . . .

I have the toy cannon ready for Charlie & Seymour, and *after I bring them to the boys,* we may as well for all purposes not deny our engagement any longer—the *report* of those cannon to the average hearer, will announce our engagement all night—that delicate little attention to the little brothers will fix it all right, My Beautiful, My Own. Now Katie, Sweetheart, Darling, Beautiful, My Own, if you have not formulated the programance for the dinner May 31st, for the "passing" of Katherine Seymour *Paul,* do so at once, so that you may outline it all to me, when I come—you have carte blanche—*to get you,* I will do anything that moves your fancy—make the ceremony what you please, the *only* condition that I impose is, *that I be in it.* You have not sent me your last photo, and even if it is marred by others, your being in it, makes me want it—the Loveliest Thing that a camera ever *hopelessly tried* to catch is in it, and for that *shadow* I want it—for that laudable effort for the *unattainable,* I will prize it, Beautiful, Beautiful, Beautiful Love.

Greenlee actually spoke (although humorously) of the *passing* of her in this letter, as if by marriage she would be obliterated. Obviously, no such conscious intent existed, but no wonder she was afraid. Feminist Nancy K. Miller has pointed out that marriage and death are the only two possible ends for fictional women and has added that they are, frequently, one and the same. Greenlee's next letter, written March 17, admits to his "vanity" in *obtaining* Katie:

> My Beautiful Love, I have the right to be the vainest man in the world after getting that letter of yours this evening, and when I think of the *loveliest thing in the world* loving me and wanting to see me bad enough to get up at 5 o'clock in the morning, I am *vain* and know that the world will think something of me when it finds all this out. I will be to see you a little before nine Saturday morning, unless I am the most disappointed man in the world,—the victim of some *fearful and uncontrollable restraint;* and if you desire and yearn to see me half so bad as I want to see you, Beautiful Angel, I will be satisfied, *that* I am loved— and *that I am loved,* will satisfy me, with life and all in love that life brings to us, My Love and My Own. . . .
>
> I think our engagement is very well known now—a drunken darky stopped me on the street and *pleasantly* referred to it to-day—it amused me and in no wise put me out of temper, even considering the source; the *pleasure* of the *theme* was paramount.

A barrage of letters followed. Although Greenlee's from this period are missing, obviously the two exchanged ardent endearments as the wedding date neared. On May 2, 1898, Katie wrote:

> I love you more than ever before. . . . And I was just as crazy for a letter from you this morning as if I hadn't had one for a week and it seems more than a week since you went away. It was such a lovely, lovely letter, Dear and it was so sweet of you to write last night and tell me you had had a happy visit and that you loved me harder than ever. I am so perfectly crazy about you, sweet thing, and I want you *always* to love me harder than ever and never to have any more sense about some things than you have now.
>
> Mamma says she doesn't think it would do to invite Miss Ott[24] to the wedding and not any one else in town . . . but she wants you as soon as possible to send a list of *all* the people in Rockbridge and everywhere except Harrisonburg to whom you wish cards sent. I'm going to leave the whole thing to Mamma as much as possible.

I went to church with Mr. Coleman [ex-beau] last night, and wished all the time for you, love of my soul. I told him we were to be married on the 31st and he was lovely — said it met with his entire approval and he was glad to hear it as he had never known two people more suited to each other, and added that if he could have chosen the one person in the world for you and for me he should have made exactly the arrangement we have made. . . . Sweet, sweet love, I love you more deeply and truly and tenderly . . . . Don't let the extent or lack of extent of your worldly goods worry you, precious thing. I am not marrying you for a fortune, dear, but simply because I love you with all my heart and soul, and know that without you the world would be desolate and life empty and vain. . . . I would rather endure trials and *arrows,* if need be, for you and with you, than have any life of ease and happiness without you. But we are so entirely one now, dear, that I cannot even fancy any life without you. To be your wife seems the only *possible* thing.

A week later, she wrote: "Dr. Firebaugh [another beau, apparently] was here last night and was properly regretful at losing me, and sent his regards and congratulations to you. . . . Virginia Fletcher and Lucy Effinger met me on the street a few minutes ago and tendered me their best wishes and unanimous support. . . . I'm scared today — scared nearly out of my wits, but I love you just the same and there is no danger of my getting too much alarmed." She added a P.S.: "Mr. Keester has just come in & is being gay."

Many a bride-to-be must have been frightened, in that Victorian silence (and thus, misinformation) about sexual matters. Women still were politically without strength, with only their bodies for bargaining power. Childbirth still killed, and reliable birth control was nonexistent.[25]

It is particularly ironic that Katie's early letters, so shiningly full of hope, addressed the very things that would so soon become festering wounds. She wrote: "I am not marrying you for money"; "I am glad you will not leave me but once or twice more"; "If you asked me not to do a thing, I'd gladly yield"; "I cannot imagine a time when I would cease to love you"; "your will is my pleasure, and your pleasure is my will"; and "in spite of all the remarks about the foolishness of being married so young, and the warnings about what a serious and dreadful thing we shall find it and all the small worries, I am glad and happy as I have never been before, for I love you and you are lovely, and if only I do not grieve and disappoint you too much I think we shall find life very much worth living." This phenomenon is not uncommon; all who are in love try to talk themselves out of worrying about the things that worry them.

Katie instructed him not to do anything to worry his mother: "I am inclined to think it would be better to invite to the wedding only the people she would invite to a reception. As it is to be only a quiet house wedding I think people would understand that we couldn't invite everybody." It is possible she is just being diffident when she writes: "I only wish I could give my heart's beloved something more worth having," but the remark may also betray an underlying doubt about her own worth.

When she thought he wasn't being attentive enough, she grew coy, then loving by turn, then businesslike, then philosophically hopeful, writing on May 14:

> Perhaps in view of the fact that you waited until yesterday to answer my letter I ought to be extremely haughty and reserved and not write to you until tomorrow, but I love you, precious thing, and I choose to tell you so today. You are the very sweetest thing in the world, and if I am so perfectly crazy about you now when I only see you occasionally what will become of me when I am with you all the time? Oh, I never dreamed that I could ever love any one so. . . . Mamma wrote yesterday or the day before to your sisters asking them to stay with us, and I truly hope they will do so for we have been strangers long enough, and we would all enjoy having them. . . . The hat that goes with my traveling dress was sent home a day or so ago, and it isn't a bit like a bride!

On May 19, 1898, Katie expressed disappointment that Greenlee's mother, Aunt Mag, and sister Fannie had decided not to attend the wedding. At that time, only sister Jennie planned on coming. Katie chatted of her old beau, Professor Keester: "I think you had perhaps better write a note to Dr. Firebaugh and Mr. Keester and ask them to come. While I was waiting in front of a store for a package yesterday, Mr. Keester came along with an extensive smile, and got in and drove home with me. He still thinks it the funniest thing that ever happened and wonders how you ever screwed up enough courage to ask me to marry you. My fellow citizens are very sweet about lamenting my loss. And, Mr. Keester tells me that I am the *most* serene and happy of brides." In daily letters, she complained about the "churlishness" of the postmaster, chatted about who was and wasn't coming to the wedding, and chided him: "And don't call the things your sweet people send me 'plunder,' or I shall refuse to speak to you when you come. But I guess I'd better be very careful and respectful between now and the thirty-first so you won't change your mind." Of their forthcoming honeymoon, she wrote: "If you object to being busy until the last minute I am sorry you are so perished, but think how we will enjoy just loafing around for a week or so without any depositions or divorce cases or invitations or dress-makers to bother us." In one letter, she regretted deciding against a church wedding: "All my friends are bitterly reproaching me for not having a church wedding and for some reason I am rather sorry we decided not to though on the whole I think the quiet wedding sweeter and in better taste—don't you?"

Greenlee received many letters from his friends congratulating him on his coming marriage: an example is from his old friend and professor James Quarles, who had once offered him a job: "I have not the pleasure of knowing Miss Katherine Seymour Paul; but I can felicitate her upon the prospect of soon becoming Mrs. Greenlee Davidson Letcher, because I have the honor of knowing him reasonably well. I am sure that he will prove a knight loyal and true to her highest interests. . . . I pray, dear Greenlee, that she may be to you what a good wife is, the best, the most helpful of all earthly friends. May your lives, like sweetest music, blend in perfect harmony. Affectionately yours, James A. Quarles."

A week before the wedding, Katie wrote Greenlee that "Miss Maggie Freeland sent *her* sweetheart and his sweetheart a beautiful lamp yesterday. I wrote this morning to thank her for it and to ask her to come down next Tuesday. Next Tuesday, dear,—less than a week and still I'm not scared.—I forgot this was a business letter and that I was not going to tell you how I love you. Mr. Keester walked home with me yesterday and showed me your note to him. . . . Precious thing, do you suppose Mr. Letcher [Judge Sam Houston Letcher] really might be here? He is *so* overpowering that even Col. Lehmen will faint and fade."

As it turned out, Katie was not the only one with misgivings. A letter from O. M. Yerger, the Episcopal minister who married the couple, must be addressed. It stands out oddly, for it refers to a letter from a man supposedly madly in love, only a week before his wedding, written to his *fiancée's* clergyman, inquiring about her character. It was too late for any ungentlemanly reconsideration, so why did Greenlee write and ask Mr. Yerger to write to him about Katie? Yet he did, for Yerger's May 24, 1898, reply was among the papers.

> My Dear Mr. Letcher: I know nothing that will give me a sadder pleasure than to comply with your request. I have known Miss Katie for five years, and during all that time, I have seen many things in her to admire and nothing with which I could find fault. Perhaps, I may give the best

explanation of my admiration of her worth by saying that if I had a brother, I would be every way delighted by having her for a sister. You will pardon me for predicting for you both a happy home and for affirming my belief that if the marriage is not what it ought to be, it will not be Miss Katie who is to be blamed. I am glad I feel assured that you will be tender and considerate of the great gift which she will bestow upon you. Very sincerely and affectionately yours, O. M. Yerger.

There was no name for depression at that time, and it was not understood by many of Katie's physicians, but there is evidence that she suffered from the malady for most of her life. Heilbrun writes that "forbidden anger, women could find no voice in which publicly to complain; [so] they took refuge in depression or madness" (15). Lilian, Katie's sister, suffered from an unidentified form of mental illness so severe she spent the last thirty years of her life in a mental hospital, the family saying only that "Lilian went mad." The records at the hospital where she was incarcerated have unfortunately long since vanished. Their brother Charlie and sister Virginia evidently had mental problems also, as hinted at in letters.

The symptoms of depression include loss of pleasure and effectiveness, leaden feelings, forgetfulness, nervousness, difficulty in concentrating, brooding on the past, withdrawal from life, and an almost endless array of physical symptoms. About three times as many women as men suffer from it. Greenlee, blessed with a sunny and even nature that nothing disturbed for long, shook off any problem as weakness, lost himself in his work, and urged Katie to do likewise. Greenlee also attempted to bring difficulties into the open, but Katie, from all the evidence of the letters, simply refused to discuss problems, instead apparently brooding on them, then erupting in anger inappropriately.

The reason for Greenlee's letter to Dr. Yerger a week before the wedding is, I feel sure, that he was already disturbed by the nameless ghost that haunted his beloved, perhaps only anxiety then, but soon to be manifested as lifelong depression. The intense energy of early love changes everyone temporarily, and apparently it masked for a while the symptoms that lay close beneath Katie's surface, symptoms that would leave her only briefly, when a world war and her part in it focused her energies outside herself. Katie always said (even to me) that she didn't care for most other women. She wanted to listen to talk of politics; women, she elaborated, only wanted to gossip. And so she isolated herself, perhaps suffering from agoraphobia. Her only friends, with one exception, were her mother and siblings.

Katie was the oldest of six children born close together, the next born only one year after her. Baby John Rockingham Paul may have been sickly, for he died at two. His birth and illness might have shoved her out of the spotlight too soon — leading her always to conclude that the world was a woeful and chilly place.

And what of their choice of each other? Greenlee met challenges head-on his whole life long, and may have unconsciously believed that he could make her whole by just loving her *more*. On a more obvious level, Katie must have been attractive, as she had several suitors; in addition, she was the daughter of a prominent judge, and Greenlee could not have been unaware of her ornamental value to the ambitious life he had set his sights on. She was well bred, popular, and affluent.

Katie had to have been, as all women were then, aware of the economic advantages of marrying Greenlee. He had a sterling academic and professional record — *and* he was the son of an ex-governor. She could have reasonably expected that they would be not only secure financially and socially but probably quite well-off. What Katie did not bank on was that Greenlee, caring so little about the acquisition of wealth, gave away much of what he took in — in his open-hearted civic-mindedness, his forgiving of rents and payments, his disinterest in gaining wealth.

So it was not until Greenlee was already committed to Katie that some of her symptoms began to appear. Even if Greenlee had second thoughts, as his letter to Yerger may suggest, young love thinks it can overcome all obstacles. Neediness and fragility may well be attractive qualities at the start of a relationship, appealing especially to a male need for domination. Victorian women were still the "weaker vessels."

Women at that time must have feared all sexuality: their own as well as their husband's, living as they did in the dark loneliness of ignorance and Victorian shame about the body. In fact, it is said that Queen Victoria once instructed one of her daughters on the child's wedding day, to "close your eyes and think of England." Although his earliest letters are missing, Greenlee's life themes were already evident: side by side were his passion for his work and his passion for Katie. But when reality hit, maybe as early as their honeymoon, from which Katie returned, as her mother observed, "pale and worried," and maybe even earlier, it was by that day's standard too late for any change.

Katie in her wedding dress, May 1898

2 Early Marriage (1898-1901)

MAY 31, 1898 LETCHER-PAUL.

Harrisonburg, VA., May 31. — A beautiful wedding was solemnized this afternoon at the residence of Judge John Paul, of the United States District Court, when his eldest daughter, Miss Katherine Seymour, was married to Mr. Greenlee D. Letcher, of Lexington. The marriage was witnessed by a small company of relatives and intimate friends of the couple. The bride was given away by her father, and Hon. S. H. Letcher, Chairman of the Board of Visitors of the Virginia Military Institute, a brother of the groom, acted as best man. A sumptuous Lunch was served after the ceremony, and the bridal couple took the afternoon train for a northern trip. Mr. Letcher is the youngest son of the late Hon. John Letcher, Virginia's famous war Governor. He is a member of the Lexington Bar and has represented Rockbridge county in the House of Delegates.

The Harrisonburg paper dilated on the wedding, describing the "apartment profusely decorated with roses and smilax," and Katie's dress, "fine French organdie over white silk, with valenciennes lace." Of the groom it reported, "The son has inherited the political talent of his father, having been chosen . . . to represent Rockbridge in the House of Delegates when he had barely reached his majority. His social qualities are remarkable and his faculty for making friends is practically without limit." Attending the wedding from out of town were Katie's old beau, William D. Coleman, then of Danville; Professor Keester of Charlottesville; Aunt Susie and Uncle Rock Paul of Roanoke;[1] several Lexington colleagues of Greenlee's; his sister, Jennie; and Governor J. Hoge Tyler.

After the wedding, the couple spent ten days or so in New York City. A letter from Katie's mother soon after hints that the honeymoon was a disappointment — but in fairness, what honeymoon is not? Afterwards, Kate Paul wrote, "We all lost our hearts to Miss Jennie, she is so sweet and entirely satisfactory — and we don't worry at Jules' [Daingerfield cousin] envy of your in-laws."

Because the wedding was small, dinner receptions were planned for later in both Lexington and Harrisonburg. Ottobine, referred to in the following letter, is a large farm and mill west of Harrisonburg that has been the Paul family seat since its purchase in 1830. Sister Lilian (Idge) wrote Katie on June 4,

*Greenlee's wedding
picture, May 1898*

Mamma received Mr. Letcher's letter this morning and we all enjoyed it immensely, and have been congratulating ourselves on our new brother-in-law. I will be so sorry when Virginia [2] gets married because I never could spell the plural of brother-in-law. . . . Aunt Susie,[3] John Gray [John Gray Paul, Susie's son], Charlie & Seymour went to Ottobine today and as John went to a picnic at Rawley and Bunch [Virginia] was sick, Mamma, Papa, Mary Morton and I had rather a small dinner party. I have just completed a type-written list of your goods & chattels and so far you have 134, *tres bien*. I enclose a list of some more presents received. Had a lovely letter from Miss Virginia [Jennie] this morning. . . . There are several letters here for you, one from Prof Harrison [of UVA, married to Elizabeth Letcher, father of Letcher], which we opened to save you the exertion saying that you are not expected in

The Paul house in Harrisonburg on Greenlee and Katie's wedding day, May 31, 1898

Charlottesville, on account of Letcher's whooping cough. Mamma says the Reception will be next Friday night so if you come on the afternoon train it will be all serene. . . . What do you think of the menu?

SUPPER (FRIDAY) 18 PEOPLE
Fruit Cup
Cream of Pea Soup
Rolls   Butter
Sausages   Oysters in Brown Gravy (ramekins)   Sliced Ham
Egg Plant   Candied Sweet Potatoes
Waldorf Salad
Caramel Ice Cream   Peach short Cake
Coffee

Although Lilian's letters are cheerful, from the beginning of the marriage, Katie's mother seemed concerned about her eldest. She was a typical Victorian mother, however, and could bring herself only obliquely to address her worries. On June 12, she wrote: "Dearest . . . When your carriage disappeared down the street yesterday I went up to my room and locked the door, with a feeling of desolation you can not understand and which I will not sadden you by attempting to describe."

She went on to say she was herself again but then returned to the "worried mode," writing, "But we miss you! every hour in the day—I keep finding myself thinking 'it's time Katie was coming home from down street' or there's something I want to tell you or to ask you and I half rise from my chair and then it comes over me that you are gone."

In this and later letters, Kate Paul shook off her blue mood and proceeded to describe (rather insensitively) all the gay visits, parties, churchgoing, hayrides, and ball games that Katie was missing. "After ten last night Mr. Coleman came as usual and later Dr. Lenny, Gov Conrad and Ernest Wilton. . . . This morning we went to church, very hot *and* perspiry, and listened to a very young and unfledged freshman who soared into dizzy heights of eloquence while Mr. Yerger regarded him with the countenance of a sphinx, and Dad nudged me maliciously."

Kate Paul was a power to be reckoned with. She was one of two members from Virginia of the Board of Lady Managers of the great world's Columbian Exposition held in Chicago in 1893, and postmistress in Harrisonburg for twenty years, following the death of her husband. She was outspoken in the cause of women's suffrage. And she was not sure she liked her eldest daughter's husband.

She returned in a later letter to the theme of Katie's fatigue, and there seems to be a great deal between the lines:

> It distressed me to see you looking so tired. . . . You *must* not overtax your strength; tell Greenlee. . . . I know your sweet new mother and all the other nice in-laws are as good to you as can be and will do all they can to make you happy—I know Gov is sweet and kind and considerate of your wishes and will take the best care of you, but there is unavoidably a great deal of excitement and perturbation attendant on the entering upon a new life, a new home—new acquaintances, and I want you to spare yourself all unnecessary fatigue.
>
> Mr. Greenlee Letcher promised to take your part till you got acclimated, but if that protection isn't sufficient for that irrepressible young man just hold up his mother-in-law as a horrible warning—picture the terror in store for him when that dreadful personage comes to make you a visit!

Another note ended, "Write and tell me every thing—If Gov is too bad, pack your kit and come home—but be sure to bring Gov with you. . . . When are you coming back?"

Kate Paul was eager to write, a few days later, on June 13, of how cheered she was to receive a "satisfactory note": "For I confess I had been haunted by your tired sad face on Saturday. . . . My child, I am so glad, so glad you are happy—it almost compensates for losing you to him that you are in such tender keeping and that your heart is satisfied." She went on to apologize for overreacting, and ended, "[Y]ou know sometimes a tooth will keep us hurting for a little while after it's out."

Returning from their honeymoon, Katie and Greenlee moved in with the seventy-five-year-old Mrs. Letcher, her sister, Aunt Mag, and whatever grown children, all older than Greenlee, were then still living at home—a houseful of elderly people so different from the youthful Paul household, with Katie's youngest siblings hardly even of school age.

The living arrangement must have been unsatisfactory, for in only a few weeks, the newlyweds moved out, renting a small house at the end of July. Kate Paul fended off Greenlee's endless invitations to visit them in Lexington:

> I appreciate and thank you for your kind and urgent invitation to come to the reception to-morrow evening. I know it will be as enjoyable as charming hosts and hostesses and pleasant guests can make it and I should so enjoy meeting the nice and clever people who will be there. I am pleased that you wish your repressive mother-in-law to be present. Any request of yours my dear boy, to the half of my kingdom, if I had one, I'd take pleasure in observing, but you know that for an old lady like me [she was all of fifty-one]—and I feel positively venerable since I became a mother-in-law—it isn't always convenient to leave home. I know Katherine will enjoy it as she would enjoy a Chinese mob if you were in it, and as she is already so fond of your sweet mother.
>
> I'm glad you like your little life partner; I think you'll find that like the wedding game of the Vicar of Wakefield's wife, that she has "qualities that will wear" and it is quite a coincidence that she seems to entertain similar sentiments in regard to you.

Early in his marriage, when he was campaigning for the Virginia House of Delegates, according to local retired lawyer Henry Foresman, Greenlee was holding forth in the courthouse green, making a campaign speech. Someone from the crowd jeered, "Hey, Gov, if Republicans are so bad, how come you married one?" Greenlee hollered back, "I got the only good thing in the entire Republican Party!" In his notebooks Greenlee recorded many jokes, among them that the definition of a Republican is "a sinner mentioned in the Bible."

But Greenlee was just being a politician when he returned the comment; in fact, he gloried in his newfound Harrisonburg family, speaking often of how lovely they all were. And certainly they seem more spirited than the Letchers. The "mother" letters are a study in contrasts. Kate Paul's letter tugs at the heartstrings, and we can see her ambivalence, including her final plaintive refrain, "When are you coming back?" Rather than encouraging Katie to stay in Lexington and become a wife, Kate Paul urged her daughter to come home at every opportunity.

Early on, Katie established her habit of returning home at the slightest provocation. And early on, she was spurning not only the hospitality of her mother-in-law but also the gestures of welcome and friendship among the Lexington folk.

While Greenlee never denied Katie's intellect, his view of her insisted upon softness and gentleness, and whenever she was unkind or cold to him, he begged her not to be so. He asked her not to be who she was.

From the beginning Katie found his focused and absolute adoration unbearable. Her family's idiom was lighter, and her responses, after the first flare of romance had settled to a low flame, were, even when loving, more matter-of-fact.

Greenlee wanted to communicate. He had the gift of thinking his life, his friends, his wife, and later, his children, the finest imaginable. Katie frequently found his cheeriness irritating and did not hide her preference for being home in Harrisonburg. She spent more time there than she did in Lexington, even in the first year of marriage. It would not be unfair to say that, in a sense, Katie Paul never left home.

When Greenlee was in Lexington, she often removed to Harrisonburg. When he had to travel, she also took the opportunity to go home. And he began traveling almost immediately. He was still struggling and apparently often had to take cases fairly far afield from Lexington.

Katie must have resented being left alone even while she recognized the necessity of his being gone. And her family was not subtle in trying to reel her back in. On June 13, her father wrote amusingly, "A book agent captured Mama today, on some 'Weary Willie' story about trying to raise some money to take the course at Washington and Lee University. I think Mom has an idea, now that you are going to stay in Lexington, that it is incumbent upon her to help sustain all of its institutions." On June 19, not three weeks into the marriage, Katie's grandmother,

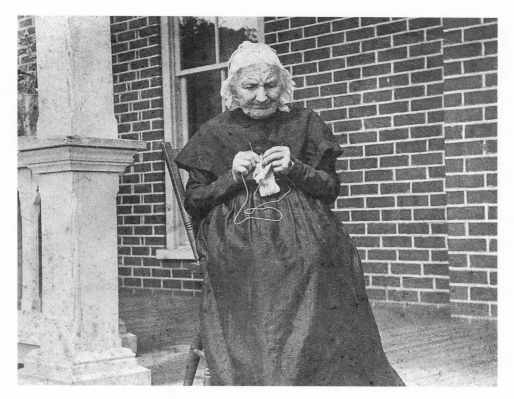

Maria Whitmore Paul, Katie's grandmother, on the porch at Ottobine, c. 1898

Maria Whitmore Paul (1814–1902), wrote plaintively from Ottobine, where she lived with two of her unmarried children, Abe and Fanny Paul.

> My Dear Grand Child, Your remembering me helped me wonderfully, I am much more feeble this summer than last, but as I am passing my eighty-fourth milestone I can't expect to be strong and vigorous. I appreciated Mr. Letcher's letter so much I swear I will like him. . . . I suppose you are going to the Bar Association, your Papa and Mama are going. . . . We had a week's visit from the boys. Poor little Seymour got quite homesick. I told your Papa if they were willing to come to send them out while he was away. . . . Don't be too anxious on the housekeeping. If your influence will be like the majority of housekeepers you will have enough of it in a lifetime. Accept my warmest love to you and Mr. L.
>   Yr. affectionate Grandmother, Maria Paul

On the sixth of July, Kate Green Paul wrote to her daughter, rather lamely excusing herself for not visiting them, and blatantly attempting to get Katie back home. Jennie Rogers was Kate Paul's sister from Fauquier County, with whom she apparently got along raggedly.

> I have intended as usual—but the weather was first too hot, then too cool and then I was too lazy. We're glad you are coming Friday. Of course it is convenient—the idea of *you* asking if it suits us for you to come home! You certainly are getting stuck-up since you've "been sleeping in town folkses' geese." . . . We shall all also be very glad to see your puritanic worser half. . . .
>
> There is a Ball at Massanetta to-night. All send love, Mamma. . . . Of course I take it for granted that you are going to stay awhile and let Mr. Letcher come back for you. We can finish packing your goods and chattels—and you can see all the folks—Aunt Jennie is arriving soon.

Katie's being in Harrisonburg necessitated the first of many domestic exchanges between her and Greenlee. On July 13, 1898, he wrote, as he would for the rest of their lives, to her in Harrisonburg:

> My Darling Katie, Have just reached home today. First thought is of my Angel, I love you, I love you, I love you, Beautiful Darling. All asked after you before they ever showed interest in myself.
>
> Brother [Houston] left this morning for his talked of trip, I suppose to the Eastern Shore of Va. with the R.R. Commissioner, but Mother's ideas are a little vague about it. He will be gone 4 or 5 days and they all seemed glad for that reason, not to mention any other, at my return. They wanted to see you, but said I did right not to insist on your leaving home so soon—and all send love to My Angel. . . . I can not tell you how lovely all your good people are, and how grateful I am for their kindness to me and hospitality—give every one my love and a kiss, especially your sweet Mother. . . .
>
> I enjoyed my stay immensely & will return as quickly as I can, even if your Mother dont want me to come back until the last of next week, for fear I will take her baby from her. Angel, I am mighty lonely without you, but your happiness is my first thought, & I will let you stay just as long as I can, Sweet Angel—for you are the sweetest thing that God ever made. Katie, please by *first* mail send me my bunch of keys—I am at a loss without them.

Mother tells me that Miss Ruffner invited you to a Dining which she thinks was in your honor, but she told her you were at home. . . . Talked all the way from Harrisonburg to Staunton with Fred Effinger whom I like very much—he expressed the greatest desire to know you. He was most complimentary to your Father. He gave me much advice, the principal part of which was not to bother you again for ten days & wanted me to promise to mind him, but I told him I could not promise that. . . . Beautiful, Beautiful, Beautiful Angel, *I love you,* & am following your advice & not let anything weigh on my mind, & will continue to do so, if I can. Love me Angel, while I am gone, and be happy, & intuitively knowing it, I will be.

This letter indicates that Greenlee discussed a sexual problem with another man. Perhaps that was not unusual among men at the time. Greenlee carried on valiantly, despite sexual rebuff and anger (which would unman any groom), and, characteristically, made the best of things. His next letter gives us the first clue about her unhappiness. Greenlee wrote it on July 14, when they had been married barely six weeks:

My Dearest Angel, I kiss the carnation in the thought of my love, as I start to write my love to my love. Your lovely letter I got as I rode out to the Sellers property, & when I got there I hitched my horse & left the "madding crowd" and went down to the lonely grave of Patriarch Sellers and read the sweetest letter that a man ever received and devoured the kiss at the end—a kiss from the sweetest lips that ever breathed love, Oh Beautiful, Beautiful Darling, I love you, I love you. . . .

Yes, Sweet Love, I slept quite well last night from 10 to 6:30, and both ends were bounded by thoughts of you, I slept from those thoughts and awakened into them, and all through my sleep I loved my love, and all day I love her. Have felt pretty well but been too busy to think of myself all day.

Saw the Doctor this morning and the kind good man laughed at me and guaranteed personally that a few weeks would see me all right, said our experience was the usual one, & that I had pulled up very rapidly, but that right now it would be well enough not to hurry back to you, but Angel, I swear, this advice will be hard to follow. . . . I enclose a letter to your Father endorsing Hart which please hand him—in it refer to the date, *14th,* as the anniversary of his most gracious consent.

> Sweet old Aunty [Maggie Holt], and all the rest sent love & say they
> miss you as they never dreamed they would. I think Jennie will come
> back with me, she is in love with your people & gratified by their
> thoughtfulness in wanting her. I enclose a letter from Mother to you.
> . . . The keys came all right, many thanks, Sweet Angel. . . . Oh you are
> the sweetest & loveliest thing on earth.

Greenlee, although restrained, did allude to sexual matters occasionally. The
letter to Judge Paul was on behalf of a friend of Green's: "Mr. Geo. L. Hart of
Roanoke, who desires to be Referee in Bankruptcy—he is an earnest and outspoken Republican, and a man whom I feel certain would fill the position satisfactorily." Greenlee ended, "Thanking you again, for granting an infinitely more
important request to me on *this* date a year ago, I am with love to all sincerely
yours, Greenlee D. Letcher."

We can read an implied criticism of Katie's behavior in the gentle letter from
Mother Letcher, who as wife of a governor had once been a formidable political
force in the state in her own right. Even when Greenlee was away, Katie had so
little to do with his family who lived in the houses all around them on Letcher
Avenue, that one is forced to conclude she didn't enjoy their company. This letter
implies that Katie, in being absent, was not quite fulfilling her obligations. It
reads, in part,

> I wrote to you yesterday but Green was in such a hurry to get his off
> that he left mine out—We have missed you so much—I know you are
> enjoying your first visit home hugely—You have had a good many calls
> and several invitations out—Jennie will go to the Ruffner's to-day. I
> think the dinner was given for *you*. . . . Bertha Howell[4] is invited. Mary
> Quarles and the Prestons both invited Jennie to go in their carriages.
> Miss Preston invited her first so of course she will go with her, that is
> if it does not rain, it threatens just now. Jennie is sorry she cannot go
> down with him [Greenlee]. She is busy putting up fruit for the winter.
> Lex. is very quiet now, at least for young people—Mrs. Harris is no
> better—Mrs. Campbell's baby is still quite sick. Jen. spent yesterday
> with the Davidsons & called on her way home—Fan. says she will try
> and remember all your callers—Mag. is fixing up an old dress and I am
> trying to make a wrapper, so you can imagine us as we are—Hous. has
> gone to a Rail road meeting—We have had such cool weather lately.
> . . . Mrs. D. Pendleton came yesterday to invite you to tea Friday—

Green will give you all the news but I know his letter will be taken up with regrets that you are not with him. All join in love to you & all the family. God bless you. Yours very affectionately, Mother [Letcher]. P.S. Jennie has just returned from the dining—says she had a delightful day— . . . I think you must have treated my *baby* well as he is looking better—Goodbye—Yours affectionately. Mother.

PS If you see a fine piece of white Tarleton in your travels around town, get me a half yd. I suppose the quality I want will be about 50 cents a yard—I cannot get any here—I want it for caps.

The picture of sober industry in the Letcher household contrasts with the frivolity of the Paul household. Katie did not return on schedule, citing in a note to her mother-in-law her mother's "indisposition" as the reason, and Greenlee wrote back, innocently solicitous of Katie's mother, promising Katie a house of their own, and obviously trying to smooth out difficulties, on July 18,

My Dearest Katie, Your letters, so full of the love my life and heart crave alone enable me to possess my soul in patience until I can return to my heart's home, to you, Sweet Angel, My Own, My Love, My Life. . . . The Doctor told me to-day that Mrs. Harris could move and expected to do so & give us our house by August 1st, of which I am very glad, as the sooner we get settled the better and also because both of my Sisters with their families are expected in August, and this would crowd things here.[5] So Sweet Angel, if you love me enough to follow me, look forward, (but suppress too much sadness), to coming with me home early next week. . . . [B]ut please My Little Angel, write so that I will get your letter Wednesday evening all the same, because if I find none when I get back from Buena Vista, *I will die*. . . . No Angel, I don't object to your laughing at my clothes—*love me* & you can laugh at them all you have a mind to—I am very certain you love me for neither my money nor my clothes, Old Woman. I know now that your love will stand every test and I feel safe & happy beyond all words, and I love you to, and beyond, the verge of the *infinite*. Jennie will be down to-morrow evening, & her brother [that's Greenlee himself] will follow as quickly as he can. . . .

I am so sorry you see cause to be solicitous about your sweet mother's health—don't be worried, I guess it is just the warm weather, which I expect is her trying season.[6] I love your mother, Angel, with a love akin to yours, and every time I see her, her charm and sweetness grow on me; I only hope she loves me & feels toward me as I do toward her.

In another letter two days later, he spoke delicately of their personal problem, almost certainly sexual in nature: "I look forward with confidence to the time when we will not even consider all this a misfortune—it is high proof of our absolute love, there could perhaps be no more searching test, and I look forward with perfect confidence to a happy issue for us." And he held out another carrot: "Yes, my Little Angel, we are going into our own house next month."

Finally Katie returned from Harrisonburg to Lexington, toward the end of July, when Lilian wrote,

> Dearest Katie, thou hast left us—And thy loss we greatly feel, etc. this poem being so well known I can't quote the rest even with substitutions. . . . [W]e had a postal from Papa this morning but no word from the fair Virginia. Please excuse these blots but Miss Brighty *must* do something characteristic. . . . You and I anti-moustache fanatics should look on the face of the Rev. A. P. Funkhouser. (A more diabolical thing you never saw but I suppose the result is quite reasonable, for the less seen of him the better—in more ways than one.) Mamma and Aunt Jennie [Rogers] have not so far gotten into any "discussions" and I am hoping the armistice will continue. It is after ten or rather the train has come and of *course* all are in bed except me. . . . All send best love to Miss Jennie. With Spain asking for peace it looks as if our part (the division to which Bun belongs) of the Society for the Prevention of Cruelty to Animals, otherwise the U.S. Army won't be in the scrap and Bun can't kill my 266 Spaniards.[7] . . . Oh me! Oh my. We have not heard a thing about the Roller dance and not a soul will get married—so there is no news. . . . I am ink from top to toe, as you may imagine. There was an agent here this afternoon, but ah, I settled him, he was a callow country youth with spectacles. I scorned his little black grip with me eyes, and the poor boy turned away crushed and heartbroken. Give my best love to Benedict.[8]

There follows a list of all Katie and Greenlee's wedding presents, pieces of silver ranging from oyster forks to coffee pots, pearl-handled knives to chop plates, chairs to lamps. Here, as she will later, Lilian willingly does Katie's chores for her.

The newlyweds moved from the Letcher house around the first of August, and Lilian's sly references on August 2 allow us to see Katie's determination to move. That move didn't go over swimmingly with Greenlee's mother.

> We received your letter this morning and are so glad you are going to Hang Your Crane, also that you didn't shuffle the poor old lady off this mortal coil by your insistence. . . . The peace still continues between Mamma and Aunt Jennie but they come "near it, mighty near it." Your friend Mr. Coleman is at Collicello.[9] Daddy and the boys are getting ready for the mountains with great preparations. . . . Mamma is trying to get out of the Kentucky trip by various excuses.

There follows a chatty description of a dance past, an upcoming dance, who has spent the night, who is coming to dinner, a ball game, John and Seymour's search for a lost "dorg," and a mischievous reference to their contentious Aunt Jennie. It is easy to see how the somber life in Lexington might not be so appealing as the gala milieu of Harrisonburg. Lilian ends by sending "Love to you and the robber," and encloses a note from Aunt Jennie Rogers:

> My dear Catherine, I have missed you so much from the home circle here, and had so much hoped you would get back to see me, that it is with feelings of each disappointment, I shall go away on Tuesday next, and had it not been in view of the fact that you were just in the midst of preparations for housekeeping, would certainly have made another appeal to my dear nephew [by marriage] Mr. Letcher to bring you back. I have enjoyed your Mama and Papa, Lilian and the boys very much but of course could have taken in a great deal more had the vacant chairs been filled by you and Virginia. Hope you will soon realize your fond ideal of home, and be fully established in your own house, for I like to think of one so well calculated to make home life all it ought to be, as being appointed to that realm. With very much love to Mr. L, you may tell him, that while I am perfectly happy in him as a nephew, I have not as yet been able to forgive him for taking you away just as I came, and will write to him when time has softened these rebellious feelings. Remember me kindly to Miss Jennie. I feel as if I knew her too, and would like so much to have farther acquaintance with both her and Mr. L; and now I beg, that you will sometimes think of Aunt Jennie, and write to me, when you can catch a time.

On August 27, sister Virginia, who had returned home, wrote: "I have intended to go see about the carpet but have not been down town but once since I got home. . . . I want to see you so much and tell you about my trip. . . . Harrisonburg is as usual getting lively. . . . Of course the horse show was the event. . . . Our urchins were disappointed when Hensie D[aingerfield] only carried off a red ribbon . . . Mrs. Rosenberger had a party Wednesday night but I did not go. . . . Thursday night the young men gave a hayride and I went with *Ernest* Wilton! Last night Winfield Liggett took me to Mrs. Miller's watermelon feast. . . . I promised the urchins a cake and must go and make it."

Virginia also noted how pleased everyone was at S. H. Letcher's appointment as judge, making him the second judge in the family, and adding, "Seymour is disturbed because he is afraid you won't know who people are speaking of when they say 'The Judge.'"

It is interesting that the family referred to Greenlee as "Benedict," "the robber," and "your puritanic worser half." Katie's grandmother wrote, "I swear I will like him," as though to do so were a difficult thing, and Aunt Jennie Rogers spoke of being "not yet ready to forgive him." Although any comment by itself may have been written in humor, a reader might conclude that the Pauls were not as smitten with Greenlee as he was with them.

Meanwhile, Greenlee attended to business. This letter was forwarded from the mother of an inmate at the state prison:

> I wish you to take this message to Mr. Letcher. . . . His of the 12th inst. rec'd with gratitude for the clemency extended to me therein. I do not wish to molest him. But his missive was so delectable and elaborate, also knowing he is a gentleman so magnanimous, I again appeal to him for maintenance, beleiving [*sic*] he will not defer writing immediately if not sooner informing me why I have not been released. My deportment is without maculation and I hope for his lenity to think not I am too importunate. Please . . . let me know weather [*sic*] you received this letter or not and when to expect a letter from Mr. Letcher. Your devoted Son, Fountain Lewis, Va. State Prison, Barber's Cell.

It is not known if Greenlee secured the man's release, but possibly he did, for later in his life he had another "delectable" letter from Mr. Lewis. Katie spent Thanksgiving in Lexington, visited by her sister, Virginia, who was attending Stuart Hall, and Virginia's friend, Mary Morton. On Thanksgiving Day Kate Paul wrote forlornly, "We are all well and looking forward to an unusually quiet

Thanksgiving: with you, Virginia and Papa all away we will have a small party to eat our nice, big turkey." She ends by saying, "Give much love to Mary from us all and tell her we want her awfully at Xmas if we can get her."

Telephones came to Lexington in 1894, and numbers were assigned in order as people were connected. The Letchers' number was 60, four years later, suggesting how slow the newfangled telephone was to catch on.

Katie went to Harrisonburg for the 1898 Christmas holidays, and Greenlee joined them for Christmas Day. Two days later, back at work, he wrote her with his usual generosity, to ward off her return to a cold house:

> My Dearest Angel, I telephoned home telling them to tell Maggie to make the fires as soon as she came to-day, and Fannie answered that word had come that Maggie would not be there until tomorrow, so I at once tried to telephone you. I was some time getting the message through, then Sipes & Harris's Office failed to respond, and then I finally got Mrs. Eishman at the Clarendon to take the message for you. I told her to send it up & pay the boy 10 cents, which I would hand her when I came down; or to tell you to pay him. I feel lonely, Angel, at the disappointment of not seeing you this evening, but will make up for it by that many more kisses tomorrow evening. Sweet, sweet, sweet angel, I love you, love you, love you, with *all* my soul. Thank every one of your lovely people for me for the delightful Xmas I have had—they could not have been nicer, and I could not have enjoyed myself more. I enjoyed every minute, and unless they kick, we will spend every Xmas in the same way.

In February, Katie returned to Harrisonburg, two months pregnant. She spent nearly her whole pregnancy there, with Greenlee visiting as often as he could get away. Despite his loneliness without her, he carried on cheerfully, traveling widely and enjoying life. She appeared to love him dearly when they were apart. It seems to have been a foregone conclusion that her pregnancies, lyings-in, and births, would occur at her childhood home, though in fact it would not happen that way.

From Harrisonburg, Katie was capable of warmth and generosity: "I wonder if my precious old man is writing his promised letter to me now and if he wants to see me as much as I want to see my brave Sweet Thing. I love you so, and it isn't half as much fun to be here without you." She wrote, "My arrival was, as you may imagine, rather a surprise to Family, but they took it wonderfully well and seemed quite pleased to see me, and only regretted that you hadn't come too. Indeed everybody I see asks so promptly if you are here or when you're coming that I begin to feel quite jealous and a secondary consideration."

In Harrisonburg, Katie resumed her life as it had been, attending church and social events (which she rarely if ever did in Lexington), entertaining drop-ins, and stopping by to see old friends: "On the way home I stopped to see the Deviers and Mr. Deviers hardly noticed me but inquired at once 'When's Lee [Greenlee] coming?' in a tone which seemed rather to resent my taking it upon myself to come without you. . . . Mrs. Deviers and Miss Teensie both look very well." Hortense Deviers was Katie's age; the family were lifelong Harrisonburg friends. Miss Teensie is someone Katie always visited while in Harrisonburg; she may have lived with the Deviers.

The next day, Katie inquired solicitously, "Did old man sleep all morning and get a good rest?" She crooned, "I know he's getting fat over at Mother's house with Fannie's good things to eat." Away from Greenlee, she was able to write: "Sweet thing, I miss so not having you here, and I don't know how I'll get along two more days without you. I love you harder than ever and want dreadfully to see you —and you surely won't disappoint me by making your coming any later than Tuesday night. If you find Tuesday evening that you can't come, I hope you'll telegraph *not* telephone."

She instructed him to water the plants, to send her a pattern she wanted a jacket from, to send a cactus to Fannie, and not to forget to tell Brother Houston how much everyone in Harrisonburg thought of him.

He replied at length on February 5, 1899, how much he missed her: "You are *all* my heart craves, and as I sit here and feel your absence in every vacancy, and in every silence, (which emphasizes every tick of that beautiful green clock,) I *know* what a desolation that life and my life would be without you, Sweet, Sweet, Sweet Angel."

He wrote asking her to check on whether the bills were all right and described working so hard on the "Insurance Policy, the Day case, and the Rockbridge Alum Springs case" that he didn't get home until one in the morning, but admitted "I did not work all the evening as I took Wilkerson first to the Patent Medicine Man's show, where I thought of you and got you some elegant tooth-powder and soap. It was not extraordinarily good, but I got one or two laughs out of it which paid me for going, while also Wilkerson seemed to enjoy it beyond measure."

He wrote endless paragraphs of his love and yearning for her, reiterating how he loved her family, adding, "All at home send love and Mother says she had intended to invite us both over to dinner today to eat her turkey, and was sorry you were not with me." He wrote of his bitter disappointment that he was too busy to visit. "The Day case keeps me, which I think now looks encouraging unless something goes wrong. And to guard against that possibility I must stay over to see Day tomorrow evening." He continued, "Mrs. Bev Tucker telephoned up this morning to ask me if you would attend a Euchre [card game] party in Lent, that she could not give it any other time and that anybody else she wanted had said they would come to it. I told her that I guessed you would come and that you would write her from home after I went down."

But despite his protestations, Greenlee was not lonely. He ended one letter, "I must go to the Depot to mail this, and go to Col. Mann's after that, [and] Miss Maggie's house, so I will kiss you Good-night, with all the love of a heart and life."

Katie was *still* in Harrisonburg in April. Elsewhere in the world, in 1899, Detroit was beginning to manufacture automobiles; Jello and Welch's Grape Juice were newly invented, a worldwide cholera pandemic began. People listened to "Maple Leaf Rag" on the piano, and "My Wild Irish Rose" topped the hit parade for that year. The Yukon yielded gold, and Robert Service penned the ballads my grandfather loved. Greenlee visited Harrisonburg when he could get away and wrote from Staunton, Clifton Forge, and several places in West Virginia, always yearning for her. Typically, he wrote, "I can not finish this as I have but a moment waiting for my train—but I write to tell you *I love you* and am homesick for you, Sweet Sweet Angel"; he wrote also of daily frustrations: "I fear the servant mixup will keep you from me longer than Thursday. I expect you had best write to Maggie to come. . . . [F]or although she is of a temper not the best and a manner not the most winning, yet as she cooks pretty well and is clean, seemingly honest and without encumbrances, I guess we will do worse to change."

On May 15, 1899, Republican President McKinley campaigned at Natural Bridge, introduced by Democrat Greenlee Letcher. This says a great deal about Greenlee's all-encompassing tolerance. Katie missed the event but possibly Greenlee was trying to lure her home or at least gain favor by inviting McKinley to stay with them, as Katie was of course Republican. That night Greenlee wrote: "And to think that you did not know how I loved you early this morning, when I laid everything aside to write & tell you." He sent her roses, stamps for her little brothers' collections, circulars from Lexington merchants; he complained about having to work late every night. Through the summer, he traveled to West Virginia, and to New York, where he ate oysters and thought of her. He attended funerals, commented on some poetry in *Harper's*: "It's right good. It all interests me very much." His promoters were clearly looking out for him: from New York he wrote to Katie,

"Got an Immediate Delivery letter from Miss Maggie Freeland telling me Strother[10] was [here] & to call & I will do so if I have the time."

Greenlee connected with old friends: "Met Broadway Rouss [G. W. Rouss, VMI '97] coming from the funeral this evening—he invited me to see him, & was very friendly." And he begged her, "Make Mother & the kids [John, Charlie, and Seymour] come with you and the sooner the happier I will be, for the house looked terribly desolate Sweet Sweet Angel, without you—*the soul is not there* when you are away." Obviously referring to some discussion about where she would have the baby, he wrote, "You are right, Dearest Angel, in not being willing to go home in September—it would derange your good people too much."

And she wrote back, more lovingly the farther away he was: "Although I suppose this will either be forwarded to you at home or dead-lettered, still I cannot refrain from writing to tell you how I love you." She wrote of the weather, of reading a novel, of her mother's making her a shift, of a dressmaker's altering clothes for her changing shape, of Lilian's running to the post office, of everyone but her going to Ottobine on a picnic. In her delicate condition, she believed she could do nothing.

But she clearly didn't write to him often enough, for on July 26, 1899, he wrote, from New York, "No letter has come from you and I am brokenhearted and don't know what to make of it."

However, on July 28, he wrote from Philadelphia, "I live again—as I registered here the clerk handed me your letter, and it gave me great joy, for in New York I guess I about devilled the clerk of the St. Denis to death by my importunity about important letters I was expecting but which never came. . . . I began to be nervous about your health." He ended one letter by saying, "I have again taken a trip to the cities and can find nothing that can touch my Angel in beauty."

By August 15, she was back in Lexington, nursing a toothache, and he was on the road again. She wrote, "In a quiet interval of the tooth I would just like to mention how I love you and how I miss you. I have no doubt about whether I love you or not, and I don't believe you have either." Pregnant, she took more interest in his family than usual, reporting to him that The Judge [Houty] hadn't been able to leave on a planned trip because Becky [Greenlee's horse] had twisted her rope around her ankle and cut it badly. When he came home, Greenlee wrote to her—she had already gone back to Harrisonburg—of his mother, whose health was failing, "Mother is about as she was yesterday, seems brighter and stronger by far than when I saw her last. Finally and in conclusion, I love you and will be heartbroken if anything keeps you away longer than tomorrow night. With all my heart's love."

Sometime in August, with the family all gathered, the children and grandchildren home, and Katie pregnant, the Letchers assembled for the family portrait. Perhaps they sensed Mrs. Letcher had not long to live.

On September 8, 1899, John Paul Letcher, presumably named for both grandfathers, was born in Lexington, and as soon as telegrams alerted the world, letters of congratulation poured in. Greenlee began writing fond letters to baby John: only ten days after the baby's birth, he wrote: "I hope you want to see me as badly as I want to see you and Muddy. . . . I hope you have been a good boy and not been out with the other boys and gotten the high coughs [hiccups?] again. If Aunt Henrietta [a baby nurse] Muddy or Granny or anybody abuses you while I am gone tell me tomorrow evening when I get back to you & I will see 'em about it."

On September 22, 1899, the young prince received from his Castleton, Kentucky, Daingerfield relatives, the following letter, notable for its choices of "gifts." (In the 1830s, Robert Letcher, the governor's first cousin, had gone west and become, in time, the governor of Kentucky.)

> My dear John P. Letcher, I was extremely glad to hear of your arrival in Lexington. I know you will adorn a name that has been an ornament to your (& my) state for long. I wish I could now, and may some day, send you a pair of dumb bells and Indian Clubs, and illuminated copies of the Bible, Shakespeare and of the Latin & Greek Poets. The Constitutions of Your State and of the United States (minus the amendments adopted under duress)—and of Jay's Political Economy to fit you for the Career to which you are born. Kiss your little Mama for me. . . . [A]nd always "kiss & love" her when you go out and shine from school or office. Your devoted cousin, Foxhall A. Daingerfield

Katie's mother stayed in Lexington for the lying-in, and for several weeks after the birth. From Covington, Greenlee reported: "I just ate supper at the same table with Jim Frazier and told him all about Little John." and from Natural Bridge, he wrote: "All at the Bridge send you love & said that they must see John at the first opportunity." Katie was his "Beautiful Angel," and he sent "All my Heart's Heart's love." From Bath County, he wrote, "Beautiful Thing, I am just too worried for anything in the world—we just got into the trial of our case this evening, what frightens me is that we may not finish tomorrow, but I hope we will—for Sweet Sweet Thing, I do want to see you and Little John the worst kind of way, and if I don't very soon, I'll just die—the only consolation I have at all, is just to tell everybody, everything about Little John."

On October 4, the new grandmother, Kate Paul, took the train home to Harrisonburg and reported the next day:

> My homeward journey was not attended with any startling adventures. I was surprised to see so many people on the train, until I remembered the Carnival at Staunton. The number increased at every station and at Fairfield another car was attached. Va and Idge met me at the station the former with a very severe cold which had kept her in bed a day or two. John lumbered up and we all came home to dinner. The two precious urchins don't get home till 4 o'clock, Charlie not till five as he has "a job," to carry the Evening News, at 75 ¢ a week. Do you remember an account in the News I read you of Mr. Sibert being thrown from his buggy? Well, Charlie wrote it! Isn't he a cute little reporter?
>
> The children have thousands of questions to ask about the baby. How big, how heavy, his eyes, his hair &c &c. John always speaks of him as the Kid and shows great interest, he says "we wanted him named Greenlee, Jr.," Va and Idge think he ought to be John Greenlee. Idge says—"Does he slobber Mamma oh! does he slobber, and have to wear a little bib? I do *love* babies that slobber and wear bibs!" I had to admit he hadn't begun this delightful accomplishment yet, but it would probably come later. They are all crazy to see him and say they can't wait. As I expected they are all furious because Virginia F[letcher] and Charlotte [Richardson][11] saw him before they did. Bun says "it makes me so mad to hear them sitting up and telling what a lovely baby Katherine has." It seems they both shouted noble about your baby and your sweet home. Tell that precious little infant Grandmuzzer did want to see him yesterday and last night so *awfully bad*. He looked *so* lovely in my last view of him in his cloak and cap. . . . Does he 'mell as sweet as ever to-day! I suppose Papa saw a good deal of the Dewey[12] parade in Washington—as he was there from 8 to 12 that night.

On October 18, Katie's mother wrote her daughter in alarm, saying she had heard at a funeral that Judge Letcher had been called home because of his mother's "extreme illness" and subsequent death. She repeated the usual sentiments, and she worried about how Katie was taking the death of her mother-in-law. Katie apparently took it just fine, inured against pain by her new plaything. She saw fit to go to Harrisonburg with the baby shortly thereafter, and on November 2, Greenlee wrote her there of how busy he was: "I was worried to death that Col. Marr[13] & Mr. Parsons stayed at my office until almost midnight, & kept me from telling both my loves how I love them." He reported on several baby gifts from his family, two silver cups, a "sack" and a pillow, and urged Katie to write to his sisters and brothers to thank them. "Haven't had time to have my hair cut, which I know disappoints you dreadfully," he added, and sent kisses to them both, directing baby John to "take care of Muddy."

Although he urged her to return, Greenlee frequently assured Katie that he wanted her to do whatever she wanted. He wrote hastily of his busy-ness, of the impossibility of visiting them, adding, "I do hope it will not be necessary for me to go to West Virginia, as it may carry me up into the wilds, which will be unpleasant."

He reported, "When I went home today Ella [Hanes, one of many maids] had cleaned up everything, made up the bed (for the first time since you had been away) and taken down the curtains, and washed them with my soiled clothes, and called order out of the chaos. She said she was well today—had gotten over the bad water at home."

On a local election day, he exulted: "The election was very quiet to-day and the result as expected—and Little John is certainly no Republican *for he is surely a winner,* and to look at him proves he is not 'Jonahed' by a defeat in the outset of life, for if he was he might be 'hoodooed' forever. Little John and I are all right with our feet over the dashboard tonight, riding the crest of the wave and sipping the foam—look at him and see if you can deny it. 'He's all right—who's all right? *Little John!*'" Since McKinley was reelected a year later, obviously, Democrats won locally. Given that Katie and all her people were Republicans, Greenlee might be accused of insensitivity in his enthusiasm.

He wrote to Katie from Richmond on November 10 that he'd seen her father, who assured him that she was "mending" at home in Harrisonburg. Typically, he protested, "I love you and am just crazy to get to you Sunday, but I fear I can not, but still I hope because I want to so much." He averred that he enjoyed her letters so much that "I look forward so to getting them I could hardly stop you, if I knew it hurt you to do it, Sweet Sweet *Sweet* Angel." Like any fond father, he wrote: "Saw Judge Graham this a.m. & he tells me he has a beautiful daughter 6 weeks old, & he and Minnie seem to think almost as much of it as we do of John." He

detailed his activities, arguing his case, obtaining money due Maggie Freeland, and
hoped he had "accomplished something for Mrs. Parsons."

As the year wound down, he recounted his after-hours social invitations: "Jack
Montague invited me to supper tonight but I was too busy, so I had to decline—
also was invited to the club. I think it very probable that I will have to go to West
Va. if so will try to come by Harrisonburg on the way back home and take you
along." Upon his return to Lexington, he wrote,

> I have not seen Ella since coming back but I never in all my life smelt
> such an odour of onions fried as last night in the house—I guess Ella is
> living on them in your absence. You had best make arrangements, if
> you feel well enough, to come back home with me on my way from
> West Va., perhaps about the middle of next week—I will determine
> certainly about going and when, tomorrow. . . . I expect on account of
> the short time between now and Xmas, and the large proportional ad-
> ditional expenses of the travel, you had best get a nurse here till then—
> then we can look for one there for next year; but of course do as you
> think most judicious.

Back in Richmond, he wrote: "The governor today asked after 'that pretty Mrs.
Letcher.' I will call on him tonight, the good man."

On New Year's Eve, Katie was still in Harrisonburg, the baby had been colicky,
and Greenlee was lonesome:

> I received your sweet letter last night after giving up hope—Hous came
> with the mail and no letter from you and he told me he had gotten it
> all, but when I went to my office after supper Wilkerson had gotten
> it—and I lived again. It made me happy it was a sweet letter for it told
> me you loved me, which I would rather hear and think about than any-
> thing on earth—for I love you with all my heart, all my soul, beautiful,
> beautiful angel. . . . I am sorry to hear of John's colic—precious boy—
> Kiss him a hundred times for Daddy. . . .
>
> Ella was looking for me yesterday & Jennie was uneasy, thought
> maybe she was going to leave us, as several people were looking for
> cooks, but she just wanted to know about your movements in view of
> her going to the country for a visit. I told her you would be here Friday
> evening. You had better arrange to bring Bunch with you Friday
> evening and I will return the same evening from Clifton Forge and

*John Paul Letcher,
eight months old, 1900*

meet you here. Unless Bunch is not coming, I do not feel that it will be possible for me to come for you. Mother & Daddy can then come Saturday evening. Tell them the Lexington Hotel just phoned me that they can go on to Lynchburg Sunday morning—as they had hoped. . . . By phone Miss Maggie Freeland just invited me to supper tonight. Now I am comfortable with both the Heater & the stove going.

The next day, January 1, 1900, he penned her a New Year's speech: "So do I, a thousand times over pledge you and Little John my hearts love, deep, pure and absolute, for not only the century beginning to-day, but for *all* time and eternity—oh, I love you, I love you, I love you, with all the love, that love can love, Beautiful Wife and Beautiful Boy—my heart's world, my soul's wealth. I know you love me, for a consuming love like mine, could not live except in love. Beautiful, beautiful Darlings."

As ever, he nudged her homeward, urging her to bring her entire family home to Lexington with her, adding, "[D]o not risk anything, Angel, either overexertion or catching cold if it be too cold."

In Harrisonburg, on January 5, she wrote him that his letter had come before breakfast, "and The Boy and I read it together. I send you the last page back so you can kiss the crumples he made with his dear little pink hands playing with it. He is so well and pretty and sweet. I wonder if any other baby ever gave any other mother as much pleasure as he gives me." She closed by asking him to bring the baby's pillow when he came and thanked him obliquely: "I forgot to tell you howdy for the check—which is more than I need even at the present drug rates." She must have hated having him in charge of the money, for although she was not shy about asking for it, she rarely thanked him for sending it.

Katie's letter ended: "I'm still feeling better but keeping very severely quiet and sticking close by the bed, demon bed. Be sure and give our love to all the folks and come down and spend Sunday with us, for we do want to see our Daddy man so much," and the next letter noted: "The baby man has just come in from a ride in the sunshine and is now engaged in taking a nap. He says he surely does miss Dad-dad and wants him to hurry back. Isn't he the most beautiful little boy in all the world?"

Greenlee continued to find life fascinating even away from his wife and baby: from Weston, West Virginia, came a typical missive:

> I reached here this morning, and have seen Judge W. Brannon, the lawyer conversed with me in the Wills matter, and in his office there was a young man, named Jake Fisher who went to W&L U. some years ago, but I recognized him as soon as I saw him, & in talking he asked me if I was married and when I told him that I had married Judge Paul's daughter, Judge Brannon said he knew your Father. Fisher was very wild when in Lexington and tells me that as he came home, he got drunk, & into a fight & nearly killed a fellow & was a fugitive from justice for a year; but that now he never touches a drop, is married, and we had a Ratification and Enthusiasm Meeting over our Boys. I also met another fellow, young Bennett, who had gone to W&LU. and he called his Father Judge W. G. Bennett who was an old V.M.I. man and his Grandfather, another Judge Brannon, who told me he was a great friend of my Father's and took the votes of 3 or 4 counties with him to the Convention that nominated my Father for Governor.

The Lexington paper reported that "Greenlee Letcher, a prominent and distinguished member of the Lexington bar, was in Weston several days last week in consultation with W.W. Brannon, his associate counsel, in the Wills estate."

Katie was wholly absorbed with the baby: "How I wish you could see the baby man now as he lies on the bed, kicking and crowing and 'joying his self right along. Poor Old Man, to have to spend whole weeks without seeing that beautiful little John."

On January 11, 1900, Greenlee wrote, "I used to laugh while at the V.M.I. at the intense eagerness of fellows looking for their mail, hanging around the Q.M.'s [quartermaster] room, and watching for the Mail, which I had never felt & could not understand—but Beautiful Thing, I yearned all day for the one train that reaches here at 4:30 and laughed at myself, as I pulled for the Post Office when I heard it blow, and waited until the little mail was distributed, expecting a letter, as Judge Brannon promised to forward any that came to Weston; and I knew how I loved you in the *disappointment* of not getting it."

Katie worried about "Gov," as she mostly addressed him, not protecting himself from the weather and working too hard. But she always returned quickly to the object of her fascination: "The Boy is well and beautiful and good in spite of the poor little gums that hurt so by reason of those far away teeth. Poor little boy, I wish he didn't have to wait so long for them," and "Little John boy has just finished his dinner and says be sure and send his love to the gov'ner—And he has put a kiss for you where I have marked it on the next page. But we wish we could put them on your dear lips instead." Of Greenlee's conviviality, she commented, "If you were shipwrecked on the coast of Patagonia I believe you'd run across old acquaintances or make new ones and be invited to supper with the chief of the tribe that very night."

Greenlee reported: "I was broken off in my letter last night by Phil[14] hugging me, and shaming me for not naming the Boy after him—I told him that if he knew a father's love, he would know that a boy would never be started into the race of life with such a 'hoodoo.'" Greenlee moved from his usual raptures, "Sweet Sweet Thing, no power could keep me here for the winter, without you; and I just wish every minute for you & that splendid boy—kiss him for me, and then have him kiss you for me" to "Shelton invited me to breakfast with him at the Jefferson this morning, but I could not accept, as I had to get ready for argument of our case; but I took lunch with him at Rugero—he also invited James and a friend of his named Reid. Shelton is lobbying here for some R.R. Bills. They say he is doing well in Norfolk. In a crowd to-day he said if he made anything of himself, he owed it to me. Gov. Tyler invited me specially to his Legislative Reception tonight, and I thought I had better not go on account of Mother. I have met many friends and enjoyed that very much since being here."[15]

*Phil Nunn of Lexington, freed
in childhood by the Civil War*

In April 1900, Judge Paul wrote to his daughter, who was two months pregnant
with her second child:

> My Dear Katie: The little Jersey cow came around to the front porch
> this morning, looked up at me as I stood in the door and said: "Where
> is that baby you all told me about a month ago, was coming down here
> to stay awhile, and that you wanted me to help care for while it staid
> with you?" I told her the baby would be here in a few days, she said,
> "That will be all right, but ask his Mother why she don't come on with
> him? I can't be all the time waiting for her baby;" and she marched
> proudly back to the stable yard. So just pack your duds, fill his bot. and
> get your ticket at the earliest time practicable. Everything is ready for
> you, your bed in the sitting room, and you shall have fish and eggs for
> breakfast, and the young onions in the garden await your coming. The
> yard is beautiful in its early spring dress; the buds and leaves are coming

out on all the trees and bushes, and the few flowers that can are doing their best at blooming. You shall sleep so long as you please every morning, and nobody shall insist on your getting awake to hear the robins sing. Yes, come down and cheer up a feller what is realizing the meaning of the patent medicine man when he talks of that "tired-run down-played-out-feeling." I want to toss the boy and hear him laugh. No news. Morgan is still trying the "insurgents." The trial bids fair to be as long as the Ticheburne case. Mr. Keester has been on the stand today but I have not heard what he said. Abe [Abram Paul, Judge Paul's older bachelor brother] is taking dinner with us—and will testify this evening. All well at Ottobine. U.V.Va. Glee Club at Assembly Hall to-night—dance in Newman building for the performance. Much love to you all. Yours, Papa

What young woman could resist such a call? Katie hurried back to Harrisonburg with the baby, as Greenlee headed to West Virginia on horseback, where he encountered, "baby James [Graham], just 2 days older than John and next to John as fine a baby as I have ever seen—I told them so, and they did not seem to get mad." He urged her, "I hope you are getting stronger & better each day; I feel that you will, if you *rest* thoroughly day & night."

Greenlee was willing to enter an arena generally left to women, the frustrating problem of servants. "I asked after Charlotte [a potential maid], as I returned from playing a game of Base Ball on the Burn this evening, & her mother told me, she was very well—I saw Reid [Reid White, a physician] afterwards, & he said he had not seen her for some time, but would see her & let me know."

Katie nagged Greenlee to find things and bring them to Harrisonburg and was annoyed when he could not find them, for he replied, somewhat fearfully,

I have been looking tonight in the front room up-stairs for the "silk dress with dull yellow flowers," but cannot find it—will look again however, Sweet thing, & will be worse disappointed than you if I fail to find it. Excuse me for forgetting the stamps last night but I enclose you some now, with postals. Beautiful thing I am rushed to death & have only time to tell you I love you, love you, love you & am Yours absolutely & forever, G. D. L. P.S. Find enclosed check for $10.00 to pay back money advanced by you.

In the letters are many exchanges such as the one above. Katie had fairly strict rules about what she would spend *her* money for, and it did not go for food, drugs, stationery, travel, or stamps. If she had to use her funds for those, she insisted on being reimbursed. It seems an oddity of their relationship that Katie kept her money separate from Greenlee's.

She remained "frail" throughout her pregnancy, or at least described herself so, and was possibly experiencing morning sickness. Greenlee, held at arm's length, instructed her from afar: "I do want my angel to get strong and well again for she cannot be thoroughly happy and love Old Man as she then would—rest yourself & take the best care day and night, and I bet you sodas you will get all right again, and Old Man will get you that $25.00 dress and we will (with my new suit) just 'split the atmosphere' down to Dress Parade, and most everywhere." He wrote sadly, "Everybody asks after you Sweet Thing, & even if you do not care for any one here, everybody seems to care for my Angel."

It must be universal of parents to talk nonsense where their babies are concerned (for how *can* we express the *in*-expressible love we feel for our children?). Greenlee wrote (and I spare the reader many similar expressions):

> for Daddy surely *wuvs* you and Muddy and wants to be with you all the time, and he gets pow'ful lonely when he goes to bed at night now without you and Muddy for company. And I surely am glad to hear Muvver tell me you are getting all right again and will enjoy that nice game of "Ketch yer" which you & Muvver sure have such fun playing when you feel good. Kiss Muddy for Daddy & tell her he is coming to see her just as quick as he can, that she don't yearn half as much for him as he does for her—cose he *loves* her *so*. With *all* love for you both and kisses, I am your devoted *Daddy*

Greenlee was left as usual to grapple with the servant problem, reporting, "Oh, I saw Reid White again, but he has not yet seen Charlotte, saying that when she called he was out of his office, but he will send for her again & let me hear from him. Did Estes[16] get down & see our Gal Bunch? Beautiful Darling, I hope you are continuing to improve—Old Man wants you to be well enough to come with him to the Bridge next time—they all here urge me to bring you and Little John."

Estes must indeed have visited Virginia, for soon Greenlee wrote: "I saw Estes this A.M. & he tells me he has never seen anyone improve as you have done in the same length of time—I bet you money if you would do as Mother & I told you, you would get *all right, all right*—and I do so want my Beautiful Angel to get strong & well again when she will be happy, and *if possible,* more beautiful than she is now. This time tomorrow night I will be with my Angel. . . . and I hope it will not be late, for I will be very, very, impatient to get to all I love."

On May 15, he wrote from Warm Springs, Virginia:

> I reached here with Old Becky all O.K. in good time—left home about dark yesterday, & reached Millboro about one o'clock, & although I had telephoned ahead, I had a terrible time getting anyone up, & the F.F.V. passed at about 60 miles an hour, & I was afraid Becky would have a fit—but I finally got to bed & got about 4 ½ hours sleep & feel pretty tired today. . . .
>
> Sweet Sweet Angel, I did hate to leave you, & I wish you were with me here, the county is so lovely and if I could be only looking at it by your beautiful face, it would be a hundred times lovelier. Reid White told me as I left yesterday that he feared it would not be safe to take Charlotte again—he had examined her and there were dangerous symptoms.[17] So as soon as I go back I guess I will better tell Ella to be ready about the middle of next week to nurse again—but will await your direction.

Greenlee neglected to do something she wanted, for Katie wrote on May 16, 1900, "If you were within reach I should certainly break every bone in your body for neglecting to write to Frazier. I drove down town this morning to see him, but the sewer people are blasting along Main St. and have ropes stretched across so we couldn't pass, and as I was in a Fridley [baby carriage] with little John and had left Ella at home I couldn't get out and walk down there."

Charlotte must have been tubercular, for Katie wrote Greenlee, "I am so worried at not getting Charlotte back, and still more so at hearing her lungs are really affected. I suppose we'll have to get Ella again though she is far from satisfactory. Don't bother about seeing her, I will write. We put the baby man back on [dairy] milk this morning. . . . Do hope it will suit him. He seemed to think having his picture taken a most horrible experience, and looked reproachful for an hour afterward. Bunch went this morning to Waynesboro to spend two or three weeks."

Katie appears to have exaggerated her indisposition so as to stay on in Harrisonburg. On May 21, Greenlee wrote: "I am terribly lonely without you, but I feel that it would be selfish to bring you back, when you are improving." He wrote to her of people in Lexington who had died, were ill, or improving. Because she was gone, he had to tend to the daily household tasks: "I send you invitations to

Miss Eva Wise's & Miss Lucie Effinger's wedding addressed to us both. Hadn't we best send Miss Effinger something?"

Tending to wedding gifts interested Katie not in the least, for she wrote two days later, "Dear Mr. Gov—You don't know how we miss you and how long it seems since you went away. It's really uncomfortable to be as much in love with a young fellow as your Katie is with you. I think you're the only man in creation, you know, and far the brightest man of your time—and the sweetest, loveliest soul of any time. . . . The boy is getting along finally (sic) and looks beautiful today. Didn't he shout when you wouldn't take him this morning? You must be sure and come back Saturday because maybe he can't remember more than a week, and then what would you do? . . . Do what you think best about Miss Effinger and Miss Wise."

Their long-distance conversation about "help" continued, with Greenlee reporting that "Jennie tells me she heard Mrs. Graham say that she was going to get Ella Hanes to go and nurse at Lulu's—so if you want her & have not written, you had best write quickly. . . . I hear that Mrs. Harry Tucker is very ill—they operated on her for appendicitis this morning. I do pray Heaven for her."

As usual, he emphasized the impossibility of his taking time from work to visit them and reported Lexington gossip, apparently unaware of Katie's lack of interest in who was dying, had died, or had invited them to a "Wooden Wedding," or a cake and tea party, for she never commented on his news. "Morgan Pendleton told me this P.M. that Miss Hennie was probably *in extremis*—my heart bleeds for Harry. I sent word this evening by Aunt Lizzie to Ellen, & will write you tomorrow her reply." Next day he reported Hennie's death and the time of the funeral (which would keep him from going to Harrisonburg). Almost inevitably, he put duty before the pleasure of seeing Katie and John: "Old Man is heartsick & lonely, on that account & because he did not receive a letter this evening from his Angel. Beautiful, Beautiful, Beautiful Angel, in the contemplation of Harry Tucker's sorrow, I know how desperately I love you—just at the thought of him and his life's desolation, my heart is overwhelmed."

On May 29, from Edinburg, Virginia, he asked for a "smiling picture" of little John. And on May 31, he wrote to Katie from West Virginia:

> I thank God for the day of which this is the anniversary, for I love you, love you, love you, My Beautiful Sweetheart and Wife, My Chum, My Angel, My All, My Everything in life, in thought, in hope, in dreams— Beautiful Thing I love you with all my heart, my life and my strength

—and true to my love in every breath I draw, every heart beat is yours. And I do wish I were with you tonight and could hold you in my arms and kiss you and love you, and breathe into your life and soul the infinity of my love, Beautiful Dream, Dream of my Soul, Soul of my Life, Life of my All.

Although he was doubtless sincere, it's unclear how much of this intensity was merely style. From childhood, he had trained in rhetoric, and he excelled at oratory, common throughout the South in the Reconstruction period—the more ornate, the better. His gift of glib, golden-tongued speech, although out of fashion today, was certainly part of the reason for his popularity as a speaker. Yet it was not Katie's idiom, may have been a little overblown even then, and her silences— she *never* responded to such flowery sentiments after marriage—testify that she didn't appreciate it and that it embarrassed her.

In the next weeks, Greenlee wrote of Aunt Mag's failing health, of how rushed he himself was at work and into the nights, of how everyone admired John's picture, and, notably, yards and yards of varnished adoration. Day after day, he apologized for not being able to fetch them home. Occasionally, there is a reference to his uncertainty, perhaps because her prose was *not* as flowery: '[I]f I doubted your love, I would be the most miserable man on earth, for I love you with my life, body, & soul, and the thought or *imagination* simply of an intermission in your love, or a division, almost kills Old Man, for he loves you, loves you, loves you with a *jealousy* which could only exist with absolute and infinite love." But he was capable of switching instantly to practical matters.

On June 11, after traveling to Williamsville, White Sulphur Springs, and Millboro on business, he wrote, "I think it is well for you to stay at home til some of them can come with you in the absence of Old Man, unless some reason we know not of should influence you differently. Direct your next letter to me at Warm Springs, where I will be Monday night—and I will be sick at heart if one is not there. . . . If my case is not tried, I will return to Lexington Wednesday; if it is tried, I cannot tell how long it will last, but will keep you posted. I enclose an invitation for you to Mrs. Bruce Tutwiler's. Kiss the fine Boy for me."

Frequently throughout his life when he traveled Greenlee stayed with old friends from VMI or the legislature and described jovial dinners and lively conversations. He traveled often by horseback, particularly in the early days, by train when he could: "We reached here at about half past eight after a 20 or 23 mile drive through the mountains from Williamsville—the drive all the way pretty much was through the forests, cool & pleasant—we had laurel all the way and some patches of rhododendron—I thought of My Angel all the way."

He reported from Rockbridge Alum Springs—a resort complex of cottages, a hotel, a gazebo with a healing spring, an icy spring-fed swimming pool, and a promising future that never really developed—in which he'd bought half-interest,

> At the Alum, Mrs. Graham (*nee* Miss Minnie Cox) as soon as she saw me insisted on my going to see her baby, Miss Katie Logan who will be 10 mos old the 25th of this month, and I went & found a baby about half again as heavy as Little John and the picture of health & good humor, and she took right on to Daddy, and seemed to want to stay with him. Mrs. Graham was terribly disappointed that you & Little John were not with me, & insisted that I bring you to see them in Tazewell. Her child looked so well, I asked her all about its foods. She said she weaned it last Feb'y when she had the Pneumonia, & then fed it on Barley water, and now on sterilized milk, & puts a *pinch of salt* in the milk, which she seems to think is *most* important. And she says Lime Water from Drug Stores is surely good & she makes her own, & will give me the receipt for it when I go back. Her child can crawl & almost stand up, and just laid on the bed as contented as you please. Angel, I thought you were as wild about Little John as it was possible to be, but such an enthusiast as she is I never saw. After I went to bed she came to my door to give me another enlightenment about it. . . . I saw the Arch Deacon, & he was enthusiastic about Little John, & told the Supper Table how he picked him out of the whole bunch of babies on the walk to inquire about. He's a *nice* man. . . . Mrs. Coles was in the depths about Lillie—she has tonsillitis, pharyngitis or something—Catlett Marshall is at the Alum to see her.[18]

On July 10, while he was away, his Aunt Mag died, and in describing her to Katie, he gave his definition of human perfection: "Auntie's character was without reproach—she was lovely—I never saw her do anything or heard her say anything which I thought to be a detraction to herself." Mag's life was lived entirely in the service of her sister and her sister's family. She had never sought a life of her own, and when her sister died, found her own life's work over and died shortly thereafter.[19] A July 11 letter from Katie's mother expressed condolence about Aunt Mag's death, detailed a happy trip with Lilian to Washington to visit Aunt Jennie, revealed their plans for the annual trip to the Virginia Bar Association, and ended, referring to the birth of Katie's second baby, due four months hence, necessitating the alteration of a dress:

> P.S. Miss Ida made me promise to write and explain that she could not fix your black skirt any other way, to make it look right. If she had put in the new breadth it would have been too much wider than the under-skirt & not looked or hung well and if she had made it 8 inches longer in front, as your note directed, it would have been too long entirely for the back. She called me in to tell me the difficulties and it seemed to me she was right. I do not know whether you could get Aunt Susan or not. She is in great demand. But if you'll tell me what time you'll need her I will see her about it. I think it would be just as well for you to pack up, bring little John and the nurse (or let me get a nurse here) and come and stay here till it's all over. I've had the surrey fixed up and we could drive every day and the baby could live out doors. Think about it and let me know. Mamma

Greenlee, unable to return to Lexington in time for his aunt's funeral, explained, "I have been in conference all night with the Commonwealth Atty., and a Physician whom we may introduce as an Expert on the use of Laudanum etc., and I have yet to do considerable work before going to bed—so I can only have a moment to tell you that I love you, love you, love you."

Next day, July 12, 1900, he recalled that this was "the anniversary of when you kissed me the *first* time, or rather when I kissed you the first time, My Beautiful, Dearest Darling and I wish I were with you at this moment to rain a thousand kisses upon your lips & cheeks, & face and body, My Beautiful, Beautiful, Beautiful Angel, My Own, My All. . . . I thank Heaven for the moment and the day you promised to be mine, entirely, forever mine. . . . Your sweet letter received this morning & I was glad to hear from My Angel & Boy—Kiss him for me."

July 14, in Bath County, he wrote that he feared that he "was getting sick this morning, but I believe it has passed off. . . . —the Judge I believe has decided every point raised of any importance in our favor though some have been warmly contested. . . . Your sweet, sweet, sweet letter of 12th to-day received, and I am just so glad I don't know what to do, that I am yours, yours forever, absolutely and entirely yours, My Own Beautiful, Beautiful Darling—and I love you, Angel, Great Heavens, I love you."

He suggested she phone him: "Any day at *10* minutes to *3* P.M. if you can call up O. W. Stephenson's phone at the Warm Spgs, I can talk with you a moment or so—bring Little John with you & let him holler at Daddy."

But Katie went to Harrisonburg, after a letter from her father dated July 14,

> Your telegram received, sorry you didn't pack your grip and come right along. I want you to understand for all time, that this "Fambly" keeps open house for you and all of your belongings the whole retinue; "the whole shootin' match;" What that boy wants is what every free born American baby is entitled to; that is to say, three acres of blue grass sod, on a hillside, with plenty of shade trees, a big oak with a swing under it, and a fresh cow, in plenty of grass just twenty steps away. Mamma and Idge will be home . . . tonight. . . . Seymour went to Ottobine Thursday to go with his Aunt Kate [spinster Kate Paul, 1837–1905] to Mt. Solon to see Blanche Paul. He will be back this evening or tomorrow. We will take our mountain trip about the 23. Very much love from all of us boys to you Mr. L. and the little man. Yours truly, Papa

Reading between the lines, Katie had in Greenlee's absence suddenly decided to wait in Harrisonburg for the new baby's arrival. Greenlee demurred: "I hardly think it would be right for us to camp on the lovely people in Harrisonburg, with the consequent trouble and disarrangement that the situation would entail upon them; but we will talk over it on my return—as we have considerable time yet to decide that question. . . . PS How are you & Ella getting along at night?" He suggested alternatively that Lilian and her mother come to *them* in Lexington for the duration of the pregnancy. On July 17, he wrote in some alarm, "I hope you have bettered yourself by swapping nurses—who is Malinda & where did you get her, and what was the unpardonable sin that disrupted my household?" Katie apparently fired Ella and not for the last time.

In Lexington, well into the 1960s, maids were terribly underpaid for the work they did for families. Most if not all were black, the children of slaves freed by the Civil War, but not yet understood as fully human—as can be seen in my grandmother's *irritation* when a maid got sick or a baby nurse inconvenienced *her* by exhibiting symptoms of tuberculosis.

Presumably, when Katie left Lexington for Harrisonburg she let the current maid(s) go, not wanting to pay for their services in her and the children's absence. Then when she was ready to return, she prodded Greenlee about either rounding up past ones or finding new ones.

Maids in Lexington supplemented their meager incomes two ways. First, they "toted." In charge of kitchens and houses all over town, they ordered and charged groceries for the families they cooked for, ordering more than they needed, and took about half the groceries home with them at night. It was probably the case that baby nurses who didn't have access to food in this way were paid higher wages. Toting was understood and accepted, not judged as thievery.

The second way this underprivileged group got along was by individually bargaining or striking for higher wages. This too was understood and accepted, for good maids were absolutely critical; families often "bought" maids away from one another for a dollar more a week, and maids quit employers who wouldn't raise their wages and went with families that offered them more money or a better situation, such as fewer children to care for, shorter hours, or Sundays off. A threat to leave could elicit higher wages. Similarly, the black community (who knew the whites intimately, being in their houses all the time and, in a sense, invisible) knew who was difficult to work for, who was generous at holiday time, who was stingy about toting, who could be threatened for more money. Maids might refuse to return until the price was right, or they might leave another family precipitously for the lure of higher wages or less demanding bosses. Many a white friendship was broken over the "theft" of a choice servant.

The white community (which knew and cared little about the servants' private lives beyond what affected them) knew which maids were useless and which were hard workers, knew who was dishonest, who knew how to clean a house properly, who cooked tasty meals, and who couldn't fry bacon without burning it. It's easy to see why the subject of "Help" dominated the town's conversation when I was growing up. My grandparents' experience with maids coming and going, leaving them in the lurch, demanding more money, or being lazy or dishonest was typical. Everyone envied the women who had what they called "jewels" as their household servants. Aunt Henrietta, Julia Trader, and Aunt Sarah were baby nurses, designated "Aunt" because of the presumed superiority of their positions. Other servants were gardeners, cooks, and housekeepers, and over forty are named in these letters. Because women did not run their own households, "good he'p," as it was called, was absolutely crucial to the smooth operation of any house, the skillful raising of mannerly children, the harmony, in short, of domestic life. Katie was careless and cavalier about servants, leaving Greenlee to scramble mightily to discover, obtain, keep, or replace them.

From Harpers Ferry, West Virginia, Greenlee described his day on July 30 to Katie, who was in Lexington: "I took dinner at home [Harrisonburg] to-day &

enjoyed seeing the folks very much, and was delighted to put Idge on the train for Lexington before I came on. On the Southern train I found Gen. Roller[20] who was on his way to Webster Springs in West Virginia where I am going—he has a case in Judge Bennett's Court he tells me, and I was very glad to catch up with him, & have company. There was also a Drummer named Loewenbach from Harrison-burg, who goes a part of the way with us. We have just taken supper here & walked up on Bolivar Heights, & our train goes west in about 50 minutes."

A contented answer came from Katie, postmarked July 30:

> Only a line, precious Dad-dad, to tell you how we love you and miss you every minute. The baby Man watched you out of sight this morn-ing with the most wistful look in his big blue eyes, as if he understood how long it would be before he'd see his Dad-dad again. He has been so good and sweet and playful all day. . . . How we both wish you were coming down in a minute to take us driving. How did you find the folks at home? . . .
>
> Dear, you are the sweetest and best thing in the world to me—a hundred times better than I deserve—I make times pretty hard for you as it is, but just think what life would be if I didn't love you, and be thankful it is no worse. Precious thing, don't be away long but hurry back to me and the Boy—

From Webster Springs, West Virginia, Greenlee described his journey on "the roughest road I have ever seen almost" but had a wonderful time and wrote her ex-citedly. "It is a great day here—Court Day and the Hotels are full of guests. Mr. Brannon[21] & myself as yet have been unable to get a room, but through his influence, we are promised one." He described the arrival of General Roller in a "Road Wagon," and told her about drinking the mineral water, "the most peculiar taste you ever saw." He adored the excitement and crowds and described showing *everyone* pictures of the baby. He told of a twenty-mile horseback ride to see a friend. He mentioned the illness of the other side's lawyer, while commenting that he was praying for his quick recovery. Greenlee Letcher was the sort of man to wish even his enemies well.

Tireless, Greenlee went from there to Abingdon, Virginia, and reported meet-ing a man who knew Katie: "Mr. Page came in & told me he had had the *pleasure* of meeting you several times & I told him he was a lucky man, and he said *I* was lucky—truthful, good man." He ended: "I pray you are well My Life, My Soul, My Hope, My All, and that a kind Heaven will be good to us, and save you from any danger, My Own, My Beautiful, Beautiful Darling." His reference is certainly to the fact that her second baby's birth drew near.

Greenlee's sister Jennie married Walter LeConte Stevens in August of 1900.[22] Katie may not have attended the wedding, as she was about three months away from delivering her second child. In Lexington at the time upper-class women did not appear in public when visibly pregnant, a custom lasting until well after World War II.

The following Sunday (mid-October) Greenlee got home in time for the baptism of young John, with Katie's parents and brother Houston to stand in as godparents. Although the event was duly noted in the family Bible, no mention was made of whether Katie attended, but the baptism may have been performed at home.

The Letchers' second baby arrived safely (in Lexington) on November 15, 1900, and was named Greenlee Davidson Letcher Jr. but called "Bruddie." Within days, Greenlee was back in Richmond for a legislative session, writing, "I have bragged on the *whole family*," but only days after he returned to Lexington, Katie took both babies to Harrisonburg for a long Christmas stay.

That year Katie's seventeen-year-old brother John was a "rat" (freshman) at VMI, and cadets were not allowed to leave post for Christmas. In one letter, in an effort to prevent John Paul's going AWOL for a day, Greenlee told the cautionary story of a cadet who had left VMI on Christmas against orders, had been discharged, and how it "*ruined his life.*"

Greenlee took pity on the poor "rat," and, returning on Christmas Day from Harrisonburg, Greenlee went down to VMI and collected up John and a "brother rat," named Sam, and that night reported to Katie: "I brought John & Sam to my office & ordered oysters for all, & we all refreshed the inner man,[23] & John & Sam went to Barracks, & I went to the Clerk's Office & have been at work ever since (10:35), & now will go to my lonely home & dream of my Beautiful Angel. . . . [Y]our people are too sweet & lovely for anything—give my love to all & with kisses to our splendid young fellows."

But next day's letter to Katie hinted at problems: "Your sweet letter just rec'd— a letter from my *wife*—the wife of my soul, my life, my home, my all—with no feeling of gift or bounty, awakening repulsion, when she receives the little I can give, but the consciousness of sharing *her own,* with no resulting obligation there from of any kind—and I love you that way, angel, more than all words can tell, for in it I feel that nearness of identity and oneness of being, which is the merger in infinite love."

Alone, in Lexington, Greenlee could not find any silver spoons or the key to the wood-house, and was unsure about whether to hire Julia Trader as a nurse for the little boys. He had no difficulty, he reported, in setting up The Wonder, a heat stove that had been their Christmas present from Katie's parents. He thanked Katie's mother for a paperweight with little John's picture in it. In the following days, he reported to Katie on presents awaiting the *boys* in Lexington, "a box of blocks and a toy fiddler. Miss Bettie sent a ball, and Miss Marie Lewis sent a toy representing two nursing dogs—all very cute & I think the beneficiaries will be wonderfully struck with admiration & delight." He nudged her gently:

> I was tickled to death to get your postal & to know you were thinking
> of me and that the *men* sent love to Daddy—but, Sweet Thing, Old
> Man will understand it, if you have not time or opportunity to write
> every day—he will be terribly disappointed, but he will philosophize
> and know that had you done it, you would have overexerted yourself &
> Little John & Brother would have blamed selfish Daddy. . . . I told you
> last night that Miss Maggie Freeland sent us a lovely table for the
> Parlor. . . . I am working day & night, so as to have more time when
> you return, so that I can see my Angel and the *fellows* more & thus get
> the maximum enjoyment out of life. Because Beautiful Darling, Old
> Man does love his family—and realizes the kindness of Heaven in
> them.

For Katie's Christmas present, Greenlee deposited $100 in her personal account, a huge sum, roughly the equivalent of half a year's salary for a full-time servant, as can be seen from the letter as it continued: "The Trader girl was at my Office this P.M. & said she would come with you when you returned, I told her I would let her know a few days ahead. I liked her looks and manner very much. I told her she was to take care of the children, clean up the house and generally do whatever you told her, & we would pay her $16.00 per month; that she was to stay in the room next to you in my absence—to all of which she assented."

On January 2, 1901, he wrote the "first love letter of the 20th Century to my Sweetheart," full of his usual expansiveness, but adding, "To feel that you may be filled with a repulsion or fear when you come to me at times plunges me into a sickening heart stupor—for I love you with all the wild, infinite love and passion of a soul and body that knows no other love, nor thought of love; and to imagine that I have an aspiration of soul or a pulsation of heart that is not answered makes me unhappy." Perhaps this was as frank as any discussion on sexual matters could be for Katie and Greenlee. As historian Suzanne Lebsock and others have observed, the widest blind spot in the American past concerns sexuality and fertility.

Greenlee continued to describe his train trips and boon companions, including a drummer, a general, and "Roy Mitchell, [who] invited us to bring the kids down & spend some Sunday."

Life continued as it had, neither of them aware that tragedy loomed on the near horizon, although Greenlee described "an inexpressible anxiousness, which comes at times to make me unhappy and fearful, [which] consists in the terrible suggestion that you do not love me *soul* and *body* as I love you, which love from you my whole being craves, and *cannot* do without." Yet he never seemed lonely, reporting visits, kind words, and gossip: "I was at Miss Maggie's last night *and* had some delightful egg-nogg, & they all expressed so many kind thoughts for you and Little John, and well wishes. . . . Old Mrs. Norgrove fell down the steps. . . . [T]hey thought she would die but I called just now to inquire after her, and they told me she would recover, the Doctor thought."

Katie directed him to find and hire a new baby nurse for when she came home, and he replied,

> I saw Mary Morton [a black woman with coincidentally the same name as Katie and Virginia's friend] this evening & she says Sol is mightily cheered up now, about living with us; and she was mighty glad, as she did not know what she would do if Sol left her & went to Petersburg. She says she will be ready to move down when I tell her you are coming. I enclose you a dun for your dues to Ladies Aid Society—return it & I will pay it for you—who is the Treasurer? Ask [your] Daddy to get Brother 50 cigars like the ones he smoked from Van Pelt, which cost $1.80, & I will hand him the money when I come down—if it is any trouble tell him never mind. And I only ask him to do it, as otherwise I fear I will again forget it. Give my love to all & tell Sister Bunch we are expecting her to come back with us.

Enclosed was the notice,

> December 28, 1900
> Dear Mrs. Letcher: The annual assessment of the Ladies' Aid Society is now due. Will you kindly hand the amount, $1.25, to the Treasurer.
> Yours very truly, Mary H. Gibbs, Sec'y.

When Katie wrote back, she remarked, "I don't know who is treasurer of the Ladies' Aid, probably Jennie though I didn't even know I was a member" and left it at that. To be fair, her temper was shortened by an earache: she added that her ear "tuned up again last night and nearly set me crazy, but Dr. Neff was here this morn and gave me some medicine so that I'm tolerably comfortable now." Evidently this was an attack of the mastoiditis that was to plague her the rest of her life.

The epitome of the proud mother, Katie wrote: "The boys are well and beautiful and good. I don't know which is most beautiful, big white John or little red Gov." Not only named, but also nicknamed, for his father, young Greenlee was called Buddie, Bruddie, Brudder—and as he got older, Gee. One assumes the older baby's pronunciation gave him his nicknames for "Brother" and "Greenlee." She continued, "Mr. & Mrs. Keester called last night, but as I had used up my allotted trip down stairs I only saw her. . . . Dear, dearest love, you don't know how I love you, and long for you all the time." Greenlee wrote that he could not get to Harrisonburg to see her but described himself as "grieved beyond measure to know that you were suffering from your ear, Sweetest Angel."

Members of his family sent a book, a cravat, crocheted shoes for both boys, and a "sack," for the new baby. He went around to supper at family members' and friends' houses and urged Katie to "write them all and explain how you have been sick and I have not a moment for anything from business." He told her, "After getting your letter this evening I have determined . . . to stick just as close to my Angel as I can."

He again urged her to bring Bunch back home with her, perhaps sensing that she'd be more likely to come if she brought one of the family along. On January 7, he expressed concern that young John's teething was giving him so many problems. He wrote that he'd filed for three divorces that week and was working on a land suit. He told her of meeting with another lawyer whose "clients have contracted to buy the Tin mines at Cornwall, & they desire me to abstract the title for them."[24] He wished to discuss a fee connected to a business matter, commenting, "will advise with you about the fee when you come home. On that, as in fact *all* matters, I find your judgment is better than mine." He closed by asking her to "tell Bunch we will take no excuse from her, but will bring her back with us bodily, if she will not come otherwise."

In replying, she wrote, "Mr. Gov—Your letter this morning was what all your letters are—sweet as sweet can be and a happiness to me. The story of the Philadelphia lawyer is good news and I'm truly glad to hear you have decided to let me umpire the fees hereafter, for if you keep to your present schedule of charges you'd soon be in the hands of a far worse referee—the bankruptcy kind." The boys, she added, "are beautiful and sweet as they can be. They've both been asleep the whole morning."

Greenlee threw himself wholeheartedly into the work of the mining company, writing that "the lawyer who came to see me from Philadelphia . . . employed me to look up the title . . . & intimated that there were other matters later that would be given me, when the Company began operation, on a large scale as they expect to do, & I do hope & pray that I will be able to handle their business successfully & satisfactorily, as it may develop much to me." Greenlee worked valiantly to justify the company's faith in him, asking her to enlist her father's help in hiring a full-time stenographer.

But Katie was not inclined to be helpful and made the following reply: "Papa . . . is, I know, so very busy that I didn't say anything to him about the stenographer, and as it is raining I could not go myself. I don't think Mr. Shaffer is here now, but I could ask Albert Lewis and 'Deck' if they know of anybody and let you know tomorrow if you telephone me to do so. I hope you can get Miss Deaver— and keep her."

She described how John slept while being admired by a friend, then ended, "If you can't come Saturday you needn't come at all, as I am quite capable of personally conducting the boys and their body servant from here to Lexington. But you'd better come Saturday—in fact you *must* come because I want to see you—*bad*. When will you take breath and rest a little, poor hard pressed old man?" She obviously viewed his working hard as a *choice* he had made rather than a necessity. Greenlee had a cold throughout the Christmas season and begged off going to fetch his family home. About his legal work, he remarked that "it worried me not getting back this evening, as every minute counts with me now."

Two days later he wrote about another case: "All the Parsons are very well, but are beginning to realize the fact that after paying all debts they will have little left, but if they only meet the situation, they will be all right." His philosophy is here in evidence: you don't need money to survive, only honor and courage to "meet the situation."

Greenlee continued to ask Katie to look for a secretary in Harrisonburg, find what she would cost, and if she would come immediately. Despite her snubs, his letter ended: "[I]t set me way up to think my sweetheart wanted to see me, and it is a severe, almost breaking strain on duty, which keeps me away from what I love." He explained that "the option to the Tin Property has but a short time now to run and I fear too short for me to do what I am employed to do, & as there is so much at stake, especially in future possibilities that I must forego seeing my sweetheart tomorrow, and I am disappointed & sick at heart over it."

Katie did not respond to his requests, and eventually he found a secretary on his own. On January 13, 1901, he wrote, "I do wish I were with my Angel and my Kids. . . . I do love the whole outfit just about up to the limit—and I am the luckiest dog in the world and have about all the law allows, as young Williams said when I told him I had the prettiest wife in the world, the most splendid boys on earth and the biggest house in Rockbridge."

The bleakness that was to come on them drew nearer. On January 15, he wrote, "I do look with so much anticipation and happiness to *have my home* again tomorrow; and I hope you will be comfortable enough and well enough to be thoroughly happy. I hope little John's croup has gone, and that his teeth don't continue to bother him so much."

The next day he wrote that "Sol said last night that Mary would be here early Monday to clean up & have things in shape for you; and Mrs. Rhodes said Julia Trader would be here Tuesday morning. And I feel that domestic affairs are going to be more prosperous hereafter with the new arrangements."

On the seventeenth, Greenlee wrote that he wanted to come for them, "but the abstract in hand is so pressing & the time so short, & the results of the work so important, that I do not feel that I can lose a minute unnecessarily." In that letter he asked for some law books "under the bed" and added, "I regret beyond measure that Bunch is not coming with you—how soon can she come? . . . I am sorry to have troubled you about the stenographer, but I was desperate. I have gotten a Miss Clemmer from Fairfield who came highly recommended by Prof. Dunsmore, & I hope she will fill the bill. . . . Yearning to clasp you in my arms again smother you & the Kids with kisses."

Katie came home with both babies sometime after January 17. Apparently the Letchers had a week or so at home as a family, in that darkest month in the mountains of Virginia, for Greenlee wrote no more letters; in fact he wrote none that survive for the next four months. Just at that delicious age when language has begun, and the naming of the world is a daily excitement, when a child has so recently lurched from crawling on all fours up to the uncertain balance of the toddler, just when his carriage is that of a cheerful drunk, when parents can begin to see what kind of child, then adult, this baby will become, John Paul Letcher was struck down. The next few notes are all we have of his death.

January 30, 1901
Oh, Katie: Keep up a stout heart, we are hoping and praying that the morning will find little John better, and if we can do anything, you know we are more than willing. With much much love, Jennie

JANUARY 31, 1901
It is with deep regret that we learned of the death of the eldest of Mr. and Mrs. Greenlee D. Letcher's little boys on Wednesday night at the home of his parents in Lexington. The little fellow was about sixteen or eighteen months old, and was a remarkably fine child. He died of spinal meningitis.

January 31, 1901
Dearest Katie,
My heart has been with you all today, for only today did I know of your loss. Sister Lizzie

The high death rate of children in earlier times must have created a fear of death so strong as to retard the forging of strong attachments to infants and small children. But this clearly was not the case with the Letchers. For devout Christians, death was a reunion with God in a perfectly happy Paradise; but it is not clear that Katie, at least until much later, was convinced of the truth of Christianity, and even if she had been, her pain at losing baby John was terrible and pushed her further into depression. About forty letters to the Letchers around the time of John Paul Letcher's death have survived; Thea Lewis, a friend from Harrisonburg, wrote, "My dearest Catharine, I was so deeply grieved today when I heard of your great bereavement and only wish I could say something to comfort you but know too well from my own bereavement that words are futile at such a time." Greenlee's old friend, James Quarles, wrote, "Life is a house of two stories; one of which is a basement, much under ground and cut off from the fullness of light. Here it is that we live our imperfect lives, in cold and damp and dark, never finding the realization of our hopes. . . . The upper floor is lifted into the light and glory of undimmed effulgence; not dazzling, but mellowed with the radiance of an infinitely gracious love. Now live those whom you and I have most loved upon this lower range of being, and *there now* is precious little John." Sister Lizzie poured out her heart to Greenlee; she had herself lost two children in infancy. Sister Lilian wrote: "Let not your heart be troubled, your little one is safe in the arms of Jesus. Little John is safe. Lovingly, Lilian"

Katie's mother went to Lexington at once to be with her eldest and favorite child. In a letter sometime later to Lilian, she blamed Greenlee for John's death, because he kept the house so cold. From Harrisonburg, on February 2, 1901, little Seymour wrote to Kate Paul, who was in Lexington with Katie, a letter calculated to cheer: "We are well except Virginia, who has the grip or some kindred ailment. She has not been down this morning, but beyond that I can say nothing as to its seriousness, except that Dr. Neff was up to see her yesterday evening. Papa says it is a slight cold. Chickens, dogs, cats, turkeys and ducks all well."

Not surprisingly, Katie and Greenlee in their letters to each other are silent on the subject. One letter to Katie from a Kentucky cousin refers to "your dear, piti-ful, note." And Lilian wrote: "It was so sweet of you to write and tell me that little John boy did not suffer." Nell Paxton, a contemporary of my father's, reported that local folklore had it that the reason Katie's eyes were "so bad" later was that she had cried so much over John's death that she burst blood vessels in her eyes and ruined them. The baby's death was also thought by the town to have marked the beginning of Katie's self-imposed isolation (although I believe those seeds were sown much earlier).

When Mrs. Paul returned to Harrisonburg on Feb. 11, she reported to Katie that she and the Judge were "starting tomorrow for the sunny south," that a cousin, Peyton Gray, had been to tea, that "he sent much love and sympathy to you." She wrote: "Gennie Fletcher was here this morning. You know how she wor-ships babies. She showed so much feeling and understanding of your grief that I can always hereafter overlook her oddities. . . . Mr. Keester and Virginia had wanted to write, but felt they could not say anything but what would add to your sorrow." Kate Paul, perhaps a smidgen insensitively, spoke of Herbert Thomas, a past suitor of Katie's, still coming around. He was "looking very well and is much improved in so many ways, called Sat. night and inquired particularly about you. He took Bun driving and to-night chaperones her to a small card party at Ediths." She commented that Greenlee "works too hard," urged Katie to get up to "go down to the kitchen: it will please you to see how neat and clean and orderly every-thing looks there. You must take a little promenade on the front porch every evening and you ought to take your time, to help supply little brudder's demands. That precious little urchin!"

Katie and Greenlee—I can imagine this as a ploy on his part to distract Katie in her grief—began looking for a house to buy, for up until then they'd been renting, building no equity. There is much correspondence on the subject: Mears Williamson decided not to sell; Mr. Barclay could find them nothing; Mulberry

Hill cost too much. Those letters all mention John's death, typically, "My love & sympathy to your little wife. I hope she & the new Baby are both getting well & strong. You have had too many sorrows of late years, Mrs. Letcher and Miss Mag, and now this blackness in your life."

Inevitably, life returned to normal for Greenlee, who began his travels again. He appears to have recovered his balance quickly. One must suppose it took Katie much longer. His first letter after the death (that has survived) came nearly three months later, and, to no surprise, is subdued, ending, "I write only to tell you that I love you & that all my heart is with you & Buddy. Yours, G.D.L."

On May 31, he wrote her a third anniversary letter which included a restatement of his adoration and the hope that "through all eternity we shall never be separated even in thought for an instant for I love you my Beautiful Wife with all my heart and body, all my life and soul—I love you in every thought and with every breath, and all in all."

They did not buy a house then, and they didn't build their house for another four years. There are no more letters until early July, so probably Greenlee stayed close to home to support Katie through the long days and nights. Then, she returned with Gee to Harrisonburg, and he wrote to her from Natural Bridge, from Millboro, from Staunton, from Harper's Ferry, as ardently as ever. On July 9, 1901, he wrote,

> It was raining so hard when we passed Winchester that I came on here instead of cutting across to Martinsburg as I had purposed—I leave at 9:45 for Fairmont. I reached Harrisonburg just as a storm was coming up but John met me at the Depot and I got home before it broke by running as much and as fast as an old man was capable of. I found all well and enjoyed my 3/4 of an hour's stay very much. Bunch will be up Friday—write to her at once that you are expecting her—she said she had not heard from you. I gave your little package to Charlie. Did not see Seymour—he was at business. Saw your Uncle Rock, and after Daddy's nap, I saw him for a few minutes. Mother set my dinner aside for me which I enjoyed very much. They all asked after you and Buddie. Beautiful Angel I love you, and hate beyond measure to be away—think of and love Old Man, as he thinks of, and loves, you, all the time.

What Greenlee and Katie did not write of often "shouts" as loudly as what they said. For example, Greenlee sometimes wrote directly of his fear of Katie's not loving him, while she invariably ignored his anxiety about her loving him. Perhaps he could only shape his fears on paper. He expressed great relief when things went well—but even then, Katie never commented.

In her mourning year, 1901, Katie also coped with the second baby, diminished energy, and the final illness and death of her father. We can imagine her reminded each moment of baby John as she attended to the new baby, or later to her father—while, of course, Greenlee, who had to go on making a living, could re-immerse himself in the world of his work and friends. In his travels, he reported sleeping well even upright on trains, and carrying on business after only three or four hours' sleep.

Greenlee seems to have been a general practitioner of the law, taking whatever cases came along. Early in life, he did lots of trial work, according to the late Henry Foresman, a Lexington lawyer. Later, Greenlee was considered something of an expert on the subjects of land disputes and mineral rights. He at least twice defended people he believed had been wrongly accused of some crime. Because he frequently took depositions (the only part of the legal trade he did not like), he apparently concentrated on civil law; at the turn of the century, there were few or no depositions in criminal cases. Often he mentioned meeting with lawyers for the other side, a process called "discovery," by which, in advance of a trial, each side learns about the other's case. There are references in the letters to business con-tracts, court appearances, sponsoring bills, land transfers, civil wrongs ("torts" in legalese), wills and deeds, collection of delinquent fees, a suit for money by a victim of a train injury. He defended black clients at least twice. He was named "power of attorney," or guardian, at least twice. He acted as agent for people buying property. Throughout his career, he was from time to time involved in George Washington's will. Although George Washington died two weeks short of the turn of the nineteenth century, he owned land all over western Virginia, and it took 150 years and the work of many lawyers to settle the tangled estate. In let-ters, Greenlee never went into much detail to Katie, but it is clear he must have talked to her about his work *because* his epistolary references are so vague.

Mention of what would be Judge Paul's final illness crept into the letters in the spring of 1901. On October 1, Greenlee wrote that he "found Daddy looking better and stronger than I had expected to see him—he was sitting in bed propped up with pillows, and appeared bright and interested in hearing of so many people asking after him, wherever I went—he or mother or perhaps both spoke of how fine Buddy looked from his picture, & Daddy seemed to think I looked better than he had ever seen me."

Not surprisingly, Katie used her father's illness as an excuse to go home, although it is unlikely that she was much help with nursing or domestic matters. She wrote to her husband lovingly: "Dear Mr. Gov—Papa slept a good deal last night and some this morning and though very weak still has been tolerably comfortable. Brudder has spent the morning asleep and has just waked up in a fine humor asking where Dad-dad is. Dear dear old beau, I do love you, and you are so good and sweet to me always."

Her father had good days and bad. On October 19, Katie wrote, "Brudder is well and sends his love. He is at present making the 'grand tour'—taking in the chickens, rabbits and other attractions." She wrote coolly, "I hope you are not having a very uncomfortable time all by your dear old self. Are you taking your meals with Fannie? I was disappointed at not getting a letter from you this morning but hope for one this afternoon." In one letter, she wrote that "the baby man and I love you all the time even if you do put on airs and say it is only when you are away—you dear, spoiled old thing. I'm sorry, sweet old man, that I'm so hateful sometimes, or most times, that you can even say that though I know you don't mean it." In other words, *she* knows he doesn't mean it when *he* says she's hateful. The statement reveals her confusing ambivalence. Actually, she was doing to Greenlee what he did to her: denying that he meant what he said. They talked *past* each other.

The domestic difficulties did not abate: she directed him, "About Martha Adams—you had better phone Mrs. Pendleton yourself—Jennie is too apt to get mixed up on the servant question."

Judge Paul eventually died of congestive heart failure on November 2, 1901,[25] leaving the family in possession of an elegant house but little more. Characteristically, Greenlee volunteered immediately to be a legal advisor, and wrote, "I talked over the family's affairs considerably with Mr. Sipes, & we arranged to examine them fully as possible Saturday when I come down—Mr. Sipes spoke of writing for Uncle Abe to be with us. By careful and economical management, we have nothing to fear, but I will talk fully with your mother when I understand the situation better."

Back in Lexington, he anticipated Katie's return: "I sent up to Mrs. Dold's[26] this morning but she could tell me nothing of Ella—who else do you think would know anything?"

And still after all, he could and did write, on November 7, "Beautiful, Beautiful Sweetheart, I wondered whether you would have any time to write me today, and my heart beat as I ran over my letters to-night & dropped all the rest when I came to yours."

Still Katie stayed away, and still he tried to find a servant to ready things for her return: "Mrs. Dold told me today that Carrie had heard from Ella in *Boston* to-day, but she said nothing of coming back. That Mr. John Banks had married another lady—ain't that too bad? I am terribly terribly lonely without you & Buddy but do whatever you feel is best for the lovely folks at home. . . . Insist that Mother come with you when you come."

She replied: "Guv—Brudder man is taking his nap after a very busy morning. He is *so* sweet and *so* smart for he knows a picture of 'kitty' when he sees it and can say Katie. Mamma says she cannot go back with us—that she can't afford the expense. Won't you please sir, send me a few stamps? And bring some money for Julia when you come. I am going to try Cresoline for Brudder's cough which continues though it does not seem to get any worse. . . . You are a sweet old dear and I hope you are satisfied that I love you and that Brudder does not forget Dad-dad-dad."

Greenlee's sister, Lizzie Harrison, wrote to Katie on the death of her father, adding, "Jen wrote me . . . about dear *little* Greenlee. She is perfectly devoted to him. How I would like to see the dear little fellow. I know he is such a pleasure & comfort to you *all*. Mr. H- & L-[Letcher] join me in love & warmest sympathies to your mother & your dear self." Little Gee Letcher, then and later, was, in the eyes of all, the "perfect" child, relaxed, bright, sociable, handsome.

Katie took Lilian back to Lexington with her, doubtless still reeling from the loss of her child and her father so close together. Letters from her mother reveal Kate Paul's struggle, adding to Katie's burdens: "Dear, precious little comforter! His sweet little face and dear little ways cheered us in those dreary days as nothing else could. . . . I try to be busy all the time so as to keep gloomy thoughts away," and "By dint of keeping busy from morning till night I manage to make the heavy days pass." The prospect of poverty was always with Mrs. Paul: "It would touch a heart of stone to see poor, dear, ease-loving, dress-loving, good-time-loving Bunch making over her dyed clothes and darning the boys socks." In one note, she wrote that "Seymour is sad to-day. I had wanted him to sell his dearly beloved ducks but he pleaded eloquently that they would begin laying so early in the spring and lay so many eggs that I consented to keep them until on a visit to the stable lot I found that out of the flock of ten eight were *drakes*."

Kate Paul kept Katie apprised of domestic activities at their house and a plan to foil an unwanted suitor, writing that "by Thursday or Friday we'll have Idge ready to ship to you. The sooner the better I think for Tommy seems bent on showing that he is not going to take our advice and keep 'out of the game.' He was up Tuesday night. Sent a bushel of carnations Thanksgiving Day and he and Joe H were up last night. Idge is very stately and went on with her sewing upstairs while Bunch, Tommy and the boys ate pumpkin pie."

Lilian, when she arrived in Lexington, reported at once to Mrs. Paul that Katie was unwell. Of course Kate Paul immediately wrote to Katie:

> I feel much concerned about you. Idge says you have such a bad cold and Greenlee said the doctor had been to see you. I do trust you are being prudent and sensible, both in taking care of yourself and about weaning Brudder. You know you are awfully weak-minded about Brudder, and I know you will have a hard time teaching him to eat, but you must persevere both for your sake and his. You ought not to keep us all anxious about you by yielding to what I know is your natural inclination whenever the dear little urchin howls. I certainly would love to see his sweet, pink, little face. Tell Lily Ann [Lilian] we miss her very much and were glad to get her letter. . . .
>
> I suppose Greenlee will be down Monday, at least I hope so. Rock departed yesterday and dear old Abe came in with a big basket of sausage and spare-ribs.[27] I've had several very sweet letters from friends lately. Give much love to John [at VMI] and tell him we are all right.

3 *Domesticity (1901–1916)*

The roses nowhere bloom so white
As in Virginia
The sun shines nowhere quite so bright
As in Virginia
And I believe that Happy Land
The Lord's prepared for mortal man
Is built exactly on the plan
Of old Virginia!

—ANONYMOUS, "DOWN IN OLE VIRGINIA"

Greenlee continued to protest his homesickness while going on to every new adventure, while Katie stayed home or returned to her family's home. Her family appears to have experienced financial problems as a result of Judge Paul's death. Greenlee's idea was to buy or build a big house as soon as he could and have all the Pauls move to Lexington with them; he seemed blissfully unaware of their lack of enthusiasm about the prospect.

The original "networker," Greenlee took a great interest in things political, both local and global. He is an interesting contrast in utter self-confidence and co-dependence. Although he'd go miles out of his way to see an old friend or a VMI contact, and he appears to have known and loved, and been known and loved by, *everybody,* yet his anxiety about Katie's love is wrenching.

Kate Paul, after a life of leisure and frivolity, sought and won the demanding job of postmistress for Harrisonburg, an appointment she held for the next twenty years. On January 29, 1902, Katie's mother wrote:

> Bun is sewing on the machine up-stairs, I am mending and making over some sheets, in the setting-room. The boys have just gobbled up their dinner and rushed off through the snow to school. Charlie and Rob are bent on a sleigh-ride in the old historic yankee jumper. . . . There are "no new novelties" in the P.O. contest, as I suppose you learn

Katie and Gee, 1902

from the news. . . . You have been constantly in my thoughts lately, for I know you have been living over the sad days a year ago—but try not to grieve. Think—the child has been a year with God—a year of perfect blessedness; think of the two little Johns and Papa together."[1]

In February 1903 Katie conceived their third child, and they began talking in letters about building a house, apparently unable to find an appropriate one to buy. Greenlee repeatedly urged Katie's mother and siblings to make their future home with them in Lexington, arguing that the boys could go to VMI, and the girls would enjoy "plenty of company."

Mrs. Paul didn't even like to visit, and clearly did not want to live with them. As Katie and Greenlee began to build in Lexington, she sold the elegant house in Harrisonburg and moved to a more modest one a half-mile away.

On the seventh of February, Greenlee reported from Washington on business that he "found Mr. Attas lawyer, & a Mr. Alexander waiting for me—. . . [T]hey promised to make me a written proposition and an advance to take back to Mrs. Morrow. Tomorrow I will see Flood, Martin and others about Miss Maggie Freeland's bill, & see Judge Payson re Mrs. Parsons mother." H. D. Flood, a Democratic senator, carried the Tenth District in 1904.

The same letter reports that Greenlee got "Bruddie a toboggan cap and a bird whistle this evening. I wearied the clerks at the overcoat counter this evening but without luck so far. . . . We all will take a Lobster Supper at Harveys and go to the Theater afterwards. Little at the Theaters apparently." Greenlee was the same way about entertainment that he was about food: he thought it was fine whatever it was and never judged.

Greenlee wrote the same sort of letters to Gee that he had written to John. And he continued to write love letters to Katie. "I am writing you early in the morning, about the break o'day, to tell you how I love you—it is the last thing I think of when I go to bed and the first when I awake, Beautiful Angel." On July 31, from Cumberland, Maryland, he wrote, "Found all your good people well yesterday & Mother at once told me that she had not answered your letter as she expected you & Bruddie just whenever you desired to come. Of course I said nothing to her indicating that any doubt existed in your mind as to your invitation or welcome. Bunch & Idge also expressed the hope of your coming with Bruddie." Whether this doubt in her mind was occasioned by considerations of their poverty or by a misunderstood intimation by Katie in an oversensitive mood, we cannot know. "I told Hugh[2] & Miss Descher to forward my mail to Weston c/o of Hon W. M. Brannon, until further directions so don't you bother about it."

Greenlee advertised weekly in the *Lexington Gazette,* along with other lawyers in town. The personals often reported on his travels: "Mr. Greenlee D. Letcher is in Welch, West Virginia, this week on Business." From West Virginia, he wrote, on July 31: "No news—simply to tell you *I love you,* and wish that I never had to leave you, for I do love you, and love the home you make for me and would rather be there than at any place on earth. My Own, My Beautiful Darling, I thank Heaven that I left happy in your love—Try and not say or do things which make me so terribly unhappy, even temporarily, for I love you as no man ever loved a woman—the infinite and terrible and jealous passion of my love for you brings Heaven and Hell close together."

On August 3, he wrote her in Harrisonburg, "I have received no letter from you but I hope when I return to Weston to hear from my Beautiful Angel & to hear that you & Bruddie are well. I have met here some friends, W&L U. boys of some years back, and Mr. Thomas the engineer of the C&O [Chesapeake and Ohio RR] came up last night and introduced himself—he has a corps out about 50 miles from here & I gather a route across West Va. is trying to be found to connect with the C&O. If this is finally done, property should advance in Harrisonburg. It seems to be the impression out in West Va. that such a road will be built." On August 5, he wrote: "I settled with T. M. Holbrook this evening, which is the last thing that has been bothering us—if you see Hugh tell him to tell his mother, as it has been worrying her badly for some time. . . . My Beautiful Angel, I got the first letter from you late last night, & it made me happy. I have had quite a pleasant time here, but I want to get back to you & Bruddie, and I am losing heart about going to Niagara on account of homesickness for all I love."

On August 6, Greenlee wrote: "I expect to get off in the morning & Judge B & myself go over the land—an interesting function that will attend our visit will be the dedication of a church site on the Wills land—the people are laughing about our locating a church & say Kodac [*sic*] pictures of it will be taken and enlarged for Judge B. to use in his political campaign."

On August 8, 1902, he made the decision to go to Niagara: "I leave in the morning at 5 A.M. for Fairmont & will go to Pittsburg Sunday & I think from there to Niagara Tuesday. Write to me at Cataract House, Niagara Falls New York." He added, "I think some intermediate letters from you must have been sent to Addison & have not returned, as these letters were the first to give me intimation of your being in Harrisonburg. I know you are enjoying yourself with your sweet people—what did you do with Ella? . . . I am tickled to death to hear that you and Bruddie talk of Daddy, kiss the splendid fellow for me & tell him how I love him, & do not forget how I love you my Darling, my Beautiful Darling."

From Wheeling, West Virginia, on August 9, 1902, he reported, "I came here today at Mrs. Morrow's request to have a conversation about investing her money with the gentleman with whom she had been stopping when here. I will go on to Pittsburg either this evening or tomorrow, & if homesickness for you & Bruddie don't overpower me, I will go Tuesday to Niagara. . . . Thomas [perhaps Herbert Thomas, one of Katie's old beaux] was telling the people at Webster Springs that I had cut him out with you—you never told me of that."

He continued to report on his social life, which appears just as active as his professional life:

> I have just talked with Hamilton over the Phone & he invited me around to his house, & told me that he was talking of me last night to R. P. Hobson of Merrimac fame, who was his guest, and the great Hobson told him that as a Kappa Alpha he had heard of me—I am sorry I did not get here last night and meet him. He is lecturing around here at Chatauquas. Hamilton said Congressman Dovenor was also talking of the destruction of my father's house during the war by Hunter.

On August 11, he wrote from Pittsburgh, "My darling Katie, I have spent most of the day riding on the Trolley lines to see the city. Went to see West's Jubilee Minstrels & enjoyed them very much, & am just starting out to see Fra Diavolo,

an Opera I believe. I wish you were with me Sweet Angel. I will start in the morning for Niagara Falls, & as the ticket to Toronto Canada is only $1.00 more, I will
perhaps go on there." All was grist for his mill; minstrel shows and opera alike received the same benevolent approval.

So, despite Greenlee's protests of homesickness, he was willing to *extend* any
journey to see yet another place. It is easy to see how this tendency might, despite
her needing to be away from him, still annoy and anger Katie. He wrote a running
account of the trip: "I left Pittsburg this morning & we are now running along in
sight of Lake Erie, which seems to rise to meet the sky at the horizon. I see the
smoke of four steamboats in the distance. I have been thinking about you a heap
today and loving you, my Beautiful, Beautiful Darling, and I would be so delighted if you were along, for I love you and want to get back to you so bad, that
I am desperately homesick and lonely and would not have now been on my way to
Niagara had I not written to some people that I would have been there."

In a letter written on August 12, he commented that "I have written to Fannie
that I did not know your plans, & if you stayed at home longer, I would take my
meals with her if perfectly convenient until your return." Apparently, Greenlee did
not keep a cook employed while Katie was away.

He reported having sent "Bruddie this morning a picture book which I bought
thinking the animals would please him; and I enclosed a song book I bought at the
West Minstrels for him to give to his maiden aunt Virginia. . . . I have seen and
heard of nothing on this trip that strikes my fancy like you & Bruddie, & I love
you—harder than ever—I do love you so, and if you & Bruddie only love me like
I love you, I will be perfectly satisfied."

From Niagara Falls he wrote: "Beautiful Angel, I went through the gorge this
evening & wished for you all the time to see the "beeg wa-wa," it was grand & I
will never rest till you come with me here. Beautiful Thing I do love & miss you
so, & see no girl here as pretty as you, but there are several beautiful girls here, &
one especially." But Greenlee was no philanderer; his remarks were only innocent
admiration.

Back in Lexington, he wrote to Katie, still in Harrisonburg,

> I have missed you & Bruddie very much to-day & talked to old Rock
> [a horse] about it and he seemed to consider your absence regretfully
> out of his eyes. I slept or rather stayed in bed till eleven today & will try
> & get to bed early tonight, & I hope another night's good sleep will
> make me feel all right again—I was more fagged by my trip than I had

thought. . . . I went up to see Carrie yesterday about Ella but she pretended to know nothing—I told her that you would be much surprised to hear of Ella's leaving, but of course Ella had a right to go if she desired. I told her that Pat had told me that Ella only expected to stay a month, but Carrie said she did not know but would write & find out. I told her to tell Ella that if she expected to come back & wished to live with us I had no doubt you would make some temporary arrangement till her return. She said she would write soon to Ella & let us know her reply. I regret Ella's going but as she left only two days after you left, and a ticket was sent her, I do not think it would have been prevented if you had remained here. Tell mother I will send her our old refrigerator as a present, if she will promise to come back with you, & make us a long visit—and to bring you & Bruddie back to me *soon*.

A day later, he addressed another problem: "I think it will be unwise for us to stay in the same room with Bruddie, both for him & for us, so explain to mother that we will fix her up nicely & cozily in the room next to the Dining Room, if you think as I do about it. I feel it would be too dangerous to constantly risk waking Bruddie up as I did the other night and it would be an almost intolerable inconvenience and as I think we could arrange it to make mother perfectly comfortable in the room down stairs, it would be useless to risk the above." Katie may have been keeping him at a distance by having the baby in the room with her—and with *them* when Greenlee visited. In fact, within a year, she was sleeping by herself in her own room in Lexington. In Harrisonburg, she always slept with the children.

Katie remained in Harrisonburg. He wrote, on August 18: "Your sweet letter rec'd this morning *and I love you*. I sent the old Refrigerator to the Depot this evening. . . . Tell Mother I send it on the condition expressed—that she come back with you very soon, & make us a long visit." Possibly he had picked up a virus on his trip, for he ended, "I want to get to bed early as I feel pretty 'rocky.'"

On August 20, he wrote:

Your postal & letter rec'd & I was so delighted at the thought of you & Bruddie coming back that I at once sent Hugh for Ella Hanes & she promised to come up to my office but did not, & I then went to her house myself but could not find her & left word for her to come to my office to-night, which she has not done yet. I will try & get to see her tomorrow again. . . . I have been working hard & have not felt very

chipper but I slept better last night & feel better to-day. I hope the Refrigerator will get there safely tomorrow & Mother will be pleased &
will be up with you & Bruddie Thursday or Friday—for I do love you
& Bruddie & am mighty lonely without you—I love my home and
what makes it.

Possibly his indisposition was caused by worry over the troublesome state of his
marriage, about which he seemed unable to do a thing—as well as the worry of
not being able to secure servants.

The next day, he continued: "Beautiful Angel, I appreciate how I love you when
I know how lonely I am tonight not to get a letter from you this evening for the
second day—This world would be a poor old world without you, my Beautiful
Darling. Ella Hanes called today to say that her mother was sick & she could not
work for us but would look around for a cook for us. . . . Mother wanted me to let
you stay till the first of September—I miss you terribly but of course you must
not let that govern you, but do what is best for you & Bruddie and for your pleasure. Tell Mother I let you stay provided you bring her back with you."

From his perspective, what more could Katie want? He gave her perfect freedom to make her own decisions, and he was doing everything he could to give her
what she wanted and needed. Still, it appeared that it was not enough. Being the
man he was, he never gave up trying. He wasn't afraid of working hard, but he was
used to winning when he did—an article once described him as a "snapping-
turtle," who, once he had hold of a case, "never let go." This tenacity worked in
most of his life, but not with the one thing he worked at most diligently.

On August 25, he had been to visit her in Harrisonburg, for he wrote that he

got back from the Bridge at 15 minutes to nine tonight, and I hasten to
write to tell you how I love you, & how I enjoyed my visit over Sunday,
& how happy I am in your love, and the consciousness of it—for I love
you Beautiful Darling with an undivided love, and a jealous love, and
from your loveliness to me and love of heart and body you gave me, I
am happy and free from these doubts that damn. I love you, My Own,
My Angel, My All, and if anything occurs to make me doubt your love,
it blights my days and banishes sleep at night, but I enjoyed my visit to
you more than I can tell, Sweet Angel, and I am happy in the thought
of it beyond words—Be kind to me, Beautiful Darling, and love me,
love me, love me, without a shadow of turning or doubt, for all my happiness, my life, my *soul* is in the keeping of you and your love for me.

His pathetic gratitude obviously grated on her sensibilities. Not once did she respond to such a comment.

On the 26th, he wrote:

> I note in your letter just received that "*all the folks* were so glad to hear" that I intended coming back next Sunday—but nothing is said about you and Bruddie—now Beautiful Thing, unless you and Bruddie want to see me *most* as bad as I want to see you, I will have pressing business somewhere else, either at the Alum, or Natural Bridge, or more probably with my old friend Morpheus over Sunday, which will prevent the "folks" from being delighted. . . . Do something for your cold Sweet Thing and get rid of it—don't let it hang to you whatever you do. . . . Give my love to all the folks who would be glad to see me. With all the love of my life to you & Bruddie.

Without doubt there was a serious lack of harmony during this time. Greenlee's manner of directing her to not let her cold hang on must have annoyed her. That he had to tell her to banish the baby from their room, that she may have used as an excuse to avoid intimacy the cold she claimed to have, indicate that she wished to avoid sleeping with him. Her grandmother was evidently dying, for Greenlee referred to that fact the next day. He finally had good news about a cook: "Ella Hanes saw me this A.M. & told me that Sue Harvey would come to see me about cooking for us—that she was now at Frank Smith's and that he was going to Staunton soon—that she had 2 boys, Henry who worked at Fannie's and the other, she did not know where he was. She has not seen me yet. Ella says she is a *lovely* cook. I hope your cold has gotten better—take good care of yourself Dearest Angel for I love you & Bruddie needs you. . . . Love to all, with kisses for you & Bruddie."

The next day, he wrote her the sort of letter we can now be sure she did not want to receive:

> Your nice long letter came this evening and Bruddie's letter written & crossed on both sides and with them my loneliness vanishes. . . . Beautiful Thing, I love you and anything that comes from you in love, makes me happy beyond anything in the world, and Sweet Angel, don't leave anything in love for me to take for granted, but love me demonstratively and tell me so, tell me so, with your soul and your body, with your heart, and eyes and lips and all—tell me, tell me for I love you

with every thought and every second of time, and the visible return of your love makes me the happiest man in the world, Beautiful, Beautiful, Beautiful Darling. . . .

I, of course, will engage no cook—*that* you should have taken for granted. I will go to-morrow to take affidavits at the Misses Fontz's, & expect to get back tomorrow evening—sorry you are not here to go with me. . . . I found today that I had lost my pocket-book, and I cannot recall seeing it since Saturday evening at Sipes & Harris's office when I gave you $10.00. I left $5.00 in the purse. I guess it slipped out of my pocket at some time. Look all around home for it.

What he needed apparently she could not give: *love me freely, totally, with abandon.* He passed along a tidbit: "Cousin Mary Davidson told me this evening that the cook she had expected to get, Susan Harvey, said she was going to cook for you & so cousin Mary then got another. I told her that you had never engaged her—in fact neither of us had seen her, that a woman had spoken to me of her, & I had sent word for her to come & see me but she had never come. She said she was a good cook." He explained that he did not want her to spend her gift money from him on Bruddie or the family but only on herself: "I mean that money for your personal uses simply, or rather what you want independently, & with which I have nothing to do." The arrangement of having their money separate must have been unusual for the time. Perhaps Katie demanded it.

On September 4, he seemed to be grasping at straws: "Your letter marked with love and kisses received this evening and it gave me happiness—for I love you." He then congratulated Lilian, who had decided to become a nurse, and began her studies that fall, 1902: "My best wishes go with Sister Lilian in her chosen life—she deserves the happiest & the best. . . . Tell her we will expect a part of her holidays always in a visit to us—and tell her that the Doctor or patient whichever it turns out finally to be, will receive our blessing & congratulations." The family reverses upon the death of Judge Paul may have been the impetus for the young women remaining at home with no matrimonial plans on the horizon to go out and earn their bread, for Lilian did become a nurse, and Virginia became a teacher for a while, then later worked in the public library in Harrisonburg.

On September 7, Greenlee wrote to his "Darling Katie, I am happy to feel that I will have you & Bruddie back this time tomorrow for I do miss you so, and life has not much of its light without you. . . . Capt. Moore lost his cow last night which I regret doubly, on Capt's account as well as our own, as the milk we got from Mrs. Moore was the best we ever got. . . . Tell Mother I have done a good week's work in one line, having gotten three unhappy people divorces this week. I have had a touch of neuralgia this evening—the first I have had for many a day." Neuralgia, though the word specifically means "nerve pain," appears most often to mean "headache" throughout these letters unless some other site is mentioned, such as "neuralgia in my hip."

But the next evening, September 8, 1902, Katie had still not come home, and Greenlee wrote:

> Darling Katie, My Beautiful, My Angel—the consciousness of how much I love you and how much you are to me, comes to me, when I realize the disappointment I feel at your not getting here this evening as I had expected. I put my best clothes on to-day just to meet my Sweetheart this evening—but of course you are right in this as in everything else & I will look with yearning for my love to come back to me tomorrow evening. . . .
>
> I expect it is very well for Julia to come in the morning to straighten up what looks like the most veritable bachelor's den, & make up the bed after a six weeks state of unfettered disregard, but unless Hannah comes with you & helps with the "big man," I expect you had best have Julia. . . .
>
> I got the flowers this evening, & took them to Little John's grave, & I felt so forcibly how, three years ago when I heard his first cry, the horizon of life, and eternity itself, heightened and broadened. I was up to his grave also yesterday evening & wished for you. No fear for your love comes to me there. Once when you were away, and I felt depressed I went there in the night.

But Greenlee was not one to let gloom hover for long, and the reader can almost see him shaking off such doleful thoughts, for he continued: "Mrs. Hubard, Taz's[3] mother, who drove over from the Bridge, was asking most interestedly after you. Also Mrs. Estill this evening—I went to ask after Dr. Estill, he is quite ill with appendicitis & a complication of troubles with his liver, but he was resting easier."

On September 22, 1902, Katie was back in Lexington and Greenlee was once again off on his travels:

> We left Millboro this morning a little after six, & got here for Breakfast & have had a very pleasant day, & have seen and met a good many

pleasant people—Miss Davis, sister of Richard Harding Davis, whom I have known here for several years invited Judge Anderson[4] & myself to eat Dinner with her to-day, but found her table full and went to the Maury's table, who had invited Benton & myself to eat at their table while we are here. Slim Willard invited me to take Dinner with his wife and himself at the Hot Springs today but I told him not to expect me, as I could not spare the time to drive over there—I wanted to get through and get back to my Angel. . . .

I talked today with Senator Morgan & want to have a long talk with him about public matters while here. There is still a large crowd here—greater than ever before at this time. . . .

Beautiful Thing, I don't see anything here as pretty as my Angel, & nothing that can keep me contentedly away from my angel. . . . I called this evening on the Andersons and they asked most particularly after you & Bruddie, and invited us to come over next Summer & make them a visit—I thanked her very much & told Mrs. Anderson, I knew you would appreciate it. I have enjoyed myself very much here, and I only wish that you could have been with me.

It took little to lift his spirits: "My Darling Katie, Your sweet letter just received and I thank you for the love that is in it—I love for you to love me and am the happiest man in the world in your love—for I think of nothing else, work for nothing else, live for nothing else—*I love you.*"

But he was evidently displeased at the same time. Apparently Katie had chosen to keep the baby in the room with them, against his express wishes.

I will be unable to come down (to Harrisonburg) tomorrow as I have several matters in Court, and probably two of them to argue. But even if I had the time, I would be afraid to come, as I am so nearly broken down tonight, for with Bruddie not getting to sleep till 10 or 11 at night, and crying out in his sleep several times in the night and waking for food between 5 and 6, it is impossible to get any continuous sleep that does any good—now Angel, be strong minded and wean the kid for this thing continuing for night after night will shatter the nerves of both of you. This life and tissue-giving nourishment of your milk has long since weakened, and the only affect of continuing nursing is detrimental, and destructive of that continuous & deep and undisturbed sleep that is an absolute essential to health—the baby is like one wait-

ing for a train, his sleep is worth little or nothing to him. Each time that
I have slept in the room with him this summer, it has almost broken me
down. Now my Beautiful Angel for the sake of everything, wean him at
once—I know you love him to be at your breast; it is natural and a
physical delight to you, but give it up for his sake and yours, & both of
you save your nerves.

Katie made no reply. On October 3, she bought a buggy for the baby, and
Greenlee, ever agreeable, wrote, "I enclose a check payable to Fridley for $1.50 in
full for the buggy. Miss Jennie Bacon[5] is in my office and says that she can let you
have milk. She will let me know when she gets her cows from the country."

But things were difficult, and Greenlee risked a great deal in writing to confess
that he felt at times in danger of losing his self-control:

Your sweet letter rec'd yesterday evening & your love makes me happy
after it. I slept last night without a care and feel splendidly to-day. I love
you Beautiful Angel, and with your love and the consciousness of it
with me, I am the happiest man that God ever made; as without it, or
the doubt of it, I feel, and am, the meanest man the devil ever regarded
with satisfaction. With the certainty of your love, *I am certain* that all
the pure, good, high and happy aspirations that you have brought into
my life, are impregnable; but when doubts and disbelief of your love
force themselves on me, damnable thoughts and purposes creep up,
which although I turn from as a death-dealing contagion, yet the absolute integrity of my "moral-grip" is wounded—but I pray God, that
no moment of uncontrollable depression or resentment may come, in
which I might lose it, and I swear before God to you, that it shall never
be lost as long as I am conscious of *your love*. Your love is the inspiration and symbol to me of all that is good, and beautiful and true, and if
it failed me, all things would sink with it to the level of the false and
wrong, and carry down at the same time my dreams and purposes. Love
me, love me, love me, My Wife, My Darling, My Angel, love me—and
not only love me, but tell me so and let me know it all the time, and as
you love me and regard my happiness, do and say nothing which would
bring a doubt to me. Let us swear to each other that neither will ever
purposely do anything to bring a doubt of love, and unhappiness, to
the other, but will do everything in reason to impress on the other the
existence of perfect love—Such life to me would be ideal and no words

would measure my happiness—for I love you, Divine Woman, to the fullness of every power and faculty that God has endowed me in soul, mind, heart and body, and hence no thought nor aspiration but that begins with you and ends with you, and your love; and if you failed me, the greatness of my love, would be the measure of my curse.[6]

In that letter, he did not return to his other self, interested, optimistic, social. But later that day he wrote her another letter, in which he commented, "I think there will be no trouble about the delegate of the Daughters of the Confederacy, as Fannie tells me that some people up town had spoken for them & there would not be enough to go around, & she would tell Jennie to put ours with one of them. I told her if there was any doubt about this that we would board her somewhere." Almost certainly, Greenlee had offered their house, and almost certainly, Katie did not wish to have a visitor and told him to uninvite the guest.

In October, Katie's grandmother died and was buried at Ottobine. The family undoubtedly gathered for the funeral, giving Katie yet another excuse to stay in Harrisonburg instead of returning to Lexington. Something unpleasant happened at the funeral, to which the following from Greenlee alludes: "It was a gratification to me to be able to go to Ottobine Thursday, & I am doubly glad . . . if our people appreciated it. Give my best love to mother, & if my blundering in what I conceived to be your happiness gave her cause for worry, tell her that you were not in earnest about what you said to me, & that everything is all right and that we are loving each other harder than ever before—and be sure & bring her back with you. . . . [And] telephone me at once so that I may get a bed & fix up the Parlor for her." It seems that, no matter how he tried, he could not win.

The reader may have inferred that his mother-in-law, who heard only Katie's version of things, was not entirely supportive of Greenlee. She seemed ready to criticize him and obviously didn't like visiting them. But marriage at that time, with rare exceptions, held until death's dissolution of the bond.

Six months went by without any more letters. Perhaps Katie stayed home in Lexington, and perhaps Greenlee did too. In the spring of 1903 he went to Richmond, then to Bath County. During the winter Katie became pregnant with their third child—and demanded her own house, for nothing had come of her earlier efforts to separate them definitely from the rest of his family. Although there is a brief flurry of letters on the subject, again it was dropped, at least in letters, perhaps because a child was on the way.

From West Virginia, Greenlee wrote, "I have been taking Depositions a good part of the day, and will continue all day tomorrow, & hope then to finish, but it is by no means certain that I shall. . . . Brother telephoned me that he would make me a proposition for part of the front lot, but did not tell me what it was. . . . I told him to talk to you." Houston owned a narrow but deep lot on the west side of Letcher Avenue, which ran between Washington and Lee and VMI. The lot, only 100 feet wide, began at the street, went up over a hill, with a long slope down to Woods Creek in the back.[7] At my father's death in 1994, the lot was sold to VMI. Today the schools abut each other.

Greenlee ran into old friends in Bath County, bragged on Bruddie, took depositions, and noted: "I enjoyed my trip regardless of the bad weather most of the time." At one point he told Katie, "[Mrs. Eubank] says I have been saying that I was going to bring along you & him so long that she believes I am ashamed of you, as I don't do it," and in another letter wrote: "I was disappointed at not hearing from you and Bruddie, but you have treated me kindly and I can not complain."

He attended church, played whist three nights in a row with three women from Charleston, commented vaguely on "a very interesting damage suit" he was pursuing, and wrote, "I got your letter about the lot and I hardly felt I could give as much for a lot as a part of the front lot would cost me and then build a house on it at a cost which the location of the lot would necessitate. So if he is unwilling to let me have the rear lot, I guess I will let Frank Moore[8] bid on the Mulberry Hill property for us." Greenlee was thinking of ways to keep Katie at home: "I sincerely hope Mother will consider favorably coming with us for the education of the boys, and her living afterwards with us. . . . Everybody here is most pleasant & lovely to me, and the fair is delightful and I am enjoying every minute." On April 26, 1903, he wrote her to tell "Frank Moore to go ahead & bid on Mulberry Hill unless he hears something from me to the contrary. G.D.L."

A letter two days later noted:

> I got your letter this morning which told me of Bruddie's croup & I hope that splendid fellow is all O.K. again—kiss him & love him for me & tell him Doddy is coming back to him & Muddy as soon as he can. . . . Brother offered me ½ the lot from front to rear or rather 50 feet next to Mrs. Blair's for $1500—This is a very fair offer as he has been offered $3500 for the whole lot, but I told him I would think of it but you had set your heart on the back part, & I hardly felt that I could afford such a house as the front lot would require. But we will talk over it. I wonder if Frank Moore bought Mulberry Hill for me today. . . .
>
> Tell Hugh to tell Miss Dixon I will return Thursday evening late I hope.

Greenlee did not care where they lived, but Katie insisted on the creek and the woods for she loved picnicking, wading, and gathering wildflowers, according to my father. She transplanted wild daylilies up by the house, for there was always a bed of them along the south side. Mulberry Hill, one of Lexington's fine houses, must have been too expensive. The subject was not mentioned again in letters.

In the end they bought the entire lot from Houty. Greenlee returned to Richmond for the spring legislative session and wrote of seeing a play; of many dinners, lunches, and even breakfasts with friends and clients. He expressed the hope that "you & Bruddy & Julia [the nursemaid] reached home all right, & are having a 'goot' time as that fascinating little Dutchman Bruddy would say."

Katie was now pregnant for the third time, and at some point during this period consulted a physician, perhaps a psychiatrist, in Baltimore. There is the sense that Greenlee made Katie "nervous" as the letters below from and about Frank Smith imply. Greenlee's zest for life wavered as Katie rebuffed him. She spent the entire third pregnancy in Harrisonburg, returning to Lexington *only* when Greenlee was not there. Although we can only intuit her reasons, this was apparently an unhappy time for them both.

He wrote: "I enclose a letter rec'd from Dr. Smith; I have written him that I would be detained here longer than I had expected & tell of him I feared that I could not bring you on at this time. . . . *If I telegraph you,* reply if you could meet me in Baltimore Friday. I expect I had best meet you at the R.R. station in Balto."

Dr. Smith's letter must have been typical of letters about medical issues of the time, when even less than now was known about the causes of illness. For many years the Baltimore physician listened to Katie's complaints and offered reassurances and some medications, but perhaps his most valuable contribution was his sympathetic ear. On May 18, 1903, he first wrote to Greenlee:

> My dear Sir, Your letter about Mrs. Letcher arrived this morning. From the history you give of the case I am inclined to the opinion that all the various manifestations might be due to a nervous condition rather than to organic heart disease—which would also be in accord with your family physician's view. Before, however, making myself absolutely responsible for any opinion it would be necessary for me to see the patient. Now as to the time of course that depends a good deal upon the feelings of the patient. If her nervousness is largely increased by doubt as to her condition, the sooner we clear up such doubts the sooner we might look for improvement in the nervous symptoms. . . .

I could see you at my office at 4 P.M. on Wednesday or Thursday (or could make an appointment on Thursday for some other hour). Please let me know what you wish. In case you decide not to come please tell Mrs. Letcher that there is no reason that because Judge Paul had heart disease that she should have it. He probably acquired it years after she was born. I should very much like to help his daughter. Again so far as her nervousness is concerned please tell her that I expect a decided improvement in the fourth month.

In conclusion I would say that often a thorough examination & the knowledge of what is and what is not the matter with them does a great deal for such patients. If Mrs. Letcher comes please let her bring a specimen of urine with her which should be as fresh as convenient. My fee for examination would be $10.
Yours faithfully, Frank R. Smith

Greenlee chatted on, writing that "Miss Sallie Thomson says all the hill seems lonely without Gee Gee and it surely does." He arranged an appointment for her (and himself) with Dr. Smith and wrote: "I hope to be down on the Wednesday morning train early, & you meet me. . . . I enclose check for $6.50 making $25.00 in all for your trip, which you can take as an anniversary celebration. I will try & get the little overshoes & scissors to you by tomorrow's mail. I hope, I hope, that I can find them."

He told her about the delegates staying with Fannie (instead of at their house), noting that "[they] are very pleasant—one is a Col. Denson of Birmingham, Ala. an ex-congressman."

Ever hopeful, Greenlee commented after the trip to Baltimore to see Dr. Smith, "Sweet Thing, I hope today's sleep will make you all right, & you will have no bad affects from our jag. I had a good time Beautiful Angel, a good time; and enjoyed the trip so much, that I wish we could have stayed a week longer. Make Mother get ready to come home with you. . . . Sweet Sweet Angel, I love you & so enjoyed being with you all the time on our trip."

Greenlee continued to seek her help with finances: "If the enclosed acct of Miss Harman is O.K. send it back & I will send her a check. Please *at once* mail me the K.A. Charter, among the papers in Idge's top drawer."

Seymour, Katie's brother, wrote: "We were talking the other day about how much formality is necessary to bring you down. This letter is very informal, but I hope it isn't ineffectual. . . . Charley will quit about the first of August. Lil will get home about then. So we can have a great re-union."

Dr. Smith's follow-up letter to her visit is a wonder of rhetoric saying very little. Clearly, he had no idea what was wrong with Katie, other than homesickness, or a need to be somewhere else other than where Greenlee was. So he chose the optimistic view that her symptoms would "pass off." Sadly, no acceptable alternative existed for a woman who wanted out of a marriage. "My Dear Sir, I duly received Mrs. Letcher. We are confronted with a very difficult problem and one that is very hard to meet. It seems to me that should the difficulty continue it would be well to let Mrs. Letcher go home for a month or so and see whether the thing will not pass off. I have written Mrs. Letcher that the matter is perhaps only temporary and that there are prospects that her nervousness is only temporary. With kind regards, I remain very sincerely, Frank R. Smith."

Today Katie would probably have chosen to separate from Greenlee, but of course she could not afford that. It appears that she felt trapped and miserable. Surely sex was a big part of the problem. Back in Bath County, Greenlee wrote, in mid-July, "I write this while depositions are going on, just to say that I have arrived safely but almost frozen—cold as winter. I trust you and Bruddy are safe at Nuzzer Mama's and well. . . . I have had time only to write you . . . while Depositions were being taken—then even for that moment, when I centered my thoughts on *all I loved,* I feared something in the evidence would escape me."

Despite the pressures he was under, Greenlee kept his sense of humor: "I got a telegram from Capt. Press Moore last night saying he had as I requested by letter put off our case in Lexington which was set for Wednesday; so I will stay & try & finish up the case here before leaving. The Old Capt sent me a 30 word message that cost me 65 ¢, which he ought to have put in 10 words for 25 ¢. In the precise prolixity, I could see the Old Capt photographed. He wrote it like he had been writing a deed. If it had been from Hop or Morgan Pendleton, I would have felt certain it was a joke." He ended by writing, "Beautiful Angel, I love you & want to see you—if you want to see me. With love to you & Bruddie."

Day after day he worked, wondering if the other side

> is trying to wear us out. Our depositions are slowly dragging their length along—much slower than I had anticipated—but I am enjoying myself though working hard. From after breakfast until 6 in the evening we are hard at it. . . .
>
> I have met some people here but am so busy that I cannot cultivate any new acquaintances. Some old friends, I find, who are very pleasant and nice. A Mrs. Newcomb from Louisville I found was a Miss

Churchill, that I knew in the days gone by. Hunsdon Cary, an old Cadet & a K.A. is here. I called on Mrs. Geo. Gibson at her cottage this evening—she has spent every summer here for 15 years, I think. I called at Mr. Anderson's this P.M. but they were out. Beautiful Thing, I see no one here as beautiful as my beautiful Angel.

Of Dr. Smith's letter to him, he wondered, "Do I read between the lines of his letter to me that we should be *separated for a month?* If so Beautiful Angel, for your sake, I will try & do it—I do want you to be well and happy, & will do anything to accomplish it."

Coming back from West Virginia, he sounded a little discouraged: "I hope to get started to Lexington by 9 or 10 & reach home for Dinner. I telephoned last night for Fannie to expect me. This will make it impossible to get to Harrisonburg —I feel lonely but I guess it is better for you, that I do not come. I sent you Dr. Smith's letter the other day, which I presume you got." While Katie stayed in Harrisonburg, Greenlee provided her with a running account of his time: "I have been going pretty continuously today. Went to the Presbyterian Church to hear Mr. Robt Campbell preach this A.M.; went this evening & called on Brown Ayres family at Mrs. John Anderson's & afterwards went to Col. Moody's. After supper I called on the Misses Grahams, & will go over to the Depot to mail this letter tonight yet—all with new shoes on. . . . I wish I could have seen you & Bruddie to-day, but for you better not, I guess."

Greenlee had many health "notions," as the following example shows: "I am so sorry to hear of Bruddie's croup—what in the world caused it? Had he been going barefooted—this tends to keep the whole body cool, & of even temperature & is generally thought to prevent croup entirely. I wonder if he could have laid down on the ground? Or played in the water near the stable? As his tendency is to croup, . . . be extremely careful with him."

And he mentioned the lot on which they would build their future house: "I asked Miss Ruth Anderson to tell her father to call at my office as he came up in the morning when I will see if anything can be hoped from Mrs. Blair. The back lot won't do. I will try to find the things on the list you sent, & send them by Mrs. Colvin to you. . . . Let me know if you need any money yet & how much. I enclose some stamps (10) & several postals. *All,* all I got. . . . With love to all."

And soon he wrote, "I am glad to hear that Bruddie is doing well, & I have looked up the things on the list sent and will send them by Mr. Colvin tomorrow. I also send to Bruddie a bag of animal crackers. I hope to Heaven I got the right things. I enclose a check for $5.00—be as careful as you can, as today I had to go in Bank and borrow $250.00 to keep things going. You did not send Mr. Boley's letter as stated in your letter."

He reported that a friend, Mrs. Mallory, had a boy. He seemed impressed that "she said it was to be named Frank Mallory & she wanted it to be the same size as Col. Mallory & look exactly like him. . . . Some women seem to think something of their husbands, don't they? . . ." We can see him here wishing that his own wife were so adoring. After some news items, he promised, "I will water the flowers tonight when I go home."

On July 29, he wrote forlornly, "I got a telegram that said not leave for W. Va. before next Monday, but I expect I had better not stay overnight if I pass Harrisonburg for your sake. . . . I do hope you will get all right again."

In early August, he wrote, "If Dr. Smith meant for you to be a month from me, I guess I had best try to stand it, & see if it will do you any good." He told her, "We were invited to a card party at Mrs. S. B. Walker's tonight, & I told her you would appreciate the invitation & regret that you could not go. I will take Jennie. Mrs. Coles[9] also has a ladies Tea tonight at 6:30 & Jennie said you were missing all the gaiety."

He wrote, the next day, "Dear Katie, Your postals rec'd this A.M. I have been all right, though not sleeping as well as I would like to." One can imagine him tossing and turning, blaming himself perhaps, wondering how things could have gone so wrong, and worried sick about Katie, about Bruddy, about the baby due in November. His month-long banishment must have stung. He was here confronted by something he didn't know how to deal with: by now it is clear that he believed that if he just loved her hard enough, she would have to love him back. All his life his optimism, his determination, had won him friends and accolades. Now that it wasn't working, he didn't know what to do.

Katie could not live *his life agenda for her*. She couldn't leave, and she couldn't give him what he so desperately wanted. So he just kept communicating, although he must have felt near despair: "Enclosed find accts of Boley & Bruce's meat bill—examine & see if they are all right. Bruce included Glass & Co., & I thought I had paid accts to them in the last year, but cannot find a receipt since July 1, 1902." "Beautiful Thing, I love you & want to come to see you bad, but I do not know but that I should not."

He went once, early in August, to see them and afterwards, wrote: "Beautiful Angel, I love you, & enjoyed my visit to you & Bruddie so much—and seeing our lovely mother & the byes [boys]. Sweet Thing, my cup of happiness would be full if life was fraught to you with the delights and happiness that it brings to me and if they came to us together; and I pray that Heaven will yet be kind to us together—for I love you with every pulsation of my heart, and every aspiration and yearning of my soul and body, and if that love was returned I would be the happiest man in the world." As always, the world intruded: "I enclose Mrs. E. A. Sale's[10] card which I found under the door today. Also invitation to Judge Love's daughter's marriage—tell me what to do. Also acct of Miss Jennie Bacon for 80¢ is it all right? Also acct of Irvine & Co, examine it & let me know if it is all O.K. & return all the accts I have sent. I sent 2 Saturday." Most sadly, he wrote, "Tell Bruddie Daddy won't come any more to see him till he writes me to come."

But Katie's symptoms persisted, and Greenlee sought medical advice locally: on August 4, he wrote:

> I saw Dr. White to-day and he says that the trouble you have is caused by pressure of the child on the arteries, preventing the blood from circulating normally, that you should take exercise by walking but when not walking you should lie down as much as possible as this relieves to some extent the pressure; that your clothes should not bind your body any, but should be held up by suspenders from the shoulders; that hot sitz baths are all right; but you could also use a rag saturated with vinegar and water in equal parts, hot. He said he thought this was better than boric acid. I told him I would keep him posted. I hope Sweet Thing you will get relieved, & not suffer.

He carried on valiantly: "Tom Rice sends word that the lamp cannot be fixed, —so I will get another & send with your overshoes & dress tomorrow by Mr. Colvin."

He continued to report on the babies being born who would be his baby's contemporaries, and on the illness of a friend's wife: "I talked with Hampton Wayt yesterday evening on the train, & he told me his wife was very ill—had fatty degeneration of the heart—I was so sorry to hear it." He regretted not being able to attend the bar association meeting and continued to discuss money matters with Katie. He sent her a skirt she wanted, and overshoes, and warned her about "a new alcohol lamp—be very careful about letting any alcohol drip on the lower part and trim, as I expect that is what caused the other to melt. We can probably send the other to the factory to be mended—so keep it carefully." And the letters all end with something along the lines of "I hope to be able to come down next Saturday, but I don't know whether I ought, Beautiful Thing."

On August 8, 1903, she finally wrote him: "Your postal about the papers came this morning. They are not in your mail, but there is a registered letter at this P.O. which may be what you want. I cannot go up to see about it but will have it forwarded in this uncertainty. Buddy is well, with a wonderful appetite. Love from us all, K—"

This sounds as if she were contemplating not returning to him at all. It must have been a rare word from her, for he responded with delight: "My Darling Katie, Your postal just received & I am delighted to hear that a good appetite is [Bruddy's] and Nature's Gentle Nurse stays with him—two better companions for that splendid fellow could not be found." He did not respond to her allusion to "this uncertainty."

He continued to write: "I got your letter yesterday after writing my postal and was so sorry to hear of your feeling badly & headache & I hope you are all right now" and "I called on Jim Quarles & his wife last night & they all asked after you & Bruddie & Miss Mary was telling them what a magnificent fellow Bruddie was." His friend, Jim Quarles, had remarried after his first wife's death.

Greenlee continued to write to Katie daily:

> I am getting calls made. Friday night I called at Dr. Manley's[11] & ran in on prayers. Last night I called on Mrs. Cox & Frank Junkin, but as they were just getting in from the Natural Bridge I did not sit down. This evening I called at the Moody's. The Col. & Mrs. Will Moody[12] leave tomorrow. Tonight I called on Capt Blake who came yesterday. He & his wife will leave Tuesday for Florida. This evening I had a call from Mr. Strauss & his wife from Richmond. He is a part owner of the Paper Mill at Big Island, where I went some time ago. I brought them in & got some ice from Fannie & gave them some beer. I may have to sue his Company. Everybody asks after you & Bruddie. I got a ripe tomato out of the garden yesterday—there will be plenty shortly. I negotiated with David Chandler to plant celery as soon as he could; & told him you wanted as much as he could plant. . . .
>
> I have had a terrible time with a rat that had been caught in a trap in the basement, & had almost lost his identity before I discovered him with my eye.

Greenlee took an interest in everything: house decorations, how much to spend for wedding presents, what Katie wanted planted in the garden. "Just paid my party call—Mrs. Walker was out, but found Mrs. Paxton in. She & Matt asked after you & Bruddie."[13]

On August 11, 1903, a Tuesday, he wrote: "I have heard nothing from you since last Monday morning—I do hope you are not sick, Sweet Angel. I sent you some nasturtiums this morning which I hope reached you all right, my Beautiful Sweetheart. . . . I have lost so much sleep lately that I must hurry through some work I am obliged yet to do tonight & get to bed & try to get an early start tomorrow. Yours—G.D.L. PS 194 Celery plants planted."

Greenlee's constitution was remarkable. He wrote from Bath County on August 12,

> My Darling Katie, I left Lexington at 11:13 this morning & took Dinner at the Alum, left there at 4 and reached here 9:15 tonight—too late for regular supper and some doubt about old Rock being properly cared for, but I have promised extra pay & I hope this will accomplish the matter all right. The next time I will stop somewhere on the other side of the mountain, as the night caught me on the mountain and it was so dark I had to get out and lead the horse pretty much up the steep part of the mountain, for fear the buggy would go over the side. You can imagine how tired I feel after about a 40 mile drive and a walk over the last part of the Warm Spring Mountain. . . . [O]ld Rock did noble but was somewhat fagged toward the last.

On August 13, 1903, he was introduced in Bath County to the game that became an antidote to this most tense time of his life: "Met many old friends here & people that I have met here before, & have enjoyed myself. I went on the Golf Links this evening & knocked some balls around a little—think I would like the game very much, but I am afraid to learn the game for fear I would go crazy about it like everyone else does. Your sweet letter rec'd this morning & *I love you* and am all *yours*. G.D.L."

Golf quickly became a passion, giving him pleasure until near the end of his life. He became so good that he won local, then state, then regional championships.[14]

His wife away and pregnant, himself banished from her presence, Greenlee's hurt and bafflement turned inward, affecting his digestion. On August 17, 1903, he visited them, and wrote wistfully afterwards: "My Beautiful Angel, I love you and in the recollection of my visit I am happy, & think how beautiful you looked this morning. I am feeling pretty well but still living on toast. Will leave at 6 in the morning for Irish Creek. Capt Moore had Rock out at the farm to-day & broke the shafts and a rein, & returned late tonight."

A postal from Irish Creek on August 19, reads, "Dear Katie, Frank Moore & myself reached here safely by buggy yesterday about midday, and have had quite a pleasant day & night here. I feel about all right again and have enjoyed my meals here very much. We go a little higher up the Creek this morning and expect to get home sometime tonight. Affectionately, G.D.L."

Although he was strong and healthy physically, emotionally Greenlee was so dependent on Katie's love that it must have been extremely stressful to hold himself and his world together. On August 21, he wrote: "I was a little lonely last night, not finding a letter here from you, but was happy this morning to get one—I love you & love to hear from you when away, Beautiful Sweetheart. You looked so pretty when I left you last Monday morning, and I loved you. . . . Use your good judgment, & get something for Miss Grace Parsons—I leave it to you." On subsequent days, he paid for a new baby buggy, commenting that the cost seemed excessive. His tone was wistful, and on August 24, he wrote, "I enjoyed so much our drive yesterday. . . . I will look for you surely tomorrow evening and will be very lonely and much disappointed if you do not choose to come, Sweet Sweet Thing. . . . I have just telephoned to Carrie Woodford to tell her to come & see me, so that I could enquire for you."

But still Katie did not return. Greenlee's sadness showed in his August 25 letter:

I am lonely & disappointed tonight at not having yet any home, and away from what I love, Beautiful Darling. Your telegram came in time to keep Geo. Adams & myself from going to the train. I am sorry to hear of Julia's sister being shot, but hope it is not serious. . . .

Mrs. Jamison came to see me today & is a most delightful middle-aged colored lady, reminding me something of Aunt Susan. Said she had lived 4 years with Mrs. Price when she was here,—she was the Army Officer's wife. She said she would cook & do the washing for $8.00 a month; and she and her husband Harvey Jamison, who is John L. Campbell's footman, would occupy the room in the basement. I like this as Harvey is one of the most respectable colored men here, and I feel it would make you feel safe when I am away. She has been up north for some time but she said if she got a satisfactory place with us she wanted to stay here. They own a house, & are among the colored élite.

Have no children. I believe they are what we are looking for. I am working very hard this week getting ready for court, & am so busy I had to decline to go to Oxford [a community several miles from Lexington] & make a speech at the dedication of the New Palmer Academy they are building there. . . .

I hope everything will be O.K. for you to come home soon—you doubtless did right in delaying under all the circumstances.

Generous and forgiving, three days later, he wrote how very disappointed he was that they were still not home but opined yet again that she was right to stay away and that no cook could be had for a week.

On August 28, he wrote sadly and simply, "My Darling Katie, I have but a moment to tell you I love you. I don't know what else to say. I am expecting Capt Moore every moment to go to work on a case. I am disappointed that you may not be able to get home this week, but whatever you do, if not *best,* is *all right*— and I will expect you just as soon as you can come and will be lonely till you & Bruddie do come." Then, two days later: "I am so sorry Sweet Angel that you have a cold & feel badly but hope you will soon get over it. When will John & Charlie come up?"

On August 29, John, Katie's brother, returning to VMI, "handed me your note & I was right home-sick for you & Bruddie. . . . Enclosed find check for $10.00 as requested. I hope you & Bruddie will be along Monday—if you don't come home, I fear Mother will never invite you back. . . . PS For fear you overlooked some expense I make the check for $12.50 instead of $10.00." On the last day of August, he wrote,

> My Darling Katie, I could not make out a word today from you over the phone, but I could understand Charlie pretty well. . . . I understood Charlie to say today he would not be up till Thursday, which surprised me as I understood all state cadets were ordered back on September 1 st.—If Charlie had such orders *by all means* send him up on the 1 st, as it will not do for him to begin military life by a failure to obey orders; and unless he has permission to delay, it may prejudice Gen. Shipp[15] and the authorities against him, and subject him to penalties. John seemed surprised when I told him Charlie would not come till Thursday this evening as he passed. I hope you & Bruddie can soon come home—I miss you. With all love & kisses for you & that splendid fellow. *I am, Yours, G.D.L.*

It cannot escape the reader that Katie could have made herself understood but apparently chose not to. On the first of September, Greenlee wrote: "My Darling Katie, Your sweet long letter just rec'd with Bruddie's negatives & I know all at home will delight to see them. . . . I will go on the early train in the morning to Staunton to argue my case before the Supreme Court, and . . . I will try & get to Harrisonburg tomorrow night. . . . I expect you had best wait for Julia, as nursing might break you down here."

Despite his focus on her, his concerns went out into the community, and his generosity attracted the generosity of others: in another letter that day, he wrote:

> I am glad Charlie is going to report promptly, as I know how much is thought of that at V.M.I. . . . I failed to tell you that Miss Maggie Free-land asked me if Charlie would want Cadet Symonds bed, books, white pants, clothes, etc, that he was a 4th classman last year & died suddenly during the summer & his mother told Miss Maggie to give them to some worthy State Cadet who would appreciate them. I told Miss Maggie that I knew Mother would appreciate them & I felt sure Char-lie would too, & I told John of it & he said he knew Charlie would ap-preciate them. They will save Charlie probably $75 to $100. John was here a moment ago & said he would get the bed in the evening for Charlie. G.D.L.

His daily letters continued, while she, apparently, remained largely silent. If there were letters from her, they have disappeared. Two weeks later, on September 16, 1903, Greenlee wrote to Katie in Lexington from Bath County, so she had ob-viously gone home as he left. Her reluctance to return to Lexington is under-standable; in Harrisonburg she had her mother, Virginia, and young Seymour to help entertain the baby—as well as her old friends. She was heavily pregnant, doubtlessly uncomfortable. In Lexington, even when Greenlee was in town he was gone from the house all day and many evenings. She did not cultivate Lexington friends, so presumably she was mostly alone with the baby and the nurse.

Yet the mere fact of her being back in Lexington was enough to lift Greenlee's mood:

> My Darling Katie, I have just finished my Supper after reaching here— and although I have just been invited to attend a dance, I will write to my Sweetheart and go to bed. I think I will mind what you say next time, Beautiful Wise Creature—I got to the Alum in good time and

got a prompt Dinner & Old Rock brought me forward finely, & I reached the Warm Spring Mountain at 6:20 and thought I had ample time to get here, but the dark caught me near the top of the mountain, & it began to drizzle a little, but I reached the top all right. But as soon as I passed the crest, it was raining pretty hard, and so foggy and dark I could not see my hand before me. I left the horse & went back to the Toll House on top of the mountain & lit my lantern & came back, & found that I was already out of the road. But with the lantern I made along all right till about 1/3 down the mountain the wind blew the lantern out. I tried to re-light it but the matches went out. . . . [A]nd there I was and could not see the horse, & precipices and sharp turns ahead. I got out and led the horse and I had not gone 100 yards before I found we were clear out of the road. I let him go & began to wander around to find the road & when I found the road, I could not find Rock & the Buggy, but in groping around I ran against him & he nearly jumped out of the shares & started to run off but I grabbed the rein & stopped him. I then just felt my way down the mountain, getting out of the road every once & a while & once, I felt absolutely lost, & almost made up my mind to sit in the rain till day. But I finally got here all right; with a very high and absolute respect for your good judgment and advice.

Fall came on, and on September 16, he wrote, "I got very cold this evening driving over from the Hot—but am extremely glad it is not raining as it was this morning when we drove over. . . . Beautiful Thing,—I am having a very comfortable time here, but wish I were at home with you and Bruddie. With all love for you both & hoping to get a letter from my Sweetheart in the morning, I am, Yours, G.D.L."

On September 18, he wrote of his homesickness for her and Buddie, adding, "On account of the terrible storm in the Atlantic, I very much fear Brother [Houty] may be delayed getting home & over here to the Court, but I hope he is safe. . . . It is terribly chilly over here—I got cold yesterday & today driving from the Hot late in the evening. I got your postal this morning & am glad Bruddie enjoyed the elephants & am sorry I was not there to take that rascal to the Circus— but I doubt if he had been willing to have left his Mama that long." Greenlee quite clearly believed that the little boy had forgotten him, being so long away from him.

Over the next week, while waiting for Judge Sam Houston Letcher to return from a European tour, Greenlee showed Bruddy's pictures around Warm Springs, visited, played whist, was wined and dined, and wrote to Katie every day. "We have heard nothing from Bro. Hous, & no one seems to know what will be done about Court." He continued: "Whether we will just sit & wait . . . or whether the governor will be asked to designate another Judge to hold the Court, & I am able to form no idea as to when I can get through & get back to you & Bruddie, where I want to be." One day, he reported visiting *seven* people "who are all enthusiastic over it," to show them Bruddie's portrait: "Miss Davis . . . wanted to see your picture, but I had none with me but promised to bring it next time—she seemed very anxious to see the prettiest thing in the world." And, "We had no Court to-day as Bro. Hous did not turn up, but the Clerk rec'd a telegram that he had landed at Philadelphia & would be here tomorrow."[16] Finally, "Brother reached here this A.M. & the work of the Court proceeded in the big case—no telling hardly when it will be finished." On September 23: "I gladden new people every day with Bruddie's photo—everybody thinks he is just fine. Kiss the splendid fellow for me." By September 25, Greenlee was frustrated enough to write, "Disappointed again & I feel like making up my mind to stop practicing away from home. . . . It looks now that I will not get home earlier than Sunday to dinner or supper." He continued: "I am pretty chilly with my thin gauze on. It's cold here. There are very few people left here now though I expect more than any of the other springs, except the Hot. Lots of rain. With love." The *Lexington Gazette* on October 1, 1903, announced Judge Letcher's safe return from "a tour of the European capitols."

Evidently Greenlee planned a dinner party by himself, perhaps to pay back all his friends who fed him while Katie was absent. The minute he got home, Katie went back to Harrisonburg, and on October 29, he wrote her there, "I transmitted your directions to Aunt Caroline tonight & she will bake the cake layers tomorrow. Fannie had arranged with her cook to cook the chickens & she has picked & cleaned them—so I told her to let her go ahead & I would pay her for it. Pretty much all invited are accepting—which I am very glad of for every reason except that it prevents me writing out more." As usual, he seemed to be thinking, The more the merrier!

On November 20, 1903, their third son arrived safely in Harrisonburg. They named him Seymour, but as he was so active he was quickly nicknamed "Buzzy" or "Buz"—which stuck the rest of his robust ninety-one years.

On December 14, Greenlee was back in Warm Springs, Virginia, at court again, sending love to "Gee Gee and you and the baby."

In February of 1904, three months after Buz's birth, Katie entered the hospital for major surgery, and there was talk of a second operation. It clearly was intended to stop or cure her mastoiditis. Pregnancy had made Katie ill, or at least exacerbated her already significant problems.

No more children were born to them after Buz, and Katie was only twenty-seven. It seems likely that in addition to having her ear operated on, Katie persuaded a doctor to prescribe a cessation of sexual activity as a cure for her nervousness. No birth-control methods other than abstention were foolproof then. The tone of Greenlee's letters changed during this third pregnancy, and rarely afterwards did he express ardor, although his *devotion* remained unswerving. Finally, Katie's letters became more cheerful for a time, as though some great burden had been lifted from her—perhaps the burden of sexual responsibility or worry about becoming pregnant again.

Katie's mother went to Lexington to help care for Gee and Buz, but everyone in both families pitched in to cover Katie's absence. Greenlee continued to travel.

In February 1904, John Craig Miller (VMI '80) met his classmate, Benjamin West Clinedinst, a New York artist, in New York, and Miller wrote to Greenlee, recounting his dream of a mural depicting the New Market charge, as a memorial to the VMI cadets who died there. Greenlee and Maggie Freeland conspired to invite Clinedinst to paint the mural, which was unveiled a decade later in Jackson Memorial Hall at VMI. Letters on the subject began during Katie's hospitalization.

On February 13, 1904, Greenlee wrote to Katie in Memorial Hospital, Richmond:

> I reached home this morning about 10 o'clock. . . . I found all well— ze 'ittle ba looked very chipper, and Gee is all right. . . . The Franklin woman had rheumatism and failed to materialize. I saw Fisher today and he promised that his wife would come to see me Monday. So you see I have obeyed orders. Everybody today asked most especially about you. I do hope you are improving. Dr. White promised today to write to Dr. Johnston fully about your troubles, & I think as soon as you cease to be sick, Dr. Johnston had best see you, & treat you—Dr. White thinks well of it. If he waits till I can come, it may be too late, or you might have to remain longer. . . .
>
> Gee Gee wants to go back with me to Richmond when I go after you. He has been mighty good tonight. . . . Charlie was to dinner today—he was elected Class Vice President last night.

He continued to report Lexington news, writing: "John told me today that Milton had fallen into some hot tar in Baltimore, & could not live"; "Mr. Colvin telephoned this morning to know how you were"; and "tell Dr. Davidson [the Richmond surgeon] to keep me posted." And always he ended with loving words: "We miss you so much, Beautiful Angel— . . . get strong & well so that we will never have to have you leave us again."

Although the baby was still too small to go on his rounds with him, Gee became his father's shadow while Katie was ill: "P.S. I took the violets to the cemetery late yesterday evening. Gee Gee is with me in the P O when I mail this."[17]

On Valentine's Day, 1904, Lilian wrote Katie in the hospital, "I know just the discomfort and nausea you endured. How I want to be with you. Don't get homesick and lonesome, longing for the kidlings. Mamma wrote me yesterday a little note and sent me the collar you lent me, thank you very much, it is a beauty." Lilian was "specialing," presumably privately nursing, in Winchester.

Kate Paul took young Seymour to Lexington while she looked after Katie's children. She wrote to Katie news of her brothers: John and Charlie were both at VMI now, Seymour still too young to go. We get a glimpse of what life at the Letchers' was like in Katie's absence:

> I know you want to hear all about the kid and kidlet so "I take my pen in hand." We got along all right yesterday—Daddy being at home, of course Gee was satisfied. He and Daddy enjoyed their usual Sabbath ceremony of bringing up coal and afterwards they and Seymour amused themselves for an hour or so thawing out the water-pipes. . . .
>
> John came to supper and Charlie dropped in a few minutes later to tell Seymour good-bye. Skimp [Seymour] left on the early train this morning; we haven't begun to miss him yet for Gee went up to the office with Daddy after breakfast. Ida was to go for him at half past ten, but Mr. L. phoned to her not to come as Gee declined to come home yet a while. We got some oranges this morning and Ida is to make jelly. Gee is developing a liking for oatmeal and ate two saucers this morning. . . .
>
> The little ba is just lovely and so good—the dear little creature is doing his dear little best to help along by being as little trouble as possible. He has for the past two nights resumed his custom of sleeping from seven until two o'clock and every day after his bath he takes a nap of three or four hours—between those two long sleeps he calls for his

bot every two hours with great punctuation. I've concluded that ye little baby as a cure for insomnia is almost equal to "murder as a means of grace."

Greenlee sent "a letter written by Gee Gee all by himself. Where I was afraid he would misspell, I showed him what keys to strike. That splendid little rascal has been working here at the office all day—came up with me after breakfast, stayed till dinner. Came back with me after dinner, & stayed till I went back late in the evening. Ida came for him about 4 but he would not go back with her. I had no trouble at all with him, but he insisted on going everywhere with me even into the courthouse, & stood right by me while I was speaking."

Greenlee reported that he would "have the oatmeal matter attended to." Greenlee's simple test of good health has stood the test of time: "Gee Gee seems to have a fine appetite & sleeps splendidly & seems all right." Of baby Seymour, Buz, he wrote, that "he was laughing in a most fascinating way at Daddy this evening— first time I have seen him laugh, & it was fine. I have scarcely heard him cry since I came back & Mamma says he gives her no trouble much at night. I have been trying to get the Fisher woman—she promised to come & see me today but did not. Seymour left on the early train this morning—Ma & all were sorry to see him go." It's interesting that it didn't even occur to Greenlee to take a turn at night duty.

He chatted about VMI, about Brother Charlie, about people who were ill. He worried that he had heard nothing from Katie's doctor, was "overwhelmed with work," and wrote: "Of course, if another operation is necessary. . . . I would lay down everything & come anyway. I have not yet been able to get Mama to write a statement of her case for me to send Dr. Davidson, saying she is too old for treatment & feels it is no use, but I will keep after her." At fifty-seven, Mrs. Paul could still have been suffering from menopause symptoms.

Lizzie Harrison, Katie's sister-in-law, who had lost two children before having Letcher, wrote to Katie from her Charlottesville home:

I felt uneasy too as soon as Green wrote me about your ear, but hoped you would in time as you recovered your strength get better from it. . . . I know how hard it was for you to leave the dear little things but Jen writes me that little Green was perfectly satisfied when they told him you were coming home *well*. I wish I had been near enough to have taken one of them for you indeed I think you might have left Green with me as you passed. I have always been so anxious about my children that I can appreciate and enter fully into your feelings. I think one had much better err on the side of being too anxious than not anxious at all as many mothers are nowadays . . . . Do be careful about taking cold, for the least cold will go right to your ear. . . . Mr. Harrison joins me in much love to you. . . . Letcher sends his love to Aunt Katherine.

Kate Paul had baby Seymour "write" to his Mama:

I've been lying in Grandma's lap for the last half-hour after my bath 'pitting and cooing and Grandma says I look so bootiful and lovely that just as soon as I go to sleep she'll just have to write and tell you how shockin' handsome and how awful good I am. I 'pits and slobbers and crows and I'm getting a double chin. Grandma says brudder Gee is so sprisingly good she's perfectly 'stonished and he seems entirely well now 'cept an occasional little cough thats not croupy. He eats lots of oatmeal and sweet potatoes. That big man you call John [John Paul] comes to see us twice a day. He said you and daddy would be glad to know Milton is still alive and has a chance of recovery. He wasn't burned so badly as they thought. . . . A big black woman [possibly Julia Trader] took care of me last night and I liked her first-rate. Grandma laffed this morning when she came down and found me cooing and 'miling in de black woman's lap. She says she's jealous. We send lots and lots of love to our dear, dear Mudder. Your little bye, Seymour

From Lexington, Jennie Stevens wrote to Katie that she and Gee were having a grand time, had been walking, riding, looking at pictures of train engines. "When I asked him what to tell Mudder—he smiled & say'd 'tell her I love her & that the kid is all right & daddy too, but that Udder Mudder is sick;' he then laughed for the last is a joke—he 'jest frolics'—I really think Brudder is the cutest & smartest little fellow I ever saw. As to Seymour, he is growing so rapidly that you will not know him when you get back. He is a beauty too and so strong & well. Your mother gets along beautifully with the children and is in good spirits." She reported on the dinner party Greenlee was hosting, for his men's club: "We are to have the Fortnightly this Friday,[18] so Fannie & I are deep in the mysteries of chicken salad, deviled-crabs, jelly, cake etc. . . . As you are away the learned gentlemen will not get any salted almonds." To name salted almonds as a specialty of Katie's might be called damning with faint praise.

Jennie Stevens, always beloved for her charm, wrote to report on Gee's sweetness and stoicism. "He had one cry for you, the evening of the day that you left, but when I told him you went away to get well, so you could take him walking & riding this summer, he soon dried up his tears & has never whimpered since. I never knew of a child his age showing such reasoning about anything, as he did about you & Green leaving him. The nights I stayed with him he was just as good as could be. . . . [H]e gave me to understand that he wanted me if he could not have Doddy."

On February 20, 21, and 22, 1904, Greenlee continued to report to Katie on everything: work, news, children, a new baby nurse: "Been in court pretty much all morning. Gee met me to take me to dinner & he looks fine & in fine spirits, & ate a good dinner.[19] . . . Charlie was to dinner, & says he is doing first rate now in Geometry. . . . Dr. Davidson just told me that Dr. White who has the grip [*sic*] sent word that he was anxious to see me, & I will go up to see him this evening or tomorrow. . . . I trust when this reaches you, you will be over the chloroform effect & free from pain. . . . Tell Miss Black or Miss Austin to drop me a postal every day. . . . Martha Fisher stayed one night while I was away & promised to stay 2 nights every week—Jennie was much pleased with her." And he mentioned Kate Paul's increasing deafness: "I told mother about the ear trumpets, but she has not determined what she will do."

Everyone delighted in Gee's good behavior, and that praise was passed along to Katie. On business in Staunton and Mount Crawford, Greenlee wrote that the "new bank was organized yesterday and although I obeyed you & took no stock yet they called me in to fix up some papers for them. I hope their bank will be a success, as the more banks there are the better for the town—and if you had not commanded otherwise I think I would have taken some stock—Don't you think you had best withdraw the embargo?" He reported on all who had pneumonia in what was a mini-epidemic, adding, "Everybody is asking after My Beautiful Angel." There was a P.S. from Gee: "Muzzer I love you & want you to get well and come back soon. I wash my teeth every day. Gee Gee"

Katie continually urged monetary caution, even from her hospital bed. Her mother kept Katie on top of the home front news, writing on February 23, 1904, "We are getting on first rate. It is now 1 o'clock and the ba has been asleep since 9:30 just after his bath. He is just too lovely for anything and I feel sorry every day that you are missing his delightful development. Gee is all right—went to dress parade yesterday and John took him up to his room where he entertained the assembled Subs [young instructors]. He's gone to help Daddy at the office today."

Sister Virginia wrote Katie from a job she was on, "Had a letter from Mamma today. . . . She seems to be getting along famously with the kidlets. Bless their dear little hearts. . . . I don't see babies anywhere as pretty as ours. . . . You wrote me how brave you had been. I think of you all the time and wish so much I could do something for you."

Greenlee, although he wrote faithfully, wrote more matter-of-factly than he had ever done previously: "Dear Katie, We have been glad to get postals or letters each day from Miss Austin & delighted at your satisfactory progress. The Dr. also wrote. I today sent check for $25.25 to the Memorial Hospital for charges to & including $17.00—1st week. . . . Gee Gee was at the office till dinner, & we went to the Drug Store & got him a tooth brush—he dropped his other one in the slop jar. I got the chloride of lime & put it in & around the cut-off today."[20]

Hospital stays then as now were not cheap, and his anxiety about finances indicate how close to the edge they lived: "I sent the check for $3.00 to the Art Collectors Club as directed. . . . Enclosed find check for $5.00—Be as careful as you can Sweet Thing about all expenditures. . . . I remitted to the Hospital this morning $26.20 for the 2nd week."

On March 6, Katie finally wrote to them:

> Dearest Mr. Gov—I don't believe y'all want me to come home at all. You are just having such a good peaceful time with old cross Mudder away and nobody all the time fussing, that you don't want it to end. . . . This has been such a pretty afternoon that the capitol square has been full of children playing and feeding the squirrels. I certainly did wish you and Gee could have been out there with them. . . .
>
> If it wasn't such a long trip I'd like for the dear good old fellow to come down and see the squirrels and the "cars what runs by 'lectricity." How I do want to see him and the precious little ba. I know I'll just sit down and "bawl and bellow" when I do.

She ends, "Oh, I do hope I'll get sure 'nough well now and not be so utterly cross and hateful. Tell Mamma her postals are such a pleasure with their cheering reports of the precious small boys. With oceans of love to each one of you. Katie"

Not only do the doctors' letters indicate that they more often than not don't know what's wrong, they all urge Katie (unwisely, as we know today) to be *inactive*. She returned to Lexington the second week in March, just as Greenlee left for Norfolk, "I reached here about 9 this morning & took a room at this swell hotel. . . . Penick & Hopkins came with me but they went on to Newport News. I have not as yet seen any of the lawyers on the other side, nor my own client, and the hour given in the notice for Depositions is considerably past. I hate to be away from home & hope to be able to get back sometime tomorrow." He closed: "My Beautiful Angel, I hope you are feeling well today, & getting better every minute & the splendid kids are good and well. I hope to be able while here to see the Hubards, Sheltons, & other friends."

On March 23, on another trip, this time to Millboro, he wrote a postal telling her that he "reached here about dark, old Rock & I both all right. I had a fine appetite & enjoyed my supper very much. Will get off early in the morning for Warm Springs. Had a chilly & rainy drive this evening. See that the stable is locked up & the rigs brought up. I told Ida & hope she did it. Love to all. Aff. G.D.L."

She answered him immediately, on March 25, "Dearest Daddy—You will possibly be on your way home before this reaches Warm Springs, but still I thought I'd better write and let you know we are all well except that Gee is a little croupy. The little kid is getting over his frequent wakes at night since his rations have been increased and sleeps to beat the band. Aunt Julia is still here. Long may she wave. With lots of love from all of us and hoping you'll be home tomorrow or Monday. Yours, Katie" There is a new willingness to respond to him, a desire to communicate that had been lacking for some time.

As long as her mother was with her, Katie stayed happily in Lexington, for he wrote her from Bath County on June 27,

> My Darling Katie, I reached here just at dark in a hard rain. I ran into three showers on the way. The first about 9 miles from Lexington which was hard but not very long. The second near the Alum Springs, neither long nor hard. The last for about 15 miles from Millboro here, hard and long. But I was well protected by the buggy top & the good lap cover, & did not get wet. . . . The other side of Millboro on the mountain, I saw a splendid red flower on a long stalk which I got for you, but I put it in the back of my buggy & when I went to take it out at Millboro I found the jolting had broken the stalk, & the flower was gone. It was the only one of the kind I ever saw. I saw some flowers like Sweet Peas [undoubtedly vetch], & I got out & gathered them first, & send them to you from Millboro. There were whole beds of them on the mountain & I wished for you, as they were beautiful. . . .
>
> I hope this rainy weather will cease & I can finish & get home quickly—for I am already homesick. With love for Mother and the boys and all & kisses for you & the kids. I am with the heart's best love, Yours G.D.L.

From Warm Sulphur Springs, he wrote, on June 28, 1904: "I think I will go to bed as soon as I tell you I love you. It rained on me both going & coming from the Hot. Everything around here and at the Hot is looking very beautiful, but I would *rather* be at home with you and those splendid kids."

And she wrote warmly, "Dearest Daddy—The sweet little flowers came this morning, fresh and pretty and a very welcome message from my true love. We all miss you so, and hope you won't be gone long. The little ba and I staid [*sic*] up-stairs with Gee last night, and Gee slept till half past eight and the little big man till half past nine this morning. . . . I hope you didn't get wet or take cold in all that rain yesterday. Take good care of yourself and let the changes do you some good. With lots and lots of love from all of us. Yours, Katie"

Another note from Katie a day or two later claimed, "The little ba scolds us all when things don't suit him and says we didn't treat him this way when Da-da was here." Things between them clearly were improved, either as a result of her oper-ation or perhaps just relief that the youngest child was safely here, and she herself was beyond that particular rough spot.

Greenlee went at the end of June to the National Democratic Convention, the first American Olympics, and the World's Fair in St. Louis celebrating the Louisiana Purchase: en route, he reported: "I saw a magnificent sunset this evening through the mountain gap, as I drove back from the Hot Springs, & told Mr. John W. Stephenson who was with me how you would enjoy to see it, and how I wished for you. . . . I was invited to take tea tonight at Mr. Stephenson's but I declined as I wanted to work, & get away as quickly as possible. Miss Haile says Geo. Wise of Newport News told her that he will marry Miss Stephenson in August. It seems to me Bunch told us this also."

In Louisville, on the way to St. Louis, of course he had a grand time: "I have been here all day or since 11 A.M. Accidentally saw Gus Quarles [James's brother?] on the street, & he & Jim insisted on showing me the town all day, & taking me to lunch and invited me to supper, but I felt that I had taken up too much of their time. I have enjoyed the day & do not regret not making my connection. Will go in the sleeper early tonight. This seems to be a fine city & prospering."

Katie answered quickly, and with humor:

> Dearest Daddy—I'll try to get ahead of the little ba while he is asleep this evening. . . . The little ba had his first chicken bone yesterday and I wish you'd been here to see how he enjoyed it. Gee and I went down street this morning and Gee had an "ice cream sody wader" which he

seemed to enjoy very much. Seymour [her brother] and Gee are at present hard at work painting the swing. Old Rock evidently believes that "when the cat's away" etc. for he is blind and deaf to all the blandishments of the boys and Mr. Childress and hasn't done a lick of work since you left. . . . I hope you are feeling well and enjoying yourself right along. Or did you take a valise full of law papers along? I wouldn't put it a bit past you. . . . With love from all of us, especially Mudder and the kids. Kisses, Katie

In St. Louis, Greenlee painted the town with his friend James Quarles and reported that he had "seen a number of friends in the Va. Delegation & others. Dr. & Mrs. Estill are here & Capt. Moore. Shook hands with [W. J.] Bryan a few minutes ago. . . . The convention will meet in about an hour. I saw Gaines & he gave me another ticket, & if I can I will give one to McPheters a nephew of Frank Glasgow, who is now living here. . . . Gaines also gave me a ticket to the Fair that he had. I am extremely glad I came. Wish you were here with me Beautiful Angel, if you could stand it, but there is a terrible jam & it's very hot. I hope you & the kids & mama & all are well. With love & kisses."

Modernity turned out to have its drawbacks, as the first two automobile encounters proved. On July 10, 1904, Greenlee wrote Katie, "Linas & Daniel Flood, James & several others & myself started to see the city in an automobile & were run into by a street car & had a narrow escape. We got another auto & started again & the auto got away from the chauffeur & we hit a horse and had another narrow call & we gave it up." In later years, Greenlee had cars. When I lived with them, he had bought a Model T Ford at Katie's urging, but he did not have a good relationship with it, referring to it as "that infernal machine." Nonetheless, Greenlee fell in love with road travel, later heading up the Lee Highway Association that built Route 11, from Pennsylvania to New Orleans in the twenties; he saw to it that the highway went smack through the middle of Lexington.

A day later, he wrote: "I was up all last night at the Convention—got to sleep at seven o'clock this morning, & tonight the Convention just adjourned about 1:30 A.M. This has been probably the most exciting & interesting Convention the Party ever held."

Katie responded, "Two postals came from you this morning and we're surely thankful none of you were badly hurt in the automobile wreck. I'm afraid that accident insurance policy is making you too reckless. Daddy dear—Don't be too much bent on getting your money's worth." And the next day, she wrote: "The

beautiful kids are both well and there seems to be no danger of either of them forgetting Daddy. See everything so you can tell us about it when you get back. With
more love than you'll know what to do with."

He reported from the Virginia Agriculture Exhibit:

> James & myself moved from the St. Nicholas to Mrs. Williams, where
> we spent a most comfortable night last night. Senator Daniel expected
> to come out to Mrs. Williams' today also. . . . We have just spent all the
> morning in the Philippine Exhibit, which was interesting but the
> weather is so hot and all distances are so great that I do not anticipate
> "doing" the whole Fair, but although it is larger than the Chicago Fair,
> yet it is generally the same, and I hardly have the inclination to walk
> myself to death to see all. I think I will be at home Saturday midday—
> I can satisfy myself by then—and get back to you and the kids, which
> beats the Fair to death with odds. . . . Beautiful Angel, I love you & see
> nothing out here as pretty as you or that I want to see as much—*for I
> love you.*

On July 12 he wrote, "I am feeling right sore today from our automobile accidents although at the time I did not realize that I had been much jolted. Jim is also
right sore. The Convention was a great show and I feel repaid for coming—it was
great and exciting in the extreme, and I feel that I have gotten a broader insight
into national politics than I ever before had—I may have read things incorrectly,
but they have awakened much thought and interest in me." Next day, he admitted,
"I have just about walked myself out, and I wish I was at home with all I love, my
Beautiful Angel. James will leave tomorrow at eleven A.M., & I feel very much
tempted to leave at 7:32 A.M. . . . . This may enable me to stop about 1/2 a day
somewhere along the road, & I may stop at Lexington, Ky., as I stopped at
Louisville coming." In the same *sentence* that he wished himself home, he still said
he would stop somewhere along the way!

After the Democratic convention, the Letchers were at home together for a
week, then Katie returned to Memorial Hospital in Richmond for a consultation
on July 16. Greenlee wrote: "After receiving a letter from Dr. Davidson this A.M.
& reading yours to mother at dinner, that an operation had been deemed necessary, I held myself in readiness to come to Richmond this evening, if Dr. D.
should telephone by long distance. . . . The letter did not say that the operation
would be serious, but I would want to be near you, Beautiful Angel, even if your
conscious suffering was the recovery from the chloroform alone." He obviously en-

joyed fatherhood: "Gee Gee has been with Daddy at the office working all day, & was asleep tonight almost before I covered him up, & I have stolen up to my office for a moment to write this letter—he seems all right, good appetite, sleeps well etc. and the little ba is fine & fat."

Whatever the problem, there was no operation, because she was home four days later. He was at Warm Sulphur Springs, from which he wrote on July 20:

> The changing of the shafts and the storm delayed me yesterday getting from Lexington but I reached the Alum before dark & got supper. Saw Miss Bettie Clarke, who asked after you, & when I told her how anxious I had been for you to come with me expressed much regret that you did not do so. I left there about 9 o'clock by moonlight & reached Millboro about 15 minutes to eleven, & not being able to find anyone to take old Rock, I went on to the Millboro Springs which I reached after 11, & got a room, & got Rock taken care of. I got an early start this morning, & reached here safely, but we have had no court today as Judge Anderson attended Mrs. Parrish's funeral. So I have been working on the papers of my cases for the argument tomorrow. . . . You had best write to Bunch, John & Idge telling them to come to see us.

His level of physical energy was as high as Katie's was low, possibly because Katie was communicating now in a way that she had not done except in their courting months. Katie undoubtedly subscribed to the Victorian ideal of woman as being without libido, but having a huge maternal instinct, thus she was free to enjoy her children. Women of that era were generally assumed to be possessed of higher moral impulses than men, and superior self-control, so she could afford to be amused at Greenlee's careless behavior (as in the two auto accidents). Men were assumed more competent but also coarser and more primitive.

Katie, in addition to having no calling but motherhood, further rejected any feminine accomplishments; she neither played a musical instrument, nor did she knit, sew, tat, paint, or do needlework. She took little interest in decorating her home, or in gardening. At a time when the idea of entitlement had not yet developed, Katie had no hobbies to distract or amuse her, yet it appears that throughout much of her life she felt entitled to her grudges and snits, perhaps because of her physical ailments. So it comes as no surprise that her happiest times were when her children were small, distracting her from herself. Thus, on July 21, 1904, she wrote, "I'll write a few lines to let you know we are all well, though when my epistle will reach you I don't know. The little ba is still worrying along with his teeth, but as it is decidedly cooler today he has cheered up considerably. . . . Gee and I went into the post office this morning to write a postal to you but there was no ink in sight so had to give it up. . . . With loads of love and kisses from self and family."

And Greenlee reported on his congenial adventures: "I argued my case today & unless something unforeseen delays me, I will go to Craigsville to the farm tomorrow & get home Saturday evening, and I love you & want to get back to you Beautiful Angel. I just called on Mrs. W. M. McAllister, Mrs. Anderson, & Mrs. Jno. Stephenson. Mr. & Mrs. Anderson asked after you & mother, also Mr. Bunting, now the Episcopal preacher at Petersburg inquired about you. . . . I have had a very pleasant trip, & I hope I shall win my case but I expect the Judge will take the papers home with him as they are so voluminous, & decide it later."

Katie answered at once, "I didn't write yesterday because I was taking care of 'yo kids' while Ida washed in the morning and afterward I had the usual neuralgia. . . . Your postal came last night. Do pray rest some if your case is delayed. You'll be breaking down again if you don't be careful. The small boys are good and sweet and well—Gee busy with a 'spickit' he found in the drawer 'where Daddy keeps his nails and sings,' and the little ba crawling and scrabbling around. We all miss you shocking bad."

Both Katie and Greenlee were more relaxed. From Fincastle in August, he wrote: "We finished the evidence in our case this evening & I guess will finish by dinner tomorrow. I will go to Salem tomorrow night & Clifton Forge Friday & get home Friday night or Saturday by dinner. Got your letter today & was glad to hear from home & to know all were well, but sorry about your neuralgia every evening. Try to get word to Hugh that I will not get home when expected & tell him to get word to Miss Dixon not to come in till I let her know. Aff. G.D.L."

The pleasant interlude was short, for in October, Katie returned to Richmond for more medical consultations. Greenlee imported Kate, Lilian, and Virginia to look after the children, while he continued to work. He wrote:

> My Darling Katie, I hope you reached Richmond all right. . . . This is a beautiful day & Gee & myself have been with Old Rock, fixing the fence and afterwards down at the creek & this put in pretty much the whole morning. He slept well last night. . . . Lilian says Buz slept late also and I had him on my lap a good deal this morning & he was just as good as he could be. Ida is just bringing him from his bath, & I will take him on my lap & have him write a few lines to you [here follows

Greenlee with Buz and Gee on a picnic at Buffalo Creek, 1904

some scribble]. . . . Mother & Lilian went to church this morning &
have not yet gotten back—it is communion day and I guess this is delaying them. Gee & I talked about you a heap this morning . . . & he
remembered you in his prayers last night. . . .

Jennie said yesterday Gee heard Buz crying and said Buz was crying
because he missed his mudder. . . . We all will go on a "picky-nick" this
evening I guess to "Buffalo,"[21] & I wish my Angel was going to be along
with us.

Next day, he reported that Gee had taken to eating across the street at Fan's table
and that the family seemed "tickled to death."

In a few days, he wrote that "we are all delighted that you reached your destina-
tion safely & that the Doctor thinks he may be able to avoid another operation."
He went on: "I have been in the police court all evening—Phoebe's [a current
maid] sister was tried and convicted of stealing $16.00 from another darky. I think

the conviction was wrong. The Mayor fined her $5.00 & committed her to jail for 30 days. I went her bail till tomorrow, when it may be appealed. I am hard at work getting ready for court next week and writing my paper for the Fortnightly Friday night, and so far, I am very much dissatisfied as to results. I hope to come after you. I can probably combine some other business. . . . Did you send a present to Miss Austin—if not get some plate or something in Richmond & send it to her at Lewisburg, W. Va. . . . With all the love of my heart & life."

And she wrote, her attitude about meeting folks and socializing so different from her husband's:

> Dearest Daddy—I'm so pleased and proud to hear the kids are keeping well and being good. I surely do want to see them dear little souls. . . . Mrs. Werth very kindly sent me a bid to the tenth anniversary reception of the Woman's Club and told Mrs. Abbot to be sure I came with her so there was no escape and poor old Katie had to invest two good dollars in some gloves and drag her weary bones to the party which was very pretty, but not specially amusing to a stranger and particularly one who had not slept at all last night as the result of Dr. Davidson's cautery, and had spent the morning being tortured by him and the dentist. Dr. Davidson's treatment has not been very painful until yesterday and to-day and I do hope there won't be any more nights like last night. I'll have a holiday tomorrow as he goes tonight to Miss Austin's wedding. I got a very beautious little sugar bowl and cream pitcher and sent them to her Monday. I think it would be well to get several pictures here—water colors—to have framed for wedding presents as we need them. They are certainly more for the money than anything else. . . . I'm too tired to write any more now. . . . With lots and lots of love to you and the precious big boy and little boy and to Nuzzer Mamma and Idge.

Greenlee reported on the home front:

> My Darling Katie, Gee worked all today morning and evening at the office, & he was exuberant when Hugh brought him your box & postal, his eyes danced when he saw the red slippers. The paints were given Buzzy but he did not seem to enter into the situation with any degree of enthusiasm. Both seem as well as can be, and Gee is eating almost normally again. He has been the best fellow you ever saw all day here at the office, going with me up to the court house, 4 or 5 times.

. . . I got over my first draft of my paper for the Fortnightly . . . but as I have to read it Friday, I expect the first draft will be the last. . . . I am glad you are putting in the time by having your teeth fixed. Idge was telling me that your landlady was kin to Miss Florence Duval.[22] . . . I enclose your Irvin's acct $16.04—as I am so close pressed for money now, I am sorry you did not defer getting the matting which I see costs $14.00. Angel, be careful for the present about every amt. you can save.

Even in her absence, he sought her help with paperwork: "I sent you yesterday an acct. of Ayres which Ida says is wrong—I noticed there were items for stuff gotten last spring. Ida says we were then getting our meals. I hope you are getting plenty of sleep & not catching any cold & will come back recuperated and spruced up. With all love."

Katie ran the household from afar with the decisiveness of a leader: "Your letter and the enclosed bills came this morning. I know nothing whatever about the Ayres bill. I suppose it is all right but why he should let it run on for six months at a time I don't know. The wagons usually come around early in the morning before I am dressed, and this cook gets the things, and this summer, since the mix-up in Shaner's account I have just had everything charged. Request Mr. Ayers to send them in more promptly hereafter." In another letter she instructed:

Will you please send me $10 of *my* moneys. Besides Miss Austin's present and a vase for future reference I had to get several things for myself which I didn't want to buy before leaving because I was so uncertain about whether I would have to go to the hospital, so now I haven't enough money to get home and I want some right away so I can make for the train the minute Dr. Davidson is through with me. Did you want me to get something here for Mr. Laird's girl? It would be as cheap and would save express. . . . Col. Maury takes his meals here, and often asks about you all. There is also a Mrs. Wise who seems very fond of Sister [Lizzie Harrison] and a great admirer of Jennie's. . . . I want to see all you fellows, *so baid,* . . . Kiss Gee and the little ba black and blue for me. With whole lots of love to them and to Mamma and Idge and my old sandy-haired beau that I know hasn't shaved since I left. *Yours, Katie.*

She added a postscript marked *Private:* "Don't think me wilfully careless when you are hard up, dear old Doddy—I had the matting put down because the bare floors are too cold in winter for Buzzy and Gee to play on and I thought the money could not be better spent than that way. Believe I love you and don't think I don't care enough for you to want to save all I can. On the street yesterday I wanted a bon-bon box but stayed my hand from getting one because it was a luxury and I have to think of essentials." In the years that followed, Greenlee and Katie had some difficulty in keeping up with the bills as they bought land and built a house.

In one letter from Richmond she wrote, "Be sure and ask Unc Houty about the lot Sunday so if he is going to let us have it the foundation can be put in and trees planted this fall." He replied, "I put Gee to sleep before coming to my office tonight. He slept like a log last night, & did not wake this morning until almost 8 & he is getting his red cheeks back again. I am so sorry to hear of your suffering under the Doctor's treatment but hope it will not last long. I wrote Houty about the lot but have not heard. With love, G.D.L."

Katie replied, on October 7, 1904: "I paid two visits to Dr. Davidson and spent three hours on my teeth today, so I've had a profitable if not a pleasant day. . . . I want to get home so bad to see Idgy before she goes. I'm glad Gee was pleased with the little shoon [shoes]—and *so* glad to hear he pahaves so good. I hope but doubt that Buz does likewise."

Buz began to be perceived by his mother as "difficult." Certainly he was highly energetic, stubborn, and quick to anger. My grandmother always said that my father hated school, hated to bathe and dress up for birthday parties, preferring, as she put it, "to go back to see a dead snake" that someone had killed.

From home, Greenlee reported, "Your room at home was papered yesterday & this morning with pink paper mother selected. Its quite pretty & I will send Hugh for Ben to come & put the matting down & stoves up." Certainly Greenlee was seeking to cheer her up. It is noteworthy that they now had separate rooms.

From Greenlee's office, Gee dictated a letter: "Dear Mudder:—I am up here in Doddy's office, workin hard. . . . [A]nd I am just dictating here at our office to Miss Dixon, our stenographer, and I send you a check that the Bank says is alright for twelve dollars and a half, I got Doddy to put in two dollars and a half more than you said you wanted, and Doddy said he would do it, and I have just gone up with Mr. Wills to the Bank, and had the check certified. . . . Doddy says he would not kiss me and Buzzy black and blue, cause we men folks don't kiss each other like the women folks do. We want to see you soon so bad. I send you a kiss right here. Gee."

Katie must have improved with the treatments; she acknowledged the check "Gee" sent and announced playfully, "What you fellows think? Mudder's been to church twice today! To St. Paul's this morning and Second Presbyterian tonight."

Another time she wrote, "You fellows and Nuzzer Mamma and Idge are awfully good to go to all the trouble of having my room papered and cleaned up now when I may not have to go to the hospital and might as well do it my fat lubberly self."

About her treatments she said, "Dr. Davidson nearly kills me sometimes with his cautery, but is unfailingly sweet and kind and places all his books at my disposal." As for social events, she wrote: "Am bidden to the Woman's Club again tomorrow, but going to Dr. D_ will prevent my accepting. I wish now I had gotten one or two glad rags but I so fully expected to go to the hospital when I came." She asks: "Did you and Gee go down to the creek this morning? I wish I'd been there too. And how is little Brudder—dear little sweet pink Brudder?"

On the tenth of October, 1904, Lilian wrote Katie this description of an evening in her absence:

Dear Katherine—The kids have both been angelic. We have gone on various drives and picnics. Yesterday afternoon went to Possum Hollow. Shortly after our return Phoebe and Ida both being away, and we scrimmaging around to find lights and get something for the baby and ourselves to eat, of course Harry Gassman called. Mamma said "Thunderation" and went on down stairs. In a few minutes she whacked the gong in grim desperation. We filed down—and took seats. The baby began to grumble and Gee wanted a dozen crackers buttered at once. Then Mamma, Mr. L. and I began to race around the table hunting for saucers, cups, oil, preserves, vinegar and potato chips. When one sat down it was the signal for another to jump up and don't stop! In hunting for the vinegar Mr. Letcher found several jars in the pantry. He couldn't tell which was vinegar so he brought them in, successively to be identified, handing them to me with a hearty "Smell this, Sister Lilian." After smelling and rejecting he would run back and bring out another. Finally my olfactory nerves, elated with the heavy responsibility imposed, told me that "this is vinegar." In the meantime the baby was dropping spoons and Harry cheerfully rambling about "Lizzie, George, Aunt Bess" etc. etc. He reminisced for quite a while. Afterwards, Mr. Wise and Dr. Latané came. Dr. L was here until nearly twelve and Idgy was so sleepy—But Buz slept on. Several times I have had to stop the conversation to go "make cook." They are such sweet little kids and do get so dirty.

Gee and Lilian on Letcher Avenue, 1904

Katie inquired of Greenlee from Richmond: "Has Unc Hooty never intimated further what he intended doing about the lot? I want to know so bad."

Greenlee answered, "Have not heard from Brother. . . . I saw Sarah Myers a few days ago & she said Carrie would be back here the middle of this month & would come in & cook for us for about six weeks until she could come." He continued seeking her help in billing and bill paying. On October 14 he wrote that he was so busy that "I fear I will be unable to take Gee to the circus today."

By November 20, Katie was home, for she wrote, on the baby's first birthday, while Greenlee was at Warm Springs, "We've just come back from church—

Gee and Buz on Maud, 1905

Muzzer Mamma and Gee and I, and Gee just pahaved elegant. I tell you that Mudder was proud. . . . Little Buzzy is taking a nap before dinner when he will have for his desert [*sic*] a slice of the big birthday cake Ida baked for him." Dinner was always served at the Letchers' around one o'clock; and supper, about sundown, was a sorry affair of leftovers scrounged from the icebox or sideboard, as the cooks had families of their own to prepare nightly meals for.

As winter settled in, Greenlee must have ceased his wanderings. The next letter came from Clifton Forge two months later, on January 10, 1905: "My Dearest Angel:—I spent last night at the farm, this morning spent the time in trimming apple trees. Mrs. Curtis was delighted with the cups & saucers, & Mark Hanna's[23] mug. After early dinner, I drove to Goshen, & the Hotel Allegheny Co. meeting was adjourned to this place tonight. I hope to get off in the morning to Hanover Court House and Richmond, & hope to get back home Thursday evening or Friday morning. . . . I wish I was at home with you fellows—no place else do I have such a good time." Three more months went by without a letter, probably indicating that the family were all home together.

Toward the end of April 1905, Greenlee traveled to Buckhannon, West Virginia, whence he wrote, "I leave in a few minutes for Weston. As I came from the train last night, I saw a crowd going into the Opera House & went around afterwards & found it was a school entertainment, & I enjoyed it a good deal."

On April 27, Katie replied:

> Dearest Doddy—I had thought I'd write a long letter to you tonight, but Busy Buz sat up till ten o'clock so I won't have much time. No news or excitement except the arrival of Dr. Trasker and the bride tomorrow. Won't Jennie's establishment be "the whole show" for all the town for days to come? Gee and Buz are well and good, except for Buz's overwhelming freshness. Gee's present excitement is a toy watch I got for him yesterday. He wears it and winds it from morning till night. . . . Col. Nichols stopped to pass the time of day yesterday and while we were talking Tyke [the dog] came up and scared the ba by opening his mouth too wide. Col. N. picked up a rock and scared him (Tyke) away whereupon little Buz began to scold and quarrel at the greatest rate, the only intelligible words in the torrent of his denunciation being "fro rock Tyke"—"bad man hit Tyke rock!" You never saw such indignation."[24] Katie wrote cheerfully, "Gee is always chattering about Doddy and sometimes Seymour takes a hand and jabbers about Da Da."

From babyhood, Buz began to develop a reputation as recalcitrant and naughty, while Gee proceeded to make top grades, charm the whole town, play the ukulele for the old ladies, and dance obligingly with the girls. My father hated his name, Seymour, and disliked formal events. He announced after the first day that he wasn't going back to school, played hookey from Sunday school, and detested having to wash and dress up for birthday parties. He always understood that his older brother was the good child, and he was the bad child.

From Camden-on-Gauley, West Virginia, on April 28, 1905, Greenlee reported rain, cold, twenty-miles-on-horseback days as he rode through vast timber tracts, apparently assessing them for a relative of Hugh Wills, the mentally retarded man who acted as a clerk for him. Despite long waits, constant rain, and exhausting days, Greenlee was able to write: "Everything has been very pleasant so far & I hope it will so continue. . . . Young Mr. Brannon at Weston today wanted me to stay & dine with him. He said while at W&L U. in 1893 he was invited once or twice to our house—so you see people don't *always* forget as you think. . . . I intended to tell [your] Mother before I left but she did not get back, that we would expect her and the children to make their headquarters with us again this summer—and I hope hereafter."

The next day he continued: "Yesterday evening Mr. Smith & I rode out 8 miles & spent the night at Mr. F. P. Cole's, got up bright & early this morning, & got him to go over the Wills land with us & we walked 12 miles over the mountains, & then Smith & I rode back here, & you can imagine how tired & 'stove up' I am, but I will write to tell you how I love you."

On April 30, he wrote: "I will leave here early tomorrow morning, go to a place mid way to Weston stage, about 12 miles, & catch a train on the Coke & Coal Rwy to Charleston, take supper there & get to Huntington that night, so that I may reach Welsh Monday, to be present at U.S. Ct. Tuesday, & I hope to start home Tuesday evening, but will stop by Roanoke to see Mrs. Parsons Wednesday, & I hope to reach home Thursday. I am tired enough to drop. With love to all."

Katie sounds happy at this period, when one of her family was almost always in Lexington with her. "Dear Mr. Gov—Your peregrinations have been such that I doubt if you have gotten any of my letters, but I do hope this one at least will reach you to tell you that the cadets have beaten Blacksburg good and proper.[25] . . . The kids are well and sweet and sunburned and send their love to Doddy. Gee's one idea is still the gasometer, and Buz can talk and think of nothing but 'on doors' [out-doors?] from waking time till bed time."

Greenlee went on having adventures: "Yesterday we could not get across the Gauley River on account of high water, but expect it to have gone down enough to-day to get across on horseback. I am now going right across the top of a mountain, & the view is grand. I wish you could revel in it. Some day I hope you can come out here with me. Hope you & mother & the kids are well & hope to be back with you all soon." Greenlee never stopped hoping she would one day go with him on his travels.

His remarkable energy continued, and on May 1, 1905, he wrote: "Left Camden this A.M. on B&O, rode 12 miles across the country, ½ on a hoss & the other half on a mule to Gassaway and reached here for supper. Will go on to Huntington at

2:46 in the morning, & hope to reach Welsh to dinner tomorrow, & get home Wednesday evening or Thursday. John Moore has just left—I wrote half of this while he was giving a man a prescription. I borrowed $10.00 from him." He met other friends along the way, always had someone to spend the night with, and found every encounter pleasant.[26] He also enjoyed incredible coincidences regarding people throughout his life, such as the one at this time: "I was called last night in Charleston up at 2 A.M. & got in a cab to go to the depot across the river, & the driver said he had to call for another passenger. After the gentleman got in on the way to the station, I found out that he was Col. Jno. Dickinson, former-in-law of Miss Nettie Preston; & I found him extremely pleasant and we have been together since & will be on same train for some hours. . . . I have been telling him about my two fine byes." This reminds us of what a small world the USA must have been a century ago, when if a man worked at it as Gov did, he could find a connection nearly anywhere.

Greenlee traveled a lot the spring of 1905, writing from Charleston:

I reached here a few minutes ago, & my first thought is to write & tell you I love you—the same which I do. I reached the Bath Alum on the other side of the mountain a little before dark & I thought I had best have Rock fed, so I stopped for supper, & then came on afterwards. The moon has not risen but it is a clear night & I did not light the lantern. . . . I could not telephone you last night as I had to hurry through a bit of supper & drive on to Craigsville, which I reached about 10 o'clock. I left Rock at Goshen, taking another horse. . . . In one of the back fields on the farm last night or this morning someone killed one of our calves and butchered it & carried away the hind quarters. I cut a piece of paper the size of a heel print I found, but could find no other clues, & I feel we will never catch the thief or thieves. I am purely tired tonight.

From Rockbridge Alum Springs he wrote: "I have just taken a delightful bath in the pool & saw a Mr. Pierce there from Bangor, Maine, who said he met me here several years ago. Mrs. Eubank was very gracious & pleasant. . . . Dr. Williams whom you met at Memorial Hospital came for a few days to-day."

In the summer of 1905, Katie suffered her first attack of macular degeneration. More common in women than men, the disease causes progressive blurring of central objects in the vision field. Even today there is no prevention and no cure, although it is known that early menopause, surgical menopause, and a high number of births all increase the risk. Katie continued to return to Harrisonburg for long periods, and on almost any provocation. When she was in Lexington, one of her sisters or her mother was invariably with her. Greenlee invited them repeatedly to come live with them; it was clear that their presence might keep Katie at home more—and keep her happier.

Kate Paul wrote to Greenlee at Warm Springs from Lexington on July 20, 1905, "Katie better than when you left though still quite weak. Her eyes have been troubling her, & I write for her. I hope in a few days she will be all right. The two little men are all right, Buz as strenuous as ever. Gee had a visit yesterday from his old nurse, Julia. The weather is torrid. All send love." Later the same day, Mrs. Paul followed up with another letter: "Katie's eye trouble seems rather serious: she complains of not being able to see at all with the left eye and also feels a good deal of pain in it. Dr. White to-day examined it and advised her to see a specialist at once. . . . She telephoned to Lilian to make arrangements and will go to-morrow. I dislike very much to see her start by herself in this hot weather, but she doesn't feel willing to wait. She does not know, of course, how long she may have to stay."[27]

The next day Greenlee wrote to Katie in great concern: "I hope you have experienced relief from your neuralgia—I expect your getting your feet wet Sunday evening wading with Buz is responsible for the acute attack Monday evening coupled with the exhausting trip to Glasgow. Take good care of yourself & get all right; but don't dissipate in Doctor's bills unless there will some benefit come of it. I want any and everything that will be for your benefit done but I trust you will be careful in every expense, as I am close pressed now and will be more so in building the house." How maddening that must have been to Katie: his diagnosis based on nothing but a notion; his caution about doctors, for how could she know what was a waste of money in that regard?

Katie apparently had the attack of eye pain while he was gone, and she left for Washington, where Lilian was working as a nurse, without notifying Greenlee, for from Millboro, Virginia, on June 22, 1905, he sent a frantic and hasty telegram to Miss Lilian Paul at Garfield Hospital: "[W]here is Katie love to her wire immediately Goshen, Va. on way to Washington GDL."

In 1905, they finally began their house atop the hill, at 302 Letcher Avenue, fifty feet or so back from the street.[28] Over the brick-lined cellar and foundation was laid a wooden superstructure, clapboard on the outside. It had twelve-foot ceilings, five chimneys, ten fireplaces, three two-story porches, pocket doors between parlor and dining room, two pantries, and a big kitchen with a wood stove. It had wide walnut front stairs and a narrow closed back staircase. The windows were big to let

Baby Seymour on the site of the new house, 1905

in light, their sills no more than eighteen inches from the floors. The second floor had six bedrooms and a small bathroom, and the first floor had, in addition to the formal half, a big hall, my grandfather's book-lined home office, and a back parlor, off of which was a water closet and stairs leading to the cellar (three rooms of coal, wood, and a furnace). The four-roomed attic was dormered and roomy. On the back porch, camouflaged by lattice, was a water closet for the servants. In the hall was a bust of Governor Letcher that stood on the massive desk that had been his while he inhabited the governor's mansion in Richmond. The parlor was formal and dark, with wine-red velvet drapes and tasseled velvet couches, and later, an up-right piano my grandfather took in lieu of payment for a case. The dining room had two highboys, two glass china cabinets, and a table that would seat sixteen if all the leaves were in place. In the bay alcove was a daybed on which my grandfather rested every day after "dinner" before he went back downtown to his office. Outside the dining room door, in the back hall, the telephone sat upright and black, with its round dial and its separate horn-shaped earpiece, on a little table at the bottom of the stairs, the thin phone book under it as long as they were alive. The house, and everything in it, cost around six thousand dollars.

Greenlee sent house plans for Katie's approval: "I enclose the letter from Mr. Sabbard about the mantels, doors & hearths—take it or send it to Mr. McDaniel & tell him to preserve it as I have no copy, & see if any of the material can be advantageously worked in" and an account of his current trip: "I got here last night after ten o'clock—was caught by a thunder storm a couple of miles beyond the top of the mountain, but my lantern & old Rock's discretion got me through all right." He reports on "elegant fare," "nice and polite people," and "the best water I ever drank" from a local spring—and of course, of meeting new and old friends: "I met here today Mr. Wm. Wheatley, a famous V.M.I. alumnus. . . . He was married in the spring & says he will bring his wife to next commencement. . . . He is fine company. Montague, Mann, & Williams spoke here today—I believe it is a mistake about Montague's being a great man—his speech today was not much, but I may be prejudiced." He added a note to Gee, "Daddy has been thinking about you a heap on this trip and misses you, but as mudder is sick I expect it is best for you to be at home & take care of her & Buz. I don't expect they could do without you. You must take good care of Mudder & everything while Doddy is away. . . . Even if Mudder had not been sick I expect it was best for you not to have been with me, as two nights I have been out till after 10 o'clock & one night in a thunder storm; & if I had not had my lantern I would have been in a bad way."

A month later, Katie was still in Washington with Lilian, staying at the Riggs Hotel, whence she requested of Greenlee twenty dollars.

Kate Paul went to stay with the children, and Katie wrote to her on July 23, "Have just seen Dr. Shute to whom Dr. Smith sent me, and he says he will not keep me longer than Monday. Says he can't say yet what the chances are of restoring the sight of the eye. . . . Am waiting now for Idge. Am writing with eyes shut so please excuse discrepancies. Kiss the precious kids for me. With lots of love, Katie." On July 23, 1905, she telegrammed Greenlee, "I've gone over to Balto to see Dr. Smith, as Dr. Shute prescribed." Dr. Shute must not have had any idea what was wrong with Katie and suggested she return to her old friend Dr. Smith, whose patient she had been in the past, and who might have been better able to diagnose and treat her. I feel he must have been a psychiatrist.

The eye got well on its own, for there is no more mention of blindness in one eye accompanied by pain. Is there an element of overdramatization in all this? Certainly it caused great uproar among those who loved Katie. As it amounted in the end to nothing, it could have been the psychosomatic symptoms of an unhappy woman. There are no more letters for seven months, and this is the year the house was built.

Charlie dropped out of VMI in January of 1906, halfway through his training as a civil engineer, because, Kate Paul reported, "he was not keeping up academically" and went to work in southwest Virginia.

On January 20, 1906, Greenlee wrote from Richmond where he was attending a Kappa Alpha banquet; he described it as a "recherche" affair and enclosed "the Menu Card & a carnation I got there, to show you that I am thinking of you— *where my heart is.*"

There were no more letters that spring, but when the time came to move into the new house at 302 Letcher Avenue, Katie was back in Memorial Hospital. It is touching how Lilian, Virginia, and their mother all took care of Katie.

Moving day was May 7, 1906. Lilian, apparently believing that Katie was too sick even to read a letter herself, or too blind, wrote:

> With apologies to whoever reads—Buz's dresses came, no gloves so far. . . . My dearest Kit-Kat, Time of your life Aunt Mary, time of your life! Sarah [a maid] and I have waded in and are making the fur fly. The desk and shelves in here, "hobbledehoy" and the pictures have all been "gone over." I know that in the long years to come you will be searching for articles required. Ella has jealously taken charge of china and preserves and won't let me touch them. All furniture here. We went to the cadets Memorial Day this afternoon. It was a beautiful and impressive sight. Afterwards, the "rats" at supper time ran the gauntlet.[29] I told Seymour I hoped *he* had not hit them, and with his usual view of the hazing situation, he replied "Oh they'd feel bad if we didn't." Last night Buz refused to say his prayers saying in the most despondent, no-hope-for-me tone "No I'se a bad boy" nor could I induce him to approach the mourner's bench. "Don't you want to be a good boy?" "No. I'se a bad boy" in a "ain't fit to get fitten" tone. Gee has had on his sandals, Buz has been barefooty today. . . . Mrs. Pendleton came over to ask about you. The electric fixtures have come and Mr. Bare seems mournfully glad to get through."

Katie's mother wrote to her on May 18: "I trust that troublesome ear can be relieved some. . . . I don't know whether you are able to see to read letters or not. . . . Virginia and I are both well. . . . She seems to have a pretty good time socially and

*Buz and Gee c. 1906, with Tyke, who later bit them and caused them
to need rabies shots*

goes about a great deal. They are now planning an automobile pic-nic party for
next week which I am to chaperone. The Young People's Whist Club meets here
next Wednesday night. Quite a number of touring parties, from Washington, Baltimore and other points have passed through here recently, among others Miss
Cannon, 'Uncle Joe's' daughter, with a number of Congressional friends."

Kate Paul reported on May 20: "Had a letter from John a few days ago. He is
very busy now. Wants to return by way of Lexington to V.M.I. finals. Charlie . . .
is well and seems pleased with his work, some of which takes him into very wild,
mountainous regions. I am so glad your house is finished and is so nice and cheerful and convenient. I've had so much experience in moving that I'd like to go up
and move all your goods and chattels in for you. I know Gee and Buz will take a
deep interest in the proceedings. I do want to see them and you *so awfully*. When
John comes home I expect to spend just lots of time with you."

That summer, when Gee was six, Ruth Floyd Anderson[30] wrote Katie a note,
letting us know that Kate Paul was under the weather and that Katie had gone to
see about her:

Dear Katharine: What a surprise it was to find you all gone this morning! I do hope you had a good trip and that Seymour had the time of his life. I know Greenlee—the much-traveled—enjoyed it. I'm sending this especially to tell you that I am beginning to know my own mind and plans for the winter and that, if you still think it best, I shall be only too glad to teach *Greenlee* every day—reading, writing (imagine my *teaching* writing!) and some numberwork. But we can discourse further on the matter when you get back. Please be sure that you think this arrangement will be best for Gee too and that you still want him to be with me at least till after Christmas. . . . I hope you found your mother much better and I know Lilian was rejoiced to see "you and your fambly." Please give my love to her and come back strong yourself.

On September 7, loyal Lilian, who had taken care of Gee and Buz, wrote from Harrisonburg where she was now taking care of "Uzzer Muzzer," to Katie, who was then back in Lexington, "Mamma is getting along well. Her eyes are better and not nearly so painful, though she is still in bed in a darkened room. Mamma says you must be *very* careful, if you are not she will send me right back. Now, will you be good?"[31]

On August 8, while Buz, age four, and Gee, age seven, were in Harrisonburg with their mother, Greenlee jotted: "Dear Buzz:—How are my troops doing during the Colonel's absence—I do not see anything here for which I would swap my troops, now I tell you, and I have bragged on my troops a heap. I wrote to Sergeant Gee yesterday, & I guess he got my letter. I got Gen. Yi's postal today & was glad Mudder & you were getting along nicely." The card was signed, "Colonel Daddy." They had begun the family game of soldiering.

At the end of September, Katie had both boys in Harrisonburg, for Greenlee wrote them there:

To the Troops: Your communication was duly received this evening & I read every word that it contained, and exhibited it to others. The Colonel called on the Gastman's, the new preacher, and the Burks's, and everywhere there is much talk, excitement and interest shown in my splendid body of troops and General Mudder—where they were, what they were doing, & when they would be back, and General Aunt Jennie, who was along, kept every audience on tip-toe of absorbed expectation in rehearing the wonderful deeds and detailing the wonderful speeches of my troops. . . . The troops must be fine & obedient soldiers and feel that the 40 centuries that looked down on Napoleons soldiers in Egypt would be a kind of a 39¢ inspiration in comparison with the 4 Generals that look on you in Haa-sonburg. Yours, Col. Doddy.

Nicknames and fantasies give us insights. Greenlee, alone among the governor's sons, bore the nickname "Gov," so he must have been like his father. After World War I, he was universally known by his hard-won title of Captain, or Cap'n (which is how "Captain" sounds in the soft Virginia dialect). He called himself "Old Man" early to Katie, hoping, one assumes, for maturity, or perhaps only reveling in domesticity. Katie, when happy, sometimes called him "Old Beau." Katie of course was mostly called "Beautiful Angel"—"Old Lady" when he was joking. *Angel* is a hard standard to live up to; it is not surprising that she sometimes dragged her wings in the mud. Greenlee glorified the military life, for he was a child of the great lost southern cause. The family developed the conceit of a military post: the children were "troops" or "sergeants," while Greenlee was "Colonel Daddy"—but *Katie* was "General Mudder." Lilian and Virginia, the sometimes surrogate mothers, fell into place as Gen Yi and General Bun; Greenlee was happy to yield to their "generalship." At some point in this correspondence, shortly after he left VMI, Katie's brother Charlie becomes Charles, as though he had felt, in not finishing his education, a need to "upgrade" his name.

The day after the letter about his troops, Greenlee wrote Katie:

> I intended writing last night but after I went to Barracks to see Seymour & then to Col. Nichols and afterwards went over the papers in a case with Hunter Pendleton till 12 o'clock I had exhausted the whole of yesterday, & thus had only today left to write to my sweetheart. . . . There is much talk here about the hazing & conditions generally at the V.M.I. but I hope things will work out all right. Geo. Woodford died yesterday morning from apoplexy very suddenly—I went to see Carrie yesterday to express regret. . . . Mary Price came yesterday to see me & said she would like to work for us—she agreed to do all the washing & the other work that Ella did for $10.00 per month. She is a strong woman, & doubtless can do it. She has her own house but said she would remain at our house at night whenever we wanted. She is separated from her husband & has no children. Jennie went for me to see Mrs. Nichols about her. Mrs. Nichols has been trying to get her to live with her but only offered her $9.00 and she promised Mrs. N. to go with her but backed out. I believe she is the individual we require if

Ella does not return, said she had heard you were so nice, she wanted to come with you. She is a nice looking woman.

Carrie and George Woodford had worked for the Letchers; Mary is mentioned here for the first time.

Greenlee good-humoredly tried to keep up with Katie's commands: "I watered your three flowers in pots on front porch yesterday, & will plant the Hysteria, or Wisteria or Vysteria or whatever it is today at the woodhouse."[32]

From "Camp Paul," sister Virginia, now also drawn into the "soldier game," wrote on September 26, 1906, in part:

Col. Doddy; It is my great pleasure to report the troops in fine health and spirits, as is commanding general Mudder. Camp discipline has been rigorously enforced. The troops have been scouting around the town and some sharp skirmishing done with bands of marauding chickens. There is much conversation in ranks concerning the absent Col. who is expected to report at Camp Paul on Saturday afternoon. . . . There has been some active work on the part of the hospital corps, rendering aid to members of the Dolls Battery who were attacked from ambush by the outlaw pup, and badly mutilated. Sergeant Buz at one time yesterday during mess, manifested symptoms of nostalgia but is in his usual health today. I enclose in this important communications in cipher, from Sergts Gee and Buz. With much love from all the camp to Col. Daddy and Lieut. Seymour, I have the honor to remain Sir,

Your ob't serv't, Bun. Brightly
(By order of Mudder, Comm'dg Gen'l)

Katie says not to ship the things for Gee unless she sends word and see if Ella will return under the old regime, she does not wish to offer any other. If Ella will not do so, engage the new cook unless new cook will want to be interviewed by Katie.

In September, while Katie remained in Harrisonburg, her children affectionately cared for, and even her secretarial needs met, Greenlee urged her once more to work on her family about coming to live with them. For example: "Tell Lilian how glad we would be to have her with us just all she can, get her own consent to stay, even to making our home her home if she would." His generosity extended to every family member: "Seymour took some supper with us at Fannie's to-night. . . . Bid my Troops Good Cheer & tell them I just miss them all the time. Ella I understand is nursing for Mrs. Weinberg—I will try to find out tomorrow whether she is gone permanently, which I expect is the case. Jennie says the only person she can think of who knows anything of Mary Price is Mrs. Goodsell & she will see her, but she thinks it doubtful if she can give any information as Mary Price has never for years worked out." In several letters he relates local gossip: "Geo. Woodford was buried this evening—the largest colored funeral perhaps ever held here—I will see Carrie tomorrow about meals. . . . I wrote to Dr. De-Schweinitz today" [Katie's Philadelphia eye specialist].

And Katie, at home with her family, instead of writing to Greenlee herself, got Virginia to be her scribe, thus adding to the dramatic impact and emphasizing her helplessness. She was quite well enough to give orders; Virginia wrote: "I am writing for Katie. She says investigate Mary as to disposition etc. before engaging. Also says tell Carrie to send supper Monday evening, says I hope we can keep her longer tho'. She emphasizes 'no bad temper in the way of cooks.' All are well; the troops are flourishing. Love from all. Hastily, Va."

On September 29, Greenlee wrote, "My dear Katie:—I was with the Heirs & Widow of Geo. Woodford until beyond midnight & did not write last night. I got the laundry bundle from Miss Truslow yesterday evening & paid her 60 cents in full. Carrie told me last night that she would continue the Restaurant business."

Katie's return home, delayed by a day, was reported to Greenlee by Lilian: "Dear Mr. Letcher—Your letter just received too late for today's train. We received a telegram telling of Uncle Pete's[33] sudden death in Richmond this morning. Katherine and the children will stay here until after the funeral at Ottobine when either Mamma or I will try to go home with her."

And Greenlee as ever was prompt with sympathy:

> Dear Katie:—Lilian's postal just received and I am sorry to hear of Mr. Peter Paul's sudden death—I wrote I could come down to the funeral but I fear it would be impracticable. . . . [T]ell Gee Gertrude Pendleton saw the door open Sunday & came up to see him thinking he had come. . . . I have faithfully watered your flowers, & have mowed the grass. . . . I got Gee's letter directed by himself & an alphabet & several sketches & you say to him how much I appreciated them. I surely miss you fellows, & yearn for the home-coming. I will get my hair cut some time. Why don't that tow-headed rascal Buz write to me too—what duties are occupying the troops now?

She stayed on in Harrisonburg, and he wrote: "I hope mother improves—you must make her come up with you & stay a long time & rest good, & get perfectly well—the change will do her good. And make Idge come too—and Bunch too—."

Greenlee kept his equanimity, but it cannot have been easy: imagine this man, deserted by his wife and children, being directed from afar to attend to domestic tasks, work generally done by the lady of the house. He wrote: "Ella has never responded to the message I left with her mother to come & see me, & I feel a little loss of respect in searching after her—I expect I may as well employ Mary Price although Mrs. Pickens was not very enthusiastic over her. But the servant situation is very hopeless now, I am told. I expect we had best try this woman—what do you think? Of course, if the General orders me to scout for Ella some more, I will swallow pride & do it."

About Dr. DeSchweinitz's letter, he remarked: "I told him Dr. White said you had nephritis,[34] but that I felt he was mistaken but if he thought it predicted anything I would bring you from Harrisonburg." And he ended, "The Colonel orders the troops to be good & obedient soldiers, worthy of their *great Generals.*"

Katie wrote on the servant issue: "'No matter how hard de times may be,' Don't go to see Ella again. I've decided I won't have George & that's what she's after. . . . See Dick Washington's wife about her sister—the girl who lived with them. Ropers. I want her badly. With love from the boys & Gen. Mudder."

Greenlee replied, obedient but absent-minded, "Your letter rec'd & I will try & see Dick Washington tomorrow about his daughter. I am in the throes of a settlement with Black—last night till after eleven & tonight again. You did not tell me when you were coming—I am getting very homesick for you & the troops."

On October 8, 1906, Katie had Lilian write to ask Greenlee for money, two suits for Gee, a white feather boa, a pair of shoes, and "Please look in Katherine's room on a chair or almost anywhere and find a big hat box containing red roses please leave roses in box, put Gee's clothes in box and look on shelf and on top of wardrobe and press and around generally until your eye falls upon a white felt hat, untrimmed, please put this in aforesaid box."

Katie wrote him: "Dear Daddy, Your letter has just come. I suppose you'd better engage Mary though I feel in my bones she is just another Jennie Jefferson." Greenlee replied, on October 10, "Your letter & Lilian's rec'd this evening & I will endeavor to perform to obey all orders tomorrow morning. . . . I will count on you all & mother & Lilian coming up without waiting for me. I can not stand being without you fellows much longer. Find enclosed check for $10.00 as requested."

And later the same day he wrote:

> My Darling Katie:—I got the hat, roses, suits etc. off this morning.
> . . . I also engaged Mary Price to do all the washing, housework etc. for
> $10.00 per month & I told her you would be here this week or early

Buz and Lilian in Harrisonburg, 1907

next. . . . Tonight is very cold & I hope you fellers will not take cold—
be mighty careful with yourself and the children. Tell the troops that
Aunt Fan & Jennie often talk about how they miss them, & want to see
them back. . . . I know you will be relieved to know that Black will leave
the Farm. He says he has a position with the Hot Springs taking care of
the Dairy which will pay him $1200 a year. . . . Sulley Paxton & Mrs.
Williams were married today—She was recently divorced & there is
much talk here about it all. G.D.L.

On October 12, Katie wrote pettishly: "Can't you come for us? And what is the
status of the cook question? Also send me $5 or $6. . . . General Mudder."

Finally she and the boys came home. The absence of letters for eight months following indicates that the Letchers were home together with the children. As the years go on, there are generally fewer letters. The late Henry Foresman, who knew Greenlee well in the early days of his own practice, told me that in later years business came to Greenlee instead of his having to go out of town to find business. He added that Greenlee was not unique in not worrying about bills, but that the assumption at the time in Lexington was that all men were gentlemen and would get around to paying their debts sooner or later. Foresman referred to that time as "the Golden Age of law, before it got mean, grasping, and dishonest."

In 1907 Greenlee made a banquet speech to the Editorial Writers' Association of Virginia entitled "What Citizens and the Newspapers Owe Each Other." He noted that the Press is "the people's university." "In the fight for ideas," he said, "it is a fortress." "You," he told the audience, "are the owners of great power." He quoted Napoleon: "Four hostile newspapers are worse than 1000 bayonets." He compared the news to a giant, claiming it should be used "with greatness, and bigness." "A newspaper is a welcome guest in every house," he noted, because it brought news, entrances into and exits from the world. News writers, he said, should be carriers, not makers, of news.

In July of 1907 while he was making that speech, Katie was in Harrisonburg. Seymour had just graduated from VMI. Greenlee urged her to go with him to the bar association meeting, and of course she replied: "It would be impossible for me to go to Bar Ass'n, as you know but you ought to go and in case you have decided to do so be sure and telegraph me so I can stay here." Two days later she instructed him: "Send a note to Hetty as soon as you get this and see if she is coming back— if she is not—bespeak Jennie's woman while she is gone or Rosa Miller's little Hannah as a third choice. Then if you will have the grass cut we will try to get home Monday evening."

In October 1907, the *Rockbridge County News* announced that the family dog, Tyke, had contracted rabies and bitten one of the Letcher boys, and perhaps both, and that they had gone with their mother to Richmond for the dreaded rabies shot series, twenty-one injections given in the abdomen. My father's story was that the dog bit Gee but that he had to get the dreadful shots too. If the sufferers were "good," a chocolate ice-cream soda for each boy would follow. These events led to a famous saying of Buz's, repeated snufflingly each day as they got on the streetcar to go to the doctor's: "I'll go but I won't like it." This saying, passed on to me by Nainai, later referred to anything anyone didn't want to do but had to.

From Ford's Hotel in Richmond, Katie, with both boys, wrote:

Soldier boys Buz and Gee on Letcher Avenue, c. 1907

Dearest Doddy—Gee-Gee very brave. . . . Please send us at once some ammunition, as the kids' shoes and other things have brought us to our last dollar & though I have tried to be and have been very careful to buy nothing we could do without. . . . Hurry Mary up on the washing & bring or send us the boys' clean suits & a gown and change of underwear for me also my white waists. You will find some of my things in the bottom drawer of my chest of drawers I think—what I want is a pair of brown gloves—dark red. . . . The hotel is full but with a most quiet crowd—I do hope you can come to spend Sunday. With love from us all to our Dear Colonel.

She had numerous other requests, and the reader must imagine the scene of poor Greenlee forced to invade the ladies' lingerie section of Adair's, the local department store, with Katie's list: "Has any letter come from Cloak Co.? In the bottom drawer of my bureau you will find some diaper cloth napkins. Will you send them with the other things and if you don't find a woven corset cover with the other things please get a 25 cent one from Adair's and send it. I'm freezing but dare not spend this last dollar till another comes. . . . Getting along all right. Bring or send Gee's gum coat with other things."

When Katie was absent, Greenlee took solace often in his new hobby of golf. Lexington had a small golf course in the early years of the century, and Greenlee played often. He became a champion, winning tournaments and collecting trophies in his determination to excel.

On October 16, 1907, she reported: "Troops doing well. Buz getting as brave as Gee about the 'needles.' Don't forget the cook." A few days later, "Troops well and General still alive. Buz has acquired some "schluits" [suits] and our funds are again running low, so when you send money for R.R. tickets please enclose some extra" and on October 20:"Troops getting along finely. *Don't forget to see the Long's cook at once.*" Finally she wrote: "The troops are well and fairly good. They are both quite heroic now about the 'needle.' A postal from Sister invites us to stop on the way home. Please write at once & tell her I am too tired.[35] If the other cook is not to be had, engage Ellen Douglas to come Wednesday for a week or two. Have Hetty come Tuesday & clean up the house—or Nannie Jackson. With love from us all."

On October 21, she wrote: "Troops well & doing well. Buz reveling in new suits which he exhibits to the nurse with great pride." And finally she asked, "Have you a promised domestic? If not do not expect us. Do not send any check for watch as it is behaving wildly."

In 1908, their friend Colonel Nichols was named VMI superintendent. In February Greenlee's friend, Maggie Freeland, the generous boardinghouse owner, had an illness, went up north for an operation, and it was Greenlee who met her train in Buena Vista and arranged for nursing care, until she died.[36] On March 23 of that year, William Jennings Bryan came to dinner at the Letchers' and insulted Katie's sherried grapefruit. In May, John D. Letcher ceased his global meanderings to marry Loulie Taylor in Norfolk, and Greenlee attended the wedding. Greenlee attended the summer Democratic Convention, this time in Denver. Free mail delivery in Lexington was begun that year.

Letters for 1908 began when Katie took the boys to Harrisonburg for the

Greenlee golfing on the Lexington links with Estes Vaughan and Ned Graham, date unknown

summer. There, her spirits were high, and on June 2, she wrote: "Troops discharged excellent discipline & conspicuous gallantry enroute. They desire for you to purchase more chick food at once as rations for their beloved little chickens. . . . [T]ell Ella to give the ferns in pots at the end of front porch some water please. . . . Hope you are getting along all right and eating onions & sleeping late to your hearts content. *No onions after Wednesday.* We expect you Saturday. How does your speech come on? They have so much music, singing etc. I think you will not need to make it over 20 mins. With love from all. K."

And Greenlee replied: "My Darling Katie:—Your postal rec'd & I was glad to hear my brave soldiers have demeaned themselves in approved style. I have missed you fellows, now I tell you. Ella watered your ferns this evening while I was at supper as you requested. I will eschew the onions, not *chew them.* On Adair's bill were 3 buys, $2.25, $3.00 & $4.00—is that all right?" He went on to add: "The bodies of the 2 students who were drowned Saturday have been recovered—one after services in the chapel was sent to his home at Raleigh, N.C. & services for the other will take place in the morning. . . . [W]ill try & make my speech in 20 minutes as you suggest."

Katie noted: "The troops are well, and doing well except for an excess of energy. . . . [T]ell Ella to get three or four gallons of cherries and preserve them. Am afraid they will all be gone before I get back. . . . *No more onions* remember."

Greenlee had a high time in Denver, and Katie and he wrote back and forth: The troops are well and as good as it is in small boy nature to be, and the rest of us including Rock [the horse] are well. . . . We all miss you dreadfully."

On July 9, 1908, he wrote: "Reached here [Denver] about 8:30 & went to a meeting of the Delegation—afterwards four of us at about 10:30 went to look for our sleeper, which at this writing about 11:15 we have failed to locate although we have tramped the freight yards in the dark & mud & are now in the night freight office waiting the return of the yard master. We may have to sit up but hope not. . . . Have Ella run the surry under the shed. Hoping to get back in time to take my soldiers swimming Sunday evening. With love to all. Yours G.D.L."

From Harrisonburg, Katie wrote on August 20, 1908: "We arrived safely but in pouring rain which has kept troops indoors & made me long for the playroom. I enclose keys to the chicken house."

Typhoid fever swept through Virginia late that summer, especially in the Valley, according to newspapers. On August 24, Greenlee wrote to his mother-in-law:

> I reached home from Irish Creek yesterday, and Katie told me that you
> had written her about the sickness of your cook. I hope she has not got

fever, and that she is better. Is there fever prevalent now about H-burg? If she has the fever, I would suggest that you at once have the most complete fumigation made of your house etc. and all clothes. As you doubtless have heard in the newspapers . . . in Richmond the theory is that a great deal of the fever there has been traceable directly to a single servant who worked in these different families, and carried the germs, and the papers say that a similar case was reported from New York I believe it was, where the cases could be traced back to one servant.[37]

Greenlee continued on his old theme: "Katie and myself want you all just to close your house up and come up, and write Charley to meet you here, and spend his vacation here all together. Can't you do this? With love to all." Greenlee's utopian fantasy of everyone all happily jostled together in their house, as it had been with his family in his formative years, is as touching as it is naive.

He wrote of forgetting appointments to be measured for a new suit *and* to have a haircut on the same day, of all the invitations to dinner he received, and added: "Fannie asked me today to come down & take my meals but I told her we were afraid to let go Ella for a single day."

A remark of Greenlee's may help explain Charlie Paul's suddenly dropping out of VMI: "I see in the paper tonight that Maj. Hawkins, the Engineer for the V.M.I. that Charlie was bragging of in his letter, suddenly died." Lilian, not Katie, wrote to invite him to Harrisonburg: "[W]e will expect you and hope you can come and stay over Sunday at least. . . . Gen. Yi."

Katie wrote only: "The boys and I will be up tomorrow evening, as we have persuaded Mamma to go on her trip Saturday before the boys come. Be sure and notify Ella. With lots of love. K."

Mostly she sent postcards assuring him of everyone's well-being. On one she wrote: "Dr. Firebaugh took me out this morning for a ride in the joy buggy.[38] We've got to have one, Doddy."

On September 21, she complained of "having a depressingly quiet Sunday as Charles and Seymour took the troops with them to Ottobine." She went on: "About Hannah Leftwich, I spoke to the successor of Ella about coming back when I returned. If she should not show up then we might try the said Hannah. But I think we had better not fly to evils that we know not of as long as the present incumbent is pleasant and good to the children, when we know nothing whatever about Hannah except that she can or will not do the washing."

Katie was good at delegating work to others, and any excuse would do to stay in Harrisonburg. "If you are going to Covington tomorrow I will not come till you are safely back. . . . If you can I wish you would let the cook know that I will not be home before Thursday or Friday—her name is Lee Strother and she lives in the same house as George's mother right behind Sheridan's.[39] Also ascertain if she is coming back."

Katie continued to direct Greenlee to take care of domestic matters, asking him to "telephone to Fannie & ask her to water the flowers in pots on the front porch and out by the trellis on the side next to the kitchen porch. Did Burke [gardener and handyman] white-wash said trellis—and, if not, why not?"

She even taunted him a bit: "Sorry you didn't like my riding a few hundred yards out this road with Tommy Erickson. You wouldn't be willing for me to go up to Rawley with Mr. Housey Ott would you? It is to laugh at you Daddy, you dear old goose. Lovingly, K."

Thus ended the letters for 1908, signifying that they were surely reunited in Lexington. On January 20, 1909, Greenlee was honored for organizing the VMI Alumni Association, and wrote a thank-you letter to General Nichols, the new superintendent, which reads in part: "My dear friend, . . . It is a gratification to look back and see several of the creations of my thought and initiative made permanent factors . . . among others, the annual alumni reunion with an alumni day during commencement, and a review before the alumni."[40]

In April, Katie's brother John wrote her from Charlottesville, where he was studying law, asking Katie to intervene with their mother in introducing his girlfriend to the family.[41] His letter tells us how John valued Katie's judgment and feared their mother's fierce maternal instinct.

As usual, in 1909 Katie went to Harrisonburg for the summer, and it appears that Greenlee stayed home all that year. The boys, six and nine, attended the Covenanter Camp near Lexington, for a couple of weeks in the summer, and Buz wrote to Katie: "Dear Mother, I have come back from the camp. I had a fine time at camp. I hope you are all right. I found a rabbit nest today. It had 4 little ones. Yours truely, Buzz."

Katie apparently dispatched Virginia to Lexington to take care of Gee while she took Buz to Harrisonburg. In a spiteful mood, she wrote to Greenlee, on July 31, 1909, "Dear Doddy—I reckon you think I'm a gay deceiver—if so, you know how it feels to be the deceivee for once, you that are all time going away and leaving your family and your lady love. I was coming today, but Mamma and all of them (Seymour and John) seem to want me to stay, and Buz is calming down so that I think the change is good for him. He has been a perfect angel. . . . With love to old Gee and you and Gin. K."

And a month later, she was still in Harrisonburg, writing: "The kid is so good and the callers so scarce that I'm going to stay a day or so longer. *Expect* to come tomorrow evening so stop at the train on your way to the 'winks' [links]. All the folks were greatly disappointed at your not coming Saturday. Would have sent this by morning's mail but didn't decide in time. With lots of love. Tell Jennie to just go ahead with the washing. K."

Katie must have gone home, and fallen ill again, for on September 27, Kate Paul wrote her daughter: "I don't know whether you will be able to read a letter yet, but I'll write a short one anyhow. I've been thinking about you all a great deal. I hope you are beginning to improve and that the urchins are all right. . . . I want to come back to your hospitable home as early in Oct. as I can but can't say exactly when. Hope you can hold on to your cornbread and potato now." The reference suggests a stomach upset. That fall, brother Seymour went to Panama to work and was followed by Lilian, and later Virginia.[42]

The Letchers got a new colt that summer and named it Starbright. On October 8, 1909, there was a United Daughters of the Confederacy convention in Lexington at which Greenlee spoke. In Harrisonburg, Mrs. Paul prepared to move to a smaller house. Katie and Greenlee received from her a table packed, according to Kate, "with her legs sticking up in the air and her body enveloped in a bed-tick. According to the rate at which freight travels on the B&O she may reach you by New Year. I could find only two slats—the others I suppose the Wilchers used for kindling. She bears the marks of long and hard usage but if fixed up will last a long time." Kate Paul warned Katie to keep the kids in, for there was diphtheria in the county and

> several deaths among the colored people. A number of persons have taken their children from school and the Board of Health has taken charge of the matter . . . . I want you and your tribe to come down about the 20th or thereabouts, and spend the holidays with us. Of course this includes Greenlee too, for as much time as he can spare us. Charlie expects to be home about that time. He doesn't say how long he can stay. John writes that he won't be home till about Xmas. I had a long and very sweet letter from Frances [John's affianced girlfriend] the other day. I'd send it, but haven't finished deciphering it. . . . Hope your Fortnightly[43] will be a success, intellectual and gastronomic.

Another gap in the letters of several months suggests that Katie was home, and Greenlee did not travel. There are big gaps in the mail for the next few years, as the following letters attest. In April 1910 Katie went to Harrisonburg, since that spring all the lights in Lexington were out for "several weeks" from the burning of the electric light transformer. At Easter, April 27, 1910, she wrote to Greenlee from Harrisonburg:

> Dear Doddy, You would never know dem darlings, they is so good. They behaved like young eyed cherubim all the way down on the train. Gen. Yi looks very well but is busy getting ready to go back next week and says she will not have time to come home with us. She and I are going to dinner with the Deviers today. . . . Tell Janie [a current servant] the kids enjoyed the lunch very much. Are you eating onions right along? It has been very cold here. Sleet Monday night. . . . Charlie went away yesterday. He looks much better than when he was at home last time though he is right thin. With lots of love from all of us. K.

Lilian came home from a nursing job for an Easter visit. Katie remained in Harrisonburg, explaining that she was staying "because the kids are so good." Greenlee wrote back, urging her to bring Lilian home with her. On Tuesday after Easter she wrote: "The kids are not so bad yet and Gen. Yi insists upon my staying until she goes—so I suppose we will linger on." Although she spoke of going home, on May 2 she was still away or back in Harrisonburg again, for she wrote: "Dear Doddy—The kidlets continue so peaceable I will continue to stay. . . . [W]e expect to be home tomorrow evening so tell Quartermaster Janie to have supper ready for us. . . . We were all much entertained by Starbright's desire for a midnight supper and the tact and resourcefulness she displayed in getting it."[44]

Halley's comet passed over Virginia in May, 1910, and my father always remembered that it looked like a "horse tail" in the sky. The Harrisonburg paper of May 10, 1910, reported that "the naked eye is all the telescope even a prohibitionist needs to see the tailed monster without being accused of things." On May 29, Katie wrote, still in Harrisonburg, "Buz still much intrigued by the comet, and wants to know when it will come back. Would have come home today, but Aunt Fannie [Paul, not Letcher] will be in town tomorrow & I waited to see her. If you can't come down tomorrow we may come home—or we may wait till next week—so you'd better come. If you do will you look in the press in my room & bring a pair of new low shoes you'll see there without any strings in them."

That summer, a letter from Lilian in Panama to Katie mentioned a beau she had acquired named Jack Flynn, remarking drolly of him: "[He] . . . is well and not breaking too much furniture."

Katie continued her directives to Greenlee from afar: "If the Peters people send the rest of the plants, have Burke plant the Japonica in the places where the hedge on the Blair side is thin, the Barberry up the Hoge side, and the Evergreen Thorn in the beds in front of the front porch. The other plants could be set out in the beds along the trellis for the present."

In July 1910 from Harrisonburg, apparently planning to return to Lexington, she then changed her mind: "I've been harrowed by the thought that maybe you didn't get my message in time, and left your golf to go to the train. If you did I know you're on a mad. . . . I intended coming this evening but it is so fearfully hot that I'll wait till in the morning—so don't 'buy a tiger,' dear mother will be home soon. Tell Gin everybody wants to know when she's coming home." Apparently sister Virginia was visiting in Lexington while Katie visited in Harrisonburg. Undoubtedly Katie projected her own "mads" onto her easygoing husband who rarely let anything bother him except Katie's unkindnesses. Greenlee's letters to Katie are missing from this period, possibly left in Harrisonburg. On July 26, she averred: "I think we'll stay a day or so longer as the kids seem well & satisfied. Let me know as soon as possible when you will be home so we can be there too. Am now setting out for to have their pictures taken."

Katie's feistiness appears to be a subconscious intent to make Greenlee suffer as she felt she had. Knowing Greenlee, her jibes probably went over his head. On July 27: "Two letters from you this morning and we were glad to get them but awfully sorry you hadn't gotten ours in time to have spent Sunday at the Alum. Since you are going back there today we will wait till tomorrow or Wednesday morning to come home—*and you be there Wednesday evening* or we'll have a mad on you. The kids are revelling in a straw-stack and seem very much satisfied. With lots of love."

In the one letter from him from that period that survived, Greenlee assured Katie from the Alum of his "yearning" for them and wrote, on his return to Lexington, "I came from the Alum today with four of the Post Masters. Starbright became foundered in some way & I could not drive her home—so had to leave her at the Alum. I enjoyed the Post Master's Convention very much—met a number of pleasant good fellows. We had a most enjoyable Smoker last night & the Punch was much complimented. The Alum is filling up—from 125 to 140 now there, & they are on the whole as nice a crowd as I ever saw there. We interspersed the Smoker with speeches, dances, songs, violin solos etc. etc. Everybody, especially the ladies seemed to have the time of their lives."

He went to meet her train but "was disappointed. Rec'd. your postal tonight. . . . Hope you fellers all reached Nuzzer Mudder's safely & that the troops all are

Buz and Gee in Harrisonburg, summer 1910

demeaning themselves well. I missed you fellers surely—& that is no mistake— for my night latch key would not open the door & I have just tramped to Freed- man's Hill at Francine's direction & then back to Deaver's Alley to get the kitchen key from Ella. I hope I will get in now & not have to sleep in the yard or wood- house. Tell Gee that Huger & myself beat Hopkins & McCrum 1 up on the last hole after them being ahead almost all the time."

She replied: "Dear Doddy—We were glad to get your letter and the story of your adventures getting into the house. The kids are well and doing well except that they have both stepped on bees and gotten stung, Gee having a badly swollen and very painful foot. . . . When you pack your grip look in the two middle draw- ers of the bureau in the upper hall & bring the kids some underbodies, nighties and drawers which you will find there. Now don't say you can't find them!"

In September 1910, Katie's friend, Frank Smith, obviously following a consultation, wrote one of his gentle and reassuring letters:

My dear Mrs. Letcher, The specimen sent me yesterday was entirely satisfactory and your kidneys being sound, your general condition always has a chance of further improvement in every way and therefore in the neuralgic and nervous condition. Well, what are you going to do about it? Can your life be made satisfactory, if you don't have pain too often—most certainly, because after all pain is a dreadful thing. But as your experience has taught you and these around you, you have borne an immense amount of suffering bravely & fortunately have come out better than might have been expected. Now about the future. I feel sure that your life will not be as limited as it is at present for all time. Gradually you will find other pleasures and interests. And yet I think I am wrong in saying that your life is limited even now. At any rate it is far broader than that of many of my patients & acquaintances. If you can take charge of the household to the satisfaction of your husband and at the same time oversee & bring up two children I think you may consider that every day you have done your share of work and that every day has been worth while. As I told you in my office do not try to nurture a New England conscience in a Virginian body & in a Virginian climate. You will do no better for it & it will keep you dissatisfied. You speak of your nervousness and I do not underrate it or the discomforts (discomfort is a mild word but let it go at that) that it entails. I suppose you may be surprised to know that I encounter an equal degree of nervousness in patients every day. Of course you may say that this fact is no comfort to you—that the fact that other people are in a similar condition does not make your condition any better—& truly it does not, but this knowledge may prevent you from feeling that you are quite alone & apart in your struggles whereas people are fighting the same battle all around you. Again I am not flattering you when I say that you have shown a great deal more grit than many of my patients and that I can feel that there is something to work on because you have courage (as you have shown) and it is only in your blue moments that everything looks almost hopeless. I believe you will find that these "downs" will come gradually less often and I should strongly advise you to let the hyper scrupulous part of your conscience rest & be assured

that you are doing your part to the best of your ability & with satisfaction to those immediately around you. I told you about the rest (or relaxing) in the middle of the day, about the drives, & about looking for sources of amusement. Probably your friend the clergyman's wife[45] can invent something in this line because I do not think you are getting quite your share of amusement. I have missed a good many points & if you will write me any questions I will gladly answer them. With kind regards to Mr. Letcher & best wishes.
Yours very sincerely, Frank R. Smith.

Another gap of several months ensued. In February of 1911, Gee and some friends started a newspaper, "The Juvenile Times," soon changed to "The College Hill Herald."[46] In March 1911, Greenlee won a golf cup on the fifty-fourth hole. Also in March of 1911 the *Rockbridge County News* reported that "Greenlee Letcher fought for a bill to 'compel the rich to pay their full share of revenue.'" Katie's brother, John Paul, retired as state senator to become judge of the U.S Court for the western district of Virginia, appointed by President Hoover.

In May of 1911 Katie returned to Harrisonburg and left Greenlee with the job of having the house repaired and painted, as it was then six years old. In a series of postcards, she told him: "We arrived safely but late after a most tiresome trip. Tell Mr. Bare to make the house a shade lighter if any change is possible with only one coat, and as soon as he is ready to begin send a special delivery letter to Burke telling him to come and take down the roses"; "Don't let painters glue up windows"; and "Did you get Burke to fix the roses—if not do so at once on peril of your life."

Greenlee snapped to attention: "Before you wrote me, the painters had gotten the rose vines down—I pray Heaven they did it all right, I do, I do. They had painted a part before I could tell them about your desire to make the color lighter." In other letters, he adjured her: "Communicate to the Troops the Colonel's desire that they be good soldiers, & deport themselves well" and wrote "I miss you fellows, I tell you. . . . Love to all, with all my heart's love, yours forever, G.D.L. PS Tell Nuzzermudder & Charlie to come back with you."[47]

Of course Katie took the boys, eleven and eight that summer, to Harrisonburg, writing on July 21, 1911, "Dear Doddy—We got here safely and the kids are doing very well. Gee reads most of the time and Buz has gathered up a choice collection of white and 'cudden' [slang for colored] boys. . . . Went down to see Mrs. Deviers this morning and found her much improved. We will be home Friday, bringing

John Gray Paul, Gee, Aunt Susie Paul, Maggie Showell, Letcher Showell, and unknown cadet, 1911

Katie with Buz and Gee, c. 1911

Muzzer Mamma with us." On July 24, she wrote: "We will be home tomorrow evening but don't leave your golf to come to the train. You can tell Uncle George or Mr. Miller to look out for us. The troops are well and fairly good discipline maintained. K."

August of 1911 brought an interesting letter from Katie's only close nonfamily friend, Nancy Bell. It dwells on Lilian's romance with a Mr. Flynn, in Panama. Nancy began by apologizing for writing on a note pad but added that she didn't mind writing many pages, for "you always eat twice as much when the biscuits are small." For eighteen pages, she begged Katie to visit them in Louisville, citing circus, concerts, shopping as lures for her, Buz, and Gee.[48] But something happened to the romance, for Lilian returned in November of 1911 still unmarried.

In November 24, 1911, Kate Paul wrote to Gee on occasion of his being named to the Honor Roll,

> My dear Gee, A little over ten years ago I and your grand-father were in Jacksonville, Florida. Mr. Dick Leggett of Rockingham, who was then living in Jacksonville, came to the hotel to see us and brought a copy of the Rockingham Register. The first thing I saw in it was the honor roll of the Harrisonburg public school and I felt very proud and very much pleased to see the names of Charles Paul and Seymour Paul at the head of the list. That's how I felt the other day when I saw "Greenlee Letcher" in the honor roll of the Lexington school, for you are younger now than Seymour and Charles were then. I know Daddy and Mudder and Uncle Hooty and Aunt Fannie and Aunt Jennie and Uncle Steve were all pleased. That was a fine way to celebrate your birthday week. I hope you and Buz and Hunt [Hunter Pendleton] and all your boy friends are well and suppose you are enjoying the football games. Lilian, John and I send love to you all. Nuzzer Mamma.
> PS We have two dogs now—Gabe and a black-and-white fellow he's brought home to live with us.

No other letters survive from 1911, but the *Lexington Gazette* reported on November 11 that Greenlee was once again victorious "at the 54th hole of play at the last put."

In January 1912, the *Lexington Gazette* reprinted an excerpt of Greenlee's speech to a VMI veterans' group, another variation on the theme that molded his early character:

Following the toast of Col. W. T. Poague to Capt. J. P. Moore and the veterans who died the previous year, Mr. Greenlee D. Letcher, having been designated by the commandant, arose and said: "The fame and greatness of Lee and Jackson, for whom our Camp is named, and the Confederate armies they led, is a common heritage and belongs to all, but the Sons of Veterans have constituted themselves as it were, sentinels to keep the bivouac and camp fires burning—they and their children throughout all the coming years, while the brave soldiers sleep; and I have been honored by our commandant in being asked to propose a sentiment to our patron saints, Lee and Jackson, immortal commandants, awaiting the reassembling of their matchless armies —glorious and deathless on fame's eternal camping ground—in heaven's battlements, at peace, beyond the clouds and stars."

In January of 1912, Lilian wrote to her sister, trying to boost Katie's morale with this sweet speech:

> Dearest Katie: Many, many happy returns of your birthday. May you indeed live long and prosper greatly. It must be a great satisfaction to you to think what a satisfying and true person you are. Most people absorbed in "household dooties" forget their own famblys, their original famblys, but as we said Christmas, you are a sort of beacon light to us all. Seymour in New York writing to Mamma, comparing material and intangible beauties once said that no art nor structure there could equal "the beauty of Katie's character." I don't say this just because it is your birthday, but think you should know what people are saying "behind your back." Mamma I suppose told you we had a little visit from Mr. Flynn. The worst thing about this gentleman is you miss him when he's gone! I do hope you are all well and enduring the cold weather. Much love, from Lilian.

Katie replied, in a rare, vulnerable epistle:

> Idgy Dear, Your birthday letter made me cry to think that such a snarling, hateful venomous wretch as I am should have a fambly so loyal and loving and deserving of better things. It's a sorrowful thing to be growing old and feel yourself such an absolute failure and futility not to mention being worse than that, and your letter was unspeakably comforting as it was utterly undeserved—as sweet and as funny as Seymour bloodying his own nose in defense of John. Can't you and Mama

make up your minds to venture on that awful old train and come and see us right now. I want you so bad. With loads of love to you both. Katherine.

If there was any doubt as to Katie's being depressed, this letter would remove it. Yet the letter from Lilian must have pleased her greatly, for one senses that Katie believed that *only* her own family understood her—not Greenlee and not much of the rest of the world.

It is hard to avoid distorting the portrait of Katie and Greenlee, because the letters were written only when they were apart; yet in the many months lacking letters we must imagine them together, talking daily, raising the children together, sharing their lives. As those times are invisible to us, we cannot know whether they existed in cold silence or in warm harmony. As I recall them, Katie was slow and quiet, and Greenlee would blow in like a flurry of autumn leaves at the end of the day, full of stories, jokes, sermons, news, anecdotes about folks he'd been in contact with during the day, which she found amusing. Although the letters do not lie about their relationship, they may not, it is well to remember, tell all the truth either.

February of 1912 found Katie in Harrisonburg, writing Greenlee once again of her delayed return: note what keen interest her own family matters held for her, when she hardly pretended interest in his family. She took Buz with her, leaving Gee in Lexington, although her reasons never appear. Perhaps she just gave in to Buz, who was famous for hating school, and didn't insist that he attend.

Dear Doddy—I find that tomorrow is Court Day and the train will be so crowded that I'd have to sit anywhere I could get a seat and couldn't have much chance of dodging open windows so we'll have to wait till Tuesday to come. Have Miss Bodell phone to Thompson's to tell Mr. Norris not to save his surry for us Monday evening, as I asked him to. Also if you go to Mrs. Graham's[49] to supper tomorrow night *get Fannie to come up and sit till you get back*—and get back early. . . .

Found Mamma and Idge well and had the pleasure of bringing them their first news of the success of John's maiden speech—of which Old Pop Keester who was on the train on his way from Richmond told me before I saw it in the papers. Tell Gee I find it lonesome with no pirates along and want to see my bold bad buccaneer so bad I don't know what to do. Tell him I just love fellows with skulls and cross bones on their arms. With love from us both.

Katie wrote on February 21, 1912, indicating that Buz had been sick: "It is sleeting and raining and so damp that I am afraid to start with Buz. He has been downstairs yesterday and today and seems very chipper, but Gen Yi and I thought it safer not to take him out in so much dampness. Negotiate for the bus or a closed carriage to take us over [from the train station to the house] tomorrow evening. Will phone or telegraph if anything prevents our coming—but fully expect to be there tomorrow evening. With love to you and Gee. Tell Maggie to give the flowers a drink. K."

Kate Paul must have been sick in May, for Katie took Buz to Harrisonburg and wrote Greenlee on May 12 that "Mamma seems better & I think she could sit up if the weather was more encouraging. You & Gee take good care of each other and don't forget to pay Rosa her well deserved money. With lots of love."

Katie spent most of the summer in Harrisonburg, but she never went to Louisville to see Nancy Bell, despite two other letters of warm invitation. Meanwhile Greenlee gave the Buena Vista High School Baccalaureate speech. In July, Buz, and Virginia's arrival home from Panama, became the excuses to stay: "Dear Doddy—The mileage book and the money arrived safely, and I ought to have acknowledged them at once, but the excitement of Virginia's finally arriving prevented my writing. . . . Buz has found some boys and is so well content that he has just informed me he "doesn't 'spect to go home for 'bout four weeks"—so while I have a chance I'll continue to linger but not four weeks. . . . How are you getting along as to eats etc.? Onions I suppose. Let us have a postal at least every day—I talk as if we expected to spend the summer. Lots of people ask about you. With lots of love. K."

Katie's ear flared up in midsummer, and in July she went to Richmond to have it treated. Gee went to camp from Lexington, and she received a postal from him: "Dear Mother—We came back from camp yesterday after having a good time. Although we had a fine time it couldn't compare with our previous ones, it was too much like a kindergarten to suit me, but neverless [sic] I was sorry to leave. There's nothing much happening here so I dont have much to say. I hope you'll be back soon since we are very lonesome without you. With love. Gee."

Katie returned to Harrisonburg, writing, on August 5, 1912: "Dear Doddy—I hope you and Houty didn't damage yourselves by your bachelor housekeeping. How is the white rab? I suppose Gee & Hunt are busy with their camp preparations. Did you send the mileage book and funds? Be sure & get the buggy fixed to take us to the Alum. Expect us when you see us—tra-la! K."

In September 1912, Katie went from Harrisonburg to visit the Bells, her lifelong friends who were now located in Fairfax at the Theological Seminary, leaving her mother with the children, writing to her husband: "I expect to proceed upon my way to the Bells' tomorrow. . . . Did you take those children swimming this evening? It was surely a good hot day for it. How is old Buz? And how is old Gee? Tell Mamma I found the folks all well and even John proud of the tea,[50] which was a glittering, a howling success."

On September 3, she wrote from Fairfax, "I arrived safely at noon. . . . It is lovely out here and of course I am rejoicing in Mr. & Mrs. Bell." The next day she noted: "Your letter and check came yesterday. Thank you. I hope your Patterson case came out all right in Staunton. . . . If I don't get back Saturday don't forget to pay Rosa $3.00. The other one $1.50 I reckon we will go in to D.C. today. Love to all."

Later in September, Katie took Gee and Buz to Rockbridge Alum Springs and wrote several postals home that included such remarks as "Gee is beginning to pine for his happy home and Hunter, and Buz too is languishing. And as a rain seems to be impending I reckon we won't stay much longer, though I'd like to stay and stay. . . ." "We are anxious to hear how the tournament came out . . . The boys are holding out better than I expected. They go in the pool twice a day and yesterday they lured Mudder in. . . ." "The kids seemed to think you a magnificent example of fidelity to duty when they heard you had stayed to vote for Martin when you might have ridden in an automobile instead. . . . They are always going home tomorrow—but it continues to be tomorrow."

A rare letter came from brother Seymour, from Ancon, Panama, in the Canal Zone, on December 13, 1912. The letter included a black silk and rhinestone evening bag.[51]

In 1913, Seymour Paul married Kate Pittman of Vicksburg, Mississippi. In February of 1913, Greenlee went to the Johns Hopkins University Hospital in Baltimore for a week for a mysterious operation, from which he recovered enough to participate in March in a golf tournament in North Carolina. While he was in the hospital, Katie sent him a snapshot of Buz barefoot in the snow, holding a cat.

From Pinehurst, North Carolina, Greenlee wrote to Katie, on March 3, 1913, of a "difficult but interesting" trip, no hotel rooms available in the entire area, and "a strenuous day" in the golf tournament. "My game put me into the first third— Vaughan did not do so well—he was right smartly down in the mouth. Don't say anything to anyone about it. He may pull up tomorrow & I may go down. There are 214 Golfers playing to-day from all over the country."

On March 5, he wrote of being "beaten," then following around "Staff, the

Buz barefoot in the snow,
Letcher Avenue, February 24,
1913

famous Yale athlete & Cochran of Balt. [as they played] a match. . . . I also saw Travis, a national champion play Welterman, champion of Massachusetts. This was worth the trip alone. There are at least 400 men, women & children playing Golf here now."

On March 6, he wrote: "Vaughan won his game today & he is high up in the air. Mr. McCormick, the father of Mrs. Whiting, took lunch with us today—quite a pleasant gentleman." He added: "Am lonesome for you."

Katie wrote him at the Berkshire where he admittedly badgered them into "fixing up a supply room" for him and Vaughan:

We miss you to beat the band—even the dashing and worldly Gee says,
"Gee, it's lonesome witto [without] old Pop—no fun at all. When will

he be back?" Gee has been at school since Tuesday, though his cold still lingers. Buz was croupy last night, and I kept him in bed to-day. But Dr. White thinks he'll be all right tomorrow & is lots better this evening. . . . Dr. White says there are a number of people sick with pneumonia. . . . A letter from Aunt Susie says Rock continues to suffer terribly and is very weak, though the doctors say he is doing fairly well. The cadets got back at 11:30 last night but I haven't seen John Gray.[52] . . . No news of any kind. The horses are getting along all right. With love from all of us, K.

Katie's opinion that there is no news was a concept alien to her husband.

In 1913 Katie was again in Richmond Memorial Hospital for a month, from July 11 to August 10, for another ear operation. Meanwhile, Lilian kept the boys, who went to camp and attended Bill Cody's Wild West Show, which my father talked about as being a highlight of his childhood.

Having to spend high summer in the hospital, at first Katie seemed cheerful: "Dr. Bowen says the improvement continues to be most satisfactory." Then a week later she plunged into the depths, writing dismally: "I feel like beginning my letter with 'Good-bye forever,' but I'll only say 'Don't expect me till you see me.'" She refers to her physician as "that boy doctor . . . [who] still does not say when, only always 'a little longer'—and I realize that there's no time like the present while Gen Yi is there with the kids—but it's mighty hot and mighty tiresome."

Greenlee's letters are missing from this part of the correspondence, so probably Katie left them in Richmond. But her responses tell us what was going on: "Houty came yesterday to take me to church but I had no church clothing along so he paid a call instead. It was so sweet of him to think of taking me. . . . I'm so glad Buz had such a gorgeous time, and to think he has another week before him. . . ." In a postal she remarked that "Dr. Bowen seemed much pleased with the improvement this morning. Says he hopes it will be more rapid now. Still doesn't say when I can leave. It has been fearfully hot and I am getting very much aweary." And:

> It is fearfully hot again and yesterday and to-day I've felt it greatly, though a shower this afternoon has cooled the air delightfully. I reckon you think I talk a heap about the weather but it is mostly weather here. To add to my heat-induced grouch the ear was very uncomfortable yes- terday having been burned out with nitrate of silver. Dr. Bowen said I looked much better this morning. I asked whether he intended Dr. White or Dr. Switzer to treat me when I went home and he said he

would prefer Dr. White. I told him you wanted Dr. Switzer, but he said
that the treatment would be very simple and he would rather have it
done by a general practitioner whom he knew *under his direction* than
by a specialist of whom he knew nothing—that the specialists in small
towns were usually men who had studied their specialties for a short
term only and had had little experience. . . . I am most anxious that the
whole treatment shall be absolutely under Dr. Bowen's direction and
control.

On July 12, she wrote: "Do Gee and Buz start camp today? I reckon there is considerable bustle and stir going on—I surely am glad for them to have the chance
to go. Won't it be a seventh heaven to old wild man, tree-dweller Buz? And Gee
can be again the greatest talker in the camp which spells happiness for him. Aren't
you getting mighty tired of board bills and doctors bills for me? I feel like the ele-
phant in Nang—Took every cent of his salary to keep the beast in hay."

On July 15, Katie had a long letter from Lilian, who was in Lexington taking
care of her nephews, on furlough from taking care of Uncle Rock Paul in
Roanoke. Miss Maggie Ott had been "presented" the same winter night in 1895
as Katie and Virginia. Lilian's amused observances offer us a window into life in
the Letcher household while Katie was gone. "Miss Maggie Ott is married! I am
simply delighted that she has escaped the serfdom of dependence, washing milk
buckets, picking potato bugs, cooking and the taunts and jeers of wealthy relatives.
Her marriage is the culmination of a romance of twenty years, parted—
reunited—It is for this her hair has stayed bright; and her dresses red. I'm terribly
pleased."[53] Lilian continued; this time Maggie was the current cook. The other
woman was the mother of another sometimes servant, Phoebe. It is so like Greenlee to insist on the black woman staying for breakfast.

We have had two visits today. Phoebe's mother was here quite early and
on the Colonel's invitation took breakfast with Maggie. She had three
letters to write, and no paper nor stamps. Of course these were forthcoming. She sent her love to "my little girl, tell her to come back soon,
if the Lord spares her and nothing happens." On Saturday she is going
to the country to visit her adopted son and see a preacher 'dained. She
says Mrs. Letcher is so clever to her, she always gives her some of the
children's clothes to take to the little boys so they can go to Sunday
School. I hesitate at giving away anything, but having found two pairs
of trousers quite too small for Buz, also a waist, I gave them to her. She

was very grateful and said in the most gracious way, of course she couldn't expect me to give her as much as Mrs. Letcher always does! Well, as the Ol' Marster was sending the sun down pretty warm and not waitin' for her, she'd better move along. The naive way in which she makes known her wants, artlessly weaving them into the conversation of Mrs. Letcher's "cleverness". . . . The other caller presented a slip of paper on which I read "Will you kindly loan a dumb Spanish printer out of a job 15 ¢ to buy some glycerine to use on my vocal cords." Think of all that coming right to one's own door! I am sure he was not an imposter. I spoke to him in Spanish and if anything could have surprised him into speech, my Spanish would have done so. After he left I wondered why in the world, if he was dumb, he wanted to grease his vocal cords.

And she pictured the boys getting ready for camp:

Gee and Buzz had quite a packing. They were not very particular about taking everything on the lists but were very careful to take a comb and brush each. They found brushes but no combs. With one accord they began to hunt combs; everywhere they hunted, upon everyone they called, for combs. They seemed to forget all else. As I knew they would not touch them, I did not insist that they buy them. Gee found one to his satisfaction, and when I went to look over Buz's things I found an old side comb of yours, to *his* great satisfaction. When they tied up their kits, Gee gently unwound something from a baseball bat, and put it around his bundle. Buz had nothing, having given his rope to Jack [Mead][54] as Jack's bundle was heaviest. Buz hunted high and low, then decided he would go up town and buy one. He was sure he had some money but finding none, he ran around and gathered up a lot of brass cartridge shells, took them up town, sold them for twenty-cents, bought a rope, fishing tackle and candy in about ten minutes. About the cot, Buz and I had our one and only row since you left. He was deeply opposed to taking it, as the other boys were not doing so. I reasoned with him, to no avail. He cried. I was firm, I was very cross with him. He persisted, and said he had rather stay at home than take a cot, and was ready to do it; as the hour for taking the things up was almost past, I didn't want him to miss the camp and gave in, with tears and kisses from us both. Dr. Graham told me the beds and bedding were kept dry, protected from wet by trenches around the tents, and thought it quite safe. I did the best I could to get Buz to take it; but he would not have gone, and I didn't think you wanted that: Gee promised to inform Colonel if he took any cold. . . . I received a letter from Aunt Susie. She is most unhappy about Rock and wants me to return. A letter from Mamma who had heard was to the same effect. I think I had better go Saturday, that is, day after tomorrow. Maggie can take good care of things, and look after the Colonel. I think she is perfectly honest and she is quite intelligent. I am sorry to leave but I think I should and the children I feel are safe and happy. . . . If you are not back by the time they are, both were to stay ten days, and if you'd rather I'd be here I can come home this way, otherwise I reckon I'll go straight home, though as Aunt Susie says she wouldn't think of taking Rock to Ottobine, away from doctor, etc., there is no especial reason for me to go that way. You must stay there every minute the medico says, my little one, and anything I can possibly do, to content your mind, command me. I have tried to keep some account of the exchequer, it doesn't seem to come out quite straight; I think once or twice I gave the kidlings some money for soda, and bought berries etc. I failed to record. Maggie can quite well keep the house clean with only the Colonel here, she says she will *not* go away before you return. I will tell her if she does, Ellen can take her place. Ellen has not been well and while the children are away, she can take a little rest . . . . And if you are still away when the children come back, I could quite easily stay with them. The Judge [Uncle Houty] told us of seeing you and how you were looking well. Miss Jennie returns Monday, Miss Fannie I know not when. I've played tennis once or twice with Eloise and Lizzie. I've enjoyed being here so much, the outdoors, the sleeping in the sweet cold air, the sunshine and the shadows, the Beautiful Mountains, the children's interests, you and the good Colonel, my golfing and tennis, the cardinals and goldfinches, the trees, the clouds and the doves calling from the hills. And they all await you, my little one. . . .

I put your ferns on the shady side of the summer house within reach of the hose. They seem safe there, the rabs showing no taste for them, and Maggie can move em if necessary. The younger children rode to camp in big wagons. Much love. . . . [I]f you have survived this epistle. . . . PS In our difficulty or rather disagreement, Buzz was quite honest about his feelings. So don't let him think I'm a tattle-tale.

Katie reported to Greenlee on July 15 from Memorial Hospital that "Dr. Bowen says I am still more to the good today. . . . A letter from Mrs. Bell says she will be in R- [Richmond] awhile next month. Wish it was now. You must drive out to see the kids Sunday and take some water-millions to the camp."

On July 18, she wrote, "Dear Col. Doddy—I am quite cheered up—Dr. Bowen says at the present rate of progress he thinks I can leave next Tuesday—I hope so for it is awfully hot, and I was beginning to feel discouraged about the apparently slow improvement. But maybe it isn't as slow as it seems. . . . Tomorrow is your birthday. Many happy returns, and a successful golf game to celebrate the day!—I had wanted to have a party and call the neighbors in to drink your health. . . . Tell Houty all the ladies were just *so* worried to hear he was a bachelor—such a fine looking man wasted!

Aunt Susie, privately called the Empress for her imperious ways, wrote to Katie from Roanoke on July 19, 1913:

> John Gray has just gone to the train to get Lilian & I will begin my letter to you. Rock has said each day—write to Katie—I want her written to often. He is so pleased to get your sweet little notes. Did not sleep last night which always means a bad day. . . . I am having a nice supper for Lilian. *Monday* Dear Katie—See how I am interrupted! This letter still not finished. Lilian got a telegram and wants to leave this morning to take some position to nurse a typhoid fever case. It was too bad for she was such a pleasure to Rock. He is easier today but very weak. Lilian seemed to think he looked pretty well, and thought I was doing exactly the right thing for him. Enjoyed your cheerful little postal even though you are sick & suffering yourself. I do *trust* your ear is better? & that you will have no serious growth. I am just sorry for you poor child. . . . Thank Mr. Letcher for his nice letter.

On July 20, Katie wrote to Greenlee from the hospital, asking his advice, which she hardly ever did:

> After I got Lilian's letter saying she was going to Roanoke yesterday I hoped you would take a day off and come down to spend Sunday here, and felt quite jilted when you didn't. . . . I told Dr. Bowen this morning that if any treatment had to be given in Lexington you preferred it should be done by Dr. Switzer. I am only anxious that it shall *absolutely* under the direction of these doctors so that they will be responsible. If the job can be completed here by staying ten days longer I think that

would, if possible, be the wise thing to do rather than risk a backset and the loss of all the time and money spent here. What do you think?

She urged him to "go out and see the kids this afternoon. Wish I was there to go along. I haven't seen anything here as good-looking as they are. As the feeling comes back to the ear the treatment is at times very painful. I will surely be glad when it is over. . . . Have Jennie and Fannie gotten back yet?"

She wrote another letter on the same day: "I surely do wish I was going to Whistle Creek with you fellows and Nuzzer Mamma this evening. Make Buz keep to his old limits if he goes in the river,[55] and *please* you go with him." She was concerned about the cost of staying in Richmond and worried when Lilian left to see Rock in Roanoke: "I am writing to Idge if possible to go back to Lexington the last of the week when the kids get home and to let you know whether she can do so. If she cannot, please send to Nuzzer Mamma and ask her to come up and stay till I get back. *I don't feel satisfied unless someone is there.*"

Lilian wrote to Katie on July 24:

> Dearest Katie, Life is just one moving picture after another. Saturday I tore my heart up by the roots from your house and went to Roanoke. I found Mrs. Welch with Aunt Susie so there was really no reason for haste on her account. *Rock* was glad to see me however. He is very miserable, sick and suffering. Sunday morning I had an urgent telegram asking me to come to Winchester. As I knew you are to be home tomorrow, I consented. There seemed nothing else to do. I came home this evening, go to Winchester in morning. If by any chance you are not-at-home Saturday, Bun can come up with kids.

Katie continued to complain of ear pain, and sent Lilian's letter on to Greenlee. John and Louise (Loulie) Taylor having invited them to Norfolk for their wedding, Katie commented to Greenlee:

> I telegraphed you to write for Mamma or Virginia, as I cannot be satisfied to stay longer unless there is someone *in the house* to look after the kids and see about things generally. . . . If neither of them can come I will come home and let the treatment be finished there. . . . It was certainly nice in Brother John and Miss Loulie to ask us down, but even if you could come Sunday I would probably be sick and unable to go. . . . Now aren't you all the rattling blades; going to Hot Springs to play golf with the millionaires! But it will be a delightful trip. Also it

lets you out—nobody can say after this that you are the craziest golfer of them all when Bennie [Huger] leaves a brand new baby to go a-golfing! The idea! With love to you and the returning campers.

From Harrisonburg, Kate Paul wrote to Greenlee: "I know Miss Jennie would gladly help you in any way with the children and that she can do it far better than I—but Katie always worries so about them when she's away, especially if there is no one there at night, that I think on her account—to prevent her worrying and make her more willing to stay as long as she ought, that I'd better come so I will do so as soon as I can; but don't bother about meeting me. Shall come to-morrow if nothing prevents."

On July 26, Katie wrote: "The doctor says his job is 'looking beautiful, just beautiful.' . . . I was relieved and delighted to get Nuzzer Mamma's postal saying she was on her way up."

Katie reported to Greenlee that her doctor had prescribed for her "try[ing] two weeks of treatment with sleeping outdoors and taking milk and eggs and iron tonic. What do you think?" She added, "I'm so glad the troops had such a big time at camp. I fear they find it very tame being 'town houjies' [var. of hoodlums?] again."

Greenlee, following the tedious and expensive treatment, wrote to Drs. Bowen & Wright a long and stern letter emphasizing the critical nature of Katie's illness. At the end he summarized: "I feel that it is a matter of so far reaching consequence to me and mine that this treatment should be handled by a specialist so when you send your bill please send me a report on her case and enclose a letter to Dr. Switzer with *specific directions*." He ended:

> P.S. What I am now about to say is strictly confidential between a patient and the Doctor and under your professional confidence. When Dr. J. P. Davidson operated on Mrs. Letcher for mastoiditis he told me that Dr. White's treatment of her ear was not the proper treatment but added that almost any general practitioner would have done just as Dr. White but that a specialist would have treated it differently. I have never told Dr. White this nor have I told any one outside of my family, and I don't want you to do so of course. For some time recently Dr. White has been treating Mrs. Letcher's ear suggesting hardening of wax which I felt was not a correct diagnosis in view of the odor from the ear, and I feel that the delay for the last few months has been inadvisable and I feel that it would have been avoided if a specialist had been consulted

earlier. You can therefore understand my urgent reasons why you do not send any letter of instructions to Dr. White but send them to me to be used as I see fit or directly to Dr. B. W. Switzer. Dr. Wright agreed with me the first morning that I talked with him that it would be wise to let the specialist here continue your treatment if it was necessary to be done at home, and I regret to have to write this post script but from Mrs. Letcher's letters it would seem that you insist on sending her back to Dr. White and I therefore write frankly so that no possible mistake will be made about this. Under Dr. White's treatment here before she was operated on for mastoiditis for years she suffered from her ear and the last few months terrifically, all of which I feel would have been avoided had a specialist seen her earlier. And the delay I fear almost caused her death. I trust you appreciate the spirit in which I write this and that you will not make it necessary for me to communicate this to Dr. White but that he will understand that the gravity and danger in the situation requires the watchfulness of a *specialist* rather than a general practitioner. G.D.L.

In Lexington, Greenlee attended a concert, occasioning Katie's remark: "So sorry Gee and Buz weren't there to hear Polk Miller."[56] She wrote on July 29, "Dr. B- said of course he would write the letter as you wished. Says 'it won't be long now,' but I reckon that means next week, so don't expect me till I get there."

On August 5, she was still away and apparently planning on being there longer, reporting: "I have just come in from a quest for a new boarding place and think I have landed on my feet, having taken at Mrs. Bowers, 115 E. Franklin, a small room but with two windows and on the shady side of the house, with private bath—room & board at $10 per week. That bath all my own sounds too good to be true doesn't it? I do hope I won't have to stay much longer. It is so fearfully hot and while you and the troops are a rum lot I do want to see you all *so bad*."

But the very next day she wrote, "It is so noisy here, I may move again, depends on how long I have to stay. Am crazy to see you fellows and don't feel as if I can wait much longer—even the Bells being in R- is small comfort to me. Will see them this morning," The day after that, August 7, she wrote:

There was a little shower last night which left a pleasant breeze this morning. Have not been to the doctor's yet. The cooler weather and the Bells have cheered me up to the point where I reckon I can make up my mind to stay peaceably a few days longer, but I've been feeling as if I

just had to get home no matter what Dr. B- said. About Ellen's $2.00 I
engaged her to cook while I was gone, but when Maggie turned up I
told Ellen if she would stay and do the cleaning I would pay her $2 for
it instead of the $1.50 I usually pay because Maggie then expected to
go to the springs and I wanted to leave Idge a cleaner who could take
the cook's place if necessary. It was more than the work was worth but
the best I could do at the time. Love to you all. Don't under any circumstances get Lily Leech to clean.

And, the next day: "Alack, alas! I was coming back thinking to pack my grip and
get away tomorrow or next day and now Dr. Wright says two or three days longer."

She wrote on August 9, 1913: "Dr. Wright still much pleased with progress and
thinks I can leave in a day or so—but you will be out with the boys at White Sulphur and I'll have nobody to row with so there will be no use coming. . . . See Dr.
S- before you go and give him letter of directions so he'll be ready when I get there
to continue treatment."

On August 10, she wrote:

> As long as Nuzzer Mamma's there and you've got a good cook and
> everybody's well and nobody needs me in the least I don't see any use
> taking risks. . . . The Bells left yesterday afternoon. . . . I certainly en-
> joyed seeing them and miss them greatly. Wish I could see the Wild
> West show—or at least one certain member[57] of it. I reckon Gee has a
> lonesome time with no base-ball and no camp. Does he play tennis
> any? How does Nuzzer Mamma seem to be standing you fellows? I
> hope she keeps well and isn't damaged by the heat. . . . How goes the
> golf? And how is Mr. Bennie's new boy? . . . I reckon you wonder what
> I do with the money you've sent—nothing and yet somehow it melts
> away, medicine, washing etc. I've been here so long my clothes are wear-
> ing out—had to get new shoes to-day.

Katie returned home on August 14, which was the day that Greenlee left for a
golf tournament. Apparently he sent her word by Houty to write to him in Hot
Springs, Virginia, for she wrote: "Dear Doddy—How could I know you wanted
to be written to when you play golf? I knew Houty had told you we were all well
and getting along all right. It was not forgetfulness but lack of news. Everybody is
much pleased at the Golf victory—people you'd think didn't know there was golf.
Saw young Ben Huger this morning. He's just lovely and exactly like Mr. Huger.

Didn't ask for Miss Lucy as the nurse said she was getting ready to go out. With loads of love from all of us."

For all his devotion, Katie could act as though she thought he didn't care about hearing from her. It seems that his travels and his golf allowed him to escape the dark muddle of his marriage. In September, she apparently went to Harrisonburg without a word to him, for she wrote, on September 15, 1913: "Well here I am visiting Nuzzer Mamma. When it was too late to stop me the folks got a letter saying a couple of companies were coming so we couldn't go. Are you fellows getting along? Love to you all. K." Three days later, she wrote: "I'm waiting over till tomorrow afternoon, when Nuzzer Mamma is coming up with me to stay a little while. . . . Have just been over to see Miss Teensie and Mrs. Deviers. Are you fellows most frozen? We are. With love to you all. K."

Rock Paul died in Roanoke on November 24, 1913. On December 11, 1913, the *Alleghany News* ran a feature about Greenlee Letcher, claiming that he "reminds you of the famous bulldog Dixie: . . . so with Letcher; when you get him on a case you have to prize him loose and herein lies his success." The piece ends by saying, "He surely am some Bryan admirer."

In 1914 there are references in letters to Katie to "your accident this winter" but nothing more specific. Virginia was away teaching. From Panama, Seymour, who had become the director of personnel for the Panama Canal and Railroad, wrote to Katie on March 11, 1914, in part:

> Dear Kit: . . . A lady from Richmond asked me the other day if you were not the president of our county suffrage association, and I had the pleasure of affirming it. I don't believe any great advance or purification of politics will come from woman's suffrage but it seems to me the ballot is an essential right; one to which working and property-holding women are obviously entitled. . . .
>
> Government impinges on everyone—everyone is more or less directly affected by it, and every member of society, excepting the unfit, is entitled to a voice in the way society's government shall act. . . .
>
> Virginia says Charley is doing well. I am mighty glad of it, and only wish he would write to me sometimes.

"Leading Spirits Women's Suffrage" was the name of the Rockbridge group Katie chaired, although the group is not mentioned in local papers. The political activities of women on their own behalf may have been equated with tea parties, only less acceptable to the male-run newspapers, and therefore unmentionable as news.

Katie wrote Buz a postcard from Harrisonburg on March 27, while visiting her mother: "I just saw a barefooted boy out of the window and he looked as tough and husky as you do. I wanted to ask if he'd been barefooty all winter, but his legs looked too white for that. Don't send in your Jackson composition till I get back. Mudder"

In 1914, Uncle Houty suffered a stroke in the spring. In April Greenlee went again to Pinehurst with some of his cronies to play in international golf tournaments. In his absence Katie reported that Houty was "about the same." She regaled him with mention of some baby alligators someone sent their neighbors, the Meads, saying they are "all the news."

But April 8 saw Katie back in Richmond for more treatment for her ear, and Lilian went to Lexington to look after Gee and Buz. On Easter 1914, Lilian wrote to Katie:

> We had a lovely Easter day and since we could not have you with us, to hear you over the phone was next best. The day began quite early with Buz up, in the cool gray dawn hunting eggs. He scurried around and I scurried, around. While we were scurrying, a rabbit, a real rabbit, and not ours, jumped out of the bushes and ran across the yard! After this I *know* the rabbit brings Easter eggs. Was ever before Fact a more ready aid to romance? I was delighted. We got a little basket at Mrs. Petticoat's for Uncle Houty, put some grass and Easter eggs in it; and filled it with lovely yellow jonquils from Mr. Boley's, from Nannie Patton's garden I think; and with lilies of the valley from those sent by Mr. O'Flynn which came fresh and lovely.[58] The little basket looked very pretty and Buz said Uncle Houty liked it. Took some flowers up to the cemetery, bright ones to please the baby eye. The morning was lovely, clear and warm, the church was aglow with yellow flowers and the music was full and triumphant; I liked the sermon, and the beauty of it all caught one up nearer understanding of "the communion of saints." John Gray went to Roanoke Saturday. We had Houston [Showell, Maggie Letcher Showell's oldest son, at W&L] and four rats to dinner. . . . We fixed the table with a bowl of flowers and some little concerns from Pettis, and the cake had a little rabbit on it; a beautiful yellow and white cake, coconut. Buz gave Aunt Sarah and Fannie some eggs to take home.[59] We persevered in conversation and as the ratlings [cadets] were right talkey we were just about our "seventhly" in topics

when you called and gave us a "and finally.". . . . I know they had names,
but as the Colonel had said he was going to invite so-and-so, I stuck so-
and-so in my mind, four so-and-sos, but what does it matter, a few so-
and-sos, more or less? All went well! . . . Gen. Nichols having
unfeelingly limited their permits, the kids and I went to the children's
service, which was as always lovely and sad.[60] I dote on the *abandon* of
the occasion; the children, dogs trotting at will, with intermittent notes
of whispering, wails and rattles. It was a lovely day and we wished so
much for you. It was for me such a happy contrast to last Easter. Gee is
tonight at a party given I believe in honor of Miss Lois the Fair. Buz
went to the egg hunt at the rectory. . . . There is a wedding invite from
Mr. & Mrs. Smith in North Carolina. Col. [Greenlee] says requires
only cards! Let me know where yours & his are and I will send. Valentine and Mrs. Causey, Mrs. Mallory & Mrs. Wise were here today. . . .
Love from all.

On April 15, Katie must have been feeling especially mean, for she wrote to
Greenlee, with no "Dear Gov," at the beginning:

I telegraphed you apropos of the Flood Portner present. We don't owe
them any wedding present and to people with all that money anything
we might send would mean absolutely nothing—might possibly seem
like boot-licking. It would be much better if you wrote him your cordial congratulations and good wishes. *These is my intuitions.* Moreover
I'm broke. . . . Also Flood doesn't need that present as much as we need
the money which would be $10 at best. . . . If you still insist wire me the
money and I will—with great reluctance—get the present. . . . *Be sure
and get Aunt Sarah to stay the nights you are away.* . . . What do you hear
from Sister [Lizzie, who was ill] and how is Houtie? Are you fellows
doing any better about coming to your meals for Gin Yi and Aunt
Sarah than you do for me? With love to you all, K. Can't the Bristol trip
wait till I get home?

There are no more letters until July 13, when Greenlee was doing business in
Greenbrier County, West Virginia, and Katie wrote: "The campers have been
packing and unpacking and repacking all day—all of them—the whole neighborhood. . . . Went down this morning to see how Houty was. Found him quiet
and about the same." A couple of days later, she wrote that "Gee got safely off to

camp, but poor little old Buz after all his packing and chest building came down with high fever and a bilious spell Monday night. He's all right again to-day though and will go out in a day or so. Am just going down to take some cantaloupe to Houty. With love and congratulations on your game. K." And on July 17: "Buz is up and about again and I hope can go to camp tomorrow or Sunday, but I don't want him to go until he is quite himself. Uncle Steve[61] has been staying here at night. No news in town that I have heard. Am sending you the papers. *That little piece is writing to our oldest son!!'*

Buz finally got to camp, and on July 20, wrote: "I am having a fine time and I ant [*sic*] sick. I have had a good time here. Yours truley, Buzz."

In August Katie took Gee and Buzz to Harrisonburg, and the boys went to a camp near Elkton, Virginia.Katie seemed happy there, and wrote: "This is a most beautiful place. The river broad and shallow, but deep enough for swimming and boating. The boys seem to be having a good time—especially Buz who has plenty of boys his age. The P.O. address is Yancey. . . . If you think I'm not a camper you ought to see me now." She wrote, on August 14:

> Gee & Buz are just starting with a crowd to Elkton which is only four miles away. . . . I came in from the camp yesterday to help Mamma with her guests.[62] . . . Left the boys to come in with the rest of the outfit tomorrow. The box you were mailing for me and the *check* came this morning. Thank you for both. Saw the Bells at the train this morning. Buz seems to have gotten entirely over his cold .. . . Gee will be home tomorrow evening and Buz and I Monday. Hope you have been getting along all right. . . . Send me $10. . . . Ask Caroline to tell Nannie the wash lady not to send for the clothes till Tuesday.

Katie went again to Philadelphia to see Dr. DeSchweinitz, then visited the Bells in Fairfax, returning not to Lexington but to Harrisonburg.

Uncle Houty, Judge Samuel Houston Letcher, died that fall after three strokes.[63] Mrs. Paul wrote on October 7 of the confusion and chaos of replastering, repapering their house; of a visit from Gee; of Virginia's return from somewhere, "pale, tired, and thin—for her"; of Lilian visiting; and of John taking Frances to Johns Hopkins "about her lungs and other troubles." From the end of summer 1914 until March 20, 1915, there are no letters or postals, except one from Lilian in November to Buz, when he was sick. It was written in verse, and ended: "The birds fly high into the blue, How high they'll go, who'll tell you true? But each sings to the others, higher and higher, Seymour Letcher I truly admire!"

Katie in garden, 1916

Virginia was unwell, having to "sit on air cushions all the time." In November of 1914 Greenlee's widowed sister, Lizzie Harrison, of Charlottesville died.

The first correspondence of 1915 was a note to Greenlee, who had gone in March for the third year to play golf in Pinehurst: "No news of any description— except that Lafayette beat V.M.I. yesterday and Gee says the anti's beat the suffragists in the school debate today. . . . I hope you are having a great time and drinking in the golf celebrities. With love from all of us. K." And next day she wrote that there was no news "or excitements of any kind except that Pinkie Penick's Uptowns beat Buz & the Bear Cats 25 to 23—so Buz is much cast down."

Ten days later, on April 1, 1915, she wrote, "Dear Doddy—Hugh, in great excitement as usual, insisted upon my enclosing this letter from Judge Brannon. The boys have just come in from the base-ball games at W&L & V.M.I. It is still cold with high winds and clouds of dust. Fannie's arm is getting better, and Bro John *writes*—not telegraphs—that Miss Loulie's finger is improving—also his rheumatism. With love from us all. K." The enclosure, from Brannon & Strathers, referred to some land that Brannon would try for the next five years to sell to Greenlee.[64] It appears that it was land adjoining some that Hugh Wills owned. Hugh wanted to buy it; Greenlee thought the price too high. Eventually Greenlee did buy it, and it may have been the land on which Greenlee sold the mineral rights, later on, to Esso. In later life Greenlee owned several pieces of land which he'd bought speculating that great riches might lie beneath the surface.

Four months elapsed with no letters. From Harrisonburg on July 23, 1915, Katie wrote to Greenlee, then golfing at White Sulphur Springs: "Couldn't prevail on Mamma to go anywhere so here I still remain. Hope you are all right again and having the time of your dreams. Don't hurry home because I plan to be there when boys get in from camp. With kindest regards. K." The next day, she wrote that "we went to the movies last night to see a most beautiful Western picture with buffaloes & Injuns galore."

On July 26, 1915, Katie reported to Guv on a trip that would prove to be fateful: "Your card came this morning. Glad you've had such a pleasant trip. Went up this morning to see the Roller school and was very favorably impressed, though everything is torn up now on account of the new barracks. With love, K." The Letchers believed in public education, so probably it was Katie more than Greenlee who decided to send their promising, studious Gee to Augusta Military Academy near Harrisonburg for his last two years of high school.

On the first of August, Katie and the boys were again in Harrisonburg where the boys took the train to the camp at Yancey. Katie noted: "We ended our wild rush by getting here in time for Buz to get right on the C.&O. train with half a dozen others en route to the camp so all's well etc. . . . Found everybody here well. Send letters here for present. With love. K."

Two days later, she wrote: "Went out to camp Monday & finding Buz a little droopy brought him in yesterday to keep him quiet for a day or so. The coat came safely. Thanks to Ca'line [Caroline]. Tell her to have the parlor curtains taken down & have Milton tack paper over the window over the cellar door." On August 5, Katie wrote: "Looked over the bills and sent them back to you yesterday. All are O.K. Buz is better today but I won't let him go back to camp for a day or so yet. Spend my time playing set-back with him. . . . Did you write and enter Gee at the Roller School? I talked to an old cadet from there yesterday and he said 'Nobody'll ever make a mistake sending a boy to Roller.' He had a regular V.M.I. kind of enthusiasm for the school and the Rollers themselves. With love. K." On August 7, she wrote to thank him for "the papers which came today. Buz is quite chipper again, but still on bread and milk and I have not let him go back to the camp yet. Give Caroline $1.50 to pay the wash lady, and Caroline herself $4.00. . . . Mr. Yancey telephoned to ask about Buz & said they were all well at camp."

Gee wrote to his mother: "I got your card the other day. Buzz has arrived and is all right. . . . I hope you can come out sometime. If you have not arranged to already, send the camp some ice cream. With all love. Gee."

Katie reported to Greenlee that "Buz went back to camp Saturday, but I did not feel well enough to go with him. . . . Went to church yesterday to hear Bishop Gibson. The camp breaks up Friday."

Frances Dannenhower Paul must have been sickly from the beginning, for Katie wrote on August 12: "Dear Doddy—I enclose Miller's acct & one from the laundry which I had overlooked. Both are O.K. The camp breaks up tomorrow. . . . No news. Frances seems to improve steadily, and is surely a sweet little thing. Virginia & Lilian are still away, though both expect to come home soon. I enclose a card from Gee. There is breakfast—so I must stop."

Life at the camp was quite informal, for on August 13, she wrote Greenlee that "Mamma and Frances and I drove down to the camp yesterday and found they were going to stay till Monday instead of breaking up today. Gee, Buz and Ben all seemed in excellent health & spirits. You'd better stay at the Baths over Sunday. With love."

She sent the boys back to Lexington on their own, and wrote, on August 17:

> Dear Doddy—I suppose the campers arrived safely. I got a chair car to keep Buz from poking his head out of the window & Gee and Ben from standing on the platform. . . . Tell them Burbridge[65] will come up with me Friday morning. Also tell Buz that Burbridge came by to see him this morning not knowing he had gone. . . . I drew fifteen dollars on the check you sent thinking that would be enough but I will have to have another ten for the Winchester trip. . . . Hope Letcher [Harrison] will still be there when I get back. Give him my love. With love to the troops. . . . P.S. Let me know if you hear anything from the Starchers[66] and don't hear anything if you can help it.

On August 19, Katie wrote: "Dear Colonel—We won't get back till late I think so I won't undertake the morning train, but come on the Special. Burbridge will be with me so tell Buz to meet us. Hope you are having this lovely cool weather."

On September 10, Katie was visiting in Harrisonburg: "Dear Colonel—As you fellows seem to be getting along so well I think I won't come til Monday. Did you remember to pay the wash lady? Tell Buz he'd better wash his face." The next day she added: "Tell Buz he needn't go to Sunday school tomorrow and tell Caroline I say come back and get supper for you fellows tomorrow night, and not to send the clothes out till after the morning train Monday so if I come in the morning mine can go too. Have just been to see Miss Teensie and the Sipes. With love to you all."

On September 13, Kate Paul wrote a postal to Katie: "We are nearly straightened out now and Va has improved very much. . . . [H]as gone to a festivity in honor of Marguerite this afternoon. . . . Frances is still at home under the doctor's care. We don't know when she can return. Charles is coming Saturday to attend the wedding on the 19th. Can't you come while he's here? We are awaiting news from Kate."[67]

In the fall, Gee left for Augusta Military Academy, in Fort Defiance, Virginia, near Harrisonburg, writing his first postal on October 1: "Dear Mother, This is certainly a fine place. Don't send anything to eat because they don't allow it. I expect to get my uniform today." On November 1, Katie went again to Philadelphia to see Dr. DeSchweinitz about her eyes, taking her mother along for a checkup also. From the Hotel Adelphia, she wrote: "Dear Doddy—We have just arrived in safety and have such a nice room here, the Travelers' Aid agent having told us that the Bingham was so much a business man's hotel, that ladies do not usually go there. She was very firm about it. Then we tried the Walton, but their rates were higher and they did not seem especially glad to see us so we came on here where we were met with such consideration we decided they'd built the hotel hoping some day we might come. Tell Buz I thought about him all the way."

Gee wrote to his father from Augusta Military Academy, on November 11, 1915: "Dear Pop, I am so sorry that mother will not be at home when I get there. You had better write to Major at once if you want me to get that furlough. We are going to have one of our biggest games Saturday but I can afford to miss seeing it to get home. Please tell Major about my reason for going away Saturday. . . . Am getting along fine in every way. I suppose Mother told you why I could not get home Monday. If you see Dr. McClure tell him that my front teeth are now practically straight. Love to all, Gee."

From Philadelphia, on November 12, Katie wrote Greenlee:

We have just come from Dr de S. who says my eyes are not going back at all, but as well as usual and that Mamma has remarkably good eyes and only needs new glasses. We will stay this evening to have the glasses tried and go to Washington in the morning. If it suits the Bells I may spend Sunday with them and come to Harrisonburg Monday and home Tuesday. . . . Don't forget to make Gee's birthday an occasion of festivity and excitement. Write me care of the Bells. Hope you fellows are getting along all right. Tell Buz I say please wash his face occasionally. . . . "The Birth of the Nation" is running now . . . and we went last night. I do wish you could see it—and everybody else in the United States. It is wonderful, and *Philadelphia* wept at the tragedy of the South. It is hard to imagine just a movie being what it is.

From Baltimore on November 15, Katie wrote that "Mamma wanted to spend a day here so we came over yesterday. Suppose we will go to W[Washington] in the morning and home in the afternoon. . . . Hope you fellows are all right and that Gee got home and had a good birthday. With love. K."

Gee wrote to Katie from school on November 20, 1915, a letter so typically that of a schoolboy that every mother will recognize the sentiments:

Dear Mother, I suppose that you have gotten back by this time, so I thought that I would write and tell you that I am getting along fine. My birthday was a great success and I was so glad to get back home when everybody was there, only of course I missed you like everything. . . . I did not bother Pop about my birthday money since he had done so much to make my birthday a success and I thought I could wait until Thanksgiving. . . . I made another great bargain the other day. You know you told me I could have some pictures taken. Well I got in on a special offer by which I can get twelve dollars worth taken for three. Have a good deal of money ready for me Monday. With love to all, Gee.

The family exchanged letters in November and December discussing Frances Paul's illness and wondering if there was a "danger to John" of her "terrible coughing." The reply was "lung trouble—but doctors agree *no* tuberculosis."

At Christmas of 1915, Kate Paul wrote Katie: "All I can make goes towards paying the debt on the West Market Street building." On December 29 Fannie Letcher's house came near to burning down, necessitating that she move in with the Letchers while it was being repaired.

Gee at camp, 1916. Note the shadow of the camera in the foreground.

Next came parts of a torn letter from Gee with no dates and no envelope, in which he wrote of

> our dance Friday night. It was every bit as good as the college dances. Everything was decorated with the school colors—blue and white. There were about forty girls, most of them from. . . . I went to

Gee in Augusta Military Academy school uniform, 1916

Staunton yesterday and got my pictures taken. After having seen some
of the other fellows pictures I decided to get a better grade which costs
two dollars more. I did this because I knew that they would be the last
I would get before I was a first classman at V.M.I. You had better send
me a check. . . . I also saw Mary Braxton. Mrs. Holt insists on me calling her Cousin Mary, so I have to accede. With love, Gee. P.S. I continued this letter from Sunday, as I had to stop for tattoo.[68]

Meanwhile, a young girl from Lexington, Kentucky, was writing to Gee. Gee
had the reputation of charming girls and women all his life. Probably she is "the
piece" Katie referred to earlier. She wrote on December 30, 1915, while both she
and Gee were at their respective homes on vacation.[69]

On January 8, 1916, Katie "fell down Barclays' steps and hurt her back," according to a letter from Greenlee to lawyer Brannon. The injury is referred to
often in family letters written the following spring. After Christmas, Katie asked
her mother to come look after Buz, and Kate Paul wrote to Lilian: "I want to go
to Katie's but their house is so cold I feel it is risky."

The next letters are all from Gee home to his parents. On January 7, 1916,
young Gee wrote his mother: "I have arrived safely and we are installed in the new
barracks. I had those pictures taken but had to pay cash. So I'll have to get another
one and one-half buck to pay for my fatigue coat. . . . I hope you are a lot better by
now and will be up before I come home Monday. I suppose you-all are snowed
under like we are. Has Punk [Buz] been sleigh-riding barefooted. How is Aunt Fan
getting along with her house. Give her and Aunt Jennie my love when you see
them. Tell Caroline to get a move on with my cake and send it down. . . . I will
come up next Monday. With love, Gee."

On February 5, Gee wrote to his father: "Dear Pop: I was coming up Monday
but as I had my hardest exam Tuesday, Major said to wait until Wednesday. I
thought that Major came over at tattoo to approve the permits but he has stopped
doing that during exam week, so I didn't get my permit. Tell Dr. McClure [a Lexington dentist] everything is doing fine. Will be up Monday. Love to all, Gee."

Nine days later, on February 14, Gee wrote to Katie: "We have had a pretty dull
week here until Friday when the team went to play Fishburne. They came out
ahead 23–21. We had a great celebration for it practically takes the championship
for us. Last night we played the Kable Juniors and beat them 26–21. I shot three
goals from the middle of the floor, and four others. We had snow today and were
excused from church, and there is nothing much happening around here at this

time. When I came back Monday all the Holts had gone out so I went to Cohen's and got some of my beloved fried oysters. With love, Gee."

Katie must have worried about Gee's health, for on March 8 he wrote: "Dear Mother:—Cut the Calamity Ann nonsense for worry. I spent the evening playing baseball. I went down to see the Gim. He looked me over and said I was O.K. My sore throat and stiff neck are things of the past. Baseball season has just begun and you won't get me away with a rope until I come on the tooth furlough. Then I will come with pleasure. With all love, Gee."

But five days later, on March 13, he wrote a letter that is left unfinished: "Dear Mother: I've had a punk time this past week for I've been sick, sick enough to feel miserable but not enough to go to the hospital. I began to feel funny while on the train Monday. On Tuesday. . . ." The note stops abruptly and is not signed. One imagines the boy fainting at this point, a roommate's raising the alarm to the school officials, the unfinished note being sent home with Gee's effects.

A school chum named Jim Hearne, seemingly his roommate, wrote to Gee's mother, on March 17, 1916, the first of two letters he would write her in his life, one much later:

> Dear Mrs. Letcher—I received your letter of the 15th inst. I certainly am sorry to hear that "Letcher" is so sick. But being home and having the best of care he ought to be well and back among us before very long. What does the doctor say? Letcher is mighty lucky that he can be home instead of being laid up here in the infirmary. The little I did for him when he was sick don't amount to anything, just remember all those cakes "Letcher" brought back, and divided 50–50 with me. . . .
>
> Tell Letcher there is not much going on, too cold for base ball practice so they are just trying the pitchers out in the gym, started having drill with both guns and music, "Old Pete" and "Lindsey," "Legs" are having a fierce time, music seems to have a peculiar effect on them, Legs jumps all thru the exercise, and Pete races madly thru, rugs are shaken on Sunday only, been late for Reveille twice, Soup, at last is not served at lunch. This is a *complete* summary of last weeks happenings. I sincerely hope Letcher will get along alright and get back here with us before very long. All the fellows have been asking about him, were sure sorry to hear he was so sick. Thanking you for your kind invitation and hoping I may see you some time. . . . Sincerely, Jim Hearne.

Gee lingered four days at home, and then on the first day of spring, died of pneumonia, with Katie at his bedside. Lexington residents say that for two years Katie never went out of the house, and one recalled that it was this blow that triggered the beginning of her reclusiveness.

Letters poured in, 432 of them, an astonishing 38, or nearly 10 percent, from people who mentioned that they had themselves had lost children. Nearly all spoke of Gee's unusual promise: "I too have looked forward to the fulfillment of the promise of the power that was felt even in Gee's baby days. I can see those beautiful eyes now when little Gee came over even on Thanksgiving morning and sat and waited because he wanted to have kindergarten and not have holiday!" So wrote his earliest teacher, Ruth Anderson. "A finer, braver lad never drew breath" is only one expression of many similar to it. "Having lost my oldest boy Harrington, I can in some means understand what this blow means to you. I have been peculiarly interested in Greenlee for a number of years, and no boy has attended our school to whom I was more sincerely devoted. . . . He was absolutely honest and as straight as steel," wrote Harrington Waddell, the Lexington High School principal. "I cannot recall ever hearing an unkind word spoken of him," one writer said. "I so admired the exceptional promise of the boy"; "I have heard so much good of your dear boy, and my sons are so dear to me, and once I had to give one up, and I know how difficult this life has been to me ever since"; "Having with much sadness just learned of the death of your dear, promising boy, and I lost my only son about the same age, I cannot refrain from expressing to you a heart oercharged with sorrow"; "I will think of him as I do our little daughter who died. . . . They have entered spotless on eternal years"; "Gee's picture has always stood on our desk by Winston's and I will keep it there"; "He won my heart more than any young fellow I ever met." Others wrote that he was "kind, beautiful, outstanding" as well as "engaging, bright, clean, graceful."

An undated newspaper clipping tells the story,

Sad Death of Bright Youth

Greenlee Davidson Letcher, Jr., in his 16th year, son of Mr. and Mrs. Greenlee D. Letcher, died at 12:20 p.m. today at his parents' home on Letcher avenue, Lexington, after an illness of two weeks from measles, pneumonia and complications. He was a student at the Augusta Military Academy and returned home March 10th on account of illness. . . . He was born in November, 1900, and grew up to be a bright and lovable youth, with promise of great usefulness. The sympathies of the entire community go out to stricken parents and relatives. . . . The funeral will be held tomorrow (Thursday) afternoon at five o'clock from R. E. Lee Memorial church.

A note in Katie's handwriting listed the pallbearers as Reid White, the Letchers' doctor; Dorsey Hopkins and Scott Huger, Lexington friends of Gee's; and Jim Hearne, his AMA friend. A second clipping from March 25, 1916, describes the funeral:

Funeral of Greenlee Letcher, Jr.

The funeral was at Lee Memorial Episcopal church at 5 o'clock in the afternoon of March 23. . . . Before the remains were placed in the casket the family gathered around it, accompanied by an escort of cadets from the Augusta Military Academy, and an appropriate prayer was offered by the pastor, Mr. Randolph. . . . The casket was covered with roses and carnations on a green background. At the center was a shield, presented by the cadets and bearing the letters, "A.M.A." Among the many floral designs sent by friends were crosses from the scouts and campers of both Lexington and Harrisonburg, with whom the deceased had been in camp last summer. The church was filled with sorrowing friends, both young and old, who followed the remains to the cemetery. At the hour of the funeral in Lexington a memorial service was additionally conducted at the Augusta Military Academy, in which all of the cadets took part. The hymns sung at the church were, "Abide With Me," and "Paradise, Oh Paradise"; at the cemetery, "Nearer My God to Thee."

Katie's brother Seymour wrote from the Panama Canal on March 23, 1916: "Dearest Kit:—We have just received poor Doddy's [Greenlee's] cablegram. We are shocked, and stunned. . . . I wish there were anything we could do to help you."

Also on March 23, Miss Teensie, whom Katie never failed to visit while in Harrisonburg, wrote: "Truly, God's ways are past finding out. I will direct this to you, dear Greenlee, so that the heart-broken little Mother need not see it, only let her know I have written and am praying that she may be sustained. . . . He was so bright and handsome, so full of brightest promise. My anxiety is great—for Katie, and your other son, and for you. . . . With sincerest love, Cousin Teensie."

A childhood friend of Gee's who had grown up next door wrote: "My Dear Mrs. Letcher, Mother has just sent me the paper with the acc. of dear Gee's death, . . . [W]hen I first saw it the tears just ran from my eyes. Once more telling you of my tender sympathy, as Gee was always one of my best friends and playmates. I hope I always remain your friend. Jack R. Mead."

*Robert E. Lee Memorial
Church, Lexington,
Virginia, c. 1900*

Virginia Paul, who was working in Florence, South Carolina, wrote to her sister: "My precious Katherine, It is so terribly hard to feel that all our love can not take this burden from your heart, when we would so gladly bear all we could to lift any shadow from your dear life. I think of you every single moment and of your wonderful strength and courage. If it had been possible my own life would have been such a little thing to give to have saved him to you. Our splendid boy. Virginia."

Greenlee's sister wrote from Burke, Maryland: "Dear Green and Katherine,

Houston's letter has just come bringing the sorrowful news of our loss. Dear, bright, handsome Gee,—it seems impossible that he has passed from sight. . . . We pray for you both in this hour of desolation and suffering. . . . Lovingly, Your sister, Maggie Letcher Showell."

Cosby Bell wrote, "Dear Mr. and Mrs. Letcher:—The word that came to us this afternoon over the telephone has shocked and appalled me in a way that I cannot put into words. Two years ago the news came to me in almost the same way of my younger brother's death."

Greenlee's godmother, Robert E. Lee's daughter, wrote to Katie: "Dear Mrs. Letcher—I can never tell you how distressed I was at hearing of dear Greenlee's *death*. I loved him dearly—& he was always so sweet & *affectionate* and I remember so *well* his coming up & kissing me *last* fall & I so surprised to see a man instead of a little boy. . . . I think of you all all the time, and wish I could help you in some way—Affy, Mary Custis Lee."

A sympathetic mother of a classmate who seems not to have known Katie personally wrote: "Our two youngest children, Dan and Ellen, were schoolmates of Gee. . . . They both admired and loved him, and in their behalf as well as my own I would love you to know how impressed and saddened they seem by the sad tidings . . . and how sorry I am for you in this great baptism of sorrow that of giving back to the invisible world the fresh bright-manly young life of your son, untarnished by life's conflicts and trial. I hope you are well and that your eyes are giving you less trouble. I remember they were not strong when we lived in Lexington. Very sincerely yours, Fanny C. Wilson."

The next letter is from the girl "Katharine" who had written to Gee earlier in the year: "My dear Mrs. Letcher, You don't know how sorry I was to hear about Greenlee. Jack Mead told me last sunday night it shocked me so that I haven't been [able] to do anything since then. Greenlee hadn't written to me since the last of February, but I had no idea that he was even sick. In his last letter he didn't say anything about being sick, but he said that he expected to go home. . . . The first person I thought of when Jack told me was you, his dear mother and how you have suffered. If I had had any idea that he was sick I would have written right away. Please send me a picture of him. . . . With all my love, Kat Marshall."

Gee's first cousin, Letcher Harrison,[70] then a student at the University of Virginia, who had lost both his own parents recently, wrote: "My dear Aunt Katherine, You know how dearly I loved Gee, and what a terrible blow this is to me. . . . It seems as though all of us had been through more than we could bear. . . . Now I have nobody left. You have 'Buz' to love and devote yourself to. And Gee lived long enough to show what a splendid boy he was, and yet remained unstained by temptation and sin. Such a memory is priceless."

Lilian, who served her family selflessly, apparently flew to Katie's side. She stayed with Katie for many months after Gee died, leaving her only to go nurse their brother's fiancée, Frances Dannenhower, through her final illness. On August 1, 1916, four and a half months after Gee's death, Katie wrote to her while she was briefly in Harrisonburg, "Darling Didgy, You don't know how I've missed you, but am so glad for you to be out of this sorrowful house for awhile. I can never, never tell you what it has been to have you here, what it meant to have you always with Gee when I was so blind and helpless I was only in the way, and to have you here through all the endless days since. I don't know how I should have ever gotten through them without you—there was never anybody so sweet—let us hear how Frances is. With greatest love to you all, Katherine."

In 1931, when Buz was in the Marine Corps, Katie wrote him a remarkable letter about Gee's death. Although out of sequence, it seems to belong here. His mother wrote him rarely, but Daddy kept in his shaving kit one letter from her, received while he was stationed aboard the battleship *Oklahoma:*

> My lovely Buzz, The roses came Easter morning fresh and beautiful. How like you to send them. Later in the evening I took them up to the cemetery where the grass was soft and green. Somehow since you went out into a bigger world and found your heart's dream and have seen all the beauty of seas and sky and new mountains and forests I am so much happier thinking of Gee in his new world. Of course he was always just away, but he is nearer now. I ought always to have been happy to have him there, remembering how after an hour's delirium, his fever and restlessness faded from his face and he lay for a little quiet and very beautiful and turned his head from us and looked up with such wonder and love in his eyes seeing something or Someone wonderful and lovely beyond our knowing—and was gone, to be "this day in Paradise." Mother.[71]

4 *War and Healing (1916~1919)*

Oh, we'll rally round the flag, boys, we'll rally once again,
Shouting the battle cry of Freedom,
We will rally from the hillside, we'll gather from the plain,
Shouting the battle cry of Freedom.
We are springing to the call of our brothers gone before,
Shouting the battle cry of Freedom,
And we'll fill the vacant ranks with a million freemen more,
Shouting the battle cry of Freedom.

—GEORGE F. ROOT, "THE BATTLE CRY OF FREEDOM"

Katie, despite her own pain, saw that a major distraction was in order for twelve-year-old Buz, amid the gloom of their lives, as they struggled to find balance in the face of such a senseless loss. She found a dog. Howard Keeler of Airedale Farm Kennels in Spring Valley, New York, wrote, on April 17, 1916,

My dear Mrs. Letcher,—

[T]he puppy leaves this evening. I doubt whether he will get there much before Wednesday morning. We are providing food but the Ex. Messengers are not always faithful in feeding so he may be rather empty and hungry. Therefore, feed lightly in the first few meals until his stomach gets used to food. . . . The registration papers will be made out in your son's name and will be mailed as soon as I get the returns from the American Kennel Club. . . . I think that Master Letcher and The Scout will have great times together. The pup will respond to kindness very quickly and will repay in affection and fidelity many times over. Some time I would like to have a picture of the Boy and the dog. Especially the boy. Sincerely, Howard Keeler. PS You might let me hear of his arrival.

The next day, Mr. Keeler wrote again, this time to Buz:

My dear young Friend,—I sent your puppy late this afternoon and he ought to get to his new home before you get this letter. I am sure that you will like him and that he will find a friend in you. . . . An Airedale loves to be petted just the same as a child does and in return he shows a great deal of affection for his master. Talk to him just as you do to your boy friends. He will soon learn to understand everything you say. I would like to hear from you whenever you feel like writing. Sincerely, Howard Keeler.

The dog arrived safely, and the kindly breeder wrote once more to Katie, advising her not to get the dog a distemper shot, as in his opinion they were useless: "A dog will not get the disease unless exposed to it—any more than Master Letcher will contract a contagious disease. The main thing is to keep the pup in good strong health, so that his system will throw off any germs that he may pick up. I would keep him supplied with green bones with meat on, to chew. Nothing makes a dog grow like the yolk of one raw egg daily." Although Buz enjoyed the dog, it was Katie who became absolutely crazy about Scout.

Letters like the following one must have arrived often in the weeks after Gee's death, as news spread slowly in those times. Phoebe had worked for Katie and Greenlee and knew Caroline who was currently working for them. On April 9, 1916, she wrote:

> Mr. Letcher dear Sir: I thought I would write a letter to see if you could give me a little advice about that place of ours. Lucy say that she was offered a hundred dollars for the place. And did she say anything to you? Caroline has the deeds and she wont give them up. And how much will it be to have them renewed. Mr. Letcher if it any way I can borrow any money on that place if it is please let me know because Mr. Letcher I need the money you know I am blind and I can't get no body to help me but Gertrude and I need the money. Give my love to Mrs. Letcher and the children. Tell Semore that he forgot my Christmas present and now it is all most Easter and I am looking for a Easter present. How is Mrs. Letcher's eyes. My eyes are not any better, but I am going to the Providence hospital next week. Phoebe.

Kate Marshall wrote to Katie on May 21: "My dear Mrs. Letcher:—I can not express my thanks to you for sending me the photograph, it was so kind. . . . Greenlee had promised to send me one at Xmas. We were such good friends, and

Buz, Greenlee, and Scout, 1916 or early 1917

he was so nice to me while I was there. He was certainly the fineness [*sic*] boy for any one to know, and a good friend, though he was much more to me than a friend. The night that I met you I felt as if I knew him better, he was all ways so anxious that I should meet you, his dear mother. I knew then that you meant everything to him. . . . I cannot write any more now, but when you feel able to, will you please write to me. Give my dearest love to Buzz. Lovingly yours, Kate Marshall."

In June of 1916, Katie's cousin, John Gray Paul, graduated from VMI. From Harrisonburg in the summer of 1916, John Paul wrote to Kate Paul, who was in Lexington with Katie, a long letter, saying that Frances was under the weather and that he was sorry to hear that Buz was too. Greenlee ventured out for a golf tournament at White Sulphur Springs, and Katie wrote him that Charles, her brother, was very worried about Frances and that Charles could "be more worried than anybody I know. . . . Buz has not written since he went back [to camp]—the little rascal. I suppose he thinks it isn't worthwhile till the dog finds another skunk. Hope you are having good weather and a pleasant time. We have had a lot of rain since you left. Jennie had a letter from Letcher yesterday, but I haven't seen it yet. Fannie [Letcher]'s cold continues to get better. Scout misses Buz, and howls miserably at night. With love, K."

Already the dog was working its magic on Katie. She sounded more cheerful and balanced when she wrote: "Dear Doddy—Your postal came last evening and we are glad you are having good weather for your golf and meeting the nobilities. So well did the post card work that *I told you* to write to Hugh, that he brings the mail a dozen times a day—every time a train goes out or comes in. . . . Buz is having too good a time to write. Fannie is busy moving her things into the little house.[1] With love, K." In September of 1916, Katherine Herring, a contemporary of Gee's, wrote:

> Dear Mrs. Letcher, Aunt Nan came yesterday and in looking at our kodak pictures saw this *snapshot* of "Gee" and thought you would like to have it so I am enclosing it. This is the best picture taken at camp and if it should be a comfort to you would show there was a divine reason that it should be so good of him especially. His friends talk of him so often and only wish we could express our deep sorrow and sympathy. Sister has returned to Kentucky but I will go to Hollins College this year so will not go back till June.

Katie and Scout, in the Letchers' backyard, 1917

Not surprisingly, Katie's health flagged following Gee's death. Such a blow as she had had, science now knows, compromises the immune system, and hers was never strong. Katie's sister Virginia, teaching in New York, wrote to thank Katie for a check: "It was dear of you, and just like you to send the check, and until you are a rich school teacher you can't know what a help it was in my wild endeavors to get a few things." She alludes to difficulties at home: "I think matters at home will right themselves; but if Idge can I would like her to go down for a few days. *Gin*" P.S. Kate and Charlotte should be home by now. Can't you see Seymour's grin?"

Gee, left, *at the Covenanter Camp on North River, summer 1915. Katherine Herring, a friend of mine all her life, and the mother of a close friend of mine, Henry Herring Eichelburger, sent this photo a year or so after Gee's death. She always remembered what a great friend Gee had been to her when they were young together.*

In mid-August, Greenlee was in Weston, West Virginia, where Katie wrote him: "We had a very quiet Sunday yesterday—only Hearne for dinner, Hardkins having gotten smashed up some in the game Saturday. After dinner Butler, son of the man you know so very well and were so exceedingly glad to see, came—a very attractive rat he is too. Buz and his Scout are well. Hope you had a comfortable trip." Hearne, Gee's AMA friend, was a VMI rat.

Two days after the previous letter, she wrote:

> Dear Col.—Your letter came yesterday with its many and various tales of adventure with trains and ladies and their valises. I always told you that politeness didn't require you to ask every girl you meet on the street to marry you—maybe you'll believe me after toting those valises.

That's a joke, you understand—seriously it is lovely to think of people like that in the world—you, and the man who adopted Nuzzer Mamma and myself in Baltimore—that must have been in reward of some of all your goodness to lone feminines—Buz went yesterday to "The Birth of The Nation" and was very much impressed. He really saw the wonderfulness and the greatness of it. . . . Scout cut his foot the other day, but is getting better now. Hugh brings the mail ten times a day. . . . I enclose a card from Letcher. Affectionately, K.

Other letters continue to refer to Katie's "recent illness" or express hopes for her good health. But great tragedy sometimes humbles a person, and at least for now she was kind to her husband.

From now on, nearly every letter of Katie's mentions the dog. In September of 1916, John and Frances Paul visited in Lexington, where Jennie Stevens had a welcoming party for them.

On October 24, 1916, she wrote to Greenlee, once again in Weston, where he was "looking after the interests of Hugh Goodson Wills, who owns over 1000 acres of coal and timber land there":[2] "I suppose you will be starting home to-day or to-morrow, but I'm sending this anyway to let you know we are all well and Scout's foot is better. We let your Fortnightly people know you would not be there. . . . Anyway you must be having beautiful rides through the mountains with all the red & yellow leaves. Aff' K."

All the fall of 1916, Buz had an unidentified recurring sickness that must have been especially alarming to his parents. As he recovered from a bout of illness that laid him low for his thirteenth birthday, his father and Dr. White agreed that they might avoid further sickness by keeping Buz out of wet shoes—and the only way to do that was to keep him out of shoes, period. So for the next five years, he went everywhere barefoot: school, church, parties, and dances. He delivered newspapers and eggs barefoot, and he entered VMI barefoot as a rat in 1920. At the beginning of his second class year he finally put shoes on again.[3]

On November 11, 1916, Katie wrote Gov at Pittsburgh, where he had gone on business, "Dear Col., This is just a line to say that Buz is coming on finely and there is no longer any cause for uneasiness. He is in fine spirits and Dr. McClung thinks he can go back to school in a few days. . . . No news of any sort since you left. Am hurrying to get this in the mail. Love from us all. K."

Dr. Smith from Baltimore wrote to Katie in December of 1916, with his usual grace and tact:

My dear Mrs. Letcher, I received your letter in August and later on I heard you were sick. I hope you are getting better. A very dear friend of mine died some months ago and left a devoted wife. When I see her she speaks freely of her husband. She will say in the course of conversation "Oh how Jack would have liked to hear that" or "Would not that have amused Jack!" In other words her grief is lightened by keeping her husband with her, just as he was in health. . . . Different people have different ways, but I think her way helps her to live and be a comfort to her family even in spite of her deep sorrow. With kindest regards, Yours very sincerely, Frank R. Smith.

PS My sister writes this morning that one of her sons has been killed in the war. Another has been wounded but has recovered & is going out to India & probably Mesopotamia. And yet she writes with cheerfulness!

The United States had been neutral in the great war in Europe that would come to be known to later generations as World War I, which began in 1914 with the assassination of Archduke Ferdinand of Austria-Hungary. However, the sinking of the passenger ship *Lusitania* on May 15, 1915, aimed against Britain but killing 128 Americans among nearly 2,000 casualties, led to strong feelings of hostility toward Germany on the part of Americans. At the end of 1916, Germany announced that it would pursue unrestricted submarine warfare in an attempt to break England's control of the seas. In February of 1917, the United States broke off diplomatic relations with Germany in protest of that action, and on April 6, the United States entered the war, although American opinion was not uniformly supportive. Greenlee Letcher was 100 percent in favor of entering the war, despite the resignation of his old friend, William Jennings Bryan, as secretary of state, over the matter. Letcher Harrison went to France as an ambulance driver with Pershing's army almost immediately, and John Paul enlisted.

Greenlee had for some time made speeches and written articles averring that the Germans must be stopped. He had missed out on his family's deep involvement in the Civil War; his oldest brother had been a surviving member of that romanticized band of youths who marched off to New Market and fought and died like men. Greenlee had grown up near VMI, and trained as a soldier there. Although he chose the law, he clearly yearned to be a part of the military. Unfortunately, he was also fifty, a full five years above the age limit. He battered at the doors that prevented him with his usual arsenal of optimism and determination.

In April of 1917, he tried to enlist in the army but was rejected as too old. At the time, he appeared to react to this rebuff with resignation. But two months later, while walking uptown one day, Greenlee met up with his old friend William A. Anderson, a state senator, who looked up from a letter he was reading, and said to Greenlee: "Gov, you may be the man I'm looking for." The letter was from Adjutant General Joseph Lane Stern, and the gist of it was that five batteries had been raised for a Virginia regiment of field artillery, but they could not raise the sixth one to complete the regiment. If the regiment could not be completed, the Virginia artillerymen would be scattered and their ranks broken up to complete other regiments around the country. The Virginians could serve together only if the state could raise that sixth battery. Greenlee, in the meantime, had learned that National Guard units could be composed of older men; having already been turned down because of his age, he figured the only way he could get into the service was if he brought along a National Guard unit. He and Anderson discussed what a splendid thing it would be if the old Confederate veterans would agree to sponsor them in this crisis of a world war, as it would "symbolize a loyalty to the rejoined North and South." Inspired, Greenlee contacted veterans for support and inspiration and began a campaign to raise the sixth battery. They nicknamed it "The Rockbridge Battery" after the Civil War Rockbridge Battery. A war battery required 199 men; after great difficulty and much oratory, they raised only about 160 recruits. But Greenlee thought of a way beyond that difficulty; he applied to the governor of Virginia to accept these 160 on a *peacetime* basis, which required only 135 men in a battery. Adjutant General William W. Sale said it was impossible but urged Greenlee to go to Washington and try himself.

In the middle of these plans, Lilian married John H. Flynn of Pittsburgh in Staunton, Virginia, on June 14, 1917.

Although opposed to the war, William Jennings Bryan made headlines by saying: "The quickest way out is straight through." Katie's brother, John, joined the army, writing to her in July from Fort Myer, Virginia, where he was in artillery training, of how difficult it was to learn so much in so short a time, thanking her for cakes she had sent and describing a lecture he had attended: "He [the speaker] advised us when German airplanes flew over us to stand still. . . .[F]or 'there is no better target for bombs than a lot of silly faces staring into the sky.' I see Frances nearly every week-end. She seems to be feeling very well and looks well, but the drainage still continues."

On August 1, 1917, Greenlee went to Washington three days before the deadline for the formation of National Guard units, to call on Senators Martin and Swan-

Lilian Paul, Kate Paul, and Jack Flynn, on Lilian and Jack's wedding day in Staunton, Virginia, 1917

son and Congressman Flood. He made them go with him on August 2 to see Major General Mann, head of the National Guard. He tried to see Newton Baker, the secretary of war, whose secretary told Greenlee he'd have to go to the end of the line and wait his turn. He hijacked and bribed a black messenger and insisted he take him to the adjutant general's office. It was filled with "distinguished look-ing people," so he sat down to wait, discouraged, until, to his surprise, he was called ahead of all the rest. He explained to Adjutant General William Sale how many men he had and the urgency of having only two days left. Sale told him to go back to Richmond "and I'll telegraph you my decision." Greenlee did as he was told, and three hours before the midnight deadline, the telegram arrived at his hotel: "Muster in the battery, with Greenlee Davidson Letcher as captain."

All that night and all the next day he telegraphed and telephoned back to Rock-bridge County and told the men to spread the word and gather. He took the train to Lexington that night, which was a Friday, bought tickets to Richmond for all

Greenlee and Buz,
August 1917

the men out of his own funds, and the mustering of the battery into the Virginia National Guard was completed before midnight Saturday. He bought a life insurance policy on himself for $45.85.

Greenlee feared that he would still be rejected, writing Katie: "I will be deeply disappointed if for any reason I am discharged but I expect it is probable. I would hate to leave my Battery and be unable to tender the service I had hoped to give, but whatever comes I will try to accept it philosophically."

Before he left Lexington he paid a call on his godmother, Mary Custis Lee. He told the Daughters of the Confederacy in a speech in 1936: "In the fall of 1917, when I last saw Mary C. Lee, I was warned that for her to see me, her godson, in the Uniform of the United States, would awaken resentment—but not so—she received me with loyalty, interest, and kindness."

Greenlee and his men trained in Richmond (where Katie and Buz visited him), until September 20, when they shipped to Camp McClellan, Alabama. He reveled in the training and turned out to be a natural leader, despite his irenic disposition. Katie's patriotism rose to the fore. On August 3, 1917, she wrote him in Richmond: "Dearest Doddy—Yes, it's all right whatever comes. After seeing your volunteer boys Wednesday night and all those people at the train yesterday less than ever could I try to hold back any man who belonged to me. Buz was much mortified at my having cried—dear game little cuss that he is. Pinkie [a kitten] has been leading a hard life this morning—Scout chews her up whenever he misses you, which is all the time. With love to you and every boy, Katie." In August and September, the letters flew back and forth between them: on August 4, she wrote: "Dearest Col., I am here at the office paying the rest of last month's bills. Miss Georgie [his secretary] is writing collection letters. . . . Kept letter from man who wants to sell Houston coal land, knowing you can't bother with it now."

And Greenlee replied:

> My Dear Katie:—Your letter received & I was glad to get it—I have not had a moment to write to you fellows since I have been here—did not have time to get dinner either yesterday or day before. This is a new world indeed. Everything seems to be running along all right, but we have not yet gotten organized into the Federal service. A number of difficulties have been run across. The Doctors threw out over 20 of my recruits today and I feel very badly over it. They will go back I presume tonight. The examining doctors here seem very strict. . . . Tell Buz he is in charge of the Post and must take good care of everything while I am gone. Give my remembrances to Scout, if he has not forgotten me. P.S. We finished the organization of the Battery tonight & I feel relieved—been at it with the army officers night & day—I am a Captain in the U.S. Army now & trust I will be as well disciplined as I have been by General Mudder. May Heaven be with us both.

Katie responded:

> Dear Captain—We were so glad to get your letter and to hear you had a chance of coming up Sunday for we do miss you so. It was hard luck

about the men falling out so on the medical examination, but the draft figures everywhere show about that percentage failing to pass. And you put it through—I am so proud of my old hoary headed captain in spite of all the hardship and weariness ahead for you and the loneliness for Buz and me while you are gone. And you'll be such a comfort to your men with your unfailing courage and patience and spirits. . . . With greatest love and hoping to see you Sunday. K.

Greenlee did not get leave to come home.

Katie wrote him again on August 8: "Dear Col. Doddy—We have no news, but you will want to know we are getting along all right. Buz and the other boys go every day to the V.M.I. pool. Scout, to cheer himself up yesterday went out and acquired a smell so hideous that we spent the day fleeing from him, much to his enjoyment. We've heard nothing from Letcher and John or their prospects [in the army]. The country won't hold me if they don't get something good. Have you heard anything from Charles or John Gray? With love from both of us. K." All the brothers, cousins, and Lilian's husband enlisted to fight the Germans.

As Greenlee became involved in the war effort, Katie experienced a renaissance. She mobilized herself, went to weddings, parties, and to his uptown office to work with his secretary, "Miss Georgie," on bills and correspondence. She helped Buz start an egg business—his boyish war effort. Both Katie and Greenlee were infused with patriotism, and the reader feels the excitement, the high purpose, that both felt. He wrote:

> My Darling Katie:—I am thinking of you fellows a heap but I am under pressure day and night—I have not eaten a regular dinner since I have been here—just get something to eat & get to bed when I can, but I think the thing will gradually settle down to regularity soon. The Rockbridge Boys all seem to be happy & getting along all right, except Wilson fainted yesterday which I hope was only what happens to cadets frequently in hot weather. It is quite warm here. The men are suffering from blistered feet, in which I sympathize, as the Army shoes here have given me thunder. Kicklighter passed here last night for Lexington & will return in a few days to come with us. . . . Charlie [Katie's brother] is off on leave of absence to North Carolina—will return tomorrow morning. I expect to be able to make him First Sergeant. He is looking well. A Fort Myer man was here last night, & wants to come with us as a Sergeant rather than take his chance of going into the Draft Army

with what he may get from Fort Myer. It is gratifying. . . . I hope to get home Saturday evening but cannot be certain yet. I am homesick for you fellows & old Scout & Pinkie & Caroline. We want to recruit to war strength—talk to Mr. Anderson, Ruff & Ainsworth about it & see if they cannot get some more men. The 2nd call in many places is already out. Tell them to get good men as I was thoroughly mortified that so many of the ones I brought were rejected as unfit. I have to stop. With all the love of my heart & life.

Katie replied: "Dear Captain—(How I am proud to write that!) I got your letter this morning and am so glad to know you and the boys are getting along all right in spite of the heat and busy time. I called up Maj. Anderson, Mr. Ruff & Mr. Ainsworth and they said they would do all they could. Mr. Ainsworth has two good men to send you Monday. I am glad to hear Charles is going with the Virginians. With loads of love to you, Charles and the boys. K."

And he replied, on August 14:

My Darling Katie:—Box just came, & it was so sweet of you to think of this, and I love you, Beautiful Thing. . . . Just came from Memorial Hospital where Privates Yates & Goode are, & was glad to learn they had no typhoid. They have a little malaria and will be out in a few days they think. They are in the Memorial Hospital and this was the first time I have been there as I recall since you were there, & the memory of the day you were operated on came vividly back as I passed the door of the Operating Room and I was grateful to Heaven at the thought of the difference. Had a pleasant talk with George Ansted today, an old V.M.I. man and now Mayor. I will have to close as I go to the Drill formation to give the men a little talk. Several of the Rockbridge boys will go home Thursday taking advantage of an excursion to Staunton. . . . Love to all.

On August 16, 1917, Katie wrote:

Dear Captain Letcher, Your letter has just come and we are glad to hear your men are better and that you've had at least an hour off to go to the Club and see some of your friends. The . . . excitement . . . yesterday was Nancy's wedding. Mrs. Bell spent the night here as Mr. Bell was out of town, and she says Nancy was most lovely and that she liked Mr. Elcock so much. Buz went, all scrubbed up—and barefooted—and seemed to have a very happy time—wore his loudest tie. And Nancy sent me her wedding bouquet. Wasn't it sweet of her? Father De Gryse [a Catholic priest] married them and I'm sure he met some of the town people. Hunt and John White have been staying here at night. We do miss you so—but we're terribly proud of our captain.

Lilian wrote to her brother-in-law with her usual generosity and grace:

My dear Colonel: You cannot know how pleased and how very proud we are at your energy and patriotic endeavor in raising your company, and how happy over your success. How pleased "Honest John" and Sam Houston and all the brave and hardy men who have gone before would be. But just what they expected! And how delighted and satisfied Gee must be. He is near and knows, I feel. What a heritage for our precious Buzzie. Of course it is just this spirit that has created and preserved our country. Tell Katherine I have seen on several houses a placard, somewhat after her idea—only it should be a shield. "A Man from this House is serving with the Marine Corps"—or "in the army." Everywhere we see people anxious to help and earnest in endeavor. The hotel menus are giving war portions, really about one-half the usual service on Mr. Hoover's advice. Jack's endeavors to enlist, like Charles', have so far been unavailing for active service abroad, tho we still hope. The Blaw company expects a visit from the French Commission next week regarding aid the company is to give in furthering French work. The construction companies are requisitioned by the Government, and if need be the organization sent abroad. A friend of Jack's, Mr. Harrison who was with the Red Cross in Belgium, has had thrilling experience, and Jack's sister-in-law, a sweet little French girl, on a visit home, saw the mutilated children from Belgium. I have connected myself with the Red Cross here which is quite active. At one of the branch chapters not long ago, a woman was arrested, found putting ground glass in dressings.

Katie, with more energy than she had ever had, entered into the war effort: on August 17, 1917, she wrote:

Dearest Col.—I am here at your office to talk to Miss Georgie who is sure some hardworking little recruiting sergeant. She has been up to see about the posting of the new call. They say it will be done tomorrow.

Have been too busy. Mr. Anderson has not sent out letters to these men—says it "does *no* good, perhaps harm"—which it couldn't do—Do you want them sent from your office? Have 75 on hand. Medical examination of second call begins five days from now. Lorenzo Wilson has just been in to tell me that Capt. Letcher sends his love "and don't he look fine in his uniform?" Kester was gone to Buena Vista today to try to get some men there. Bless their hearts! Hugh has just brought the mail. He is still protesting against your going to the war—the utter folly of going where there are bullets when you might have stayed at home and now he's like "Frank Glasgow . . . who says bet he'd never go to the war with such a law practice as Green Letcher has." Which must be a slander on Mr. Glasgow—or he's a slander on his boys. Also . . . be sure and write to Mr. Shields who comes to the office every morning to ask about you and breaks down about your going. Does John Gray go to Ft. Myer or stay with you?"

She reported on their son: "Buz is busy organizing a dance for tonight—trying not to get too many "sad birds" on hand. . . . Would it be better to send out the same letter as before or copies of Mr. Paxton's editorial of this week? [It] stresses the home people are of utmost importance."

Greenlee wrote on August 18: "No promotions will be made here for anyone yet. The paper suggested we might be ordered away this week but no one at the Armory seems to know. I hope to come up Friday night returning here Sunday night. I am homesick for you fellows. Tell Scout he must stop devilling you all. This is a great life and considerable fascination about it. Love love love. PS Tell Ainsworth, Ruff, and Mr. Anders to get me some good recruits—new ones come in every day but I want some more old Rockbridgers!"

On August 19, 1917, he wrote: "Dear Mudder, I am disappointed at not getting up home, but the Colonel has shut down on all leaves of absence until he is authorized by the Eastern Department. I hope to get home next week. . . . After dinner he [a Colonel] took me in their ford out in the country to call on our officer from Fort Oglethorpe who is now Captain of the Howitzers. We must have a ford after the War. You would have enjoyed the outing. When you write put in four small safety pins. Love to all." He reported having class forty-five hours a week and drills in between.

On August 21, Katie wrote: "Dear Captain, Here are your safety pins. . . . I think they could have gotten still more recruits and they seemed to make a fine impression. Miss Georgie tells me two are leaving for Richmond this evening. I do wish you had gotten the ones who got into trouble with the train jumping. Mr. Jackson speaks so well of them. If I had known in time I would have lent them money for the fines so they could have gone on with Kester. I have been up at Dr. McClure's having a tooth done this morning. Everybody asks about you. Buz . . . spent this morning at the mill. Gen. Yi looks very radiant and sends much love to you. . . . I don't know whether you saw this letter from Mamma or not. Lots of love. K."

Even his mother-in-law now blessed him with her approval, writing to Katie:

> Aren't you just busting with pride over the Rockbridge Artillery and its captain? I am. I think it was such a fine thing to organize the company in the face of discouragements and indifference and such a noble example to the older men of the state who are so situated that they could go—and to many of the young men too! It is a record for you and Buz and Buz's children's children to be proud of. . . .
>
> I suppose there will be tedious times before they get to the training camp and very hard work while they are there, but I hope they can all stand it and will come out all right. I enclose a letter from Charlie. Please return it as I want to show it to John and I also want to keep it— in case. I am . . . so thankful to have such sons. . . .
>
> John has been recommended for a captaincy in the Artillery. Haven't heard about Letcher H. but take it for granted he will get a commission. But why—why—Why! should such men as Doddy, Letcher, John and Charlie have to fight to defend the Decherts, the Newmans and such! It certainly gets my goat!—and the Dunkards! Virginia had a long letter from Kate [Seymour's wife] yesterday; she seems to be having a lovely time socially and enjoying herself in spite of threatened appendicitis. Haven't seen Fannie or Abe since my return.[4]

Katie wrote to Captain Letcher, on August 27: "Dearest Doddy—Let me hear what you expect to do, so if you will be in Richmond awhile yet we can come down, for we want to be there with you if you are going to be too busy to get home again. And I am anxious to get Buz away from here before the paralysis[5] reaches here. I've been so mad with myself for not coming over to speak to your recruits . . . . Hugh has come so I must stop. Loads of love. K."

In other letters and postals, she wrote that Charles, ordered to another unit, "was so sorry to leave you and also that he says 'the Colonel's (Greenlee's) battery will stand out from all the military organizations because the Colonel's personality is giving it an ésprit through its men unique and distinctive.'" And she says to her husband: "You . . . are doing this exactly as it should be for the spirit and devotion of your men. We are certainly proud of you."

While Katie and Buz went to visit Greenlee in Richmond in September, the maid, Caroline, wrote the following note, exactly as printed: "Dear Seymore—Your card received, found Scout geting on alright. Clifford wore over to see me Sunday. I spent most of the day up to Dr. White & Scout went with me Dr. White sayed Scout wore the findest dog in town. I hope you are all well. Caroline."

Katie wrote after their return: "I thought the men and their people stood up to the going wonderfully well. Such a crowd on such a night and at three in the morning, looked as if there was after all appreciation of the sacrifice you soldier men are making." On September 19, she wrote: "Dearest Col, Buz and I got here Monday night to be most rapturously greeted by Scout and to find that Caroline had supper ready for us and a bright fire in the sitting room. Jennie and Fannie were here and they both wanted to know all about you. Mr. Anderson came early yesterday morning—and I tell you I was no modest violet about the Rockbridge Battery! He seemed much interested and pleased to hear all I had to tell."

The next day Katie wrote: "After I got unpacked and the house all opened up and straight yesterday I wrote checks for all the bills and redirected your letters. When I went up to the office to get your checkbook I met 'old Holt' and B. Estes. They both asked all about you—and they and Frank Moore and everybody else tell me to call on them for anything they can do. Everybody is so kind and good, and people—the real people—have such a fine appreciation. Missing you so, K." She is hardly recognizable as the exhausted, sickly woman she had been.

On September 20, after an overnight leave in Lexington, Greenlee and his men shipped out for Camp McClellan, Anniston, Alabama, where they trained until the next June. Katie stayed well, writing on September 21: "Dearest Captain—Just as I was about to begin a letter Satterfield came in, hoping to find you still here. He sent his regards to you, and to Capt. Satterfield. With him was a quiet sweet boy named Carter who is here [VMI] after three years at A.M.A. He came I suppose because he had known Gee. He says Buz must surely go there. I liked him very much. We miss you dreadfully, but oh, your visit home was such a help to me—and I am so glad I went as far as Glasgow to have had that hour on the train with you. If it should be our last together before you sail I could not have wanted more. K."

About that time, Lilian wrote that "Mr. Flynn is hoping to get to go to France before long." Buz gathered apples and made apple jelly that month, and Katie wrote to Greenlee: "A funny interest for him, isn't it?"

Katie reported on a visit from the Mallories. "When I spoke of your 5 hours' drill a day she [Mrs. M.] made 'miration and said, 'Do you think you could stand that, old Man?' And I wish you could have seen his [Mr. M.'s] face light up as he said, 'Yes, I could.' Wanting to go and having to stay—that must be the hardest thing."

Under certain circumstances, stress can strengthen the human immune system. It cannot be coincidental that Katie's stamina picked up when she was needed. As must have been the case with many wives, the war was a time when she came in to her own. She helped organize dances, took an interest in local news, and in the town's business. She assumed the correspondence with Judge Brannon and other of Greenlee's friends and associates. For the first time in her life, she had a job, things to do.

In searching for a reason for her sudden admiration and support of her husband, she clearly loved a fighter—she often wrote about the dog and his fights—and with the daily irritations of life with him now gone, she saw her husband in a different, more heroic, light. Although he was too busy to write often, she kept up an amusing account of things at home. That she was well in those two years argues for her lifelong parade of symptoms being at least in part psychosomatic. In her war letters Katie responded to her husband with the enthusiasm and love befitting a devoted wife. She reported constantly on their feisty dog: "McBryde said Scout was the finest Airedale he had ever seen, the largest one, and with the finest bearing." She even seemed fonder of her husband's family. She heaped scorn on men reluctant to go to war or women reluctant to let them. "Poor Mrs. Bare is said to be nearly distracted about her son. It is all so terrible for all the poor ignorant people who don't know, or care."

Greenlee was the oldest battery captain in the war and ever after was affectionately called "Cap'n." He allowed no foul language and no roughhousing. He bragged in later years that Lexington was the smallest town in the United States that was the home station of a battery of field artillery. The battery won constant awards for spirit and outstanding performance. Nell Paxton recalls that Greenlee took a fatherly interest in his men and was forever writing people in Lexington in what *he* felt was a reassuring manner, to the effect that the beloved husband or son "hadn't been in battle yet, but don't you worry, he will soon!" He remarked often to Katie on how well he felt, despite primitive living conditions, exposure to terrible weather, and demanding and anxiety-producing duties.

On September 24, Katie wrote:

> The schools opened today and Buz was put on the Vigilance Commit-
> tee to prevent hazing, a brilliant scheme of Harrington Waddell, wasn't
> it? They had just as important and exciting a time as they could possi-
> bly have had breaking the newcomers. Buz has just come in flushed
> from a delightful morning. . . .
>
> A colored boy—I refrain from adjectives—hit Scout, who was
> going his way peacefully, on the leg with a rock and cut him so terribly
> that he would have bled to death in a very little except that we put ice
> on the cut to check the blood till Dr. Glover could get here and band-
> age it and then I had to sit up with him in the kitchen all night to keep
> him from tearing off the bandage. He was very weak for a day or so but
> seems all right now, and the cut is healing. . . . Jennie and Fannie are
> here every day—and always send their love. . . . I didn't pay my tribute
> to Dr. Glover who left his supper to come at once and was so good and
> so reassuring to poor little Buz. He wanted to hear all about you and
> your battery & seems to be the sort who will do his part when the times
> comes and he's needed.

On September 25, Katie wrote cheerfully:

> Help! Murder! Terrible times!—This morning I took myself over to
> the Catholic church, thinking it would be a quiet peaceful little service
> and that Father De Gryse and Mr. John Sheridan might rather like me
> to come since you are not here to do so. And Miss Jennie came while I
> was gone! And Buz says "she just most had a fit,—her hat fell back and
> her spectickles flew off,—and she kicked the cat . . ."
>
> I reckon I oughtn't to have gone, but I didn't think she'd ever know,
> and anyhow I'm glad I went because they seemed glad to see me. And
> Leo Sheridan told me how the boys wrote home about you and how
> you looked out for them and saw that they got a square deal and al-
> lowed no roughness or abuse from the drill-masters—I believe that is
> the secret of their remarkable drilling and that confident swing they
> have—When you took it into your head to go warring I couldn't say a
> word because I knew what you'd be to your men. And seeing you with
> them in Richmond and knowing what you are to them has been such a
> help to me in trying to bear it all. . . . Father De Gryse said he had

gotten a letter from you and that he wished he could go as your chaplain. He has applied twice but the Bishop has refused both times to allow him—a bitter thing . . . , isn't it? His brother is in the intelligence department, and, he thinks, has probably been one of the men at work on the Swedish business. Poor little father, I came away very sorry for him, priesting away when he wants to go to the war—saying prayers when he wants to go out and be a man among men . . .

Buz is very busy conserving the fruit crop. He nearly works poor little Cah'line to death making preserves and jelly. I wish we could send some to your men. Mr. & Mrs. Shields called this afternoon, but I had Scout down in the orchard and missed them.

On September 30, 1917, Katie wrote generously: "Dearest Captain—Next time you give up a circus to write to me I'll call you up by long distance to express my appreciation of the compliment but to insist you don't do it again. *Never* miss a show—you go to the circus and I'll know you are going to write when you get a chance. . . . A letter from Letcher says they expect to sail very soon—sometime the first of the month." In October she wrote:

Dear Captain—Your card about the sweaters, book etc. came this morning and Buz has just gone up to the post-office to get them off— I told him to put a special delivery stamp on the package so you get them at once. . . . Hugh's excitement is about a check for 8.35 & something that he says you and he & Judge Brannon had to pay as a fee in some suit in which Judge Brannon could not appear. What is his (Hugh's) part, is what he wants to know. . . .

Caroline has been at home for the past week on a rest and Julia— Gee's "Guba"—has been here in her place and I have enjoyed her brisk efficiency and the change in cooking. A new kitten has made us a present of itself—a pretty little gray beast to which I have taken quite a liking. It takes kindly to Scout's bullying and he lets it share his dinner, so they are great friends. . . .

Buz seems to be getting along all right at school and looks well. He is still on the Vigilance Committee.

Katie reported that Jennie Stevens had had a party for Mrs. Lee and had sent Katie and Buz up some ice cream.

A couple of days later, she wrote: "We are well, and Caroline came back this morning. Scout met her at the kitchen door and knocked her down in his rapture and then he and the little black bull-dog celebrated their reunion by eating up her hat, the bull pup prancing gaily with the rim of the hat round his neck. Got a letter from Letcher—What a high-flying time he is having—Lord Reading and Col. Lovington and Lord Northcliffe. . . . Buz and Caroline are now engaged in pickle making and we exhale onions, cabbage & vinegar to the entire neighborhood."

On October 14, Greenlee wrote that after a "very pleasant trip, we have been pitching tents all day. They say this will be the biggest camp in the whole country. . . . This country looks very much like the Valley of Va in scenery, mountains, but not in the fertility of the land. I like the climate and feel fine. We have our band of 24 pieces and ten buglers, and all the buglers sometimes blow the calls together. As I go to sleep at night sometimes I hear Taps blown 20 or more times till it is lost in the distance. They say there are about 25,000 soldiers here, and as many more coming. . . . This morning I went to Hdqrs and General Rafferty gave us a talk on cooking for the soldiers, all of which is under my supervision for my battery, as well as everything else. Tell Buz I go to school every day and night and have to study a heap harder than he does. At the Review Friday Maj. Couch said my Battery marched better than any and passed him with line about perfect.

In early October Katie wrote:

> Dearest Captain—Dr. Stevens got your letter about the taxes to-day. I had already paid them to be sure you didn't run late on them and have the receipts filed away so will just destroy the checks you sent. Frank Moore telephoned this morning that he had had a letter from you telling him about various things which he would attend to. He has been so good about telling me anything I wanted to know. I think everything is all right, so don't worry about things here. . . .
>
> Buz and I have been entirely by ourselves and I had gotten not to be so very scared with Scout sleeping in the room with us, but I thought maybe I'd better get a student so I've been biding my time, not wanting to take just anybody. Last night a boy who seemed to be the one I'd been waiting for came, and has now taken up his abode in the yellow room. His name is John Bate and he is from Louisville and has an Airedale of his own. He has sweet manners and a nice open face and looks as if he was a person we'd like—And I shall sleep more soundly.

From Camp McClellan, on October 12, Captain Letcher wrote: "Dear Mudder, I have but a moment before School and I write to tell you how much I enjoy your

210 MY DEAREST ANGEL

letters—keep em up! I don't know what I would do without them." The next day he asked her to send by parcel post "3 thickest undershirts and three thickest drawers and all yarn socks I have. Fix buttons before sending same. In red box by my bed. Had to break ice this morning to wash. Send Houty's spurs. Send card of largest safety pins. Tell Fannie I will write to her soon. Love to all."

In October, Katie wrote how delighted she was to

> hear of your furlough. Even little solemn Cah'line beamed and Scout pricked up his ears and wagged his tail most off. . . . Buz has been practicing with his rifle lately, but I think he is too close akin to the squirrels and rats to make him much of a hunter. Scout is very wet and smelly and happy in this rain, and had a joyous afternoon in the woods with Buzz. Is Frank Moore to take charge of Hugh's West. Va. affairs? . . . Our student seems a peaceable young person—only he smokes a pipe in his room's seclusion. He comes and goes so quietly we'd never know he was here—but it's a relief to have him at night much as I didn't want him. Shall I make you some bed-socks for the night?

Of the student: "He is poor and a gentleman, which makes him fit in very well. Since we had to have one to meet expenses, I think you'd be pleased with our selection." Another time she wrote that "Buz has gone to the Whitmore farm to get four or five pigeons, proposing to raise squabs. Fortunately they will at once fly away so we won't have to buy grain for them. . . . The only thing that helps for your being gone is what you are to your men—what I knew you would be to them."

Katie wrote in mid-October that "Buz and Scout have just gone up to Jennie's to take supper with Miss Mary Lee [R. E. Lee's daughter]." Their son was growing up, and Katie wrote on October 27, 1917:

> Buz was invited to a dance at Lucy Gordon White's tonight and having taken his last years good clothes for every day I had to hie in haste to Strain and Patton's and get him some new trousers. He is now completing his toilet and then he goes to escort Tina Mallory. He has harvested the pear crop and I am putting them in the garret to see if they will ripen. . . .
>
> W.&L. beat A.M.A. of N.C. here this evening—having sent a man down to learn their signals it is said by the cadets. People have mentioned your letter to the Fortnightly and how much they enjoyed it. We

are marking off the days till you come home. I'd ask Father de Gryse to dinner tomorrow but I'm scared of Miss Jennie. I feel sorry for that priest boy.

Greenlee wrote to Hugh Wills at the end of October:

Dear Hugh: [sent in care of Katie] I have been intending to write you ever since being away but you have no idea how the soldier's life here takes all your time. I am up by about daylight in the morning then breakfast by 6 o'clock and the whole day . . . is taken up by duty of some kind, drilling or teaching or studying or writing communications, or making investigations or reports or building or digging or something every moment. I am just finishing up the papers whereby my Battery subscribed for $12,750 of Second Liberty Bonds—our Battery led all the others. . . . Will Ruff is well and seems happy & thoroughly satisfied. I have made him Chief Mechanic, which increases his pay & privileges. Walker is also a Mechanic. Wilson, Thompson & Burton are Buglers. Kester & Chittum sergeants & Hussey & Kicklighter corporals—and all the Rockbridge boys are doing well & seem to like it.

I live in a tent on the hill looking down the Battery street, & the nights get pretty cold—had to break ice several times in the morning to wash. I think I will soon have a wood stove in my tent. . . . We had Dress Parade yesterday & I acted as Major of the 2nd Battalion—marched to the Parade Ground about a mile off with our Band & Buglers ahead of us & had Parade & then marched through the camp back. We have only 2 horses assigned to us now, but later will have perhaps 160.

Big Barney has a Foot Ball team and with the Band and 100 or more men are now in Anniston playing another soldier's team—we have half holiday Wednesday & Saturday. In the U.S. Army they have a way of making sure new shoes fit. First the shoes are fitted, then the soldiers stand in water to the shoe tops until the leather is fully soaked. Then the soldiers are put to march and march until the shoes are thoroughly dried on the feet. Hereafter, they fit perfectly.

I have a fine lot of fellows in the Battery & I believe they will do their duty when the time comes. We do not know how long we will remain here training. But the 28th Division has gone to France and we are the 29th. We are called the "Blue & the Gray" because made up of

Northerners & Southerners—we have men from New Jersey, Delaware, District of Columbia, Maryland and Virginia.

Keep everything straight for me while I am gone—I am counting on
you. Remember me to Miss Jennie, Wolf, Strain & Rather & Ned
Graham. Best wishes.
Sincerely your friend, Greenlee Letcher.

It was Katie who replied, as the letter found its way to her:

Your letter to Buz and the one to Hugh came yesterday. Fortunately
Hugh couldn't read it and had to bring it to me, so we got all the news
and were so proud to hear your Battery had led the rest with such a
splendid subscription to the Liberty loan. I hope they also won their
football game—they deserved to. I wish I had a section of newspaper
to publish your letter to Hugh for the benefit of your boys' home
folks. . . .

We had quite a wind storm last night and a good rain. No visitors
and no news to-day. I've moved the student boy down to the playroom—didn't disturb the books, only gave him a bed and bureau,
which leaves me upstairs to myself, and downstairs more to himself. He
is a good student, and one of much standing in the student body, a
pleasant person to have in the house and never in the way—very considerate always, and a nice person for Buz to know. I am so disappointed that your furlough will be so short. I had hoped you would be
here for a week—but my how glad I am that you've got one! K.

On October 27, 1917, Captain wrote to his son: "Dear Buzz, . . . They have
given us 30 men from one of the Va. regiments of Infantry which was broken up,
and we are now about full to the War Strength. The new men are not up to the
standard of the old, but I think they will make good soldiers. They all came from
Emporia, Virginia. . . . [I]t is thought we will be the next to go to France. . . . Tell
Mudder I do so enjoy her letters, and thank her for the apples for our men and the
comfort and Bathrobe. . . . Study hard, Old Fellow, and keep everything in good
shape for me. Love to you and Mudder."

At the end of October, Katie wrote that

Buz has been spending the day raking up the leaves in the yard—a
good deal of a job as the high wind which brought them all down in a
day, had scattered them to the top of the hill. A telegram came last

night—to Jennie from Letcher saying that because of a breakdown of machinery they had had to turn back and would probably not start again for several weeks. . . . B. Estes Vaughn took $25,000 of the Liberty bonds for himself and $25,000 apiece for three of his banks! And they do say that if he had headed the committee the farmers would have come across much better than they did because of the absolute confidence people have in him, instead of getting it into their heads that the government was going to confiscate the bonds later on.

And he responded: "This captain business is no joke, having to know how 250 men's shoes fit them and be prosecuting atty and judge and jury and Superintendent and Commandant and quartermaster and everything else at the same time."

On Halloween, 1917, Katie wrote: "*Now read this!* Dear Captain—I forgot to send you last weeks Co. news, so I'm sending it with this. You will notice on the editorial page a notice of the sweaters being knitted by the Daughters of the Confederacy for your battery. . . . [P]resent them to the men as seems best.—The wool is hard to get, which delays Miss Mary Pendleton's knitters. If you will find out how many more sweaters are needed she will know better how to go ahead. . . . Buz has gone out with a Halloweeners gang for their usual ringing of door bells and harmless whooping around. Miss Mary Lee[6] is a *sair trial* to the small boys all."

On November 9, 1917 the Roster of the Rockbridge Battery showed 187 men, within 6 of war strength, and 4 officers. "We marched three and one half hours up in a mountain called Rocky Hollow. Probably seven or eight miles. We had a number of Batteries pulled by horses, and a long line of men on foot and supply wagons. It was an interesting and inspiring experience—very like the actual thing I guess." On November 17, Captain Letcher assured Katie: "Don't you worry about anything. Everything will turn out right along. Just you and Buz keep well and keep everything moving right along."

And of course he continued his famous networking: "I have met Huger's cousin who is a Doctor—he is very pleasant & nice. Judge Keith's[7] nephew is Vice President of a Bank in Anniston—I have not yet met him but he has sent me word he wants to see me & have me at his house. T. A. Smith writes me he saw you in Lexington & asks me to come & do business in Birmingham. Dr. Denny[8] also wrote & asked me to visit him. Also Albert Howell[9] in Atlanta & Judge Tyson in Montgomery. I am trying to get a leave of absence in November to come home but no certainty. Love to all."

Early that month, Katie had written that

[w]e are subsisting on your promised furlough, looking forward to it all the time—for we do miss you so. Buz and the student boy went to the creek this afternoon on the spur of the moment and didn't invite me to go along, but left me here, not knowing I wanted to go, to pacify Scout who barked and howled at being left. . . . I do hope Charles will get his commission, but if they are only going to take half the men from this second camp and they are so much older men I feel uneasy about it. Letters from Lilian and Virginia and they both send love to you. . . . Virginia says Charlotte is . . . a raging beauty—and had a party the other day.

On November 5, Katie wrote:

Dear Captain—There is to be an election for Governor tomorrow, I believe, from a letter sent you by Frank Moore a few days ago. . . . I had a long letter from Mrs. Bell to-day. Mr. Bell has sailed, you know. She says of you, "I have been eagerly reading every word of and from Capt. Letcher in the Co. News. He has done such a fine thing and so well you and Buz cannot but be upheld by your pride in him." And "I enjoyed seeing Letcher Harrison at Garden City. He was simply bubbling with hope fulfilled—his eagerness and 'pep' were cheering to everyone." Buz has finished raking up the leaves and done it so well that for the first time the little hedge has been safe. Fannie and Sallie [Morrison, a friend] have between them knit eight sweaters for the Battery. Good work!

The change in Katie's tone is nothing short of astonishing. She continued:

When I read your letter about the other sergeant being called up "for to see and for to admire" the Rockbridge Battery I "jus' mos' bust," as Gee used to say, with pride and glory, and I know the boys did. . . .

I am sending you a letter just received from Mr. Herman's man in answer to mine asking if Mrs. H. could organize a knitting committee to help with the sweaters. Also my answer. I hope the buying question will not be raised as the sweaters were not intended as charity or merchandise but an appreciation of the men. It was like some old pussy-footed Red Crosser to come in and suggest that, to them as knows how

Kate Paul, Lilian, Frances, and John Paul, with Aunt Fannie Paul and Uncle Abe Paul holding Charlotte, at Ottobine, 1917

to give like the Jews do! . . . Any one who wants to see the war pushed and feel certain that there is no slacking up ought to just come and see how Col. Watts and Col. Bev. Tucker and them are wearing service hats. Does that sound like "Angel," and sweet and homelike? With lots of love—and it's only a week till your furlough. *K.* PS Florence Duval has just been here, but had no news, except that Miss Mary Lee comes over every day to see Mrs. Fitzhugh Lee *and is very pleasant!* Just think of that! Buz and I have been wrapping and coddling the pears from the tree and have ripened them quite successfully. I'll save some till you get here, and ain't it grand you are coming!

The furlough was cancelled because Greenlee received orders suddenly on November 29 to go to Fort Sill, Oklahoma, for advanced training. On December 8, Greenlee wrote from the School of Fire at Fort Sill:

My Darling Katie:—Several letters have been forwarded me here from Anniston but I have rec'd none since you knew I was coming here. I wrote you the night I got the order and a postal from Memphis & one from Oklahoma City, but have been able to write nothing until this evening, Saturday, which on the Army Post is a half holiday. We have had 45 hours this week in Classes and as I understand, 24 hours at a College or University is considered maximum. You can understand how we are worked here, & they say there is no let up in it. There are hundreds of officers here training in all branches. When we are out in the early morning we see a number of aeroplanes up flying, later you hear the guns in the west and can see the Infantry at trench warfare etc. A French artillery officer was a few moments ago calling on our Major, whose bed is just behind mine, as I caught his name, Capt. Ney—I wonder if he is kin to the great marshal. Tell Buz a Captain whose bed touches mine has his Airedale with him & he sleeps by or on his bed at night. The dog can't touch old Scout in aristocratic looks. He has little withers and his hair is not curly & woolly & his nose is too sharp—he can't hold a light to Scout. Thermometer was down to zero this morning —a Norther we have read about. I got an overcoat at Anniston before I left which is all right but all the officers complain of being unable to sleep for the cold last night. I thought my breath was frozen on the pillow but I may have been mistaken about that. We are all together— about 100 in the 3rd School—in one big Barracks room, beds in 2 rows like a Hospital, warmed by stoves the wood for which has been blocks & scraps left by the carpenters and scouted for by ourselves. I caught up on the road with the other five officers & we have our beds together & have become quite chummy. I have had a little cold since coming here but it has not affected me much. Been feeling fine, fine appetite & sleeping fine . . . . John wrote me you were "bearing up wonderfully"—I did not know whether to smile or not at the way he expressed it. Let us remember that you and Buz & myself are in a high adventure, and that we would ruin it all if any of us put on a long face or *felt* like doing so, and I know I can count on you & Buz going right along with me that way; and if the war lasts long enough for Buz to be old enough he will come right with me. G.D.L.

He needn't have worried about Katie, who was in fine fettle. She wrote cheerily of their Christmas plans without him, with no self-pity:

I am expecting Charlie in the next day or so as he reported to Ft. Gordon on the 15th. A card from Frances last night says she and John may come up for a day or two at Christmas. It has been bitter cold to-day with the snow frozen on the ground but Buz and Scout have been having a great time with the sled. . . . I am sending you the County News with the notice of Gen. Shipp's death. How we shall all miss him. I wired you because I knew Bennie [Huger, General Shipp's son-in-law] and Miss Lucy [his daughter] would want me to. I told them I had done so. . . . We watch every mail for news of you and Ft. Sill, and for your for-sure address. In the meantime I venture you letters any way because it makes the missing you a little better and you don't seem so far away. The thermometer here went down to 5 below last night. . . . Buz capered off to school this morning arrayed in two sweaters and his overcoat, a cap pulled over his ears till it met the overcoat collar and fur gloves—and his bare feet.

On December 18, he wrote: "Lawton [near Fort Sill, Oklahoma] is all right. If it is possible, and it is, I am busier here than at Anniston. Please attend to every-thing for me appertaining to Christmas. I am sorry I can't be with you fellows Xmas but 'I am in the Army now,' which says it all. Life here is strenuous but it seems to agree with me."

At Fort Sill, he worried: "I am not doing anything like so well as I'd hoped, as there is so much new and so little time to get it all up. Some of the Officers have their wives at Lawton. Lawton Hotel was raided and closed as a disorderly place, and with other women they were arrested." At Christmas, he wrote that "I had hoped for the Carpet in Arabian Nights that I might have reached you and gotten back to duty on time. . . . The War will be fought to the finish now." He closed: "May the future hold many Happy Xmas for us all together. Yours, GDL."

She thoughtfully sent him the "Literary Digest and the Co. News—hoping you might have time to glance at them and thinking the boys would like to see them-selves in the paper." Because Hugh Wills's job was to deliver mail to Katie when-ever it came, her letters often end abruptly, with something like "Here comes Hugh so I'll have to stop with barely time to send our love. . . . Hugh is raving crazy about the West Va. taxes. For pity sake write a post-card & tell him to wait till you come or something." Another time she wrote: "The Williams . . . were here yesterday to ask about you, and while he didn't say so, it was evident that the Wills land was what he wanted to find out about. Of course I was like Brer Fox and 'ain't say nothin.' I find he has talked to Hugh many times and that Hugh stands pat on 'whatever Green says.'"

From time to time, Katie reported delicious neighborhood gossip, including a tidbit about the strange and overdressed Bertha Howell.

> Yesterday I had no news but poor Florence [Duval]'s broken wrist but to-day I have the joyous fact to tell you that Mrs. Pratt has now staying with her Mrs. Black, Mrs. Allen Potts and Lily Coles, and is just reveling and basking in worldliness and frivolity—poor good little lady—letting them do her sinning for her. One morning as they were all sitting on the porch and Miss Bertha hove in sight Mrs. Potts dropped her knitting and cried, "Good God in Heaven! What is that?"—I didn't like to write that last, but it is so funny to think of such regardlessness of Mrs. Potts and her joy in being unregarded. I'm not without appreciation myself.

And: "Miss Lee is bossing the town to her heart's content—ruling with a rod of iron." And elsewhere: "I was so glad to hear you'd had an afternoon off and a Country Club for a little while. Wish you could have had a golf game. Hunter Pendleton is at V.M.I. this year and fell in the gymnasium and broke his arm, but gets around with it in a sling. Scotty [Huger] is at Episcopal High School. Well so long, and lots of love."

And Captain Letcher describing his life to his sister, Jennie Stevens, reported that he was

> up by daylight every morning and sometimes before & take a shower bath, & get to sleep about 10 at night and every minute of the day has something pressing. I . . . have everything almost to study up on—even *cooking*. I have written off for cook books—all that is under my direct care, cooks being detailed from the Battery for the purpose & you never saw such cleanliness in your life. A spot is reported by the inspectors if it exists. There are no sewers and everything is burned up in the incinerators which would attract flies. Men are required to eat everything up—leave nothing on their plates. Never to throw anything of any kind on the ground.

Among other things, he reported, "Ruth Lam, the famous woman aeronaut flew this evening over the camp—flying above for a long time—looping the loop again and again. I will go up at my first opportunity. . . . I have been into Anniston twice since here—a little while each time. We are in the mountains here and I am much reminded of our country. I like the climate and water."

Katie continued strong in her support:

> We were all so glad to get your letter and to hear so much about your
> camp life and that the Rockbridge Battery was head of the class and
> doing itself proud on the parade. It helps a lot to feel that along with
> the hardship you find interest and companionship and are having such
> satisfaction in your men. But I hate our comfort knowing what the
> winter will be to you all in the camps. I know you think I'm mighty glib
> and smart about you and the boys going to the war—"mighty patriotic
> for her men folks" but it all nearly breaks my heart. It has been some-
> thing I've never dared to talk to you about—the hurt of your going
> into all the horror and danger of it. And one evening in the summer
> when I saw you standing in the door and looking out on House Moun-
> tain and the trees and the sunset I knew all that was in your mind. . . .
> I pray day and night that God will bring you back safe—that he will
> take my life not yours.

And Katie continued to write cheerfully: "*Buz got his first partridge this evening!!*
Great Excitement, as you may imagine. Much exaltation and congratulations between Buz and Mr. Bate [the boarder]—I was glad Mr. Bate was here to properly
respond to the sight of the sad little limp bird, which they called 'a fine fat cock.'
Kept me from rising to their heights. We were all so glad to get your letter this
morning with all its news. . . . We forgot to put in the shirts; will send them. Am
enclosing insurance list." And, the next day, she wrote him:

> Buz was so elated by yesterday's partridge that he and Ben set forth
> again this morning but the rain drove them back—safe and dry in
> somebody's automobile—with only a couple of rabbits to Ben's credit.
> Buz has just gone up to Jennie's to dinner with Sallie [Morrison] and
> Fannie, and a late Thanksgiving turkey. There has been no mail for you
> except the collection letters and some advertisements. I think I shall
> have little cadet Carter who was at A.M.A. with Gee and Kent Ford
> also there with him to dinner Sunday. Then I'm going to have the
> meals sent in and cut down the expenses. Don't worry about Buz and
> me. Remember we have good little Mrs. Blue Hotel Moore to fall back
> on. . . .

On December 14 she wrote: "We were so glad to get your first letter from Ft.
Sill yesterday and to hear about your new camp and new friends. I told Buz again

apropos of the neighboring officer's Airedale that Scout ought to be there. All he had to say was, 'Now spose every officer took his dog and his wife—the dogs would be fighting and the wives would be rowing an' who'd get any work done. . .? In re (is that right?) of 'bearing up' Bro John[10] sent me a tract. Now you know whether to smile, don't you? Me a tract! With a powerful lot of love. K."

Greenlee described his arduous life at Fort Sill on December 15:

> My Dearest Angel: Your long looked for letter came yesterday and I was glad to get it, Beautiful thing. . . . We are pressed here to, and I fear, almost beyond the limit. We are in Section Rooms from 7:30 A.M. till 5:30 P.M. with 2 hours for dinner. And we scarcely have time to read over the lessons at night. Things are still crude and uncomfortable here. There are about 400 officers here now at school and they are building and preparing, I understand, for 1,000. Everything is crowded and rushed under high stress. It is very cold and (I hear an aeroplane flying over us now) this morning the coal was out and getting up before day in zero air is not altogether the most pleasant thing I ever engaged in— but I tell the men that I don't kick as it may by comparison with the future be *luxury*. And it seems to be agreeing with me all right. One day this week my right fore-finger was caught in the breach block of a cannon but luckily I think the worst (I hear another aeroplane going over) that will result will be the loss of the nail. Capt. Wiseman of the Danville Battery followed me here and is in the next Class. . . .
>
> Capt. Magruder[11] who was at the V.M.I. some years ago is an In- structor here now—he recognized me, & spoke and offered to help me in any way he could. He said Lyerly another old cadet was here as an Instructor but I have not seen him. Dunlop spoke to me—he is in the Headquarters here—I do not know whether he is an Officer or not— his people now live in Bristol. . . . If my Regiment goes to France before the course ends here I could not go with them but would have to follow after the Course ends. . . . [O]ur Regiment at Anniston has been moved about a mile away from its old place. I am sorry as I had them macadamize the paths etc. & they would have been kept out of the mud and now all will have to be done over again, & and the new place is not nearly so convenient as the old. . . . Last Sunday I went to the Episcopal church at Lawton about 6 miles off on the Trolley. The Dean of the Cathedral at Oklahoma City provided a very good

sermon—he was an Englishman. I may go to hear the Post Chaplain tomorrow. Lawton is the home of Senator Gore—the people seem very much down on him now, and I hope they will lick him good at the next election.[12] A Frenchman lectured to us a few days ago on "Position Warfare"—he objected . . . to it being called Trench Warfare. . . . A full Battery of French Guns are now here. . . .

The School here is not teaching men to manipulate & fly aeroplanes —only training Observers. Each man goes up twice a week. I want to go over to the Aviation Field when I get more time—at present I could not spare a moment (another aeroplane). Capt. McLendon just came in from Lawton—he is a fine fellow. I invited him & his wife to come to see us after the War. I lost my eyeglasses this week—look in the *bottom* dresser of my bureau & see if you can find Dr. DeSchweinitz's prescription—if it is there, you will find it in the lower drawer front left hand corner. Send it to me at once as my old eyeglasses are not so good. Give my love to Jennie & Fannie & Prof [Stevens] and with my heart's love to you & Buz, Aff. G.D.L.

Buz wrote, a week before Christmas in 1917,

Dear Pop, I have been intending to write to you for a long time but I did not find time. Scout is all right and so is Pinky and Bootsie. Grandmother is here she came on the 15. I mailed your Christmas box Monday. We got our reports at school to-day and I stood 11 th 3 better than last time and I made 90 on Algerbra [*sic*]. It is now 11 :10 and I have just finished studying. I went hunting and killed two partridges and one rabbit we hunted without a dog and this is very hard shooting. I went hunting out on the Zollman farm Thanksgiving but as it rained we had no good hunting. It has been very cold here lately. . . . [O]ne night it went twelve below. I have not been sick this year. I have not missed a day at school or have been late a single morning. Mother wants me to go to bed now so I must stop. Your respectful son, John Seymour Letcher.[13]

On Christmas Eve, Katie wrote that she had "sent some cards but no presents—whatever money I could spare going to the Red Cross and to the club started in Richmond by the Howitzer Ladies to send Christmas stockings to the Howitzers, the Rockbridge Artillery and the Headquarters and Supply companies.

. . . Buz and Nuzzer Mamma have trimmed the house with cedar and now Buz has gone off to get the Christmas tree and I think of the Christmases when he and Gee were little and we all went to get the trees.—But we must remember that through our unending sorrow we are faring on to the Land o' the Leal.[14] With our love, K."

On Christmas Day she wrote that

> Buz has been having as good a Christmas as he could "with Gee and Doddy away," as he said. He has had the student boy and three of the A.M.A. boys—Jennings, Hawkins and Carter to dinner and it seemed a very pleasant and harmonious gathering. There have been many cards . . . and flowers for me with books and money for Buz from various relatives. A pot of primroses [came] from Miss Mary Pendleton who is much better and sitting up—and lovely ones from Miss Maggie and Miss Lizzie and carnations from Mrs. Mallory. . . . A beautiful snow has been falling for the last hour—I have never seen one more lovely. Buz goes to a dance at the Mallorys' tonight—We've missed you so.

Katie sustained a fall on Christmas night, on icy steps, and wrote on December 28, 1917: "I was sorry afterward I had told you about my tumble, fearing you would be worried, but I'm almost all right again now—have just gotten back in bed after a sit up. . . . The Derbyshires' dance last night seems to have been a stylish affair—ice cream and cake and fruit punch and a huge box of Huylers— Huylers! . . . Zimbro[15] at Craigsville sends his rent most promptly, also the student boy is always there with his—have to dun Dessie McHenry but I get it."

His father wrote to Buz, on December 29:

> Your letter of 18th received and I enjoyed it very much and want you to write me every once and a while, and report everything of importance occurring in your camp—you know you have an important charge as my Adjutant under General Mudder. I hope you all have had a fine Xmas—I wish I could have dropped in on you. . . . Lots of the officers here were talking of their wives & little ones Xmas—so I was not alone in that regard. We have a fine lot of men here. I am the oldest man here—think of that. Some of them however are bald headed and grayhaired and I believe look older than I do. . . .
>
> I went in Xmas to go to church but our church was closed and I went to the Catholic & enjoyed it. The Priest gave a good talk and the music

was pretty good. . . . One of the Balloons here at the Aviation Camp blew up this week & I understand two men were killed. Every day we see aeroplanes up flying around. . . . We have had some very cold weather—and quite a cold snap is on now but we are better able to take it now as the Barracks are now in better shape. . . . [B]ut still life is not easy . . . . For 4 hours now in the morning we are outside, 2 hours drilling in locating a Battery in battle, and the next two in smoke ball practice, which is as if we were firing cannon and watching where the cannon ball goes—the smoke ball represents the cannon shrapnel shot. . . . They have been teaching us about automobiles—I wished that we had a Ford so that I might have learned all about them before coming here. It is expected in France that we will have much to do with autos. They are also teaching us to telegraph with the military telegraph instrument, which is called a Buzzer and combines telegraph & telephone. They also teach us how to take to pieces & put together cannon balls, American and French. We may use French 75's when we go over. I see in the papers that Gen'l Mann has been retired. He was Letcher's general. Kiss Mudder for me. Tell her I enjoyed the candy you fellows sent me very much. Make the very best marks you can at school & watch everything carefully while I am gone. With all love to mudder & you.

Throughout the winter months, Greenlee thanked Katie for the sweaters knit by the Lexington Ladies, seeing that his men got them and not keeping one for himself. Katie sent him instructions how to make a "Klondike bed" using old newspapers between spring and mattress, and between sheet and blanket, for sleeping healthy out-of-doors, and he responded: "I have never suffered from the cold at night since you sent me the comfort directions." He noted that this was the coldest winter on record.

Katie wrote in January that

Buz began school again to-day, poor little wight and is pegging away at his algebra and French while I write. He has been sleeping late during his holiday and got well rested up. We had another big snow last night and today so that it is now ten or twelve inches deep. Have had snow on the ground since the 10th of December, which ought to be good for the wheat. Idge reports coal is so low in Pittsburg they live on gas. Idge works for the Red Cross. . . . Colonel Tucker asked me to tell you that the Vestry had finally disposed of your resignation by refusing to accept it. The intense cold continues with the town so full of frozen radiators and burst pipes that the plumbers get no sleep at night.

In January 1918, Greenlee suffered a blow but reacted to it with his usual unflinching honesty:

My Darling Katie:—I was ordered to rejoin my Regiment tonight & will leave for Anniston tomorrow. It means that in the opinion of the Instructors I have not made good here in the Artillery Course, I presume. Six others received the same order, two of whom are Regular Army men. I do not know what effect this will have on my future in the Army. It may end it. But I will go back to the Battery and do my duty & let the future take care of itself. I have worked terribly hard here but was plunged into all kinds of things that I knew nothing about, such as electricity, automobiles, drawing & sketching etc. etc. and was unable to do satisfactory work in them, and especially in the observation of fire I was unable to see like the younger men. For the present do not go into any explanations, simply say that I was ordered back to Anniston. . . . I am very much disappointed but as my papers seemed better than some who remain here, I do not entirely understand it. But I trust it will all turn out for the best in some way. And if they are right, and I am not fitted for an artilleryman, I would not want to jeopardize my men by continuing with them. Let us feel that everything is for the best under Heaven's direction. I am glad to hear that you are getting all right again—of course I was worried but always let me know everything as I would be worried all the time, if I felt that you did not. With all the love of my life and heart.

Two days later on January 4, 1918, on a train "approaching St. Louis, Mo.," he finished the letter: "Not having mailed this letter, I add to it. Don't let its contents worry you too much . . . as I feel a consciousness of duty done throughout, that is the important matter of it all." There follows a long directive about money, the shortage thereof, ending, "but we will arrange it all right some day. . . . [W]hen untoward things happen to darken up the outlook, I realize more deeply than ever that there is little else beyond your love that amounts to much. My Beautiful Angel, I am, Yours G.D.L."

He visited briefly in Lexington on his way back, and Katie remarked in a note to Idge that he looked on furlough "bronzed but a little thin." Back in Anniston, he expected to be discharged, and four times in subsequent letters repeated: "Whatever comes I will try and accept it philosophically." He felt ashamed of his inability to learn as fast as the younger men, or to otherwise keep up with them, and feared that he'd be relieved of duty. Instead, he was made an intelligence officer.

His mother-in-law wrote him a lovely letter in January, saying how awfully they all missed him: "Dearest Green, . . . I suppose the others have got accustomed to your absence somewhat but to me the house doesn't seem like the same place— the town doesn't seem the same, without your cheerful, kindly bounce. And all our pride in your noble example doesn't compensate for 'the vacant chair.'" She goes on with news, then ends:

> I am glad to be here with Katie and Buz through this trying winter, though there is very little help I can give; my own home was too empty and desolate. "Mudder" is slowly improving and is up a while every day but not yet able to go down stairs. I suppose she has written about the Arctic weather. As "the oldest inhabitant" I can truthfully attest that I never knew such a long spell of such intense cold. We think constantly these bitter days of the soldiers in the camps and those "over there." Buz is doing splendidly and seems perfectly well & is very punctual in going to school and faithful and diligent in studying at night. He shows a strength of character and a perseverance unusual in so young a boy and with it all is as sweet, boyish and lovable as ever. You have every right to be proud of your son.

Katie meanwhile reported that Buz had gotten in trouble by writing a sarcastic poem, then been made to read it aloud to the class, and moved quickly to her favorite subject: "Scout had a very turbulent night last night because there was snow and moonlight and a grand neighborhood dog fight and he got in it, and so whimpered and growled and barked most eloquently all night long. The thermometer is up to 30 above today—a great relief from the bitter cold. Buz and Nuzzer Mamma were invited to dinner at Jennie's today but it was so slippery Mamma didn't venture, though Buz with his sure footed bare feet was undeterred."

Katie responded with exquisite grace to his disappointment in being returned to his battery without glory:

> My dearest Captain—Your letter mailed on the way back to Anniston has just come—and I cried to think of your disappointment. But you know you've done your duty and given your best and offered your life.

You can't be disappointed in yourself. I've always been uneasy about whether your eyes would pass and if not, let us thank God you found out in time—bitter as it will be if you can not go with your men. When Fred Greene was here he spoke of the great difficulty, the almost impossibility of a man of his age learning new things. And he and Charlie both, talking together, dwelt on how the offices in the training camps were going to the young men just out of college because their minds were still plastic—This is a possibility you have faced from the first and we will not be disconcerted by it. Dr. White was here yesterday and said I could begin to walk about the room and probably go down stairs the last of the week. . . . He heard Dr. Bell was coming back [from the army], his health not being up to his job. So you see it's a shifting process all along. . . . With greatest love and no regrets whatever comes.

In his next letter, Greenlee sent a check for $200 and instructions for paying certain bills, closing: "Thermometer below zero & snow blowing over me in tent, but I feel fine."

On January 8, Katie wrote supportively: "Dearest Captain—You said you supposed you hadn't made good. If you hadn't you never would have been sent to Fort Sill, and if with no previous knowledge of artillery your marks were better than those of some of the men retained I don't see how you can have such an idea—hard as it has been for you. My heart aches for your disappointment, but if it has been decided as the papers say that no men over fifty will be taken to France it will be, as Buz would say, 'just your hard ruck.' And we'll all be always proud of your taking a try at it and making the record you did in Richmond and at Anniston —just bustin' proud of you."

Katie wrote nearly every day, imparting such tidbits as "I hope this new cold wave is not going as far as your camp. We are getting so used to the cold weather we don't expect anything. As Idge writes, 'The weather just don't seem to be able to stop weathering.' Capt. Satterfield's cadet brother was here this evening with another strikingly handsome boy whose name I forgot being so taken up with his looks. His mother was Miss Lucy Boothe of Carter's Grove, a sister of Henry Wise's wife. I've heard you speak of her." And "Buz went this afternoon to the Lyric to see Mary Pickford in 'The Little American.' He thought it very good, as did Satterfield and the other cadet." She informed him also that "Poor Houston [Showell] had an ear frosted in the bitter cold where he is," that a "letter from Mrs. Bell yesterday says Dr. Bell has landed and is better so they hope no operation will be necessary. He was several weeks in the hospital in France. He only saw Letcher once—as he was leaving," and that "Jennie had a lunch yesterday for Mrs. Gibson and sent us some of the party. She and Fannie were here this evening. They are busy now crocheting 'Philips' bonnets' for the men in the regiment." Finally: "About your enlisting as a private in case you are not allowed to go as captain—I have nothing to say—I'm not fit to say anything to the likes of you."

On February 14, Katie wrote: "Dear Captain—I hope my valentine got to you in season with my love. Your letter came this morning, and I am sending Gee's glasses in this mail. I was going to send them to the navy when I got your letter. I hope they will do—Gee would be so pleased to have them go to the War. . . . Buz is going to put all his savings into War Savings stamps. He has been working all sorts of ways for me to make money enough."

Also in February, she wrote that "Jennie's tea-party for Frances went wonderfully, all report. . . . Hugh—poor, faithful, grateful Hugh—digs his heels in the ground and says 'Green saved that land for him and he ain't no Judas to be selling it unless Green says so and he'll lose every foot of it before he'll sell till Green writes it down in black and white.' So for pity's sake write to Judge Brannon and write to Hugh."

On February 23, she wrote that she was so glad "you had such a nice dinner party Saturday with your Bishop and clerics. That reminds me—the three of that tradition—that *true story* of the Letcher who had three kings to dinner at his house at one time and so all the Letchers have a right to walk right into the English court without being presented. Don't forget, when you land in England."[16]

Two days later, she regaled him with the story of a

> [t]hrilling adventure—narrow escape! The bell rang this afternoon and hearing Scout barking as if he would tear someone limb from limb I went down to find Father de Gryse come to pay his party call and ask about you. And while he was here Miss Jennie came in! And there was only one thin door between her and a Catholic priest! I just laid low and I suppose she thought I was talking to a cadet—but it was a close call. He has just made his fourth application to go to the army and been refused by the Bishop again—*wants* to go as a soldier but would gladly be a chaplain if they would consent to that. I think he had a pleasant hour being just a person.

And she entertained folks, for she wrote on February 25 that "Buz and the Scouts of his patrol went on a big hike to Lover's Leap Saturday—and saw a fox!!!! Great excitement and delight—Cadet Herman came last night. From him I

learned that the keydet most favored by a 'chicken' is the Big Dog and 'has the biscuits'—when displaced he is a 'Dodo.' All of which I enjoyed."[17]

In February, Buz made maple syrup "for the war effort." Aunt Susie Paul, visiting in Alabama, attended a review of the Division and wrote to Katie about how
fine Green and the men looked.

In February, Buz wrote his father:

> Dear Pop:—I have finished my lessons early tonight and I want to ask
> you about getting a horse up from the farm. Answer this in your next
> letter to mother. Do you think Starbright or Daisy will be the best one
> for me? I would rather have Starbright if you think she is safe but
> Daisy will be all right. I wish you would write a letter for me to give
> to Mr. Cox or Mr. Zimbro so that they will understand everything is
> all right. . . . We have been playing baseball a great deal and we have
> taken several hikes. Monday we climbed "Lovers Leap" and cooked
> our dinner there. We climbed from the river up and it was a hard job.
> Scout is all right and so is Pinkey. I stood 4th on my exam report and
> passed all of my studies. We have been having very warm weather
> lately and I would like to have the horse pretty soon. Mother and
> Grandma are both all right. Hoping you are all right I am, Your re-
> spectful son, John Seymour Letcher.

On February 27, Katie wrote: "Enclosed find addressed envelope in which
please send copy of roll of officers and men of Rockbridge Artillery. Mrs. Dold
died Friday. I sent some flowers, and a note from you and myself to poor old H.A.
Mrs. McAlphin had heard you were at home (!) and telephoned yesterday to ask
about her boy. How I wish you were—Won't there be a furlough soon? . . . Buz
wrote you last night about a horse. Mr. Cox says Starbright would not be safe."

On March 3 she wrote of a visit from one of Greenlee's men who "says he is as
happy as he is well and feels as if he 'had just begun to live.'" She took some
"chocolate and whipped cream" to a sick neighbor and was full of news: "I showed
the picture of the battery to Mr. Brady Ayres this morning and he thought they
were 'a fine lot of fellows.' Also he said tell you to drop him a card and tell him
how his boy is getting along. Here is the card. Be sure and send it. . . . A letter
today from John Gray [Paul] says he is to be married May 7th to Miss Gibb of
Warrenton. She is a very pretty little chicken I remember. . . . I saw Mrs. Turner
the other day and she asked about you as everybody does. Nuzzer Mamma is about
the same. Idge stayed over today in Petersburg with John."

On March 3, Greenlee wrote to Buz, telling him of 173 horses, and 80 more expected, that the men were learning how to care for. The weather in Alabama had warmed up, but the work was harder than ever. He related: "So many [horses] that no Battery in the Regiment have given satisfactory attention to their horses and the Brigadier General in Command has confined to Camp all officers & men of the entire Regiment, until I presume the horses & stables show satisfactory condition." He explained that his lieutenant, Rowe,

> is on close arrest in his tent—he went into Anniston to see his wife without permission & spent the night and on the way back his car broke down & Gen. Rafferty came along & caught him & ordered him under arrest and he is awaiting charges & trial. I hope he will come out of it all right but I hear the last one caught was put in confinement several months and fined $100.00. I feel sorry for him, in some way he got the idea he had the right to do it. When I heard of his wife coming down, I felt uneasy for him, as I knew he could not afford to lose any time now but did not think of this kind of trouble.

Rumor was rife, he said, of their going to France. He had just taken "a test on signaling in Wig Wag and Blinker and passed proficient—I have still to take Simaphone & Buzzer—I work on them every Wednesday & Saturday," going on to advise Buz: "You & the Scouts should learn Simaphone signalling & perhaps the others. The cadets could teach you, or you could get some out of some book. I bought Friday a splendid pair of Field Glasses, cost me $39.38—from the Government. I have not bought all the other paraphernalia, not knowing whether I would be accepted for Foreign Service—but having learned nothing to the contrary, I guess I will go ahead & get everything in shape for it." He related a cautionary tale:

> Last night I called a Private named Kennington before me to talk to him about his Discharge. The Doctor had reported him as a Moron with capacity of a boy 12 ½ years of age. He was a man transferred to us from the Infantry last fall with a lot of other generally poor men. As I had to report on him I wanted to investigate myself. He is a big fellow with a heavy face, and an impediment in his speech. I asked him a number of questions. Why he desired a discharge? He replied he was very nervous & lost his strength and that he could do better service in the Cotton Field than in the army. That a German bomb shell would

make him more nervous. That no girl was trying to get him out, but that he corresponded with several. I told him he looked mighty healthy and strong, but he replied "all that glitters is not gold."

Greenlee made him stay in the army.

Soon he reported to Katie of a kangaroo court that had developed, to try, through humor, to get soldiers to shape up; they tried a soldier "for not washing himself a good deal." He thanked her for socks, candy, and nuts. He discussed the Wills land.[18]

And he answered Buz: "I guess you will have to go on the train to Staunton & from there to Craigsville & carry saddle & bridle with you & ride the horse back. If Mr. Cox thinks Starbright is not safe you had best get Daisy. Write some days ahead, so that Mr. Zimbro can make arrangements to let you have her. Has he been paying regularly his rent?"[19]

Katie spoke of visiting him but did not. She reported how hard she and Buz worked paying bills, collecting rents, depositing checks, keeping business alive. On a piece of land he'd sought his brother's help with, she advised: "I don't think you can depend on Bro. John's attending to it because he is so busy with all his church work etc., and I'd feel better satisfied if a lawyer had it in charge." When it snowed, she commented: "Another joyous day for Scout." She noted that "Nuzzer Mamma and Fannie and Buz and Francis Mead have gone to the movies to see The Tale of Two Cities so Scout and I are here by selfs" and reported a small drama: "Mrs. Mallory offered some time ago to take Pinkie, and while I was up town this morning sent for her. I returned to find Ca'line swelling with resentment, in which Buz joined when he came in at dinner time—and now Pinkie is still here. And certainly nobody else will ever want her." She wrote that "Scout escorted Nuzzer Mamma uptown Monday and because it was court day and the town was full of country dogs . . . he got in *four fights,* and won them all. Doesn't it entertain you to think of Nuzzer Mamma in such a movie show of dog-fights?" In addition: "I was cutting some beef for supper last night when Scout came and stood expectantly till I says 'No—this is Buz's bone' when he went and lay down to wait till it was time for Scout's bone." Finally: "Buz has been busy for the past two afternoons fixing up the fence preparatory to getting his horse. I confess I am rather in hopes he will take up all his energies on the fence and forget the beast, or that the baseball season will open or something. I do not yearn to be all time chasing horses that get out and make Mrs. Anderson mad."

Katie pitched in wherever necessary, even trying her hand at housework:

"Caroline didn't get here this morning, having sprained her ankle, so I have been being cook and house-maid. A fluffy little gray cat came in from the cold—now I suppose we'll never get rid of it. Pinkie doesn't think much of it."

Katie could tell a story well: "Last night we had a grand aurora—all the northern sky a white light with a great shaft like a search light reaching up across the sky. I called the student boy to see it and dilated on how in that dear Harrisonburg, *my* home, we once had a lovely one, all colored streamers of *light*. And when this morning's paper came there were big headlines about all the colors of the rain-bow in Harrisonburg, when here in Lexington it was only *white*. The student accepted the fact that there is no place like Harrisonburg."

Of their son, she wrote that "Buz is taller barefooted than I am with heels on my shoes"; "Buz is goodness itself—his own brand—and never gives me a minute's trouble or worry any more. He has begun saving for more War Stamps"; and "It has been pouring rain all day, much to Scout's delight. He loves rough weather and he dearly loves to rush in all wet and smelly and see us flee from him and hear us squeal. Gen Yi is still here, very much pleased with herself to have finally had sense enough to marry her young man. Buz is fat and sassy and very engaging with his rags and dirt."

On the anniversary of Gee's death, March 23, she wrote:

> Dearest Captain—Your letter came this morning. I knew that wherever you were and whatever doing you were thinking of Gee. Always it is a great hurt to me that he could not have had the immortal glory of giving his life in this God's war—but I suppose immortal glory is what he was—and that somehow, somewhere he bears his part—certainly that his thoughts are of us and that his heart is with you and the boys he would have been with. . . . Mr. Hileman has ordered a granite cross—with the name and dates and below, the line, 'With the dew of thy youth,' from that Psalm about the glory in the hearts of young men. If there is anything you would rather have it can still be changed.

Next day, she wrote: "I think of you a hundred times a day. Thank you for the picture of the battery which is a most pleasing possession to me if only you weren't so blurred. I shall hang it in the hall where nobody can miss it." Katie's words here confirm Carolyn Heilbrun's claim that it has been the part of women to "find beauty even in pain and to transform rage into spiritual acceptance."[20]

Katie reported that her brother, Seymour, and Lilian's husband, Jack, were unable to get into the service. She also told of the death of Mary Pendleton, a neighbor who had been a particular fan of Gee's, in March: "With the news of Miss Mary's sudden and quiet passing, just a falling asleep, came a lovely bunch of yellow Easter flowers that she had been watching and saving to send to me, and the last thing she said the night before was to tell the girls to be sure and gather the Easter flowers in the morning and send them to Katherine for Gee."

She described the yard with appreciation: "Everything looks so beautiful here. The fruit trees, the flowers, and your lovely japonica hedge covered with the most charming little buds, the green wheat fields and brown hills roll to the mountains. It is cold with a covering of snow, but beneath we know that life and cheer prevail. Mamma improves."

On March 31, Katie wrote: "This has been a perfect Easter day with all the leaves and flowers unfolding in the sun. And such lovely flowers for Gee from so many people—masses of yellow Easter flowers and blue and white hyacinths. A great bunch of Easter flowers from Miss Jennie Bacon and some of Miss Pendleton's white hyacinths—and lovely ones from Idge and from Mrs. Hunter Pendleton and Mrs. Mallory. Mr. Graham stopped this morning to ask about you and to send his regards. He wants to put the picture of the battery up in his window so the people from the county can see it and pick out their boys."

Katie related a joke about two draftees: one had taken out an insurance policy for ten thousand dollars and the other, who had applied for only one thousand, said: "'What you want wid no ten thousand dollars insurance? What you gwine pay all that for?' The second draftee replied, 'What I gwine pay that foh? I reckon I know what I's doin—they ain't goin be puttin no ten thousand dollar niggahs in no front line trenches whilst they can put *one* thousand dollar ones there instead.'"

In April, she reported that "Jennie is having a fine tea this afternoon for Mrs. Fitzhugh Lee."[21] The same month, Lilian, visiting in Lexington, wrote to Captain Letcher (whom she still addressed as "Colonel"): "Here am I in the midst of the fambly but missing you so much—everywhere we miss you. . . . I stopped by Camp Lee to see John and Frances and found them both quite well. The camp is most interesting and impressive, and I was fortunate in seeing the Division Review before Gen. Cronkite. John left—Saturday we judge, for Fort Sill. . . . Jack [Flynn] has been in Washington three times . . . trying to be placed with the Dept. of Military Railroads in France. . . . [W]e sent you today a little box of coconut candy of Buz's and my making and hope it will be eatable."

At the end of the school year, Katie reported proudly to her husband that "Br'er Harrington [Waddell] the other day . . . said Buz is doing well at school, 'an unusually fine boy,' with other compliments to the appearance and character of that ragged urchin."

April 27, she wrote: "Dearest Captain—Yesterday morning I went over to see Maj. Anderson who told me he had written to you about getting the exemption board to assign you some men from this county. The neighborhood is quite busy to-day with Si Young's wedding, to Miss Ruth Nelly of Arkansas—a very unusually nice girl, I think. Buz is getting ready to raise eggs, and has been very busy fixing a place for his four hens and two guineas."

Testifying to her mental stability during this period, Katie seemed largely unconcerned when she wrote to Greenlee, "Here is an overdrawn notice from the bank. What do I do about it? I am economizing in every way but I don't seem to accomplish much in that line, do I? We have been having a fine spring rain to-day and the flowers and budding trees are lovely in it." It was as though nothing could faze her at that time.

She reported that "the cadet cheer leader, Ware . . . was killed this evening by a live wire, heavily charged and wet. It had fallen in the road down near Col. Kerlin's—I keep thinking of his people and knowing what they are going through."

Several times Captain Letcher got letters from the parents of his "boys." Here is a typical one:

> My dear Captain Letcher, It was a great regret, and disappointment to me—to learn from my son Minor, that he was to be taken from your Battery. He also was very sorry to part from you and his friends in Battery F. Of course he was delighted to be among the number selected from the Battery, thinking it means they are that much nearer to France—where they all long to be. Minor has written me of your kindness, and courteous treatment of him, which has been much appreciated by us both—and will be added to my pleasant memories of you—when you were at the University. With kind regard, and regret that my son is no longer to serve under you—I am, *Very cordially yours, Susan C. M. Wilson.*

Katie was even able to laugh at herself as wife: "I think it would be well for you to telegraph or write Gen. Anderson yourself—I'm nothing but a woman doddering around you know, and no woman cuts any ice except with her poor terrorized husband, who will do anything for the sake of peace.—Oh, Colonel, how you can boss and bully and walk over me the rest of your life!"

She passed along news that "Jennie had a letter from Aunt Maggie yesterday and she is the proud grand-mother of *twins,* Letcher Showell's little boy and girl," and "We got such a beauteous picture of Charles yesterday—John always sends his love to you, as does Charles who still pines to be with you."

In May, she wrote that "Buz is triumphant—each of his fowls has laid an egg today! Great excitement and visions of wealth. Buz and the Scouts are going on an over-night hike this evening."

The next day, she wrote, amused and amusing: "The hens didn't lay a single egg today—terrible disappointment, verging on consternation. Buz spent yesterday afternoon taking around the checks for the bills. He takes great interest in this, and it is a good thing for him in overcoming his idea that he doesn't know people well enough. His chickens are doing so well that I have to hold him down to keep him from getting too many. Mamma had a letter from Charlie yesterday. He is well but pining to be overseas. Hugh brooks no delay so I must stop."

She reported that Seymour had "broken into" a Texas training camp and was thrilled. She said that, in Caroline's absence, "I spent yesterday cooking and washing and waiting on Mamma to such an extent that I am unaware of anything else having happened. Buz is very busy bringing up his chickens according to his Agriculture book—dieting them accordingly. He finds them absorbingly interesting. No, he has not gotten the horse yet. I think the distance and the undertaking while he is so busy with his schoolwork has kept him from it. In the meantime, I hope the little horse is helping to increase the crops at Craigsville. Here is Hugh."

On May 16, 1918, she commented: "I just can't stand to think of your not getting home again—but I will stand it if it must be, and the more I miss you every day now maybe I'll learn not to be so selfish and so spoiled when you get home to stay. Colonel, there are going to be some spoiled men in this county when the war is over with all the thankful ladies just boot-licking them the rest of their lives. . . . No end of love, K." And she reported that Buz went swimming every day and as a result "he looks more than ever well and beautiful."

She wrote that she had a letter, "a very nice one—from John Gray's girl thanking us for the beauty plates. They are at Lawton—she and Aunt Susie." Another letter ended: "Didn't send any present to McCormicks—don't approve of divorce. Also with this most careful economy we can't afford these little things now—just can't do it and give to Red Cross etc."

On May 25, Katie wrote that "Rory James 'don't see what anybody wants to go to the war for' and thinks his brother Dr. James a fool because he has been trying to go. That other men are going, that other men must endure such hardship and danger doesn't seem to be anything at all. . . . This surely is a time of sifting out the souls of men—and a lot of people who did well enough before the war came don't do at all now. . . . I'm going to pack my grip in the morning so if you write or telegraph I can just run and jump on the train and come to see you." But they did not have a visit. Instead, on May 29, 1918, Katie wrote: "The Governor's letter and the job-or-jail rule is perturbing Hugh.[22] He told me this morning he hoped I would stay here this summer so I could give him his present job of carrying the mail and make affidavit that he is essential to the war in his present occupation." And on an envelope of a proclamation adjuring all Virginia men, white and colored, to get jobs or risk being jailed, Katie's mother wrote saucily: "Katie! Here is a notice from the Governor that you will either get busy or go to jail. He has evidently heard of this butterfly life you lead!"

On May 30, Katie wrote Greenlee with lots of news: "Oscar, Mrs. Bell writes, has been sent to one of the Georgia camps to take machine gun training with no prospect of going abroad for a long time. It looks like the sooner you volunteered the longer it takes you to get there, doesn't it?—Charles has been ordered to Camp Jackson to a replacement camp for artillery. John says he met a man at Ft. Sill who was at Oglethorpe with Charles, who said Charlie could get more willing work out of men than anybody he'd ever seen. Old quiet Charles that "talks funny and don't say nothin'."

She reported that "Buz's hens are coming across with the eggs right along. The chickens had some scraps of meat yesterday. Scout was interested very much—but when I said, "Chickens got Scout's bone" he changed to rage, barking furiously and trying to tear open the gate—on a big mad about it. Do you suppose the censor will let me write every day when you go over? You'll get motor-truck loads of letters at a time."

On May 31, their wedding anniversary, Katie wrote to her soldier husband: "Twenty years to-day. I am wearing the necklace you and Gee and Buz put in and gave me when it was ten years—and thinking of you—of all the goodness you've been to me and all the pride and glory you are now. . . . With dearest love, Katie."

Nearly every letter discussed Kate Paul, although the nature of her "neuritis" is not clear. At the end of one letter, Katie wrote: "How I wish you could wire or wireless yourself home this afternoon" and in another, "Well, if Uncle Sam doesn't want you, we sho'ly do. You can walk on me the rest of your life. Gen. Yi has just come in from church. I stayed home with Mamma."

On June 5, 1918, she wrote: "Dear Captain that never knew there was any time before eight o'clock, to think of your writing to me before Reveille. . . . Your pay check came safely—I do my strenuous best at economizing not only because nothing else would be a square deal to you but because I couldn't bear that we should have anything but actual necessities these days. I enclose for you the rest of Gee's allowance. K."

On June 7, she wrote, stalwart about her disappointment at not getting to visit, "I put the bonds in your box at the bank,—and redeposited the money I drew last week to be ready to come any minute to see you—I didn't think your letter warranted keeping it here—much as I want to come and have you see how grand and lovely Buz is, we both want more to do what you think best and what is best for your men. There are two hundred of them and only two of us, and anyhow they come first now. . . . Idge writes that they heard that the workmen in the steel plants etc. are keeping their own lookout for spies and when they locate one they take no chances, an 'accident' happens, and then there is one Hun less."

On June 9, Buz wrote:

> Dear Pop:—Now that school is over I have time to write to you. I was certainly glad to pass all my exams and to be through with school for about three months. I am sending you my report and I nearly won the scholarship. The two pupils who beat me are Winnie Thompson and Mildred McCorkle. This is the best report I have ever received. . . . I expect to go on an overnight hike with the boy scouts soon. Scout is all right and so is Pinkey. My chickens are doing all right and I get about 3 dozen eggs a week. I hope you are all right and I would like to live with you in camp. I have never gotten the horse from the farm but I expect to soon. Hoping you are well and happy I am, Your respectful son, Seymour Letcher.

On June 17, Katie wrote: "In a letter from Frances the other day she says, 'I shut my eyes sometimes and just think when John gets home what good care I'm going to take of him and how I'll make all the things he likes to eat and how sweet I'm going to be always'—And that's what we all think, Captain, all the time—How good we'll be to try to make up to our soldier men for all the hardship and danger. But somehow I can't see myself ever being good, can you? . . . But maybe even *tigers* will seem good then. With dearest love." At least now, Katie was able to see herself with some objectivity. Gone was her self-pity.

Greenlee and his men sailed from Philadelphia on June 27 for Halifax, and thence to Liverpool, Southhampton, and France. Greenlee preserved a "Royal Letter of greeting to the American Soldiers from King George V. Copy received by

Capt. Greenlee D. Letcher, Battery F, 111th Field Artillery, A.E.F. Handed to me after embarking & leaving England."

WINDSOR CASTLE, APRIL 1918

Soldiers of the United States, the people of the British Isles welcome you on your way to take your stand beside the Armies of many Nations now fighting in the Old World the great battle for human freedom.

The Allies will gain new heart & spirit in your company. . . .

I wish that I could shake the hand of each one of you & bid you God speed on your mission.

George R. I.

Greenlee tackled France the way he tackled all life, writing on July 19, 1918:

My Darling Katie, Wonderful trip and experiences, and the greatness of all this impresses me wonderfully. I hope I can be of service. . . . We are here now in sunny France and have but a moment to write. I had forgotten it was my birthday until I sat to write this: a beautiful day, I hope a harbinger of a bright good year. Give Buz my love and tell him I am counting on him to be a man and take good care of you while I am gone—and if the war lasts so long, to see him a good soldier some fine day. We march perhaps eleven miles again today—it is all serving me well so far and I feel fine, eat fine, and sleep fine, barring some sore feet.

Greenlee's letters from France were rare, and even at that fairly repetitive, as though he could not remember what he'd told Katie already, for he was still terribly busy. He absorbed France, the war, the entire experience, with his usual *joie de vivre*, writing from "Somewhere in France,"[23] on August 4, 1918:

My Darling Katie:—Another week has passed in this very interesting life & I am enjoying it wonderfully—everything seems to be moving all right. . . . I am again left all alone with my Battery as Friday my last 2 Lieutenants, Shipley and Andrews were ordered away to some kind of schools. I am attending school at our Battalion Hqrs and had an examination yesterday which I have not heard from yet. Our teacher is quite a fine looking lecturer named Howe, who has attended a school in France & seems to be bright and very pleasant. . . .

Attended the Chaplain's meeting at my Main Billet, a large stable, in which we found hay & straw and among other things a large wire vat of wood—80 men are quartered there. It is owned by Mrs. Marie Riviere who lives in a room in the building, & looks like a witch, but on the whole has been very pleasant. At the preaching, there were a few soldiers and some natives. . . .

We are on one of the National Highways of France leading from Paris to the ocean—all roads are fine. Have had a bad dry spell but yesterday it was broken by a good rain. . . . I went over to the town where Battalion Hqrs are this morning, . . . & attended the Catholic Church —it is about 300 years old—the lights & colored windows were very pleasant & the music was sweet. One day during the week as we came out of school we saw excitement & women crying, & learned that an embankment had given way & 3 children in one family had been killed & several others badly hurt—my heart bled for the poor mother. My men made up a purse to help on the funerals. Good news comes from the French-Germans returning—Soissons retaken etc. . . . A Frenchman by the name of Montaigu and his wife, a Scottish woman, who by the way appear to have the same aggressive appreciation for England that you and grandmother [Kate Paul] have for Rockingham—have been to see me to get help to take care of 64 cows to be sent there by the servants for 3 days—as I understand refugee cows for the front. I will have a Detail of my men patrol & herd & milk them while here. They have a fine chateau about 3 miles away—she says following the custom, she will adopt Staff Sgt. Dobyns, who with Corp'l Wray has been several times to their chateau. She invited me over and I will try & go sometime.[24] The cows are expected this evening. It is rumored that we will remain here only about 10 days but I do not know. It is beautiful around here & after the war we will come here together—any view almost is like a picture. The men are pleased here and as comfortable as could be expected, & we are being fed very well, & I never enjoyed what I ate as much in my life. Send me the County papers each week putting them under *one wrapper* each time.

He never abandoned his dream that Katie would one day be well enough to travel with him to see some of the wonders of his world. On September 21, he wrote from Camp de Mençon A.P.O.:

My Beautiful Angel, Yours of Aug. 4th came this week with Judge Brannon's letter enclosed which I return—See Mr. S. O. Campbell & have him send check for Hugh for $10 to pay his part of Wysong fee—it should have been done by Hugh & Mr. Campbell long ago. . . . Write & tell Judge Brannon I think we had best defer a sale till after the war but if he insists otherwise we will go with him as we are absolutely dependent on him in the matter in my absence. . . . There seems to be great news from the front but we have to thrash the Germans good to get a future and lasting peace, and I believe it will take three or more years to do it.

Captain Letcher's assessment of the time it would take to quell the Germans sounds in error, in light of the armistice that came less than two months later— but he was in a deeper sense correct, however, as World War II would break out only twenty years later, the Germans having not been thoroughly enough beaten the first time.

He reported the bad as well as the good:

Yesterday Old Man Cleary's son a Lieutenant died here of Spanish Influenza—you will recall Mr. Cleary as the custodian of the Howitzer Armory when we mustered. I will write him. He was so proud of his boy—I am sorry for him. We have a new major—a Regular Army man—Major Flunts, & I believe he is a good soldier and will be strict. . . . Inspection most of the morning, and Gun Squad Competition this evening. Kester has charge of the Gas Defense work—having recently been to a Gas Defense School. On every hand in the War there is the highest specialization in all kinds of subjects, each of them being a study and a science in itself. . . .

We are so rushed day & night that I have been unable to get to see the neighboring city & may not be able to do so at all. There are things I desire to purchase—I lost considerable belongings in a box of the Regiment which has never turned up. We have been getting up for the past two weeks almost every morning very early—when we fire as early as 3 o'clock, but it does not seem to bother me like the loss of sleep in old days did—I believe this army life will be a lasting benefit to me physically. I surely hope Charlie has gotten all right again—send him my love when you write to him. G.D.L.

September 29, he wrote, from the same place:

Buz by now is I guess at school again—tell him every day to study until he feels sure he knows that day's lesson & then anything will be plain &

easy to him as he progresses, but if he leaves a day's lesson behind him unlearned, it will plague him ever after. I have just written a letter to the War Dept directing my effects and any money to be given you if anything happens to me. I hope nothing unfortunate will happen, but of course we don't know. . . . Your word that Charlie had been made a Captain brings hope & pleasure to me—say so when you write him & I hope he will soon be all right again in health. . . . I never get the Town Papers any longer & both myself & the Rockbridge men miss them. Please do not suggest to anyone that I did not remain at Ft. Sill by reason of high marks for that would not be so, & if repeated as coming from you might subject me to ridicule in the army. . . . Tell Hugh that I have consented to sell at $40.00 per acre if Judge Brannon advises it. . . .

War news seems good but I do not feel that the end is yet in sight at all. . . . Rec'd a letter from Bro. John [Letcher] of 31 Aug. from N.C. & was glad to hear from him—I had written him last Sunday. I think of you fellows a heap, especially on Sundays & hope the war will victoriously end soon and our old happy life in Lexington resume again—for I love you & want to be with you, Sweet Angel—but I don't want to come til this war ends and ends right. . . .

Congratulations also to Seymour on his Lieutenancy. Also for Mr. Flynn—hope I will see him when he comes over. Is Idge coming also as a nurse? . . . We have had a great deal of rain here lately—heard some one refer to the Equinoctial storms and thought of Mother. I had hoped to run into Vannes today for a few hours to see the city but as most of the day has passed fear I cannot. . . . Tell Buz how much I enjoyed his letter & will write him when I can. With all the love of my life.

On Saturday, October 16, Katie wrote Lilian that she was "uneasy about Frances" and added, later in the letter: "Yes, I do indeed think Fambly ought to send the baby something really beautiful, but I move you be the purchasing agent. . . . I never did like that pearl necklace Aunt Susie sent." The baby in question was Charlotte Paul.

On October 18, from Camp de Mencon, France, Greenlee wrote that

the next time I write I guess we will be at or near the Front somewhere but exactly where we are not told. We have for some days been getting ready to go — preparing all equipment, turning in all surplus property, and cleaning up so as to leave the Camp here in perfect condition — our Guns etc are already at Vannes at the RR about 9 miles off. I have heard nothing more from the General as to my future work & I sincerely hope I will continue with the Battery — but I don't know. . . . All kinds of rumors as to the Kaiser surrendering etc are flying about but from the Papers each day, there is apparently very little change in the progress of affairs on the Western Front, though the Allies are advancing.

On October 26, he wrote:

My Darling Katie:—We have come this far with our Motor Truck Convoy—in connection with a Truck of the 104 French Mortar Battery we have with us about 16 men—the Convoy in all have about 115. We have rations with us. The first night we stopped at an old Chateau at Redon—somewhat in disrepair but evidently once a grand place. Beautifully located, overlooking the city with a drive up to it through a wood and a magnificent vista from the front—a wall all around with broken glass worked into the top to keep out intruders. We set up our stove on the road by the side of the chateau approached through a wood where there had been an artificial lake, & cooked supper & the men & all slept in the various rooms. We set up the Field Range between a large flower bed and the Chateau. In one of the halls there were 3 magnificent mirrors. The interior a maze of rooms & halls, & I imagined that at some day gone by kings had been guests there—all intensely interesting. . . . The next night we stayed near the Mortar Tank Hdqrs. in the edge of the 5th largest city in France, Nantes. The men sleeping in the top of a large barn & cooking in the yard, & myself & one of the Lieutenants engaging a room in an adjacent house in the bottom of which was a small eating house run by a woman & her daughter—they gave us their room. The surroundings & the people are so like the novels of Dumas.[25] The next night we spent in a Military Engineers Barracks in Angers. Last night & tonight we ate here, Tours. Saw a very poor Vaudeville here last night. Will go to a moving picture show tonight & go to bed early & get an early start tomorrow. Our trip has been most delightful—virtually a motor trip across Normandy. We have come many miles up the Loire—most beautiful scenery, & interesting places, quaint houses. Our trip from there here was up this wonderfully beautiful river valley over a splendid road & by quaint & lovely towns & farms & vineyards. One section was evidently a great wine producing locality—with many wine cellars cut in the solid rock in the hillside. And some dwelling houses likewise so cut. We have been here 2 nights & will, I guess be here over tonight. We stopped over near a vineyard, & all ate all the grapes they desired. Passed a number of old feudal castles—some in ruins. I wished to be able to stop & go through them & learn something of their history etc. Today went through & to the top of the great Cathedral here—the most wonderful carving, unprecedented in design & extent—extending to the very tops of the steeples which I guess were 250 feet high—every cornice, every window frame, every angle crammed with carvings, of faces, flowers, dogs, dragons, birds etc., each one worked out in detail and with the finest art. Most elaborate & astonishing, hundreds of feet above the ground. A magnificent view from the top. Napoleon was educated in the military I think, at St. Cyr near here. . . .

Unexpectedly ran across some earlier acquaintances in the army today. This is quite a military center—Hdqrs of Source of Supply with guards & many officers and soldiers in various capacities. A school for aviation & aerial training is here—Lieut. Herman & Sgt. Lee & Sgt. Gilliam, all of my Battery are here. Just learned that Capt. Buchanan of my Battery got his commission at Louisville & went to Siberia with an expedition of the army. We expect to join our Regiment in a few days several hundred miles further on—how long we will remain in billet there, do not know. . . . I am writing this in bed but hope you can read it.

The next day he wrote Katie that

it may all be over before we get there. I would like to get into some of it but you of course understand, I would not want it kept up at all for my exclusive benefit. The news from the Front is good—our troops are doing their share like men—and reading between the lines I think internal conditions in Austria & Germany are such as to hasten the final victory. However unless the Kaiser is over thrown in Germany there may be hard fighting yet, I think. . . . This is a great war, and we can not imagine the infinite energy, work & money required. I spent a good part of today in the Auto Repair Shop with our autos, and to see them in that small infinitesimal *corner* of the *whole,* the men, machines, materials, repair parts, structures, automobiles, etc., attached officers and millions of money just that one department required—impressed me with the gigantic work in which we are involved. A few weeks ago I went up in a Balloon & the same thoughts came to me then—that also was a most interesting experience. At the first opportunity I will go up in an aeroplane. . . .

I enjoyed so much seeing John [Paul] & Letcher [Harrison] at Camp de Mencon recently. John was well & looked fine & evidently everything was going well with him. Letcher was as entertaining as ever. . . . . He has been transferred into Intelligence Department, he writes. . . . Hope Charlie is all right again—I am proud of the first promotion to Captain from my Battery—20 of my men have received commissions.

On November 3, from "Somewhere in France" he wrote,

My Dearest Angel:—After an auto trip of several hundred miles, from the ocean in the West to a place evidently East of Paris—I am here awaiting the coming of my Battery which is delayed by the scarcity of transportation, I am told. Our trip across the country was most interesting & enjoyable—had in all about 115 men & 5 officers, most companionable & pleasant fellows. This is a town of about 350 people—I attended Mass in the old church—it has fine chimes & stained glass windows. It is a typical French country town. I have a very nice room, near the Officers Mess, where I now am writing by a small open fire & by the light of a candle. This town furnished about 50 soldiers, of which 17 have been killed—& this is about the way it is all over France. . . . Tell Gen. Nichols I saw Whiting [of VMI]. . . . At Chateau Thierry he received 18 wounds, one permanently disabling his right arm, & a part of his left foot was shot away. He says he does not suffer any longer & for some time has been sitting on court martials. . . . He seems to wear his honors & wounds with modesty. . . . Went for a Wild Boar hunt today . . . . The dogs started up a fox, a deer & a boar—some of them ran very close to me in the thick woods but I did not see them. This is one of the large forests, & so thick you can scarcely walk through it off the cutout places. There were along 16 Frenchmen with guns & dogs, the French Lt., & 5 U.S. officers, & I enjoyed it very much —I thought of Bro. Houston & felt how he would have delighted in it—the yelp of the dogs, the winding of the horns & the reports of guns, all were very stirring, & made a scene to be remembered.

It is certainly in keeping with Houty's personality that he'd have loved an exciting boar hunt. Greenlee continued:

> Yesterday evening we returned by a Hospital which exclusively has soldiers who have been gassed & shell-shocked—there are American girl nurses—Lieutenant Caulfield invited some of them to supper tonight, but whether they will be here I do not know. . . . Private St. Charles has just been in to see if I wanted anything—I brought him along from the Battery. He is a pretty good interpreter. He is from Wisconsin but his mother was French, & taught him to talk it. . . . Every village we go to he quickly makes friends, which gets him beds & meals. He is a good boy & with some humor—as all the soldiers generally have. I have enjoyed their humor on this trip. At Bloise, some woman came along looking for a soldier whom she described as a red-headed sergeant, & the whole outfit at once set to work to talk French to her & help her to find the *red-headed sergeant.* They looked under the autos, offered to go in all the yards & houses in the neighborhood, asked all sorts of questions relevant and otherwise, gave much advice pertinent and otherwise—and the lady had great difficulty getting away—without her red-headed sergeant—they insisted on her taking some other sergeant. Did not understand why she insisted on having a *red-headed* one. Discussed the merits & demerits of red-headed men & women generally. Wonderful the spontaneous humor that erupts on all occasions when playing. . . . Last night heard that a Frenchman in our party killed a large Wild Boar 300 lbs. with tusks 2 or 3 inches long—sorry I did not see it. . . . I hear John's Regiment is in active operations—our men fear we will not get in and envy any who are. Things look as if they are hastening to some kind of a conclusion unless Germany maintains an unexpected front.[26] Great deal of speculation as to what will come after cessation of hostilities.

In the midst of all this came letters from Katie, startling in contrast to the life her Captain was living: "Dear Captain, Buzz's class in Agriculture went on a hike to the mill today. I don't know how much about milling they learned, but they got great joy out of the girls' terror of a dead mouse. I am very proud of my grocery

*Greenlee in World
War I uniform,
1917*

bills this month—only 63 dollars for groceries, milk, eggs, and butter. Told of the
probability of peace, Hugh says he's 'getten so he don't trust them Germans.' I
hope they'll soon be so where the Allies want them there'll be no more need for
trusting."

Greenlee's training continued until November 8, 1918, when they advanced
toward the front as part of Pershing's drive, which had been set for November 14,
with Greenlee as his regiment's intelligence officer. In his last letter before the
armistice, he reported: "All the village people are very friendly to the soldiers. In a
neighboring town are some Negro Soldiers, and I am told the people make much
over them. The negroes told them that they are the aborigines of America, the Indians, and that they have very little to do with the white people for that reason—

Greenlee, far right, *drilling Rockbridge Battery, Howitzer's Camp, Richmond, Virginia, 1917*

that the white people are jealous of them, and the French girls seem very proud to have their attentions, one being engaged to a Negro Lieutenant, they say."

On November 8, 1918, they fell into place as part of the planned Pershing drive between Verdun and Metz with American infantry, light and heavy artillery, and air power, all pushing across France to capture Alsace and Lorraine and restore the "Lost Provinces," as they were known, to France, with their rousing epithet, "America's Gift." They proceeded eagerly, pumping up bravery with rebel yells, marching toward the front. But three days later, on November 11, less than one mile from the fighting, they got word that the armistice had been signed, ending the war. We can only imagine Greenlee's disappointment, mixed, most certainly, with elation over the victory.

On December 1, Buz wrote:

> Dear Pop: We are looking for you home before long and we will be mighty glad to see you. I still have old Daisy and ride her a good deal, Scout is all right and has not forgotten you, for if I call your name he jumps and listens for you to answer. Pinkey has covered herself with glory by capturing two big rats which had eluded all our traps for

weeks. We received our school reports last Tuesday and I stood 6 and made above 80 on everything. I have not been hunting for some time but I am going out again soon. V.M.I. are having the Thanksgiving hops and I never saw so many Army officers and fine-looking Marines.[27] I am going to start trapping again as soon as the weather gets a little colder. I went to Aunt Jenny's Thanksgiving dinner and it was some dinner. Uncle John, Aunt Loulie and Mrs. Lee[28] were there. We have been playing football a great deal lately and some basket-ball. . . . I certainly hope to see you soon. I know you were disappointed awfully not to get into the fighting. Hoping you are well and happy and will come home soon I am, Your respectful son, Seymour Letcher.

Katie, in her sympathetic role, shared Buz's understanding of her husband's disappointment at missing out on the action he'd waited a lifetime for:

It was surely hard luck for your boys to be in hearing of the guns and not have a chance to get in, but it's certainly no fault of theirs or yours. The long casualty lists in the papers make one's heart heavy with grief for the people who must go softly in sorrow for all their lives. I went at once to Mr. Hall to give him your message about his boy. I know he will be glad to get it. . . . We had the most beautiful sunset this evening I think I have ever seen—first all shining silver and then flaming gold. . . . The weather has been cool but clear and pleasant. The student boy who was coming the first of the year came yesterday to see if he might still stay when the students' training camp closes. He is very young but sweet and attractive and very evidently folks, so I shall be glad to have him. He will come in about two weeks. . . . The cadets are having their hops—and the neighborhood is over-run with girls of all sizes and descriptions. Why will they insist on being so overdressed, I wonder. . . . Buz was much interested in your account of the boar hunt, and we all enjoyed the hunt for the red-headed sergeant . . . . We are hopeful of seeing you before Xmas.

Captain Letcher did not come home for eight months. When the Rockbridge Battery returned the following summer, they lugged along a trophy, a captured German field cannon, which stands today in Lexington's courthouse yard.

From Brechainville, on December 4, Greenlee continued the description of his French adventure, the armistice having apparently lessened the pace of work not a whit. He implies he had been sick, reminding us how often it occurs that people hold up in crises as long as they have to, then collapse when the crisis is finally resolved. The men Greenlee mentioned by name were all friends from his VMI days:

This is Wednesday but I write as we are ordered to leave here Friday morning by overland march to somewhere I understand from 50 to 75 miles, and the chances are we will have falling weather, and perhaps cold—the weather here is most disagreeable—the cold seems to go to the bone. I am feeling better, but not entirely all right but I trust the march will serve me all right. I went last night in the Colonel's auto to General Holbrook's Reception & dance which took place at Chateau Royal, Brigade Headquarters, a wonderfully beautiful chateau, & exquisitely furnished & finished inside. Handsome oil paintings, the walls with Corinthian Pillars. The reception & dance room had a high pitched ceiling. Had the 111st Regiment Band, our band, the best in the Brigade. The young ladies were from the Gas & Sheet School Hospitals at La Forche. . . . These nurses have been over only about one month, & they have signed up, about 4/5 of them, 400 to remain here after peace. Gen'l Holbrook is a great dancer & the way he danced the "Hesitation Waltz" was crowned with laurels. Our Colonel Jones does not dance but he seems to enjoy being present & looking very earnestly. Lt. Col. Jones dances & seems to enjoy it. Major La Prade was also there dancing. Some officer told of a V.M.I. man from Richmond, whose father was a Stock Yard man being blown to pieces with 19 officers during the summer just immediately after they surfaced & nothing was found but his V.M.I. class ring. . . .[29] We are about ready to move now—but it is a considerable job to get ready—look after the food for the march, wood for cooking, oats & hay for horses, clothes & belongings for men etc. etc. etc.—It is raining today, & as it rains the greater part of the time, we expect bad weather. I wrote to John [Paul] yesterday sending him Seymour's letter & also one of Buz's. . . .

I enclose several French stamps to give to any of the neighbor kids who collect them. Of course we are all a-quiver for any news about going home but can learn nothing—some think we will be ordered back early next year, some that we will be held as a Resource Army of Classification—nobody knows & all kinds of rumors. A Y.M.C.A. has moved in with us for a few days but will not accompany us. The worker is a Mr. Parker of Connecticut, a very pleasant man. The Y.M.C.A. has done a useful work in this war.

Here he was interrupted, and continued: "*Late Thursday:*—Been all day pushing preparations to leave. Reveille at 5:30 in the morning. Hope Daisy & Scout are sticking to Buz all right—tell Buz to get a book & study horses like he would study his mathematics."

On December 5, Katie wrote, in high spirits:

Every mail I am hoping for a letter or telegram from you but I reckon I'll have to wait several days yet as they generally come two at a time two weeks apart. . . . Buz has been out this evening for a ride on Daisy. He takes very good care of her and keeps her brushed and curried and rubbed down—And feeds her faithfully and according to the best traditions of his Pa—just when Aunt Sarah has put his breakfast or supper on the table. If he would only take such care of himself! Did I tell you Pinkie had caught another rat—a third one? I think she enjoys her new-found popularity a good deal. . . . I had to help—or rather stand at attention—last night while Buz struggled with *a thesis* on "Lycidas." Poor little wretch, and poor old Milton who never meant any harm. I should think he had trouble enough being blind without being thrust upon children to be parsed and hated. . . . In the papers I sent last week you will see the death in France of Lt. Locher of the engineers—a son of Mr. H. A. Locher. The long casualty lists seem more unbearable now than ever and all the draftie boys of the 80th—they break your heart. . . . Dr. Henry Louis Smith's oldest boy, J. Henry, died of pneumonia at Camp Taylor last week following an attack of influenza. They were both with him and brought his body home Saturday. . . . Idge called me up on the long distance Saturday. She and Capt. Flynn were in H-burg on their way back to Pittsburgh. He had been just ready to sail and was greatly cast down that he never got to France. . . . Poor old Charles can't get over not getting into the scrap. I'm going to send him an editorial by Col. Roosevelt in last night's paper, very comforting to all those who had to serve the whole war over here—the idea being that the only question is whether a man *tried* to go or not. I reckon we'll be hearing from you in the next day or so now—and to think you will all really be coming home.

On December 15, 1918, Greenlee, now attempting to learn French, wrote to Buz that he was

in the house of a woman whose husband was killed during the first year of the War. We have our Officers Mess here and she cooks for us and is a good cook, and we have the most satisfactory mess, I think, we have ever had.[30] Our new Major, Quinlan, took Dinner with us today, he is very pleasant: and we had a good chicken dinner. Major LaPrade called in the afternoon to talk about a 11 mile march and Review we will have tomorrow. Today we will perhaps go 15 miles to some maneuvers and camp out and by reason of rain and chilliness, the weather is not pre-possessing. . . . My window looks out on the village church, 300 years old. I attended Mass this morning; met the Priest this evening when I took a new Lieutenant to billet him in the Priest's house. He was very nice and promised to lend me a French grammar. Some think we will start home by the middle of January but from some things I have heard it seems we will be here some time. I surely would like to drop in on you fellows Xmas, and will think of you fellows a heap, I tell you. Mr. Wilson got to Paris yesterday, and had a great Reception. I would like to have witnessed it. I hope his wisdom will help guide the Peace Conference right. I hope I can make a trip to Paris before I leave for home. The men in the Battery generally are well, all our Rockbridge men, I believe. Two are in the Hospital with mumps, and have left this morning. Corp'l Wray is one whose Brother is in the VMI band. You might tell him, but I am looking for him back now every day. Give my love to Aunt Fannie and Uncle Steve and Jennie, and a world of love for you and Mudder. Yours, Daddy.

Four days after Christmas of 1918, Katie wrote:

Dear Captain—I wonder what your thermometer is doing. Ours says 8 at five in the afternoon. Buz went out to coast but didn't stay long. He and Scout have great times in the snow. He still doesn't want to wash his own face, but he curries Daisy til she shines. She nickers when she sees him coming and seems very fond of him. . . . No news—except that the neighborhood is swarming with girls for the hops. Buz went down to look on last night—and reported "'bout a hundred girls and not one sad bird." Which is certainly a happy state of affairs. . . . Am sending this week's papers. Mr. Matt Paxton will tell you all about the weather. I see our new preacher man will be here soon—Mr. [Churchill] Gibson.[31] I think we are very fortunate to get him. I realize as never before your goodness to me. Always, K.

On January 4, Greenlee reported from Nouvelles Les Voisey, France:

Rich & happy this week as I have gotten two letters from you & the town papers, and a nice long letter full of news from Aunt Jennie, & a Xmas card from Bro. John & Sister Loulie. . . .

We have learned nothing yet as to when we will go to America, but from orders requiring Records to be put in shape, and Invoices of all property etc to be made up, I think our return is being prepared for— but when I can't tell, & I yearn to see you, My Beautiful Angel. Monday Tucker Pendleton and Bierne, both majors, stopped by to see me—they were in an auto & told me they were stationed a few miles from here but in another Divisional Area. Tell Morgan Pendleton that Tucker is looking well & seems in fine spirits, & must have a good record in the army as he has been promoted to be a major. Bierne ran a newspaper at Covington before the War. . . .

On my way back from the last court we came near having a bad auto accident when we went into a ditch in avoiding a collision with a Frenchman who would not get out of the road enough; but luckily we escaped damage. . . . Major Quinlan leaves tomorrow on a leave of absence for a week or 10 days & I will during his absence act as major of the 2nd Battalion—I want to go to Paris and Lille or Reims or Metz when I get my leave. . . . A Rockbridge sunset would look mighty good, I tell you—from *your* window, Sweet Thing. For a month here I don't believe we have had 5 hours sunshine all told—rains almost every day & night—no snow yet. . . . I am so glad Buz likes Daisy—not only the pleasure now, but it may be worth a lot to him someday to have learned horses. Tell him to learn to ride and take care of a horse—it will be to his advantage when he later comes into the Army. So sorry to hear of Dr. Smith's boy's death—say so to him & give him my sympathy. . . . A Recreation Hall will perhaps be erected here soon for our men, & we will begin again firing on the Rifle Range near here—all of which looks the opposite way from home. . . . Best wishes for the year & all the years to come & to you all the love of my heart & life.

Greenlee wrote of John Paul: "I of course am relieved that he came through safe & sound—but of course I envy him—we reached the advanced zone but did not get into the actual fighting. Doubtless all for the best however, as many of my men would most likely have been killed or wounded—and I particularly realize it, as I have just received notification tonight that my Farrier Oren K. Turner of Clinton, Okla. died in the Hospital—he was taken there a few days ago with a cold, not thought serious. I have had no details but I presume pneumonia set in— he was a good soldier."

John Paul wrote philosophically of the war from France, including some interesting thoughts on Europe's future.[32] In a P.S., he wrote: "Did I ever let you know that I had a letter from Guv about a month or 5 weeks ago. . . . I immediately wrote Frances an abject apology for ever having suggested that her handwriting was anything unlike the old copy-book." Greenlee's handwriting was indeed difficult, and surpassed in unreadability only by Katie's.

On the first of February 1919, Greenlee commented:

My Darling Katie:—I have received no letter this week from you or Buz & I am lonely. Thursday evening, I went on horseback with my Detail cook, blacksmith, runners, wagons and 30 horses and soldiers for a Division maneuver. About dark we reached Jonville where we expected to be Billeted & spend the night, but . . . found the place crowded with soldiers and had to turn to another town Barrbéville, where we lined up the wagons & picketed the horses in the snow, & got supper & got billets for the 3 Batteries—all together about 80 men & 100 horses. We officers all spent the night in 2 rooms in a great big house. We found an old couple there who looked like they had stepped out of one of Victor Hugo's novels. He had fought in the war of 1870, & his only son had been killed in this war. It was a very cold night, the roads were frozen & horses could scarcely keep on their feet, numbers of them fell with the men. Most of the way we covered leading them. We officers had supper at a French inn. The next room was filled with soldiers of an Engineer Battalion who were drinking and singing and joking. The old French cook lady & her husband, who repeated all orders in a loud & commanding tone—all as if taken from a French novel. We sat around the stove with the old couple & Major Quinlan could talk a little French to them. The old man set out some cognac, a liquor something like brandy. In the room in which we slept, a Baron, his wife & 4 children had once been murdered—but we slept well. The old lady gave me a hot brick for my bed which was very comfortable. At Reveille we left without awakening the old people.

And Katie, still jaunty, replied, using for the first time the nickname that would stick thereafter:

Dearest Cap'n, . . . Scout is very stylish and cocky these days. Did I tell you that Buz made the third best average in his classes in the last six weeks? I thought that doing well for the youngest boy in the grade. . . . I asked Scout just now if I must give his love to Mr. Letcher. He lifted his head and pricked up his ears then came and laid his head on my lap, showing plainly that he did. By the way, John said one of the Army sergeants who were so loving with Scout last spring, the one Buz said "cussed so awful"—said Scout was a damn fine dog—is now a captain of cavalry at Camp Lee. . . . I am still cookless, but Buzz is getting to be an egg prince. No end of what he can do with eggs.[33]

From Sylacauga, Alabama, on February 3, 1919, came a plaintive letter from the widow of one of Greenlee's men; one of several, it must have been forwarded to Greenlee in France.

Dear Capt. Letcher, . . . I appreciate more than I can say your kind letter. I was notified by the government on January 6 and . . . was so shocked and dazed that I got myself to believing it was a mistake. It took only twelve days for me to get word and I knew the usual time was five or six weeks so I hoped and prayed every minute for it to be untrue and in some way a mistake. I had gotten three letters from him only two days before in which he said he felt fine and never caught cold. It all seems so horrible and so pitiful for he wanted to get home so bad. . . .

Capt. Letcher, of course all I have lived for since I first heard this terrible news is letters from his personal friends. . . . It seems so far away over there and I am so eager to know all about his sickness. Did you see him any while he was sick? I wonder if you talked to him and what he said. If you did I would appreciate you writing me as I am so *anxious*. Capt. Letcher please write me your house address; for I expect to be in Virginia this spring and if I am in your hometown I would like to see you and talk to you about my husband's illness. Again let me tell you of my appreciation and I would indeed be grateful if you write me of any conversation you had with him during his sickness— . . .

Hoping you keep well and come back safely, I am

Most sincerely, Mrs. Hill.

On the ninth of February, 1919, Greenlee reported:

We are having more winter right now than ever before—ground has been covered with snow for some days & the thermometer day & night is far below freezing—and it is very uncomfortable, I tell you. It is Sunday afternoon & several of us are hugging an open fire of green wood. The French say that it will last till the moon changes—which has a homelike sound. The word of Buz skating over on Cameron's Pond brings back the thought of many a day gone by. In memory I can see the plank fence that ran out into the pond and willow bushes out in the middle of it & I imagine I see Buz there but I can not fit *shoes* on him for the skates to go on. I am sorry to hear of Mrs. Paxton's sickness —give her my love & I trust she is all right again. Also Mrs. Hancock —tell Mr. Hancock so for me. . . . From your letter, I take it Charlie is himself again.

Here continued notes about insurance and bills:

I have put in request to go to Paris for 3 days to get my Battery & Personal Bank accts straightened. Later I want to go to Brussels & London on my regular leave—but I do not know with what luck. . . . The country here covered with snow is most beautiful. Coming from the Pistol Range this evening you could see the snow covered roofs of three villages, and high hills or perhaps mountains with tops covered with dark forests with cleared land covered with snow running away up their sides. The sun was shining bright. It was most beautiful, all. An old church is just across the triangle in front of our house with several rich mellow bells. I have never learned just how they ring the hours but when there is a death they are rung from time to time during the day & night and the deep plaintive tones start far reaching thoughts. A villager fell dead this evening. When appealed to, soldiers go & help lay out the dead, but it does not seem to change the amount of their thoughts and emotions much. Wood is very difficult to get here for fires and is very high—as I figure it between $30 or $40 a cord. I think the

Frenchmen "do" us in this as in pretty much everything we have to buy from them—it is one of the untoward and unattractive things about France & French people. When the American soldier comes prices go up on him, and I believe that there are two prices, one for themselves, another for the Americans. I have heard so many state instances that it must be so. Another thing that I refuse to see is that so many fraudulent claims are set up for damages done by American soldiers, if what is told me so often is true—sometimes ridiculously outrageous. But I have been very fortunate in having very few against my men of this kind.

From the Camp Hospital in Bourbonne-les-Bains, he wrote, on February 11, 1919, that he had developed a hernia and had been sent there for an operation. He assured Katie of the cleanliness of the hospital and the "slightness" of the operation—although he opined that probably he would afterwards be sent home, adding, "of course I would regret not getting back to my Battery . . . , & if in proper conditions will make every effort to get back to them." He reported sub-zero weather and advised Katie to do whatever Judge Brannon advised about the much-discussed West Virginia land, although he failed to see what the hurry was, as "I feel that the value of this land and timber will not decline." He ended by saying, "I hope all will be well with me and I will come safely through, but my thoughts and heart go to you, and whatever happens I trust will be all right & best for all of us. Tell Buz I look to him to be a man with all that that implies. With all the love of my life & heart . . . Yours G.D.L."

Katie wrote on Valentine's Day that poor Buz was "doomed to analyze one of Mr. Cleveland's speeches, the understanding of which is utterly beyond him. Beside, it's a raw deal for Mr. Cleveland, that some cheapskate should republish his speeches and railroad them through the state boards of education to be crammed down the throats of helpless and resentful youngsters. He had enough lack of appreciation in his life-time without making a new generation hate him."

She then asked: "Who are you Democrats going to nominate next time? I bet on McAdoo.[34] As for the Republicans, there's nobody even to bet on—unless it's Taft. What there is of bolshevist and I.W.W. activity in this country the government seems to be handling with remarkable promptness and decision and as it's a mild winter with plenty of work and high wages it would hardly make much progress anyhow—not to mention the good common sense of the people. But I reckon you'd rather hear about that dear Lexington—Well, Buz has finished his lessons and decided that bed looks better than the hop." She reported that

Letcher Harrison in France, 1918

Seymour missed a promotion by armistice coming so early, and that Letcher Harrison carried "messages to Marshal Foch. He described the German general as 'all strung over with medals that jingled like sleigh-bells,' and adds with satisfaction that 'the Marshal was no slouch either as to uniform or decorations.' He [that's Seymour] admires Gen. Pershing immensely—as if I needed to be telling what *he* has already told you. I've used my eyes about up to the limit so I'll have to stop this little note of mine."

Greenlee reported on his successful operation on February 19:

> On the 11th, I was sent here by Major Warwick, Regimental Surgeon for Rupture—on only a few minutes notice and as soon as I definitely learned that I would be operated on, I wrote you. The operation was not considered a dangerous one, but . . . the only man in my organization who died in the first 17 months of my Battery's existence, Chief Mechanic Will Ruff, . . . died after this operation, and I had this in

mind when I wrote. I also wrote to Letcher Harrison at same time. The nurse just told me that *Capt* Harrison had asked over the phone about me—I presume this was Letcher & I hope it means that he has received his Captaincy. I will endeavor to write to him this morning. I write this on the flat of my back. I will not get up for 14 days after the operation which was Wednesday February 12th. For 5 days, I was fed only liquids and was very uncomfortable from the ether, & the cut & the constrained position, but have become now much more comfortable of course. I do not know exactly how I became ruptured . . . but it was doubtless from some sudden strain, or perhaps *rough* horseback riding. Chaplain Taylor has just come in—we have been taken from the 5th Army & put into the 8th Army Corps—what it means . . . I do not know. They say I will be at the Hospital here 2 weeks after getting out of bed—after that I do not know—I will not be fit for duty for some months. My present idea is to ask a leave for 2 months to recuperate by travel but whether I can get it I don't know. . . . The Surgeon came in, took off the bandages & plaster strips & took out the stitches & expressed himself as well satisfied with it, all much to my satisfaction. He was helped by a big jovial faced soldier from Pittsburg named Sorce, who had washed me—the Doctor & Sorce were amused at my desiring to get Sorce's kodak photo & have wings put on it as a ministering angel. . . . An old fellow they call General McLaughlin, has been in here several times—he is a Knights of Columbus worker—very funny. I was afraid of him as it was almost death for me to laugh. He left chocolate & chewing gum each time. Of course he is a Catholic. Knew Col. Murphy of Richmond. I invited him to come & see us when we all get home. Told him of John Sheridan [of Lexington]. He is evidently a fine comedian & I feel sure has done much good among the soldiers and especially in the Hospitals. He said he told some nurses in Paris goodbye & gave them each a little cake of soap so that if they fell over board they could wash themselves ashore. Four beds in this room— occupied 5A by Lt. Patterson, Veterinary Surgeon with leg broken by horse falling on it; 5B Lt. McBreeden of Military Police formerly Essex Troop, New Jersey, ulcer on cornea of left eye; 5C Capt. Jones Motor Truck co. of Front Royal, Va. suffering from sinus over eyes; & 5D myself. All most pleasant fellows & none under any physical suffering at present. I sincerely hope I may be so restored as to get back to my

Battery but I may be sent back to the U.S. with sick leave. But I believe
& trust it is all for the best.

On February 22 he reported that he continued to improve, and was led to believe

by the Doctors that my chances are to be in better physical condition
following this operation than ever before in my life—I sincerely trust
this may be so. This trouble, rupture, seems very common in the army.
I took the bed of Maj. Truman of New Jersey, who left the Hospital as
I came in and to-day Lt. Allen of New Jersey has been operated on for
same, & is in the room with us. He is suffering tonight with nausea,
followed by wrenching which causes him much suffering in the wound
of the operation. I hope I can do something for him in a few days when
I get up. Received yesterday a note, through Corp'l Wray, from the
Countess de Montaigu, renewing their invitation to visit them, & I
wrote thanking her & saying if I get a leave will look forward to seeing
them. It is so very kind of them. . . .

Bob Lee has just been in here—you will recall he was my first Top
Sergeant. He is now a 2nd Lieutenant. He is a great nephew of Gen.
Robt. E. Lee. He said he saw an order today that our Division (29th)
would sail for America in June. I hear music below—almost every
night some one comes & plays at the Hospital, but it is such a large
building, it is difficult to hear much of it. There are also frequent Picture Shows & Vaudeville for the Patients who can walk around.

Three days later, he wrote that the "day is going well with me, I think, from my
feelings—my appetite is good & I feel bright. The Surgeon changed the dressing
to-day & said it looked all right." He reported on all his roommates, concluding
that "they are all jolly fine fellows." He ended: "The nurses are as nice & kind as
they can be—one, Miss McCarthy from Pennsylvania we have seen most of & she
is fine. *Tell Buz to avoid all sudden or heavy strains or jumps.* I think of all you fellows a heap and hope to be with you soon. With all the love of my life."

From Memphis, Tennessee, Seymour wrote to Katie that they had just arrived
from Panama and that he was expecting to visit her in a few days, "leaving Kate
and Charlotte and Victoria [Panamanian baby nurse] here, and come to Lexington. . . . [W]ish I could stay a while, but don't know how long. The Washington
Office of the Canal is to arrange my transport. . . . I trust the old 'flu' has left no

aftermath of continued weakness.[35] Charlotte is 'sickish' today, as Abe might say, apparently a result of the irregular diet, the hours, and the jolts of the day-and-a-half journey from Columbia [sic]. She has been so well, fortunately, that a deviation is distinctly distressing."

Meanwhile, in Bourbonne-les-Bains, spring arrived, and Greenlee continued to mend:

> My Darling Angel:—Your cable received—also a letter from you & one from Buz & 3 issues of the News & Gazette—the first I have received since coming to the Hospital. It is unnecessary for me to say how welcome the letters & papers were. Apparently I am getting along fine—up a part of the time each day—with a fine appetite, & time passing rapidly. Today the Surgeon told me I would be ready to leave the Hospital March 12 or 15th & I am to apply for a leave during which to recuperate. I guess I will go to the South of France—Nice likely, and at the end of the leave the doctors will say whether I shall return to my Regiment or be sent to the United States. . . . I hope to be able to stay with my Battery & be mustered out with it—but I do not know. . . . [O]ur Division 29th is now on the list to sail back to America in June—this is the first authoritative information on the subject. . . . A number of the men from my Battery have been in to see me yesterday & today & they say everything is going well at the Battery and the men are well. Cold weather has gone & in the thaw, the roads have become in a bad condition, & many of the soldiers are working on them. France has splendid roads but they were not built to sustain the heavy truck traffic of the American Army. . . . Two soldiers were brought in on our floor today badly shot up by a Frenchman & the surgeons have been operating on them across the hall—I fear they are in a bad way. A young soldier who had his arm lacerated & broken in some machinery had it amputated yesterday on the floor. A great many operations are performed each day. Surgeons, nurses, orderlies who are members of the Hospital Unit are all attentive & pleasant but of course they can not show the *constant* attention shown in the Hospitals in the States, & there is a great deal of noise day & night—but you don't seem to notice it. I enjoy the fare, which does not differ greatly from army ration. . . . Love of my life, Yours G.D.L.

On March 16, he wrote from the camp hospital that he was

glad you have gotten over your neuralgia—I can sympathize with you as I have had a spell of it for several days past & on account of it did not leave the Hospital yesterday as expected. I am free from pain today & guess I will go to Base Hospital at Langres in a few days. I had an idea that it came from a tooth, & I had an x-ray photo this morning taken of it which I hope will throw light on it. The x-ray room is just across the hall from my room, & you can look through the body. This morning I looked through a soldier's arm who had been shot, & could see the pieces of the bullet. They use the x-ray before pretty much all operations & it is wonderful. I was looking the other day through a man's stomach. They had given him water with some barium salts in it, & you could follow it clear through his bowels. . . . My operation seems to be a complete success—the incision has closed & healed entirely & I feel no bad effects of any kind from it. . . . Tell Hugh I am sorry that Rooster got the best of him but glad he did not have blood poisoning from it.

On March 23, he was still in the hospital and wrote that he

had my tooth finished this morning. . . . I guess I will either leave here tomorrow for Langres Base Hospital or have the tartar cleaned off to-morrow and leave Tuesday—but what after Langres I don't know. I suffered considerably from the neuralgia caused perhaps by a tooth with defective or leaking filling which I trust was done away with by the dental work the Hospital Dentist has done. . . .

Tell Buz I was glad to have the news of that very important part of our family which is in his most particular care—that Scoutie, Daisy, Pinkie & all were doing well—but tell him he must break Scoutie from fighting for it will turn bad sooner or later if he continues. . . . *Dinner.* A very nice one. Beef & cream gravy, potatoes, peas, orange jelly, coffee, bread & butter. Everything prepared well and appetizing. After dinner walked with Lieut. Patterson, who is one of the men in our room, with a broken leg, now on crutches, to his billet up on the hill just beyond the church in the city. The French lady just across the street from his Billet, very rich, who owns the block, has been very nice in coming to see him in the Hospital & bringing him things to eat, flowers etc. As we passed the church the deep, rich, mellow bell was ringing. While at his Billet, another Lieut. there said they had just

gotten word that General Pershing would be here this evening & inspect the 29th Division, near here, just west of Fresnes tomorrow. I
would like to be with the Battery tomorrow & see him; but may catch
a glimpse of him here. Captain Goddard on our Brigade staff is now in
the room with us. Also Lieut. Maas of the Veterinary Unit 10. Both
companionable fellows. And I want all of them to come by and "break
bread" with us back home some day. . . .[A]fter after 3 months from the
operation the Surgeon says I can forget about it. As to politics, I do not
feel that I would care to go in at all—do nothing to encourage that.
. . . Sorry Buz was disappointed in the School Debate—but tell him
not to let failures for which he is not at fault, worry him, they are in-
dispensable lessons. . . . I want so much to see you fellows *& stay with
you, Beautiful Angel*—for I love you. . . . Almost every night here at the
Hospital there are either Moving Pictures or shows given by the Troops
of the different units—last night the Minstrel Show was by the 104
Ammunition Train & was one of the best yet. . . . Friday Capt. Jones of
the Motor Transfer Co. (who is from Front Royal & was a W&L U.
Man) went to Dijon where Paul Penick wrote me his sister was engaged
in Red Cross work, & Capt. Jones went to the Headquarters to call
on her but she was out & he did not see her—if I am there I will look
her up.

He wrote letters to his sister, Fannie, telling her that he had "seen some operations,
followed interesting cases, met pleasant officers, doctors, nurses, orderlies & men
here; and I also have seen the town which is interesting. There are hot sulphur
baths here and it is quite a Resort—it is the Headquarters of 29th Division. Gen.
Pershing has his General Headquarters about 20 miles from here."

Katie had earlier described to Greenlee how her mother and Fannie Letcher had
discovered a mutual love of the movies and went often: thus he wrote to Fannie:

At the Hospital here they have movies for the patients almost every
night—some nights Minstrels & Vaudeville Shows given by Troops organized out of the Regiments. At the movies I have thought of you &
Nuzzer Mudder—your dissipations & gaieties with her. Our sergeant
from the Regiment just was here & tells me I am looking better than he
ever saw me. . . . Dreamt about Henry Dold the other night—how
about Henry now?[36] Large fire here last week—a saw mill. The French
Fire Alarm by a Bugle interested me; there are very few fires in France

as the houses are built of stone & almost fire-proof. In haste—Love to all. Now Fannie don't flirt with Dold. Affectionately.

Back home, Frances Dannenhower Paul's already frail health suddenly took a turn for the worse. Possibly she had tuberculosis, although that is never clear. Lilian Paul Flynn dropped what she was doing in Pittsburgh and went to New York to nurse her. Katie sent some money.[37]

The next communique is a telegram from Lilian to Katie on March 30, 1919: "Frances died this morning. Will take her to Alexandria. Lilian P. Flynn."

The same day, Greenlee wrote to Katie from Base Hospital 53, Langres, France:

> I was transferred here from Camp Hospital 21 Bourbonne-les-Bains Thursday afternoon. At Bourbonne the Hospital was in a handsome Hotel Building said to have been built by Germans in anticipation of the war intending it for a German Hospital—that it was one of a number built with the same view. We there had separate rooms. Here I am in Ward 12, a long frame building with about 40 other officers awaiting being sent to the U.S. The beds are lined against each side with an aisle between, the windows being opaque yellow paper. We have breakfast in bed and get up when the nurses reach your bed to make it up if you desire to do so. After one o'clock a pass is given to go up into the city of Langres which is on a hill about a mile distant. This is an old walled city, one of the oldest in France, dating back to the Romans. . . . [H]ave only been up once & walked a part of the way around the walls which afford magnificent & beautiful views in every direction. A number of forts are around the city—strongly fortified. The Germans reached here but failed to capture it in 1870. . . .
>
> 9:30 p.m. Went again this evening to Langres & walked around the moat of the old city wall & attended service at the Cathedral—heard a sermon in French by a Priest in purple. . . . About 40 officers are here. . . . [S]ome have been for weeks here waiting a convoy train to take them to some port—no one seems to know when it will be here but it is expected daily. I very seriously believe that soon troop movement home will be stopped by reason of conditions in Europe, & the probability of Germany refusing the terms imposed on her but I hope it is all over and a lasting peace will be made.

On April 1, 1919, Greenlee was moved yet again, this time to Base Hospital 99 at Hyères, "which is about 15 miles East of Toulon on the Mediterranean Sea—

what will be done there I do not know. . . ." He went on to say: "I will have about 20 hours ride on the R.R. leaving here this afternoon at 4:30 and passing through Dijon—if I have time there will look up Paul Penick's sister."

On April 6, he arrived at Hyères, after spending a day in Dijon, writing that

> some of the Kings of France are buried there. One of the finest art museums in France is there which I went through with much pleasure. I chanced to go in St. Michael's Cathedral as a funeral was taking place—evidently a considerable personage as there were perhaps 12 priests, many acolytes and nuns—very impressive. . . . But after exhausting every effort to find Miss Agnes Penick, I had about given it up when a soldier who chanced to hear me ask caught the name, and told me a lady by that name a short time before was at the Y.M.C.A. engaged in Camouflage work in which he had helped her. I then went there and found that she, with several other Virginia ladies, had gone 10 days or so ago to Tours—you can imagine my disappointment at missing her; but the young lady who gave me the information was a Miss Alice Howison formerly of Ashland who knew Dr. Easter. I left there about 9 P.M.—a darky spoke to me at the Depot who turned out to be Wm. Hale, whose wife Ellen Hale once cooked for us—if you can get her word tell her I saw William who is well & wants to get home.

Greenlee was evidently back to his exhausting schedule and relentless socializing. Even missing his target, he connected with people and enjoyed himself.

On April 7, he wrote:

> As I write I look out on the Mediterranean Sea. This morning I walked to the top of the mountain behind the hotel and enjoyed one of the most magnificent views of mountains, sky and sea one could imagine. I am in fine condition in every way except the neuralgia sticks to me. I think it must come from my teeth, & yesterday they had x-ray photos taken of my teeth, & I hope I will be fixed up all right soon. . . .
>
> I hope to get to Nice & Monte Carlo while here—which they say are the most beautiful places of the Riviera. Capt. Ashe of Lexington, Miss. is one of my roommates here—he asked me if I was not kin to the *Murphys* of Miss. & I have a vague recollection that I am—ask Jennie. He is in the Medical Corps & has met a French Doctor who lives on property adjoining the hotel & took me there yesterday & they invited us to take tea. His niece, such a pretty & attractive girl, is

teaching Capt. Ashe French. They are all so cordial. Reminds me of my Grand Pont Chateau friends. Today is most beautiful, flowers are around, trees in blossom and glorious sun overhead. Uncle Sam certainly tries to take care of his sick soldiers well. . . .

I accidentally met on the train out of Toulon Lieut. Ball of Charlottesville, as you will recall, who was in Lexington several times with Letcher Harrison. He had had trouble with his ankle, looked well however. Neither of us recognized the other at first. The time I hope will not be so long now before I see you fellows again.

On April 13, he wrote, in response to a batch of letters that had caught up with him:

I would like to be looking at House Mountain with you from your window—I don't know of anything that would look better to me. . . . The request for Seymour's discharge and return to the Zone was surely complimentary to him—I am glad you saw him before he went back. . . . The check of G. C. Godfrey on the Nat'l Bank of Ardimore, Oklahoma for $15 was received. This I believe is all the money I have ever lost by loans or endorsements for my men. I note you notified the N.W. Mutual to give me a Paid Up Policy—and that the Alum Springs has paid $1,300. . . .

I have received no reply from my letter to the hospital at Chatel Goyan for information as to Dabney Kerr's death—I very much fear now that I will not be able to get there. It is a long way off of any road I can take, and it will perhaps be impossible to get leave or permission, and out-of-the-way travel on the French Railroads is almost impossible now. Tell Dr. & Mrs. Kerr how much I desire to do so, but am losing hope about it. I wrote for a photo of the grave but have received no reply & fear that the hospital has been closed up & the Americans gone. This hospital also is being rapidly evacuated to be closed. I so much want to get the picture to have it enlarged and framed to present to W&L U. . . .

This last week, I wrote Gen. Nichols and sent him a photo of the grave of Capt. Robt. Y. Conrad, Co. I, 115 Inf. 29 Div, which I secured together with statements from his Lieutenants giving the facts of his death. I want to enlarge it & present it to the V.M.I. and send his widow a copy when I get back. He died a hero & the V.M.I. should be proud of him. I would like for both the V.M.I. & W&L U. to get the photos of the graves and enlarged photos or portraits of every alumnus who died in the War with descriptive sketches. I went to Hyeres this morning & attended the English church there. The minister introduced himself to me a few days ago. I enjoyed it—a number of officers and enlisted men were there. This is a great Resort place—many hotels here, now being used for U.S. Hospitals. I enclose another advertising folder of this hotel with my room indicated. It is a magnificent place—wonderful mural paintings on the ceiling & the old chateau which forms part of the hotel. The grounds are most beautiful and highly developed. I sent by mail home a package containing the Leather Brief Case given me by Cadet McGill's father & some books, German souvenirs, cartridge box & cartridges etc. It was very inconvenient for me to carry them—I hope they will reach home safely. . . .

I was invited to Dunkin today to the home of a French Doctor whose Villa adjoins this Hotel & who also owns one of the islands off the coast, therefore I guess he is rich. He is a very sick man, probably will live only a short time. My room-mate Capt. Ashe, who is of the Medical Corps., became acquainted & took me over. The Doctor has a wife and 4 little children, and his sister-in-law with her daughter is visiting there. The daughter is extremely pretty. I declined as I went to the city to church but called after dinner & they handed around cake & wine & we all came over to the Hotel afterwards to a concert given by a distinguished cellist, who looked very much like Sir Moses Ezekiel [sculptor of *Virginia Mourning Her Dead*]—played beautifully. I am still bothered with some neuralgia—I think I barely escaped an abscessed tooth, which the Dentist will probably pull tomorrow and I hope this will give me complete relief. . . .

He ended the long letter, noting: "You have said nothing about Buz in your last letters—I hope he is all right & the rest of the family, Scout, Daisy, Pinkie, Wm. Ruff and Aunt Sarah.[38] Give my love to Nuzzer Mudder, & all. . . . Yours with all the love of my life & heart."

Pulling the aching tooth finally cured Greenlee's "neuralgia," according to a note on April 19. He continued his pleasant recuperation, writing on April 20 that Captains "Ashe & Pearson my roommates left a day or so ago—on their way back to America—I fear both of them have developed tubercular tendencies following influenza, but it does not seem to worry either of them. I spent Tuesday in Toulon & enjoyed the day there. I fear that I will not get to Nice or Monte Carlo now, nor to Italy or Spain. While I am waiting another officer has been moved into the room & he tells me he had mumps develop about 2 weeks ago—as I have never had mumps, I would feel better if he had not come in but—c'est le guerre." He closed: "P.S. Went over just before dinner to say good-bye to my French friends and they all kissed me on each cheek when I left, the mother, daughter & 4 children, nieces & nephews. It would have taken my breath, if Capt. Ashe had not told me they did him the same way. The mother kindly said I had been to see them too few times. . . . They have been so genial and pleasant and I feel very fortunate to have thus seen something of French home life."

Greenlee took time to write home to one of his golfing buddies, Judge Martin Burks:

> I enclose an advertisement of *Le Golf Hotel* here, for I know if you came through you would desire to stop here. . . . The Golf Hotel was for surgical cases. This hotel (San Salvadour) is for officers, sent here for recuperation—many after influenza, some with tuberculosis. . . . [I]t is a magnificent place, about in a class with our Hot Springs. One part is a magnificent chateau of the time of Napoleon III—with wonderful mural paintings rivaling those of the Congressional Library. This hotel is on the side of the mountain and the Mediterranean Sea just below— ideally beautiful. Most of the hazards on the Golf Course are made of willow wicker work, very similar to the chicken wire with which we began. My memory ran back to those days & made me homesick, & I would have given much to have had you & Estes Vaughan transmigrated here with your balls close under, using all the skill the situation required and giving vent to the language. . . . I hope soon to be back home—on our own links, & I most sincerely say I have seen nothing prettier or finer over here than the view from our 3rd Tee. . . .
>
> My life in the service has been interesting and wonderful to me—at times most strenuous and exacting, but up to the Armistice, I never was sick a moment nor did I miss a Reveille or formation that I should have attended. . . . Remember me to Mrs. Burks & Mrs. Withers. . . . Sincerely your friend, Greenlee D. Letcher.

On April 20, he wrote to Katie from Dijon of touring around, of meeting at a dance several old friends, of his improved health with the bad tooth gone, and commented that he

Chateau de Vrayhes, estate of the Countess and Count du Montaigu,
near Grand Pont, France

[m]issed my train here yesterday only by a few minutes caused by misinformation & had to wait a day. . . . Whether we misunderstand them,
or they us, or what, it looks impossible to have a French person give you
any information or direction which works out correctly—it is a puzzle
to me. I called again at the Y.M.C.A. to see Miss Penick but she has not
returned from Toul—I also missed Miss Howison, who had gone to an
Enlisted Men's Dance. Went last night to the big Opera House here &
saw La Tosca. . . . [E]njoyed it although, of course, in French. I fear
now I will not get to see our Chateau friends—sorry as they are so kind
and genial.

From LeMans, he wrote that he had finally rejoined his division with great glad-
ness and made the rounds of all his old friends. He then took "a military side car
. . . to Vevrey where I took the train for 'Dear Old Paris' as Henry Dold would
say." He saw Paris for two days, "which I very much enjoyed but saw only a small
part of what I would like to have seen." Interfering with sight-seeing was his un-
canny propensity to run into people he knew everywhere. He mentioned *five*
friends he saw in Paris, and two more he *tried* to find. He ended the letter: "I

mashed my thumb in a train door on way to Paris & will doubtless lose the nail, but I hope nothing more serious—X-ray picture taken in Paris indicates no fracture. Love to all."

On April 27, he wrote Katie a long letter, a portion of which notes:

> After I left Dijon Sunday I met Prof. Riley of W&L U. on the train on his way to the Combat area—he had with him several other professors from the A.E.T. University at Beanne, one a girl. Phone or call & tell Mrs. Riley that he was looking fine and evidently was in good health and spirits. He said he would get home he felt sure no later than he expected when he left—that is, he would not be detained here beyond his contract time. I have gotten a very nice letter from Rockenbach[39] now a Brigadier General. I sent him the Lexington Paper with mention of him in it, & he thanked me & told me to write him before arriving at Base Port on my way home. He is in command of St. Nazaire, where I now find we will embark. It will seem funny to write him now a General when I drilled him the first time when he was a Rat at the V.M.I.

Elsewhere in the letter, he wrote: "We are told we will move from here to the Port of Embarkation next Sunday, & sail without delay—if so I should be at home, I think by June 1st, & you can understand my heart flutter, Sweet Sweet Angel."

On April 28, he wrote that

> everybody seemed glad to see me, and I took up the work at once where I laid it down July 11, and things, so far as I can see, have run nicely since. I write this in a few minutes I have before inspection by the colonel. The colonel was very gracious in his welcome. I have received here to my delight the first letters for some time—yours of March 4, 20, 23, 29, 30 & Apr. 9. My heart goes out to John—I am trying to find out if he is still in France, that I may see him, if possible. His Division I hear is now in this area, & if he is with his Regiment I may be able to get to him. Before I got your letter, one of my men told me of seeing a notice of her [Frances's] death in a Petersburg Paper. It is so sad. Should you write again to her people give them my love & sympathy.

Later that day, he continued:

> 9:30 P.M.: I hurried off to Equipment Inspection and my men I think made a good show—tomorrow morning the Embarkation Inspector

will be here & inspect the entire Regiment—my accounts were gone over today preparatory to leaving. Everything is being hurried to that end—it is being speeded up. . . . I am billeted at a very friendly house—the people today asked me in to have coffee & according to custom put out the brandy & whiskey bottles—they put it in their coffee—much drinking in France. Kester they say is engaged to a French girl, . . . & wanted to marry before but there is so much delay & red tape about marrying in France, that he has given it up, I think. A number of soldiers have married over here—some negroes, I understand.

On May 4, 1919, Katie wrote: "Dear Captain—Aunt Sarah cleans us up so diligently there is nowhere for Scout to lie down, or for me to write a letter. It is nice to think now that you may have sailed before you get this one. Yesterday we had your boy Boatwright's cadet brother and Cadet Satterfield to dinner. I especially liked Boatwright and you can tell his brother he was well and husky." During this time, Kate Paul, in a pathetic letter to Lilian, complained about having "no house at all!!!"

Katie reported on a visit from Aunt Susie and her sister, a Mrs. Welch:

They got here about twelve and left at three, but in that time I had much news. It was funny how they both wanted to tell about their boys—Mrs. Welch's son being a surgeon in the navy—also she is the proudest, happiest person in having the honor to have two grandchildren. Aunt Susie says John Gray got his captaincy. . . . His company had been ordered to embark and he was right at the gang-plank when he received a telegram sending him to join a unit with the army of occupation. So he had to see his men go without him and set out himself for Germany—Coblenz, I believe. . . . Aunt Susie told me also the astonishment at Camp McClellan when you broke your sergeant for swearing at the men. This has been the first real summer day—so warm that Buz and some of the gang went in the river for a few minutes—also Scoutie—I surely want to see Scout's welcome to you for he hasn't forgotten you, and if he goes uptown with me always wants me to go to your office. . . . Jack Mead was here to-day, a very trim little keydet. Buz—only he's *Seymour* again now[40]—went to a party given by Margaret Wade, Mr. Andrew Wade's little girl, last night and seems to have had a pleasant time. He and Robbie were the only hillbillies[41] invited. He took Nell Owen.[42] I opine that Robbie finds the long and necessary accompaniment of a clean face and shiny shoes rather a heavy responsibility. . . .

Mr. Locher was here yesterday—very brave and proud and very pathetic about his boy who was killed in France. . . . His daughter is with the Y.M.C.A. and I asked for her address in case you should be anywhere near her. It was too bad you didn't see Miss Penick. We are hoping Letcher will be here soon. . . . A telegram from the Salvation Army says John has landed at New York—goes to Camp Mills.

On May 4, Greenlee wrote from Beaumont-sur-Sarthe, France:

My Dearest Angel, It seems now that it will not be long before I will see you and all I love again. We were called on today for a final requisition to fully equip our men with clothes etc. and indicated that we would leave here tomorrow evening for St. Nazaire, the Port of Embarkation and we will scarcely be there long, though we know nothing in advance. We marched from Colombiers here Wednesday evening Apr. 30, expecting to entrain at once for St. Nazaire; but we were stopped here & went into Billets—some said on account of 1st of May suspension of work all over France. Others surmised that a hitch in the Peace Conference had stopped troop movements. Today, 10 days rations were provided which indicated a long stay here—later they were withdrawn they say, & orders for movement to the coast tomorrow night. I am nicely billeted here in the home of M. Alfred Mareille, who has something to do with the Department of Justice. He was a Chasseur [hunter on horseback] in the war, received a citation afterwards discharged, having acquired tuberculosis—he is 34 years old, gray haired & bald, & looks much older. Became gray in the service. He has a wife and boy & his mother in law lives with them. They are most genial. Invited me to dinner yesterday which I enjoyed. I have taken them to several of the Y.M.C.A. shows, which they appear to enjoy hugely. Their Garden is by the river Sarthe in rear of the home & like many French gardens is very pretty & kept up with taste—a very old chateau overlooks it and an old stone bridge is just above over the river & a suspension bridge below— all very picturesque & beautiful. Near here at Ballon is a chateau built in 825 and lived in by Godfrey de Bouillere. Did I write you that at LeMans I went through the chateau of the widow of Richard Cour de

Leon—(Queen Berangis?). It adjoins the old cathedral there. I went down into the dungeons. Passages run from them for miles underground into the country. . . .

I trust that I am in good physical shape again—Wednesday I marched 6 miles after having walked in the morning perhaps 4 miles and seemed none the worse for it. . . . Col. Jones, Commanding Officer of our Regiment, asked me to write the History of the 111th Field Artillery—I told him that I would undertake it with pleasure—however it will devolve much work on me after being mustered out. The Va. troops it is understood will be mustered out at Camp Lee, Petersburg. . . .

Yesterday 22 of my men reenlisted for 3 months and started for Antwerp. I was sorry to lose them before demobilization but I made the Battery a speech following the Recruiting Officer and advised those who had no call home to do so for 2 reasons—1, that the Service needed them; and 2, because they would see a new part of Europe, and in the most pleasant season & have much less hard service than heretofore. Our Battery furnished more than any other in the Regiment, which gratified me. Other officers criticized me and some tried to keep their men out—but I believe the men will, in after years, thank me. and I felt it my duty.

The next day he wrote that he had tried to find John Paul but had learned that he had sailed already: "Tell Cousin Ella Herring that Tuesday night Frances, who is here in Y.M.C.A. work, was at Colombiers and Sgts. Boatright & Masinter brought her to my window and I had gone to bed, but I talked to her some time from bed. . . . She is well and was in fine spirits; and told me to tell Cousin Ella that her mother's baby was well & fine. She is at a neighboring small town, La Avian Petre. You must stop Scout's fighting. It is a mighty good way for him to get into all kinds of trouble."

Three times the regiment prepared to leave, only to have the orders rescinded. They had physical examinations, marches, reports, and final papers, and played a lot of baseball games waiting to go. They had reunions, theatrical shows, and good-bye parties with ice cream and cake, "the first ice cream I have eaten since leaving America. The play was one of the best I have ever seen anywhere—splendid acting—all except 2 were professionals in the service of the Y.M.C.A. Strange, one of the actresses was a Miss Jones originally from Washington, who knew Tom

Taliaffero and had attended a V.M.I. commencement and she now knows a Cadet McAdam at the V.M.I. & sent her autograph to him."

While waiting, Greenlee "one evening went to Calvoire, a shrine, where the statement of the cross and the crucifixion appear in magnificent statuary most interesting—I got pictures of it in a book of postals, & will bring them to Mr. Sheridan. Afterwards we went to a most beautiful chateau, Pont Chateau."

But Greenlee understood the tragedies of war and did not shrink from telling Katie about them. "I have lost 3 of my men here by sickness; Mitchell of Richmond with mumps; Hardy of Danville with typhoid; and Daniel—am sorry for them as we will leave them here. Yesterday Maj. Coble, Medical Corps, a specialist from Indianapolis on his way home, committed suicide in a nearby field by drinking alcohol and carbolic acid. He is said to have had some family trouble. Sad. I write in haste. P.S. Just heard of Lt. Crenshaw of 112th also committed suicide a few moments ago. Hoping to see you now very soon with all the love of my life & heart."

On May 27, Katie wrote:

> The Rainbow division has landed at New York and Jennie had a telegram from Letcher this morning which means, I hope, that we shall soon be seeing him—lovely guy that he is. . . . Buz and Francis Mead are just starting on a trip to Buena Vista to chaperone some of Mrs. Mead's girls who have been here at the hops to the train. Great excitement. Apropos of the hops and the games, Scout somewhere acquired one of the fearful smells he loves so and like Mary's little lamb of course he followed Buz to the hop, breaking in joyously and bringing the lovely smell along. And at the hop and at the games all the girls would call him to them remarking on his charm and distinction only to grow cold as soon as he approached, so that now he has grown quite subdued and has doubtless arrived at the same conclusion as Mr. Bryan's gentleman of the dance hall—poor dear little beast, that thought he was only adding to his charms.[43]

Katie continued:

> Col. Bill Shields was so pleased to get your letter. He telephoned and sent it down for me to read. Your letter of the 6th from Hyeres came last night and we were so glad to think you were seeing all that beauty after all the mud and rain. And that you had seen William Hale! I shall

Rockbridge Artillery, May 1919

find out who his wife is and let her know. We were glad also you had run up on Douglass Bolling. Jim White, Dr. White's boy who went with the tanks, has been ill a long time following two attacks of pneumonia and is in the hospital at Cannes. I wish you could have seen him, as I suppose he has seen no one from home since he left—the tank men being volunteers recruited from all over the country. . . . I told you, I think, that John's ship will not be in till May 9th. It may be better so—it will have given him a little time to realize and to face coming home to life without Frances. With love from all of us. K.

Greenlee and his men landed late in May 1919 at Newport News. The local paper greeted him with an article that began: "The County News lifts its hat to Captain Greenlee D. Letcher" and went on to detail the wonder of this fifty-year-old who survived rejection, lack of military experience, severe training, and yet triumphed. "Such an example of voluntary endurance of hardship and an assumption of sacrifice during two years of military life will, we believe, find few parallels among the millions of soldiers."

After the War, the Rockbridge Battery became the nucleus of the equestrian detachment at VMI. Greenlee kept in touch with as many of his men as he could, mentoring them until his death. Throughout the rest of his life, Greenlee sent the following missive to many of his boys, to alumni of VMI and Washington and Lee, to newspapers, and to relatives, for there are letters mentioning it, and several copies. Perhaps he was requested to send copies, in those days when they could only be copied by hand. Greenlee was proud of this advice; he had survived the war on it, and he wanted future soldiers to benefit. This document serves as an interesting contrast to John Paul's views of the army and Buz's cynical opinions of the service which appear in his letters when he served in the U.S. Marine Corps.

[no postmark or date]
Study hard as to everything that will benefit you in the Army; keep in good humor no matter how anything may puzzle you and feel that those who have responsibility and who are over you, know best and are doing everything in their power for your good and the efficiency of the Army; execute every order promptly and with the best of your ability; take the best care of yourself physically; never keep on wet clothes or wet shoes any longer than absolutely necessary; do no dissipation of any kind nor break any regulations. And look forward to going to Officers School as soon as you can, but don't be impatient. Have the most respectful and kindly manner to all officers but "boot-lick" no one. On and off duty, always carry yourself like a soldier, head up, chin in, shoulders back and body erect, and speak and answer with firmness and distinction. Keep step with whomsoever you are walking. Keep your hands out of your pockets.

Whenever an order is given to you, either individually or with others, impress upon your mind and memory answers to the following questions: (1)When? (2)Where? (3)What? (4)How? (1)&(2) That you may be at the appointed place and never be a second late. (3)Think clearly and at once as to what the order means and what your mission is. Get information if you have any doubt but do not ask any unnecessary questions. (4)How? That is, put your mind on the order earnestly and continuously and determine how you can carry out the order for the best purpose and with greatest efficiency by thought and investigation and inquiry; but make no unnecessary inquiry. Be keen without "show-off." Be alert without nervousness. Be smart and prompt without confusion. Begin and end every interview with a superior officer with the word, "sir," and look him squarely in the eyes during the entire interview.

Read this to your squad and tell them that an old Artillery Captain of the First World War sends this to you all.

Greenlee D. Letcher, Lexington, Virginia
Captain, Battery F, 111 F.a., 28th Division, A.E.F.

5 Ending (1919~1954)

Gently down the stream of time,
Floats our bark towards the sea.
Sweetly peals the evening chime,
Hear it echo, wild and free.
Friends are gone, ties have been broken,
Doubts and fears, and hopes sublime,
Careless words, so idly spoken
Lie sleeping 'neath the streams of time.

Over on that golden shore,
Forms unseen are chanting low
Strains we loved in days of yore,
Memories of long ago.
Voices now are hushed forever,
Tears and flowers strew their grave,
And that mighty rushing river
Buries all beneath its wave.

—MAJ. J. BARTON, 1869

After the war, Greenlee was offered jobs, and his admirers urged him to run for political office. But among other qualities, he exhibited great wisdom. He stayed close to home, although he remained an unusually popular speaker in Lexington and throughout the state. In 1920 he was the Lexington High School graduation speaker, with Buz in the graduating class. The *Lexington Gazette* reported: "Mr. Letcher spoke very strongly, as to the Bible in Education, and used a number of illustrations from the Bible. . . . Those who failed to hear it, missed a rare treat."

A year after the war ended, Greenlee learned that General Pershing was in this country and he wired him to ask "if a meeting could be arranged in Lexington with service men and people generally at Stonewall Jackson's grave. . . . The parade

Gen. J. J. Pershing, being introduced to speak and place a wreath on the grave of Stonewall Jackson, June 18, 1920, Lexington, Va. Left to right: Col. G. C. Marshall, Gen. Pershing, Gen. S. D. Rockenbach, Capt. G. D. Letcher, Col. A. Moreno.

Greenlee Letcher with General J. J. Pershing at Stonewall Jackson's grave in Lexington, June 18, 1920

will be composed of men on horseback and on foot, and people in automobiles. . . . [I]t will be a notable event, and everybody will help make it a great success." Pershing accepted, came to Lexington in June 1920, stayed with the Letchers, was honored by the town, and delivered a speech.

Buz and his friend Leon Johenning visited Greenlee's brother, John D. Letcher, in Norfolk as a graduation trip; Katie wrote that Scout was lonesome, although "the kittens are as cheerful and flourishing as if anyone wanted them." Seymour and Kate Pittman Paul lost a child born in Panama. Loulie Letcher died late in 1920, and her husband, John D., returned to live with Jennie and Uncle Steve. Katie resumed her old habit of spending much of her time in Harrisonburg. Any letters she wrote from there during this period have disappeared. John Paul bought a "Buic" that year, which was much admired in family letters.

There are no more 1920 letters until this one, from Harrisonburg, on December 3: a mutual affection seems to have sweetened their relationship. Katie wrote,

Greenlee and Pershing sharing a humorous moment, June 20, 1920, Lexington

"Dear Captain—John [Paul] . . . is looking better than I've seen him for a long time—or maybe I had expected to see him pulled down by the campaign. . . . Virginia is in Front Royal on a visit. . . . Tell Janie not to forget to telephone to Mr. McCary for the chicken for Buz's Sunday dinner. . . . I washed my fountain pen and think I must be writing mostly with water."

In June of 1921, Katie wrote to Lilian: "The neuritis lays its spiteful spell upon me as regular as night comes." In July she wrote:

> Dear Cap'n—Your postal has just come and I am so sorry about your cold. I do hope you are much better to-day. Be sure and send me a card

Buz with Charlotte and Kate Pittman Paul in Lexington, c. 1922

to let me know as soon as you get this. Buz [now a cadet at VMI] said he might not get up home. They had parade Wednesday. As I went to the train I saw him on his way back from Dr. McClure's [dentist]. I was dreadfully tired when I got here Tuesday, but delighted to find folks going all about the house. Virginia is looking better and the new cook seems most desirable. . . . Now you and Scoutie man take good care of each other or the Missis will come home and settle you both. Lots of love, K.

From Harrisonburg, after an auto trip, Katie wrote to Greenlee on July 28, 1921. The Henderson, called Henry, seems to have been a joint venture of Greenlee and Buz, now seventeen. She wrote that they had arrived, "Buz negotiating Staunton

Buz at VMI, 1920–24

in a way to make you proud," telling her husband that she and Buz had "oysters and coffee at Cohen's." As usual, the Paul house was like Grand Central Station, with visitors day and night: "To-day Buz and Seymour went to Ottobine. Gin was sick and had to come home from Washington so I stayed to be any use I could here." Lilian arrived with tales of "the works in Pittsburgh laying off thousands of men at a time, including Jack," and Seymour left for Panama. Katie asked Greenlee: "How does Scout make out without the Boss and his car?"

Katie went to Harrisonburg in January of 1922 to care for her mother who had suffered a broken arm. She wrote:

> Dear Cap'n—I got here on time and found Nuzzer Mamma doing
> nicely and much less done up by the shock of the fall than I had feared.
> . . . She says tell you she is greatly comforted by the tender sympathy of
> her two dear sons-in-law. When she fell before Jack wrote her 'Stop

climbing trees!' and now you send her word to "let the hootch alone!" She was very much amused by the liqueur & boot-leg letter.[1] Has Scout gotten rid of the rest of his burrs? Take good care of him *and put his tag on.* Miss Teensie was here yesterday evening and sent her love to you all.

On January 19, 1922, she had instructions for Greenlee: "I was glad to hear from you and to know Julia is taking good care of you and Scout. Tell her to order some celery and a head of lettuce for Buz tomorrow. . . . Nuzzer Mamma seems to be getting along all right, but I feel so sorry for all the tedious time before her, the weeks with her arm in a sling. . . . You and Buz put Scout's tag on and write me you've done it. With love, K." In other notes, she described her mother propped in bed swaddled in splints and bandages and wished she had been in Lexington to hear Thomas Nelson Page, a well-known Virginia writer and lecturer. And she never forgot her favorite: "Did you all put Scout's tag on? And did you pay Julia and give her a dollar for the wash lady? Are you getting on all right? And is Julia faithfully on the job? With lots of love. K."

She continued to divide her time between Lexington and Harrisonburg, writing on February 3, 1922:

> I was so glad to get your letter this morning and to hear Buz seems in good shape—I am always uneasy when he has a cold or neuralgia. . . . So sorry to hear about Scout's encounter with the barbed wire. If he loses his appetite again give him one of his cathartic pills—in the medicine press about the middle of the shelf next to top, marked C.C. pills—in a piece of raw meat or cheese. Don't you let my pup get sick. Mamma was so pleased at your writing to her. She sits up most of the time now. . . . Still has her good nurse with her . . . Miss Teensie was here last night and sent her love to all of you. She seemed so worn and depressed by the struggle for a living—I don't know when I have felt so sorry for any one. She was quite sick just before Christmas. . . . Virginia has gone to a card party with Mrs. Stebel, so I must go now and get Mamma her milk. Have marked the bills and am returning them. With lots of love. K.

Though I can find no proof of it, possibly some physicians already understood the connection between broken bones and calcium.

On March 3 she wrote to her husband from Harrisonburg: "Please do take care of yourself and get over your cold before you go back to the office. I am so sorry for you to be having it all by yourself without any Tiger to make you so miserable you wouldn't notice the cold. . . . I am sending back the bills which came just before I called you up. Everything seems very quiet here. There is so much grip that I think the town is too busy recuperating to do much else. I wish I'd had time to get to that train and come and see how you are. With love to you and Buz—and to Scout. K."

For this period there are several undated notes: "Dear Cap'n—As I've heard nothing from John I suppose he will stay over Sunday with Mrs. Dannenhower, so much as I would like to be to dinner with you and Buz I will stay over till he comes. I hope Janie has remembered to make all the provisions I told her to for Buz and his buddies. . . . Tell Buz I met Elizabeth and the baby yesterday with their imported Airedale but he couldn't hold a candle to Scout. You might also tell Scout. I haven't seen Miss Teensie—will try to get there this evening, but I continue to be awfully tired." Now forty-six, Katie had a thyroid deficiency, as will become clear.

But she was more solicitous than of old, writing: "I hope there will be a card from you to-day to let me know how Buz is coming on. Yesterday afternoon I tried to call up you fellows to pass the time of day but the telephone line between here and Staunton was out of order. John did not get back. I knew Mrs. Dannenhower would want him to stay over Sunday. Called on Miss Teensie Saturday but did not find her at home. Also stopped at the Sipes. It was so cold and windy yesterday we did not go to church. . . . Are you taking good care of Scout? Your partner can be counted on to take care of herself. Lots of love. K."

On March 13, Kate Paul in a letter to her daughter Lilian complained that the last three months had aged her "three hundred years," saying she had expected to die and that her illness had been hard on Virginia "who is not well herself. . . . Katie has been down every now and again for a day or so." She went on to describe "the fire which damaged the roof badly" and ended: "Tell . . . Jack . . . it will be a long, long time before I climb another tree!"

On one visit to Harrisonburg, Katie wrote home that she "found Mamma much better again, having gotten over the upsetment of the fire. . . . Your letter and birthday gift just received. It is so nice to have friends who don't forget one's [Katie Paul's] 79th birthday! I may come home next week & back again later but don't tell Julia. . . . You and Scout take good care of each other. K."

That summer, Buz took a freighter to visit his Uncle Seymour in Panama, stopping off in New York to see his Uncle Letcher Harrison, who took him on a two-day tour of all the speakeasies and put him on the ship with a terrible hangover. "My Big Dog," Katie called Buz fondly in letters. That was some compliment, considering how crazy she was about Scout. She wrote to Buz while he was in Panama: "Scout's eyes are well, but now he's got fleas. We have Maltese kittens. I may keep one. Love to Seymour, Kate, and Charlotte."

She wrote to Buz:

> Your letter written after seeing Haiti came . . . and we have all enjoyed it a lot. . . . But that surely was some supper for a tropic clime! . . . John drove us out to Ottobine this afternoon. It was lovely there and the place was so sweet and peaceful. Abe and Aunt Fannie [Paul] both seemed well. Nuzzer Mamma looks and seems better than for a long time. . . . Will you be coming back by way of New Orleans? I think that would be a fine trip if it is feasible. I wish too I could have had the trip with you but the next best thing is to know you are having it and enjoying it so. It is heavenly sweet of you to write me such nice long letters. I had intended to keep them for you as a sort of diary and will do so. I will be going home tomorrow, and will send you the News & Gazette. The Ku Klux had their "fiery cross" burning night before last—to my fury. With love to each one of you.

She told him to wait for a return boat and not to ship on one as a sailor, and if he had to return by San Francisco, she and Greenlee would pay the difference. At the end of August, Buz returned, bringing a parrot to amuse his mother. Loretta turned out to be smart enough to imitate many two- or three-word sayings, but she bit everyone who came near.

After Buz left Panama, Seymour wrote to Katie that he and Charlotte, who was seven,

> went swimming this morning without Buz, a pious Sunday act. I wish I could teach her to swim, but she doesn't work hard at it. However, we had a pleasant time in the Pacific, the water being clear and free of jellyfish this morning. Buz should have been with us. . . . [Charlotte] has lost two of her lower front teeth, of the first set, and reminds me in a flash of Gee and his toothless grins, that dear boy. Did I tell you how delighted I was with Buz—or wasn't it obvious? He just gave me a kind of new delight in humanity—so bright and jolly and wholesome and clean, just such a darn nice worthwhile fellow. We were mighty glad to

get a little bit of him. . . . I met someone recently who knew Green, and had the pleasure of saying he was considered V.M.I.'s most distinguished participant in the War.

There is a yearlong gap in the letters here, an indication that Katie and Greenlee were spending more time together. The next item in the collection is a telegram on May 14, 1923, from Dr. DeSchweinitz's secretary: "Dr. DeSchweinitz abroad until June he can see you both nine thirty June thirteenth. Please answer."

That date being VMI's commencement, Greenlee wrote asking for another time, saying there was no urgency. However, Katie's eyes must have worsened, for May 18 brought another telegram to the doctor: "Appoint to any date left for Mrs. Letcher. Preferably before June fifteenth. Greenlee D. Letcher."

The doctor could only see Katie on commencement day. Thus it was that Buz, going into his first-class (senior) year at VMI, telegraphed his mother in Philadelphia: "To be first Lieutenant and Quartermaster. Love. J. Seymour Letcher."

Katie was at the Hotel Adelphia on June 14, and wrote: "Dearest Cap'n—Have just arrived to find Buz's telegram waiting for me. I'll never get over not having been there.[2] Will hurry to mail this in the hope of its going out to-night to let you know I got here safely—twelfth story and rates higher than that. In haste, K."

Next day she wrote that "Dr. de S- gave me new glasses this morning and said my eyes were doing well. . . . He sent me to Dr. Frazier where I got well thumped and stethoscoped. Will leave in morning early for Washington and hope to get to Nuzzer Mamma's tomorrow night. Love to you and Scoutie."

On June 17, she wrote that she had arrived "in this dear Harrisonburg last night, and will be up Monday. Hope Annie still holds the fort and takes good care of you and Scout. With love. K."

However, Katie fell sick again. On June 24, 1923, Greenlee wrote the following, to Charles E. Frazier of Philadelphia:

Dear Doctor Frazier: Mrs. Letcher is much used up by the heat and I write to ask if from your examination you deem it important or necessary that she return at once for an operation to remove the swelling in her neck. If so let me know when she should come to Philadelphia and advise me fully with explicit directions as to when and where to come and how long she should be prepared to remain. Generally it would be hardly practicable for her to come till after the 29th June.

In view of the intense heat at this time and the difference between the mountains here and Philadelphia, I hope this can safely be postponed till fall, but I wish to be guided by your judgment as to what is best in the matter. Hoping to know you personally in the future, I am, Very truly yours, G. D. Letcher

P.S. Do you think that in this case any treatment with iodine or anything else would be worth while to try in the meantime to arrest it? *G.D.L.*

Dr. Frazier responded promptly and sensibly, on June 26, 1923:

My dear Mr. Letcher; I do not regard it as at all urgent that Mrs. Letcher should have the operation now. From my conversation with her, I was rather under the impression that she was anxious to have it over, hence preliminary arrangements to operate this week. The heat here is very excessive and I should strongly urge her to postpone the operation until fall. Meanwhile, may I caution you against the use of iodine in any form in this particular case as I am sure it would aggravate the condition and might precipitate serious symptoms.
Cordially yours, Charles H. Frazier.

But by June 28, Katie had been nauseated long enough that Greenlee felt panicky, writing to Dr. Frazier that "[s]uch sickness is recurrent to her, and once she was extremely ill from it, and now her condition is such that she feels she cannot come on to Philadelphia at present, and will have to put off any operation until fall. . . . I have not received an answer to my letter of 24th. I am of course most anxious about my wife and would be glad if you would write me fully your opinion as to her condition, and the outlook." Dr. Frazier again advised against her coming. His secretary wrote on July 9 that Dr. Frazier had sailed for Europe and would be in touch mid-September. She added: "In fixing his operating fee, Dr. Frazier would be very glad to be guided by your circumstances."

On September 15, 1923, Greenlee's sister, Fannie, died after a brief illness, of Bright's disease. Katie must have gotten somewhat better on her own, for she did not have the goiter operation in the fall.

In the spring of 1924, Buz's senior (first-class) year, Katie went to Philadelphia to deal with the problem. Goiter can be caused by either an overactive or an underactive thyroid; she referred frequently to "nervousness," gained weight at some point, and her hair turned thin and silvery white in her fifties. This was also the approximate time for natural menopause, if she had not had a hysterectomy earlier. As medical conditions often run in families, it may not be too far afield to suggest that Charles's lifelong nervousness may have stemmed from a similar condition.[3]

A telegram on April 21 told Katie a room at University Hospital in Philadelphia was ready, and she wired back that she would come. On April 23 she wrote Buz, about his current flame, a black-haired beauty named Molly Laird who stood to inherit a part of the DuPont fortune: "Have just passed Wilmington but didn't see Mollie anywhere."

From Philadelphia she wrote that there would be treatment instead of an operation, but that diagnosis would soon change. A cancer was discovered on her nose and was excised. On April 29, Virginia wrote her from Washington that she had "been to walk in the White House grounds and met Mr. Coolidge with 3 guards —nobody saying a word. But who would have a word to say if they had to have 3 guards at their heels all the time? Nobody but Cap'n could weather that!"

That spring, Katie heard from Jim Hearne, the boy who had written Gee from AMA just before he died, then attended VMI for a time. On May 5, 1924, he wrote:

> Dear Mrs. Letcher—, I was mighty glad to hear from you, had begun to think you had forgotten me, and well you might have, with a son graduating at the Institute. I know you all are mighty proud of him, and I am too, although I haven't seen Buz for so long I probably wouldn't recognize the man he has grown to be. When Mother read your letter, she said she knew how proud you were and had reason to be, then afterward with a sigh, "If you had only gone on." I never realized then, a long time ago, all I should have. I would love to see you all again, and be on hand to see Buz in full dress, and to see him get his diploma and the monogram, but I don't believe I can get away. I am still working for the Missouri Pacific, have a job here at a treating plant looking after treatment and ties on hand for the Mo. P. & Wabash. . . .
>
> You need never think I will be sending any invitations out, the only thing that would even tempt me to do such a thing would be the fact that you would come, and I would get to see you and talk over old times again, and that Mother and Father would get to meet you and Mr. Letcher. But I am well past the dangerous age [Hearne couldn't have been more than twenty-five!], my mother says we are, "The Last of

the Mohicans." . . . And you can tell Buz, from what I have observed, if he really intends to do some hunting and fishing some day, that married men . . . seem to have a hard time finding time and getting permission. . . . Don't forget us if you ever come this way. Give my best regards to Mr. Letcher and congratulations to Buz. I'll be thinking of you Mother's day. Jim.

Back in Rockbridge there was a flood on May 16, about which Katie commented wryly, in reply to Buz's description: "Wish the flood had taken the old wood fridge so we would have to buy a new one." In the same letter, she crowed: "And oh! You ought to see my good new neck! You who are the solace and delight of all my days." She wrote to Buz: "I wish I could be home tonight when you come up for your grapefruit. Pat and hug Scoutie Man for me." She reported that treatment "is just an injection, no more than a wasp sting," but on May 24, she developed a complication: phlebitis. Dr. Frazier wrote to Greenlee: "She has been a very good patient and we shall be sorry to have her leave. I think she will be quite able to take the trip from West Philadelphia alone if you can meet her as you plan to do."

On May 24, 1924, Katie was in good spirits when she wrote:

> Dearest Buz, Blooming leg doing well and everything else all right but here I am still when I want to see you so bad. I have to write lying down because the leg has to be up. Did you have anybody to dinner today? And did Annie have strawberry shortcake? . . . There is a two year old baby who has been here for months and still has to breathe through a tube in her throat but she is the joy of the place which I think is being a good sport. Also there is an Irish maid here that I would like to take home. She is aged and infirm but her wit is unfailing and her swears are varied and picturesque. . . . I suppose by the time I get home you'll be a middle-aged man with several children, but I've got a nice new neck. As Leo said in the penitentiary, 'I've met so many pleasant people'— but none so nice as you. It's a great thing to have a son who is the delight of your soul and the pride of your life. I want to see you, want to see the boys [Buz's VMI friends, whom she mothered], and be licked by Scout. *Mudder.*

In June, Lilian attended VMI finals, still the surrogate mother. Sadly, Katie missed Buz's graduation, as she was still having radium treatments. There were several exchanges between the doctor or his secretary and Greenlee, who naturally discovered a social connection, for in one letter he remarked to Miss Mary V. Stephenson, the doctor's secretary: "I wrote to your cousin Jack on a business matter and received a letter from him and he says that all your people here are very proud of you which I well understand." On June 3, 1924, Dr. Frazier released Katie to come home, and on that day his secretary wrote:

> My dear Mr. Letcher: In answering your note of May 29th I beg to say I am of the opinion Mrs. Letcher will feel more comfortable if she had some one with her on the trip home. I believe this and say it because of two or three little set-backs she has had which necessitated her remaining in bed most of the time. She has not of course gained strength on that account. I should, as I told you, be happy to be of service to her and put her on the train, but I am very sure she will be more comfortable to have some one with her. With kind regards, I am, Very sincerely yours, Mary V. Stephenson

Lilian wrote: "Suppose you will be weakish but not cripply." Greenlee, forever solicitous, went to fetch her, requesting of Dr. Frazier on June 6, 1924, "any further directions, I meant any that would appertain to taking her home or in the home afterwards." He ended his letter with the most cordial and typical sentiments, including a paean to Rockbridge County:

> It will be a pleasure to see you in this part of the country at some time. We have a beautiful county here and Dick Meade, who will be near to you, attended the Virginia Military Institute in our town, and he and his father and mother have spent parts of several summers here, where it is cool and invigorating. He is a most attractive and fine young man and our best wishes go with him and your daughter, and I hope that he will bring her here before leaving for China, as in some way I have gained the impression that his father and mother would again be here during the summer.

He wrote similar invitations to the doctor's secretary, and to Sue Geiser, a private nurse who'd looked after Katie. In future correspondence, Dr. Frazier noted: "I took the liberty, while Mrs. Letcher was in the hospital of having our X-ray specialist, Dr. Pancoast, and our skin specialist, Dr. Weidman, see her with reference to the place on the side of her nose and I suppose in course of time you will receive a bill from them. Dr. Pancoast does not think that further treatment by radium will be necessary. I am glad to hear what you have to say about the Meades."

Meanwhile, Buz, now a college graduate, in contemplating the future, had a job offer as a forester in Staunton at $1,500 a year. "It's not that bad, but I'm leaving it to you," Katie commented, damning with faint praise. On July 11, Greenlee wrote to Dr. Frazier:

> I had intended reporting to you Mrs. Letcher's condition but as things were just drifting along without anything marked to notice, I have not written. She seems to me less nervous than she formerly was though she says that she does not notice such improvement and that the purpose of the operation was that she would not get more nervous—but I think there is an improvement on this line. She is using her limb very little yet and she feels that she is unable to use it much—that is, she uses it with resulting pain and fatigue. But I hope that this will improve.

Dr. Frazier responded three days later:

> Dear Mr. Letcher; I am very much obliged to you for your check. With regard to Mrs. Letcher's condition, I do not think you should expect the maximum effect of the operation until six months have elapsed. I don't think there need be any restriction placed on the use of the leg now but of course she will regain her general strength gradually. I hope you will keep me posted as to her condition and let me know at the end of six months how she is getting along.

In August 1924 Katie wrote to her mother: "Cap'n and the golfers—six of them—had breakfast here at half past five Saturday morning, drove to Winchester, won the cup, and reached home next AM at four—a pretty good showing for doddering old-agers like Cap'n and Mr. Bennie."

Buz decided to follow his father into the law, and matriculated in the fall of 1924 at Washington and Lee University Law School. On September 12, Greenlee was Chairman of Defense Day in Staunton. That fall he presented his father's gold watch to Washington and Lee University in a ceremony written up in the local newspapers. On November 9 he was Orator of the Day for the sixth anniversary of the Armistice of World War I, at the Danville Post 10 of the American Legion. Other than occasional trips, it appears that he was not traveling as in the past, and that Katie must have been home also.

Katie visited Doctor DeSchweinitz the next June, in 1925. Buz, living at home, found law school hard going. Another year passed.

Christmas of 1925 Lilian wrote, apparently already in an institution, and indicating she'd been there over a year:

Katie, dear, Oh, this beautiful, gorgeous, king's ransom necklace!—oh it is so *lovely!* It recalls too the brooch that Mamma had. I could look at this by the hour and love to wear it as I did Christmas afternoon. I have known that I must make the best of another Christmas here. I received a sweet card from Charlotte and messages from other friends. I know what joy it was for you to have Buzz. I do wish you could corral him so that he could be near you. I hope that you, the colonel, Buzz and the others had a pleasant Christmas—with Buzz's heiresses in the background. Loads of love to you, the good Colonel and Buzz. Idge.

On May 1, 1926, Katie had another operation on the goiter. By May 16, her neck was better and she was in good spirits. While she was in the hospital, Mrs. Paul visited Virginia, who was teaching in Washington, and visited with Katie. To Buz Katie sent "Love to the apple of my eye and the idol of my soul." No letters have survived from 1926, which signals, probably, a year without the need to communicate by mail. Professor Stevens retired. He and Jennie and widower John D. shared the house that Greenlee's oldest brother (Houty) had built around 1888.

From March until July of 1927, Katie's mother's illness and death held her in Harrisonburg. A letter from Virginia to Greenlee on April 27, 1927, notes:

I feel that it would do Mamma so much good to see you and she does need cheering up so much. As far as her arm is concerned she is doing very well indeed, but the greatest worry we now have is her mental attitude. She is so terribly depressed and tired that at times I fear that her mind will not come back to normal. It is a rather critical time in this illness—this time between the real suffering and her convalescence, and the only thing to be done is to try to divert her and keep her cheered. She is not making any effort to get well, does not take much interest in anything and does not want to see anyone except her own people. Charlie is here for a day or two and that is helping a great deal; he takes her out in his car, but she will not make much effort to get about the house because, I think, she feels her helplessness so much.

He answered immediately: "Dear Sister Bunch, . . . I will certainly come Sunday if you feel that it would be of any benefit to mother. I have intended coming down for a good while but I am leading a very busy life now and have put it off. I am sorry to hear that you feel that mother is not doing as well as you would like to see her. . . . I am glad Charlie is there as I know that he is such a pleasure to her always. We so much enjoyed Charlie's stopping by to see us every little while. We tried to get him to stay over the last time. . . . When you receive this and talk to Katie drop me a postal. With love to mother and you all.

But Katie did not agree that a visit from Greenlee would be salutary, for she wrote:

> Dear Cap'n, . . .
>
> I found Mamma very weak and exhausted due I think, largely to the hot and humid weather. . . . Charles was here . . . leaving yesterday morning. Did he stop over night with you and Buz? Your letter to Virginia came this afternoon. I really think you'd be more pleasure to Mamma a little later when she is stronger—she is still very weak and nervous—and that [sic] *it's well to be careful not to be too many for the cook.* I'm uneasy about that myself all the time. I know Mamma could do without me better than she could without the cook. Virginia insists on my staying and I hope I don't queer the domestic scene. . . . How git long you all? Badly I fear with the ancient Hoo-doo [unsatisfactory maid]. How Scout? How Loretta? . . .
>
> I suppose Buz is shining up for the dance tonight. Has he got a girl? If Hoo-doo is too bad let me know. With loads of love to you both.

Buz felt little affinity for the law and began looking around for other ideas, as the following letter to his Aunt Virginia on February 20, 1927, three months short of graduation, indicates.

> Dear Aunt Gin, I'm rather late replying to your letter written just before I went up to Washington. I've been in bed with grippe for a week, that's why I haven't written. I suppose John told you I wrote to him so there's nothing I need say about it except it was sweet of him writing and troubling with the matter. . . . I went up on Monday and thanks to Gen. Rockenbach had no trouble getting an appointment with Gen. Lejeune . . . who seemed duly impressed with my reference letters. . . . I think everything is about as promising as could be expected, but . . . I'm afraid I was unduly optimistic in regard to my chances for appointment. . . . I hope you are all well in this changing weather. Mother just fired the cook today so we are in for taking our meals out, which is a horrible boring ordeal, but in this day and time it has to happen with such uppity niggers. Love to all, Buzz.

292 MY DEAREST ANGEL

Kate Paul, despite her own frailty, wrote to Katie that spring, concerned about her grandson:

> March 13—So glad to have a letter from you and hope that Buz is safely over the Grippe—sorry to hear that he is worrying about anything; he's too young for that and he will have enough to worry about unless he has better luck than most of us mortals. Can't you find something for him to do—something to keep his thoughts off his worries? till things adjust themselves—even if there is no monetary return? He has unique mechanical ability and a turn for electrical machinery. And how about surveying? Would he like that? I can't bear to think of his worrying—so young—so good-natured—so bright—I fail to see why he couldn't succeed at Law. I know he has as good a mind as some of these morons I could name down here—who are attorneys. . . .
>
> Tell that dear precious Buzz to stop scaring his poor old deaf Grandmother out of her feeble old senses by thinking about joining the Marines. Do write and tell me he isn't going. Virginia is not very well. She has had to go to the Hospital for an examination by Dr. Dearly, who warned her of high blood pressure and of incipient kidney trouble—but she keeps going constantly. Mrs. Converse is better—but is still weak and frail—Dr. Converse brought her up here the other night and he and Virginia Converse came to take her home. Mrs. Sipes (in a three-storied bonnet) was here the other day looking well and stylish. The weather is mild and the Flu seems to be abating. It has been a long time since you were here. I'll forget how to play Rum—can't you, and Buz, come down soon? We have a cook, you know. Love to Loretta, Scout and all. Mamma. PS. John [Paul] is as gabby as ever—haven't heard from Charlie lately. Have lost interest in Charlotte since she is so tall and big.

On April 29, 1927, Katie wrote from Harrisonburg:

> Dear Cap'n—I had hoped there'd be a letter from you this morning telling me how the world's serving you—or rather how the Hoodoo is. . . . Mamma is about the same. The doctor hopes to take the cast off in the next day or so, when I hope she will be more comfortable. . . . In your next letter suggest that I come home over the weekend to settle the new cook, as I hope to do. It is hard to talk to Mamma and I think the

letter would be the best way. . . . I was glad to get your letter this evening and to hear how the preacher had made everything perfectly clear. . . . Thanks for the check and the papers. I am much gratified to know Sam Houston's birthplace is to be marked for all the world to see. . . . Did Buz and Dorsey [Hopkins] go to Staunton to hear Will Rogers tonight? Did you both read the "piece" about parrots in the last N.Y. Times magazine section? You may be pleased to know they don't mean anything when they bite. Mamma improves very slowly. . . . Charlie called me from Roanoke last night. Said he was feeling better. Saw Mr. T. Harris yesterday. Asked about you.

Buz graduated low in his law class and went to work for a local lawyer. After practicing law for *two weeks* in the summer of 1927, and finding himself "unable to collect as much money as I got paid," he joined the U.S. Marine Corps. Katie made a trip to have Dr. DeSchweinitz check her eyes and instructed Greenlee: "You take care of Scoutie's eyes." On the return trip she stopped back in Harrisonburg with her mother, who was in her final days.

On July 5, Kate Green Paul died. Virginia was never truly well after that; Charlie spiraled down into a depression; and Lilian was already in a mental institution.

On July 10, Katie wrote from Harrisonburg, where she and her siblings were coming to terms with their mother's death:

My Cap'n—Your letters are such a comfort to me. I wish I could tell you how much. Your postcard has just come. Charles left yesterday for Winchester, will return tonight and is intending to drive to Lexington tomorrow and go on the fishing trip with Buz and I expect to come up with him. Am sorry Annie had to stop. I'm glad to hear Aunt Maggie [Showell] is there and Uncle John feeling better. We are very lonely without Mamma. The heart of the house is gone. She has said to me so many times that nobody else was ever the comfort to her that you were after Papa died. I had realized for the last month how ill she was but I just couldn't talk about it. With love. K.

On August 29, Katie wrote Buz, newly inducted into the Marines, the following letter:

Dearest Buzz, Well, how git long? I needn't tell you how we miss you. I'm terribly proud of the way I didn't cry. Thinking what a grand looking soldier you were I remembered when you were a tiny wriggling red baby an hour or two old and old Doc carried you over to me and said, "Now, look what you've got. . . ." Everybody asks about you. The Gen. Mallorys always, and Old Rat and Mrs. Pendleton very specially and the Mr. Entsminger who drives the bus from Bueny [Buena Vista, a town six miles distant] and says "Well Buzz'll make good. He's a fine boy and so likeable to everybody." Even Dr. Mitchell—and Miss Belle Larrick! "Unusual courage and leadership"—yes, whether you were the first man in the front line or the last man in the last ditch I've always known you'd give a good account of yourself. I can't wish more for you than that you'll be to Uncle Sam all the pride and satisfaction that you've always been to me. Mother.

At the end of August, Katie returned to Philadelphia for what was to be a routine visit but turned into an extended stay. Buzz was stationed at Quantico, a short train ride or drive away. Greenlee was dying to go to France for a reunion with his battery and other war buddies, but as Katie's health was uncertain, he could not make a decision to go. The following letters give a fairly detailed account of how their fall transpired. Buz, needing his tonsils out, chose Philadelphia where his mother was.

On September 1, 1927, Katie wrote to her husband from the Hotel Adelphia in Philadelphia:

Found Dr. Bar expecting me & by a streak of luck Dr. De Schweinitz. They want me to stay over a day or so to be looked over. Sent me this morning to Dr. Babbit to have my sinuses checked up & report to Dr. de S. Don't you forget Scoutie man's drops or I'll have to leave my own eyes to come and see about his. . . . I will have to be here several days. . . . Wire $75. Dr. Bar has me in charge meanwhile. The sinus man Dr. Babbitt sent me this afternoon to have X-ray photographs made at Dr. Pendergrasts at the University Hospital. This took $25 at a swoop so I'm writing you for more. I'm afraid you won't have enough left to go to France. Buz got in to see me last night. Seemed well and likes his brother rats [marines] very much. Love, K.

On September 3, she wrote:

Things seem to be looking up—Dr. Babbitt pleased with x-ray report and Dr. Bar says eyes show improvement—both much pleased. They will keep on the job with me over Sunday so I lose no time—all of them so kind & thoughtful. Buz in yesterday in his white uniform and my eyes weren't too bad for me to see how he dazzled the beholders. The girl in the telegraph office is Miss Leonaret—Buz and I went in. Your money order received very promptly. I'll get it collected when Buz comes in this afternoon. Thank you very much. I still had 30 left and didn't know when I might need more. My room is 4th floor & close to the elevator—4.50 a day. Write how you git long & Scout & Loretta. I hope you're getting your work satisfactorily behind you.

She wrote him the next day that she "[s]aw Dr. B. this morning & he thinks improvement continues. Weather stays pleasantly cool so far. Of course I don't go out in it to any extent but stay in to avoid glare. Expect Buz this evening."

On September 7, she wrote that she had

been this morning to Dr. Bar & Dr. Babbitt. The eyes show continued improvement. Dr. Babbitt thinks he has located the trouble and the treatment which will relieve it but says he will wait for Dr. de S-return to consult with him—rather lay his conclusions before him. . . . The treatment Dr. Babbitt says will be simple and under local anesthetic only—something like what Buzz had I gather but don't say operation to a soul in Lexington—I'm so tired of being a hoodoo. He says there is no reason you should give up your trip to France —so pack your grip—I'm awfully sorry not to get back before you go, but glad to know you're not going to have to stay on my account. . . . Buzz was in last night, very grand in his white uniform, . . . Seems to like the other boys and be interested in his work. How are Scout's eyes? You'll have to show Jennie how to put the drop in when you go till I get back.

The next day, she reported: "The doctors feel it very important for eye to correct the nasal block. They plan this tomorrow morning Wednesday under local anesthesia at University Hospital. Say this is not serious and need not change your plans." Greenlee responded, of course: "Telegram received. All right. Trust everything will go right. Sail Thursday. Love." After the operation on her nasal passage, Katie telegraphed Greenlee in Paris only: "All right—Katie."

Virginia was living and teaching in Washington, and on September 9, Katie wrote her from Philadelphia: "They are going to put me on probation with Dr. Miller for awhile so I will probably descend upon you in the next 48 hours. Wish

I could be more decently definite. With love, Katie. Will wire you from somewhere. If you have any plans don't change them on my account."

But she didn't leave, for a nurse named Tease E. Pilkay wrote to Captain
Letcher briefly on September 13: "Dear Captain, Mrs. Letcher has been getting
along nicely. Of course the first few days were rather uncomfortable, but now she
has reached the sitting-up stage and is feeling quite herself again."

And Katie herself wrote to Greenlee the next day: "Getting along all right but
will be here some days yet. Buz in Sunday & Tuesday—seems interested and
satisfied. Had spent Sunday afternoon in Wilmington.[4] Can't use eyes but hope
you can read this. Lots of Love."

On September 17, she wrote that she was still "in the hospital but getting along
all right. Up most of the day & doctors pleased with things. Buz in last night.
Gone this evening to the party for the heiress. Hope all goes well with you." While
Greenlee socialized in France, a stenographer, "N. Marie Davis, Steno," wrote correspondents for him from Lexington that he was "abroad with the American
legion and does not expect to return until sometime in October."

Katie and Greenlee returned safely from their respective trips, and in November
Katie went back to Philadelphia for yet another operation. On November 9, she
wrote, reminding Greenlee that it had frosted at night: "Thank you. Am feeling
better yesterday and to-day—pretty miserable the three days before. *Did anybody
bring in my flowers?* Don't take on *any cook* without writing me first. How Scout?
Love to you & to the folks." Her sharpness of tone was likely in direct proportion
to her pain and discouragement.

On November 10, she wrote: "Don't think much of any of the would-be cooks.
Just keep a list of the applicants and when I get back we'll take the least awful one.
Probably by that time Annie will have shilly-shallied back again. Hoodoo . . . I am
writing with my eyes closed but hope you can make out something. Buz getting
along all right. With lots of love. K."

Buzz was so impressed with the change in his mother after her operation that he
decided to have his sinuses operated on; they had bothered him nearly all his life.
The U.S. Marine Corps paid for the procedure, which, although painful, finally restored his health. He was in the same hospital as his mother, and at the same time.

On November 14, Katie reported "Buzz looking and seeming better," and the
next day she wrote:

> Dear Cap'n—So glad to get your letter with the news of the old home-
> town and of Hilah's [Pendleton] wedding. . . . Just as I thought I was

doing so fine I took a cold which I am afraid will be a further delay in getting home. However it seems better today after two diligent and far-reaching treatments and throat paintings by Dr. Babbitt. But it's hard luck. . . .

Why didn't you tell me about the shawl—long as I have been wanting a shawl? It will certainly be a pleasant present and weren't you nice to think of bringing me one. This is Buzz's evening to come to Dr. Babbitt so I suppose I'll see him later.

Greenlee must have expected her home any day. On November 16, 1927, she jotted: "The cold is improving but think you may as well go to W. Va. on 18th. I plan to go by Wash. & H'burg & stay there a while. With lots of love. K."

On November 17, she wrote:

Dear Cap'n—My cold seems better but still in evidence and I am afraid it may keep me into next week—in which case or in any case I will need some more money. As it takes several days to get it by mail perhaps you had better telegraph it if you are leaving for West Va. . . . Isn't it queer to think that population drifts to the cities—the heejus [hideous] stupid cities? I hope this part of the population soon gets back to the farm. . . .

Unless I hear from you that Annie is back looking for her job I'll write and take on Caroline for a week or so—or the old Aunt Mag Cuff. No Cephas for me. Would have written sooner about the money but thought I would be leaving by this time. . . . With love to you and Scout & the folks. Have written to Caroline to come Wednesday morning.

Greenlee replied, the only note of his from the fall of 1927: "Dear Katie: Your immediate delivery letter just received and I hasten to send you $50.00 by registered letter, special delivery. . . . Mr. Gibson just asked for Buzz' address and asked about you. Buzz wrote that he would be here Thanksgiving morning, Thursday 24th, with his friend, Lt. Rutledge. Caroline is at Mrs. Kern's. I will tell Jennie to follow up with Mrs. Strain about Annie. I understand Maggie Cuff can be gotten. In haste."

On November 19, Katie wrote that the doctors would allow her to go home for Thanksgiving and "to stay while I gather and come back a little later to let them all look at me again. Hope you and the Mayor can get in your trip before the very cold weather begins. With lots of love. K."

The next day she added: "In my letter to Caroline I told her if she could not come to send Aunt Mag Cuff, but you had better call up Caroline at Mrs. Kern's to make sure. . . . As you say nothing of your W. Va. trip I suppose you have put it off till later." Of their son she commented: "Saw Buzz this morning at Dr. Babbitt's. Poor kid, this is not so gay a way to spend his weekends as in Wilmington." In the same letter, she noted: "Tell Scout I saw this morning the only other Airedale that ever approached him—a puppy that was the dearest thing and looking like he had come from the same kennel. With lots of love."

November 21 saw her still hoping to drive home with Buz but still uncertain: "Hope Aunt Mag Cuff can come to cook for Buzz and company. I only intended to get her by the week. She is too old and feeble for keeps, and too much falls on me. With love to you, K."

Greenlee replied: "I have heard nothing from Annie at all and I therefore feel that there is no use counting on her. Jennie has written to Buzz telling him that if you should be detained by the doctors and not get here she would want him and his friend to come and stay with her. From what I can understand we can get Maggie Cuff, if you write me to do so. I was looking for a postal from you this morning." Katie responded: "If Aunt Mag is on hand tell her to have breakfast early Thurs. morning for Buz and Mr. Rutledge so they can get off to the game. With love. K."

On November 26, Greenlee wrote similar letters to three of Katie's physicians—John H. Stokes, Charles E. Frazier, and to Katie's old confidant, Dr. Smith—sending each a check and desperately seeking information that would help Katie get well:

> [to Dr. Stokes:] I would be glad of anything that occurs to you, which I should know or which should be impressed on her, as to what she should eat or do, that you would write it to me that I might have it in mind. . . .
> [to Dr. Frazier:] . . . Mrs. Letcher understood you would send some writing for her local physician—if you have not done so, please send it to me to give him . . . .
> [to Dr. Smith:] . . . While in Philadelphia she was operated on for sinus and consulted several specialists and was either in the hospital at Philadelphia or under the care of physicians during my entire absence. If there is anything which she should bear in mind, in your judgment, with reference to her mode of life, exercise, diet, etc. I

would so much appreciate it if you would write me fully that we might have it before us.

Frank Smith, always thoughtful and encouraging, responded: "I am always sorry when I hear of Mrs. Letcher's troubles but I really believe that as she gets older she will get better rather than worse. I am sorry that I have no specific medicine or specific directions for her. I believe she is following the right lines. Moderation in everything—some work, not too much. The food that she enjoys will build her up better than a set diet not agreeable to her. So far as I can judge the nervous system is in much better order than when I first saw her and that is all important."

Dr. Stokes had similar advice: "I have talked over in detail with Mrs. Letcher the various points connected with a permanently satisfactory result for her skin. I am anxious that she should do everything possible to keep herself in good general health and to avoid nervous strain. Her diet, apart from moderation in the use of starches and sugars, is a matter of less importance. I have insisted that she shall follow the good old rule of 'Do as you please' in most matters and reduce her responsibilities as much as possible for the time being." There is no extant response from Dr. Frazier.

Early in December, Greenlee fell ill, and a letter on December 5 explains:

> Dear Doctor Stokes: On November 26th I sent you check for $20.00 full to date, but I presume your bill was incurred after the items of that bill. If, however, any mistake has been made you can kindly return me the check. . . .
>
> I thank you for your services to Mrs. Letcher and am grateful that she was able to return home, as I dictate this from bed and leave tomorrow for Richmond to undergo a prostate operation. Again thanking you, I am, Very truly yours, Greenlee D. Letcher.

On December 8, Greenlee had the operation in Richmond and spent Christmas there, on the mend. Katie returned to Harrisonburg from Philadelphia to be nursed by Virginia.

Bad luck, true to its reputation, came in a streak for Katie and Greenlee, both in precarious health: Jennie Stevens's husband died suddenly on December 28, 1927. Greenlee was still not at home when, on January 3, 1928, three days after Professor Stevens's funeral, Jennie's house burned to the ground. Katie was still in Philadelphia recuperating. The house was next door to the one built in 1888 by

Jennie Stevens and Uncle John D. Letcher by the ruins of their Letcher
Avenue house, gutted by fire, January 3, 1928

Houty and his mother after the governor's death; Houty and Fannie continued to live there after Mrs. Letcher's and Aunt Mag's deaths. The Stevens house was bought in 1926 at Dr. Stevens' retirement, with John D.'s help, for fifteen thousand dollars. When Stevens died, John, semi-invalid, was living with them. Thus it is likely that much family history was consumed in the fire.

Katie, when she learned of it, wrote a postcard from Philadelphia, on January 9, 1928, mainly concerned about Scout: "So relieved to hear from Jennie in a letter to Buzz that they [Jennie and John] are all right & none of them ill from shock or exposure and that dear old Scout didn't get burnt. Sorry I can only write a few lines at a time. With love, K."

The next day, she wrote Greenlee:

> Dr. B. did a small but painful operation on the left antrim [sinus] yes-
> terday to open and irrigate it. Said to-day he hoped I would not have to
> stay much longer. So glad to hear you were able to walk a little though

I suppose it seemed plenty by the time you got back to the hospital. Wish the roses had come while I was there. *With lots of love, K.* P.S. Forgot to tell you I am wearing for your peace of mind the warmest shoes I could buy and two layer of stockings. Also faithful to overshoes.

On January 15, 1928, Katie wrote that she was "glad you are home and feeling so much better. Don't get too busy." Apparently she perceived that Scout had eye problems (like herself), for she ended: "How are Scout's eyes? With lots of love. K" She stayed in Philadelphia to be with Buz at the end of January and wrote: "Surgeon reports Buzz getting along all right after tonsils operation"; "Thank you for money—check also rec'd today. Found Buzz looking and feeling much better this afternoon. Wish I could write more than this card"; and "Blizzard yesterday but Jack [Flynn] and I got out to Nancy Hospital today. Found Buzz sitting up for first time. Had had severe bleeding from throat night after operation and of course a great deal of pain. Looks very badly but feeling more comfortable now. Surgeon said tonsils much more infected than they had expected to find." She never mentioned the fire again, or Aunt Jennie's bereavement.

Captain Letcher appears to have written to every physician Katie had had anything to do with, seeking advice. Emory Hill from Richmond wrote back on February 2:

> Dear Captain Letcher: . . . I don't know that I can make any special suggestion about Mrs. Letcher's eyes. . . . We found some sinus infection and also some dental trouble while she was here, and had these both attended to. It appears that Mrs. Letcher's vision is variable, but I hope that by care of her general health, and probably some treatment to her sinuses from time to time, she will preserve her vision. I hope that Dr. De Schweinitz was able to encourage her.

On February 8, Dr. Stokes wrote: "Dear Mr. Letcher: I have no particular suggestions to make in regard to Mrs. Letcher's diet. I simply saw her for a moment in order to make sure that she had no epitheliomatous recurrence on her nose, and have not seen her since . . . Sincerely yours."

Greenlee, always sportingly generous, naturally invited his homeless sick brother and sister to stay with them; there was plenty of room. To his gregarious nature, this was only natural, and soon it occurred to him that they should just stay on. But it did not suit Katie.

On February 26, she wrote to Greenlee from the Spruce Hotel in Philadelphia:

Dear Cap'n—Will not get away until tomorrow. Thanks for telegraphed money. As soon as Buz wrote to me about the fire I wrote to Jennie and told her how sorry I was and how glad that our house was there to be a roof over their heads till they could make comfortable arrangements while their house was being rebuilt. This was all I should have thought of doing for my own people or have ever thought of anyone doing for us. It also leaves us all free from any misunderstandings and Uncle John with his weak heart could never stand the hill anyway. Even if the arrangement was feasible it would take from me the only interest that I have left for I shall never be able to read or use my eyes again. You have your office and all your outside interests, I should spend my days in idleness and unhappiness trying not to annoy other people. They, like you, have their interests, and it seems to me asking too much. . . . Don't let us make a situation out of something perfectly simple and obvious, or try an experiment that has never been known to work. Don't you remember how you urged me to be ready to move out of your mother's house that first summer even though she had been so lovely to us? Because you said it was bound to be inconvenient for people middle-aged and settled in their ways? I remind you of this not because I was ever in the least hurt by it but because I knew then and know now it is true. . . .

It hurts my eyes terribly to write even in scraps so don't let it keep up. *K.* I will return when they are out.

It is a well-known family story that Greenlee, shocked at the ultimatum, scrambled to find Jennie and John D. an apartment elsewhere. He continued to try vainly to find out what was wrong with Katie and must often have been close to despair. He even tried to mollify her by suggesting a trip to Florida, but she wrote, rather coolly: "It is nice of you to suggest the Florida trip & I would love to go but I doubt if the doctors would be willing to have me go so far and it would be less expensive later when the season is over. So sorry to hear about Palmer's boy. Buzz & I were dreadfully shocked and distressed by Fitz Rhea's death—he was a lovely, lovely boy worthy of his blood and name. So glad you are better. K."

The illness and changes brought financial burdens upon Greenlee, and he could not meet the bills for a time. At Ottobine, Fannie Paul died on February 20, 1928, and Katie, still in Philadelphia, wrote to her husband, a mere excuse to go to Harrisonburg in my opinion, as Katie rarely ever mentioned going out to see Fannie at

Ottobine: "I have been so distressed by Aunt Fannie's sickness and death and so sorry not to have gotten to see her while she was sick. She was so fine and of high courage. Am so glad Buzz likes his new assignment. Keep his letters—they may be of interest to him as a diary later on. Preacher Boy [Churchill Gibson] makes a mistake I think in leaving Virginia—he would make a good bishop later on. Expect to leave tomorrow noon or Sunday for Harrisonburg. Putting me on probation with Dr. Miller there. Please wire thirty dollars so I don't get stranded. With love, K."

On February 26, Katie was still in Philadelphia, and Virginia Paul ventured her opinion in a letter to Captain Letcher from Harrisonburg:

> Dearest Cap'n: I am very much ashamed that I have waited all these weeks to write to you after learning that you had come home from the hospital, because I have been thinking of you constantly, so thankful that you are doing so well. . . . But somehow the days have been full and busy and get away before I know where they go, and the weeks slip by without my doing half the things I ought to do—just like all good Episcopalians—and the months even get away from me! The last couple of weeks I have been spending part of every day at Ottobine and doing what I could for our blessed Aunt Fannie—and now for Abe. . . .
>
> I am enclosing the latest communications from Katie. I have not written to her a great many times and have not discussed at all her returning to Lexington. Her attitude is past our understanding and both John [Paul] and I are greatly distressed at such unreasoning selfishness. It must be, to great measure at least, due to her physical condition and not knowing just what that is, John and I have both hesitated to write to her regarding the matter, though when she comes and *John* talks to her I earnestly hope that she will realize how unspeakable this attitude is. John can have much more weight with her than anyone in our immediate family, and he is dreadfully worried. Aside from the distress of all dear Miss Jennie had been through it was absolutely providential that she could come to you at that particular time, for both your sakes. We cannot in any sense comprehend this stand of Katie's, especially when we consider all the sweetness, and unselfish kindness that your family has always shown not only to Katie but to all of us throughout the years in which our households have been connected. We fully

understand the suffering and humiliation caused you and pray that we can in some way help you; we want you to always remember how deep is our affection for you and how sincere our appreciation for you as a man as well as a brother. You gave us a home when we had none and offered me one when our mother died and for your own dear people to be received in this way and under such distressing circumstances makes me sick at heart. With our true love always, Sister Bunch.

Katie stayed in Philadelphia several months at the beginning of 1928, leaving Greenlee, undoubtedly stung by her cold lack of hospitality, having to remove his newly bereaved sister and ailing brother from their house—when in fact his family had always lived in and out of each other's houses, at least since the Civil War.

In early March, with a clean bill of health, Buz sailed for his first foreign post in Nicaragua. At his leaving, Greenlee wrote Buz a long paternally instructive letter, including a copy of his address to his troops, but his mother scrawled a note inside: "It's all right advice but don't let it worry you. Me, I think you and George Washington would do the right thing and all you could do." One assumes Greenlee did not see her addendum. Perhaps he sent his letter to Katie for her approval before having her send it to Buz. A week later, she directed Greenlee from afar: "Ask Aunt M[aggie] or Jennie to mail Buzz—*SOS*—the little green Rumford Cook Book in the end of the big side-board. . . . With love K.P.L."

On March 6, Katie wrote Greenlee from Harrisonburg, where she had gone from Philadelphia: "I'm so stingy about writing because every time I try to write more than a line or so I get worse. Letter from Buzz. Lilian been having some fine sea fishing."[5] The next day, she wrote: "Dear Cap'n—These bills are all right. There will also be a fearful one from Dr. Keffer for putting back the pivoted teeth with gold bridging. Dr. Miller thinks I am doing as well as can be expected. With love, K."

On March 9, from Harrisonburg, she wrote: "Thank you for the paper. Have been very miserable these last few days with neuralgia or neuritis or something. John is in Richmond for a few days." The postcard had no greeting, no closure, no signature. Greenlee found a place for Jennie and John D. to live, but still Katie did not come home. On March 14, she said that her neuralgia was still very troublesome at night, adding: "I am so unsociable about writing—trying in every way to save my eyes. . . . I had hoped you would come down this Sunday but Virginia is not at all well and I think it would be better to wait another week." The next day she wrote: "If I could just keep sitting up all the time—Of course I am homesick

Buz, left, *with a string of fish he* shot *in the Esteli River in Nicaragua*

for Lexington but as long as you are perfectly comfortable I think it would be very unwise to go counter to Dr. de S- and change from Dr. Miller's experience and carefulness to Dr. Mitchell's inexperience and indifference while things are still so desperate with me."[6] On March 16, she wrote that she "[u]sed up my eyes writing to Jennie so you never got my thanks for your check," indicating perhaps that she wrote to Jennie to explain why she felt that they could not accommodate them permanently.

To complicate matters further, while in France, Greenlee had met a Scottish woman, the wife of Count Montaigu, on whose estate, the Chateau De Vrayhes, the battery lived during the summer of 1918. Friends of Clemenceau, the childless countess and her husband had taken a liking to Captain Letcher. After the war, the count desired to come to America, and Greenlee, prior to the spring of 1928, presented his case to VMI and obtained for the count a position teaching French there in the fall. The countess and count planned to arrive at summer's end in time for the fall term and, of course, they expected to be staying with the Letchers, as Greenlee had invited them to do.

In April, Katie wrote to Greenlee: "Dr. de S- saw me some days ago and said the eyes were just a faint shade better but the condition remains serious." She strung him along without saying when she'd return—"Will try to drop you a card every few days to let you know if I'm all right"—writing him: "Thank Jennie for the boots she sent—I can't write. Meant to send a message in my card" and "Glad Mr. B- is starting on his painting—make sure to keep windows locked—attic windows too—Don't let *anybody* fool around up there. Are my *closet in the hall* & room kept locked? Be sure they are."

From Harrisonburg, on April 17, 1928, Charles wrote to Greenlee:

> Thanks very much for your kind letters; and I am sorry to have missed you upon your visit ten days ago; come again soon. I believe I am making some progress, but lack a good deal yet of having the strength I would like, and am bothered at intervals by nervousness and eye-strain; however, hope to go to work soon. We miss Katie very much and hope she will be back among us very shortly; we're glad to know her doctor was pleased. Hope you are quite well now, and enjoying your golf again; I am much interested in the game, and the pro says I am doing well, but fear it will be a long long time before I can seriously compete with Bobby Jones. All good wishes.

Eventually, Katie left Philadelphia for Harrisonburg, whence she wrote that "Gin continues very miserable with her neuralgia. Charles improving. Now you stop cutting that hedge!" She sent postcards, such as "Dear Cap'n—The darker shade of Mr. Bare's sample seems to me very good. Don't you think so?" and "We had not seen that the Marines had gotten to Corinto. Seymour & Charlotte came this morning for a little visit here. Both look very well. Gin is no better, not at all well. Did I see Buzz's gray *summer* suit in the top drawer of the chest of drawers in the upper hall? If so have Brown clean it to destroy all moth eggs & put it in the cedar chest."

Virginia wrote to Greenlee again in April:

> Dear Cap'n: I did not reply at once to your much appreciated letter because I was feeling so miserable and Katie told me that she had written you to postpone your visit till this weekend. . . .
>
> We hope you will come down for Sunday and trust you can make your visit for more than a day. There is to be a golf tournament at the country club on Friday, I believe, at which several professionals are to appear and you might enjoy that. Now that you are to appear in public again we shall hope to have frequent visits from you—we have seen so little of you these past few years. . . .

Katie is looking much better and seems to be feeling very well, but as she is so uncomplaining one never knows just how she is. She has taken Buzz's departure very bravely, but I know it must have been a great disappointment to have him sent off so soon after he had gotten located where the two of you might have been with him. Charlie is doing fairly well but he is very nervous and I am worried about him, at least I worry for fear he will not rest long enough. He is waxing quite enthusiastic over golf and I know how heartily you will endorse this treatment for him. Seymour and Charlotte arrived Monday morning, walking in without warning about six o'clock. Both of them look well though Charlotte is in bed today with a cold. Be sure to come down for Sunday. With love, Sister Bunch

Katie stayed on with Virginia in Harrisonburg, telling Greenlee: "I reckon Mr. Bare had better paint the *woodwork* in the upstairs bathroom white again. If he can put a bathroom paper on the walls & ceiling in a small greenish gray pattern maybe that would be better than paint. Also want Dunn [plumber] to put in a stationary wash-stand. . . . Virginia still not well at all."

Evidently in April Jennie was still living at Katie's, for she wrote: "Think Jennie's idea of painting the doors on the back and side porches green very good but think the front porch should be painted as it is now." In another letter, she appears rather cavalier about finances: "When I left Dr. de S- told me he wanted to see me again in a month and has made the appointment for May 12th—which means poor you will have to hand over another $80 for the expedition. I will make a killing as you say by seeing Dr. Babbitt & Dr. Stokes as this is about the time they also told me to report."

About his visiting Harrisonburg, she wrote that "[i]t would be fine if you could come down Sunday morning & spend the day. I don't think more would be within view of Gin's cook. She is not well & I wake up every morning wondering if she is here. . . . Situation extremely precarious. Glad to hear the house comes on so well." At the end of April she wrote: "Do hope things will soon be so I can get back to Lexington. So glad you got here Sunday & all the folks enjoyed seeing you."

In May 1928, Lilian was hospitalized for at least a second or third time in Mercer, Pennsylvania. Although she wrote cheerfully enough to Katie, and was well enough some of the time from then on to be at home, Lilian was hospitalized off and on thereafter; however, in 1934 she was incarcerated in St. Francis' Hospital in Pittsburgh until her death in 1953. Jack subsequently went to live in South

America and the Far East, writing one letter to the Letchers years later from Rio de Janeiro and one from Bangkok. Neither mentioned Lilian.

Greenlee was now besieged with doctors' bills, and wrote, in May of 1928, to E. L. Keffer:

> Dear Doctor: Your bill of March 31st for Mrs. Letcher for $260.00 received, and I was unable to see her until this week as she has never reached home, being now under the care of Doctor Miller of Harrisonburg. If consented to by you, I will send you a check on or before June 1. I have had very great expenses upon me during recent months as my wife was in Philadelphia most of the winter under the care of several Doctors and for five weeks I was in the hospital in Richmond, having been operated on for prostate. The very great expenses instant to these matters cause me to ask this indulgence of you. Very truly yours, G. D. Letcher

From Philadelphia, Katie asked for some things to be sent her there, remarking, "Send just the hair wash & old fur collar in your bag, neither of which would be slightest use to Jennie. Wish I'd had a present for her but I didn't."

On May 15, she wrote: "I think two or three weeks more with Dr. Miller will get me in shape to risk Dr. Mitchell—awful as that is to contemplate. This will give Jennie a chance to get moved in peace without an extra person in the house. John too. Love, K"

On May 22, Katie wrote to Greenlee: "Sending you letter from Buzz. I reckon Hess had better wrap the gun he wants in burlap after oiling well and crate carefully for shipment. . . . Please send the enclosed with check to Thalhiemer Bros., Broad St., Richmond. Buzz's letters will be a good diary indeed for him to have someday. Be sure to keep them all. . . . Please send me some stamps. P.O. too far uptown."

On May 24, she wrote with some irritation: "Stop worrying about the hair wash—just put it on my mantel-piece and I will eventually use it. . . . When the men wash the woodhouse have them also do the kitchen and entry in yellow wash. *Yes,* got to have the stationary wash-stand. . . . Miss Seymour & C[harlotte] dreadfully—Charles is in Richmond for a day or so. Eyes hurting so must stop."

During this period, Katie seemed to go out of her way to be hurtful and careless of Greenlee's opinions and circumstances. She rarely began with "Dear," and she rarely signed off in a note or letter. Although she wrote of missing Seymour and Charlotte dreadfully, she never expressed such sentiments for her husband. Instead, she wrote: "The money I had left from Phila is running out so I'll have to strike you for more." She had him send a Spanish grammar to Buz, reported on Charles's improvement, and occasionally rebuked him, as in "You forgot to send me any stamps so you didn't get any letter."

However, there is a pleasant letter from this period, written in May, while Katie still stayed on with Virginia, John, and Charles:

> I think Buzz may as well have his shot-gun—it seems to me a good thing to have around and I think he can be counted on to let us know what he's about. I feel that there is no more danger from the hunting than from inactivity in that climate, and better buckshot than birdshot. So sorry not to see Aunt Maggie on her way through. Am so sorry for Mrs. Burks. We are taking our meals out a few doors away and of course I insist on paying my part—8 dollars per week. So my money has run out again paying for that and other needfuls. Charles is going golf crazy—I am watching him develop all the symptoms. . . . K

When Jennie Stevens and John D. Letcher were moved out, Katie returned, for the letters ceased for a time. In September, the count and countess Montaigu arrived in Lexington, where the newspaper reported that they were "living on Letcher Avenue and boarding with the Letchers." Katie had apparently made her point that she didn't want anyone else living in their house, unless it was a member of *her* family. Around the first of October, Buz got into a fight in Nicaragua with the bandits he was seeking and had his horse shot out from under him.[7]

On October 5, 1928, Katie wrote to Buz:

> I had seen in the N.Y. Times a mention of a fight between a small patrol and forty or fifty bandits but no names were given nor the exact locality so it was not till your letters came yesterday that I knew it was your patrol and what a desperate fight! You will know what I felt of thankfulness and of pride in you and your men. You mustn't worry about me. Of course I knew when you went into the Marines what it would be and that I too must have a soldier's heart. You are all of this world to me but nothing "neither life nor death" could take you from me. I think of the Army women in the old Indian fighting days and when the Philadelphians were new and am proud to belong to their crowd. And such a fight as yours can only make one feel that God's

policy is not weak. And always our times are in His hands wherever we are, whatever we do. . . .

I shall keep your letter with the one Charlie wrote when he enlisted under Roosevelt, and Seymour's letter to Gen. Nichols when he could find no other way to get into the war, and John's first battle. . . . I hope your garrison has been reenforced so the strain on officers and men is lightened some. It must have been fearful. . . . You must miss Lieut. Chappell dreadfully. It was surely good to know that he'd been acquitted, though. . . .

Everybody asks about you. Capt. Adams specially the other day. And Mrs. Rogers and Miss Kitty and people on the street and in the stores. . . . Oh, won't it be nice when we can be in Philadelphia again and you can see the shows and go to Wilmington and we'll have oysters at Helenes and the Cascades. Wasn't it the greatest luck in the world we had those months to-gether last fall? With love every minute, you lovely one, Mother

Greenlee must have felt proud and happy to be able to do something for the count and countess who had been so generous to him and his men a decade before. In early December, when Lily de Montaigu died of pneumonia after a brief illness, Greenlee, generous to the end, had her body buried in the Letcher family plot, where it remains today. At semester's end, the count, isolated by his poor command of English, would return to France.

On Dec. 10, 1928, the Medallio D'Honore was presented to Buz at Quantico for unusual bravery in fighting the Sandinistas in the Nicaraguan jungle. He visited home briefly before returning in January to Nicaragua.

Buzz's winning the Medallio d'Honore established his credibility as a Marine to be reckoned with. He went on to an outstanding military career, becoming the youngest battlefield colonel in World War II, at the age of thirty-nine. On December 20, Katie wrote to Buz again:

Dearest Buzz—I wish you could know how many people have expressed their pleasure and sent their congratulations about your citation and the cross. It would take all the letter to tell you. Old Abe was particularly pleased and Helen Webster had copied the citation and read it to the delighted kids. Mrs. Desha was specially cordial and Mrs. Pendleton says tell you that she said in a note to you long ago that she'd be telling some day how she "knew you when you were a boy." We sat next to the Hugers in church the Sunday morning Mrs. Lejeune left the notice for me and Mrs. Huger was the first person I told. She looked stunned for a minute, then her lovely eyes filled with tears and [she] threw her arms round me and kissed me. The Count was delighted and said "And such a splendid citation." He sat looking at it in silence, then said—"How many fine soldiers would give their lives for that." That is what makes one humble in the face of such great honor, I suppose, and must make a man to whom the cross has been given think only of trying to live up to it. With love every minute of every day. Mother

In the spring of 1929, Greenlee wrote urging Congress to introduce a bill to have a special building in Washington, D.C., for all war records, salvaged and indexed so that historians could make use of them, noting: "Certainly in the great resource of this country, the idealism of true history should not be neglected regardless of the cost."

On December 10, 1929, Buz's twenty-sixth birthday, his mother wrote:

Dearest Buzz—I'm just beginning to realize that my dream has come true—that what I had hoped you might someday have is yours at twenty-five. Mrs. Lejeune left an envelope with the clipping from the Army and Navy Journal for me at the church door Sunday. What's being a senator or a millionaire? Give my regards and congratulations to Lieut. Salzman and Lieut. Piper. Just been talking over the phone to John and he surely is delighted—quite forgot his usual stoic calm. Gin came to the phone to tell me she was too proud to speak to anyone but me. With loads of love and no end of pride that I can't put into words. Mother.

Greenlee spoke in 1930 in Richmond to a gathering of Confederate and World War I veterans:

I stand on holy ground and feel that, like the Israelites of old, I should take off my shoes for where I stand to make this response, none other than a confederate veteran has ever stood before. I have touched the hem of the Confederacy's garment in spirit and dreams. In the world war, Va. needed a battery of field artillery to complete her regiment, and when all other efforts had failed, the adjutant general's office, through Generals Stern and Sale, requested our distinguished townsman, Maj. William A. Anderson, to have Confederate veterans get it up as a mark of their loyalty to our common flag and country. It appealed to the imagination and stirred the patriotism of that noble veteran who has carried since Manassas his wounded knee, that picturesque badge of brave service to the Confederacy, a badge more glorious than Golden Fleece or Roman Eagle. That battery to be named after that immortal unit of the Stonewall brigade which was shot to pieces and reorganized four times between Falling Waters and Appomattox, the Rockbridge Battery. He associated with himself other heroes of Lexington and Sons of Veterans and the supreme honor of my life came in giving me charge of the movement, and to be captain, if approved by the war department. After apparent failure, we succeeded in the last hour of the last day, August 4, 1917, and I commanded in America and France the "Rockbridge Battery," Battery F, 111th Field Artillery, 29th Division. I do not believe a finer group of men ever served their nation.

Katie continued to suffer mishaps and illnesses, including a fall that injured her face sometime in January 1931. Scout died in February while Buz was stationed on the SS *Oklahoma*, and Katie wrote him, calling the Airedale "so sweet-natured and so good a companion," and adding: "I like to think that now he is one of the animals that the War Dept has a memorial tablet in memory of who have died for their country." She wrote later in more detail:

> Dearest Buzz—Cap'n wrote you about dear old Scoutie man. He got stronger after you left, ate more, walked a little out-doors and on two or three pleasant days would lie out in the sun. And he was sweetness itself—I never knew him more lovely. He would seem so peaceful and content lying listening to the radio that I used to wonder what dreams may come, what he might feel and know. He looked so at ease after he died, his beautiful "good feets" so lovely, lying there in the hall. . . .
>
> I'm getting over my fall, though my face still shows the bruises. Dr. Mitchell seems to have handled things very well and has been so kind and nice in every way calling up to ask how I'm getting along—which I thought very kind in any one so busy. Don't worry about me. Loads of love. Mother.

On April 17, 1931, Katie wrote Buz, who evidently worried about her apparent decline and sadness:

Dearest Buzz—You surely are a sweet thing about writing no matter how busy you are and it is certainly good to know you're having such pleasant times after the wilds of Nicaragua. But honey, you must not be giving up any chances of service you would like or that would be specially interesting on account of Cap'n and me. All we want is opportunity for you, so if the Pittsburgh and Earnshaw look good to you run and get the job—and I should think they might. And you'd get home so little anyway even in the Atlantic fleet. . . . How much longer will you be in sea school? Would I see anything of you if I came to Portsmouth? I should be going to Philly before long. With loads of love. Mother. PS Hunter Pendleton has a new little girl—in time to get in this census.

On May 21, Greenlee sent the following self-explanatory letter to Katie in Philadelphia: "Yours of Monday (May 20) Special Delivery & I herein enclose results of sweepings in the Play Room & Library downstairs & in your 2 rooms, hall and my room upstairs—you will see I found little solid dust—if a darky had done all the sweeping I did to get it, it would have cost a week's wage." Clearly, a doctor had requested an analysis of their house dust in an attempt to treat Katie for allergies. Greenlee continued: "I leave at 7 in the morning—will be at Warm Springs tomorrow, Weston, W. Va., Friday night & at Webster C. H. or Camden-on-Gauley, W. Va. Saturday & Sunday nights, getting back home, I hope, Monday night. I don't know when before I have been so crowded. . . . Love, G.D.L."

On May 29, Katie wrote to her son,

Dearest Buzz, "Oh that we two were maying" on the road from Churchville to Goshen or climbing the hills on the Craigsville farm to-day—such clear bright sunshine and a breeze to make even me feel young again. . . . And such a nice day for John to be getting Phi Beta Kappa at Charlottesville! Wrote you a brief and scrappy letter to Seattle—wonder if you got it. Told you about King and Mary being wed here. I loved it that they had run in for a minute to change their clothes and leave their suitcase in the morning. I tried to make them stay to supper when they came in to change again in the evening. . . . Love to you all the time, Mudder.

Still Katie failed to rally much, and in August of 1931 she wrote her son a sad note: "Dearest Buzz, Don't worry about me. I look forward always to when you get home, and manage to fill up the days with puttering about the house and thinking of you and knowing wherever you are you are giving a good account of yourself. With my love all the time."

In September of 1931, James A. Babbitt, a Philadelphia physician, wrote to Katie: "My dear Mrs. Letcher:—I received a very nice report from Dr. Mitchell of your condition. He says that you feel better and the nasal condition looks better than he has seen it for many years, and that you have gotten excellent results from the treatment here. I am very delighted to hear this."

In October 1931, Virginia Paul was paralyzed by a stroke and became bedridden, and Katie went to Harrisonburg often to visit her. Virginia was never able thereafter to return to her job as librarian of the Rockingham Public Library.

On January 7, 1932, Katie mentioned in a note to Captain Letcher that she would stay in Harrisonburg with Virginia until they could find another nurse.

In 1932, Buz was still stationed aboard the USS *Oklahoma*, and on January 14, Katie wrote:

> Dearest Buzz—In your letter to Aunt Jennie you told of going with Rutledge to Pasadena—to see the roses and the game—which must have been a pretty happy New Year seeing the Crimson Tide rise, and run over them. Loretta and I sat by the radio and listened to the game—(she likes all the noise and music!) and thought when we heard the roars of cheering for Alamba [Alabama, home of the Crimson Tide] that part of it was you—you that are so pretty. I just gloat over the new picture of you and when the weather is so bad and I get old and poor I go and look at you and take a whiff of Idge's lovely little flask of moonlight and flowers [4711 cologne] and am all right again. I'm sorry you'll have to be at Seattle instead of with the rest of the fleet at Panama where you would be seeing Seymour and the little Garnett Ryden [a young woman he met there]. Seymour thinks her such a bright pretty little kid and all of them nice people. . . . The weather here so bad and the walks so slippery I haven't been anywhere. . . . Go every few days to take an inoculation [for allergy] from Reid who is always a pleasure. In bed the last few days with a cold but am lots better today.

On March 20, 1932, Virginia wrote to Greenlee, alluding obliquely to Seymour's divorce, and Lilian's distressing illness: I assume Katie was not communicating with Virginia, for else why would Virginia have written to Greenlee?

Dear Cap'n, I enclose the only communication received from Seymour since his return, which sounds about as irresponsible as usual. But at least it sounds cheerful, and I hope the intervening months before Charlotte's return will go by quickly for him and that he is always busy enough to keep from getting too lonely. All of us are well. John is busy in court with an unusually long term—at present their energies are directed against a poor old broken down doctor for violating the narcotic act. My sympathies are all with him because he did an excellent job of taking out my tonsils. Abe is well but doesn't come in very often. We expect Charlie home this evening for several days. I enclose a note from Seymour. Much love to you both, Virginia.
[enclosed]
. . . Lilian seemed all right but I didn't make much progress with my suggestion as to visiting Ottobine. She beat me to it with a number of suggestions of her own, that I come home, write a book, keep from getting too fat, and others—all well-meant and sensible. Love to you all. Seymour.

In a note to Virginia, Jennie Stevens remarked that Katie had grown fat. John D. gradually became bedridden.

In the years following, Greenlee became increasingly interested in Letcher genealogy and corresponded with more and more kin from all over the country. He wrote to a Kansas cousin: "I am now of an age that these things [family connections] interest me more than they ever did before." In these letters, along with his keen interest in anyone related to him, is a record of their lives, their illnesses, Greenlee's activities, and their son's remarkable military record.

Buz was stationed on the West Coast.

On May 31, 1933, Virginia Paul died. Greenlee continued to be active and was elected head of the Virginia Blue Grass Trail Association, its object to build better roads. Lumbago sometimes interfered with his golfing. He presided at the fourth annual celebration, on August 5, 1933, of the Lexington Chamber of Commerce, which sponsored that year an exhibit entitled *A Century of Progress Exposition,* in Chicago, which included "geologic maps of Va, mineral specimens, manufactured rock products, fossil shells, a complete set of the Va. Geological Survey, a diorama of Natural Bridge, and transparencies of Grand and Luray Caverns." In 1933, Buz had a serious romance with a girl named Bunny Hammond, who eventually jilted him.

The *Roanoke Times,* on October 5, 1933, carried the following article:

Captain Letcher Is Again Commissioned

Lexington, Oct. 4 (Special)—Captain Greenlee D. Letcher has received a commission from the President of the United States as captain auxiliary in the United States army to continue in force for five years from October 23, 1933, during the pleasure of the president. This appointment made under Section 37 of the National defense act and being a continuance of the commission, heretofore held by him. Captain Letcher received his original commission as captain of field artillery, 1st Virginia Volunteers, Virginia National Guard, August 4, 1917, and was mustered into the U.S. Army August 5, 1917 as captain Battery F111 F.A. and served in the 29th division in America and France for about 22 months, later being appointed a captain in the officers reserve corps. which he continuously held until his retirement at the age of 64. He has since been captain auxiliary. . . .

Captain Letcher has the unique distinction, it is believed, of being the oldest line officer in the World War, the law at that time being that a captain could not be commissioned older than 45 years, whereas, Captain Letcher, having recruited a battery of field artillery under the sponsorship of the Confederate Veterans led by William A. Anderson was taken into the service as captain with his battery on a telegraphic order from the secretary of war, and was at the time five years older than the limit. By reason of being the home station of the battery, Lexington enjoys the distinction of being marked by a captured German field artillery piece at the courthouse corner.

On March 7, 1934, Lilian wrote Katie a note from St. Francis Hospital that indicated that she was not in touch with other family members. Although she sounds a little wistful, she does not sound "mad," as she was reputed by the family to be.

> Darling Katie, Not much to write you dearest Katie except to tell you how delicious the Valentine candy was and how much enjoyed. There is much snow and wind here, quite cold too and a flood threatening, though not this high. What a happy thought to you that you have not only been yourself but have given Buzz, the joysome, to the world. I do hope the dear lad passed the exams and will receive promotion soon. Mrs. Greenway seems to be the sensation of "the Congress." She must be a beauty as the wimmen folks are a-raving—including Mrs. Longworth.[8] "Bess" McCusick, who knew Colonel Greenway, said that he

was the one and only man T. R. wanted for "dotter" Alice. So its quite nice of her to rave over Mrs. Greenway. I do hope that all is well and that you git along. . . . Loads of love, Idge.

In the fall of 1934, Buz was stationed at Quantico. From Fairfax, Virginia, Katie's old friend, Nancy Bell, widowed, wrote her a note that must have gratified Katie immensely:

> Dear Katherine: I've just had the nicest visit from that big, splendid-looking Buz—I did so wish you were here! I made him stay for a cold Sunday night supper (I wouldn't leave him long enough to cook anything!) and I did so enjoy him. Bill Harman (Cosby's nephew, who is living with me and attending E.H.S.) sat spellbound, extracting, by a breathless question now and then, some further account of Buz's travels and adventures.—I wish you could have watched Bill's face. Buz is a delightful talker, and we roared with laughter over his absurd sidelights on various things. Aren't you ever going to be able to run up here and stay with me a while, and see Buz? I can drive a car now, so I could take you down to see his quarters—and I'd *love* to get hold of you! My love to Capt. Letcher, and very much to you—and congratulations to you both on having such a splendid son—he's one of the most attractive men I've ever seen. Lovingly, Nancy Bell.

In 1934 Greenlee was the Lee-Jackson Day Toastmaster, and Jennie Stevens spoke to the assemblage about Robert E. Lee, her godfather. On November 15, Greenlee spoke at Armistice Day in Bedford to what the local paper described as an "overflow crowd."

On February 28, 1935, Greenlee spoke to the Kiwanis Club on his kinsman, Samuel Houston, concluding, not surprisingly, that Houston was a "great American."[9] That year Buz met his future wife, Betty Marston, the daughter of his commanding officer. Aunt Jennie wrote to Buz in April: "Mrs. Morely has just called and brought me the loveliest jonquils. I will send Mudder some of them—I always want to divide everything pretty and good with her: such a 'shut in' yet so brave and bright." This despite the fact that Katie had insisted in such a cold manner that Jennie leave their house seven years before! Jennie to this day is recalled by Lexington folks as having been loving, gracious, generous, and sociable.

Greenlee continued to be a popular speaker, as he still was when we went to live with them in 1943. In 1935 he addressed the Lexington Volunteer Fire

Department, of which he'd then been a member forty-seven years, and spoke to posts of Veterans of Foreign Wars, warning audiences everywhere he spoke that had Germany won the war, she would have taken over France, England, and Italy —and then America.

In 1936 he spoke to a meeting of the United Daughters of the Confederacy, noting: "The only aristocracy recognized in the South is the confederate veterans—not based upon wealth or property, but on service and pride." As president of the Blue Grass Trail Association, he emphasized that "the object of the [projected] road is to serve the people of sections which are without railroads or improved highways . . . that the route would be primarily a farm to market road and a scenic highway for the attraction of tourists [and]is a Dutch treat work; no salaries are paid any of those who work in its interest." Today, the Blue Grass Trail, 315 miles in length, runs from Cumberland Gap in Lee County, North Carolina, to Doe Hill, in Highland County, Virginia.[10]

In 1936 Greenlee Letcher was once again speaker at the local annual firemen's banquet, where, according to the local paper, "Captain G. D. Letcher welcomed visitors in a flaming red tie, which he said was in honor of St. Patrick's Day." On May 12, 1936, the *Lexington* Gazette reported that Greenlee was instrumental in starting the first preservation efforts in Rockbridge County, through an organization called "Old Lexington and New, Inc.," which that early recognized the need to "preserve historically important buildings, and to collect and exhibit local crafts, furnishings, and art." Katie made a successful application to the Daughters of the American Revolution. In 1936 Greenlee, according to the Rockbridge newspapers, was made honorary president of the Lexington-Rockbridge County Chamber of Commerce for the period of his lifetime, "in consideration of his past service to this community and his co-operation in the reorganization of the present body."

A cousin, Nannie Jordan, in the fall of 1936 wrote to congratulate Greenlee: "How proud you and darling Katie must be of Seymour. He sent us an invitation to his wedding and we would love to be there—but Washington is about 'off the map' for us now—When you and Katie go please give him and his bride God's blessing for me—I too am proud of him."

There is a fragment of a letter to Buz from Katie, October 25, 1936: "ing at her when she'll be such a lovely bride. I'll never get over that I can't be there. . . . I hope indeed Abe [Paul] does not suffer—I hope he will not have to lie there much longer but can soon cross over the river and rest in the shade of the trees and see his folks. Give my love to Betty—and take good care of her. I hope she won't be too tired by all the wedding. With my love always and always. Mother." It appears to me that Katie at least implied that she couldn't go to the wedding because of Abe Paul's illness.

In November 1936, Buz and Betty married. A note from Betty's mother after the wedding confirms that Katie did not attend, as did a letter from Grace Dunlop [Ecker] Peter, who lived from 1918 to 1929 in Lexington and was the owner of the *other* Airedale: "Dear Mrs. Letcher, I thought of you so constantly all day Wednesday, and my heart just ached that you couldn't be here to see your dearly loved son married! You are such a wonderful, brave person—but sometimes one gets tired of being brave! . . . I am sending you this clipping which you may not have seen, so you can see that 'Buzz looked grand, of course, and his bride is lovely!'"

After the wedding, Buz and Betty visited Lexington briefly, for Katie wrote Buz: "You and Betty looked so beautiful and so quality the morning you left. I was glad to see Arkansas would see some nice people just once—also the Henderson will look all dressed up with you two in it."

Betty's mother wrote to Katie two weeks after her daughter's wedding to Mrs. Letcher's son:

> My dear Mrs. Letcher, Thank you so much for your kind invitation for this week end but as John [her husband] could not get away from the office on Friday this week, we would have so little time with you. We must arrange another date soon as the bride and groom get settled at Quantico as I am very anxious indeed to meet such a nice person as I know you to be. I intended writing to you the day after the wedding but went down to Atlantic City and spent a little over a week with a friend there who has a sweet little apartment. We walked in the lovely air and read and slept and rested and I came home very much refreshed to take up the winter duties. My Auxiliary job is a strenuous one and takes a great deal of time and energy. . . . We expect the children [Buzz and Betty] on Monday evening and as their apartment is not quite ready for occupancy they will stay here and collect and move all their lovely presents to Quantico. Everybody was so kind in saying such lovely things about the wedding. I could not see how the wedding could have been improved upon. You tell Captain Letcher that he almost "stole the show"—everybody liked him so much. We were sorry the two brothers had to hurry back; we saw a little more of Uncle Charlie who is a dear. Several friends were looking around for Uncle John but he could not stay long. We hope to see them again before

long. The silver service was so much admired—the day of the wedding I left it out for Captain Letcher to see. Everything else had to be put away. It was really a lovely sight—the best looking couple you ever saw. I shall get a nice little picture when they get home. With all best wishes to you both and many thanks again for your telegram. Affectionately, Elizabeth W. Marston.

On January 11, 1937, Uncle Abe died at Ottobine. That spring, Greenlee, his popularity undimmed by age, addressed a mass meeting of the Confederate Memorial Association, the Confederate Veterans, the Daughters of the Confederacy, the Daughters of the American Revolution, and servicemen. Once more he related his father's glories and those of his older brother, Houty, "at seventeen a Lieutenant of the Confederacy on the Staff of General Preston." He also retold the story of the Rockbridge Artillery. The *Lexington Gazette* reported that he spoke to the Business and Professional Women and was master of ceremonies at the Blue Grass Trail dinner meeting.

At a Memorial Day parade in Lynchburg, reported on in the *Lynchburg* newspapers May 30, 1937, Greenlee argued that the southern states were most likely to be the safeguards of constitutional rights and liberty in the United States "in this age of industrial strife." He called that fact an "irony of history" since the *North* believed that seceding from the Union was a violation of constitutional rights. He took issue with critics of President Wilson for taking the United States into battle against the Teutonic powers, saying it was "the greatest thing ever done." At Armistice Day in November that year in Staunton, he quoted Horace: "The brave are created by the brave."

From the Canal Zone, Seymour wrote in January of 1937 about contentment with his new wife, Jane Abbott Paul, and two sons, adding that: "I can't feel awful cheerful about Buzz's going to China. It's fine experience and wonderful travel and all that—but so far away. Maybe we should say not so far, with China Clippers flying the Pacific, but I can't think of it as near . . . We trust that even your exacting judgment with regard to a wife for Buzz is pleased with Betty. We found her mighty sweet, and comfortingly solid." He ended, unaware that Abe had died, "Is Abe any better, grand old man? He has been quite wonderful. I hope he has enjoyed like the rest of us the fact of Ottobine's remaining 'a little Ararat above the flood.'"

Modern times were coming to Lexington, for in 1937 the new Warner Brothers State Theater was opened, with motion pictures that changed weekly! In April

Greenlee and Teddy in front of 302 Letcher Avenue, Lexington, c.
1937–38. In 1937, Katie wrote Greenlee while he was on a trip,
"Teddy has been a model citizen, even putting up gracefully with the
suspicious looking man from the cleaning shop, and the gasoline smell."

of 1937, Katie wrote Buz: "You make China seem a real place and not so far away after all. Who you reckon is married now—Dumps Coe! To Mr. Sam Dunlap's daughter Mildred.[11] Old Hop may as well come in and surrender." Hop was Dorsey Hopkins, a childhood friend of Buz's, who in fact *never* married.

In 1938 Greenlee spoke at the annual Lee-Jackson dinner in Lexington: he argued for the urgent necessity of readiness for his country and for the South on the basis of past defeats. "As far back as Tacitus," he said, "the Germans have been described as vicious and warlike." In August, he suffered from something he variously described as lumbago, sciatica, and rheumatism, to such an extent that he could not play golf. His sister Maggie died while on a visit to Lexington, and was buried in the family plot. His brother John Davidson Letcher died, after many years of generally ill health.

In China, Katie and Greenlee's first grandchild was born, and the parents named the baby Katie Paul Letcher.

After Abe died, John Paul, by then a judge, moved into Ottobine, and renovated it. He had been a widower for almost twenty years.

Alice Kelly Taylor of Norfolk (distantly kin by marriage to Louise Taylor who was John D. Letcher's wife) became John Paul's second wife, as he was her second husband. Katie on the occasion of their union in 1938 wrote to Buz that she was "so tiny her cigarette seemed like a log of wood in her hand. She was a great belle as a girl and all her friends chant her praises."

In September of 1938, Greenlee's old friend, Henry B. Holmes, came to visit, and wrote Greenlee in a letter that contained a snapshot of them taken in the mellow autumn sun from the balcony of the Robert E. Lee Hotel in Lexington: "Considering the fact that we are in our seventies, I think Father time has dealt very kindly with both of us."

A letter in 1939 to Katie from Charles mentioned that "Lilian, sadly, makes no improvement and the doctors give no hope that she ever will." Charles suffered that year, according to another letter, from "his kidneys."

Throughout the years, the Virginia conventions of Confederate Veterans and Sons of Foreign Wars Veterans were held in Lexington, at VMI, through the efforts of Greenlee, and in 1939 he was formally honored by those groups. That same year he was recognized and honored by the Chamber of Commerce as being solely responsible for bringing these groups to Lexington.

Greenlee reported to the *Lexington Gazette* on an American Legion Convention in Richmond in April 1939: "The meeting was very successful, the parade being a very long one, with 23 drum corps in the line."

In April 1939, Katie wrote to Buz in China: "After the cold blowy March weather Spring has come almost over night, with the loveliest things of all to me, the blossoming fruit trees, that God should also give us all this lovely bloom as though the fruit were not enough."

In May of 1939, Seymour Paul visited the family with his new wife and their two small sons, writing to Katie after his return to Panama: "It was nice to see you, even for so compressed a visit . . . and I thank you for coming to Harrisonburg, a journey which you must have found tiresome. I wish I might have conveyed a little sense of intimacy with Jane and the young sons. They are a charming lot and I hope to bring them to the States within a reasonable time." He commented favorably on John Paul's new wife, Alice, and wrote: "Our visit to Ottobine was a great interest. John is doing extensive renovations and will make quite a modern house, in the midst of the old charm of trees, millrace, creek and views of woods and mountains. The painted barn looks as it never looked before." Seymour's "young sons" were Seymour, age two, and Johnny, age one. From 1943 on, my parents, my siblings as they came along, and I were frequent visitors at Ottobine.[12]

Greenlee and Henry B. Holmes on the balcony of the Robert E. Lee Hotel in Lexington, August 23, 1938

On July 7, 1939, the *Lexington Gazette* featured Greenlee's picture inset on page 1 against a new road, "whose champion at the beginning and ever since has been . . . Capt. Greenlee D. Letcher, who inspired his co-workers with the possibilities of a trail through the wilderness to the west. It opens up a virgin scenic land whose beauty is said to be unexcelled." Today that trail has evolved into Interstate 64.

On August 31, 1939, the American Legion chose Greenlee as its representative to its national convention in Chicago. When that same year George Catlett Marshall spoke in Lexington, Greenlee escorted Marshall, head of the U.S. Army, to

Left to right: *Greenlee, Betty, little Katie, Buz, and Katie, on the front steps of their house at 302 Letcher Avenue, Lexington, November 1939*

the platform. To the Women's Club of Clifton Forge, Virginia, he gave a history of the American constitution, emphasizing the dual roles of freedom and responsibility.

Greenlee spoke at another Lee-Jackson Day dinner in November 1939 and was honored at a dinner of the American Legion, Rockbridge Post. A member of the Layman's League at the R.E. Lee Memorial Church, he organized suppers at which church members could discuss how best to serve God, America, and community through the church.

In November of 1939, Buz and Betty and baby Katie, then eighteen months old, returned from China and visited Lexington. After a ten-day visit, the family drove to San Diego, Buz's next post.

In January of 1940, Greenlee dedicated a bronze plaque put on the cannon captured by the Rockbridge Regiment twenty years before; in his speech, entitled "A Lesson from the Past," he expounded on his growing concerns: he urged preparedness and noted that the lesson learned from the Civil War is "that the side

Greenlee in his uptown office on Washington Street, Lexington, c. 1940

which commanded the sea wins." He emphasized that this fact should "govern the mind and purpose of our nation today." Recalling World War I, he warned against Germany, Italy, and especially Japan. He cited Tacitus as the first to call the Germans a hardy and warlike people. Greenlee repeated, in every speech he made during this time, that the Germans and especially Hitler were not to be trusted. Time and again he urged personal, local, and national preparation for war.

In February 1940, in a letter to Buz, Katie wrote that the "snow has been bothering my eyes." She had become almost blind.

In 1940, the centennial year of the R.E. Lee Church, it was decided to commission a church history. The superintendent of VMI, Charles Kilbourne, believed that the church had been challenged by VMI—because the military was not a favorable environment for "religious contemplation and studies." This was just the sort of thing Greenlee loved to get his teeth into, and, in taking on the job, he was able to show a statistically high participation record among local college students in the church's affairs, as well as a remarkable longevity of vestry service.

Greenlee's enthusiasm led him to make many bad investments through the years, and his trusting nature was such that after he died, and my father cleaned out his office, he found over six thousand dollars' worth of IOUs to his father, which Greenlee had never bothered to collect, many of them from people who'd borrowed from him over and over. He never locked his office and is said to have stored valuables in the woodstove, a place he figured thieves would overlook. But on one or two occasions he forgot the next day and burned them up. And yet, puzzlingly, apparently his reputation as a fine lawyer was never tarnished.

Buz, despite his early glory, was passed over for promotion, and wrote in 1940: "Selection is not working right." He complained to his father that "CO's don't bear down hard enough on no-account officers" and that they "passed everyone, and so the selection board can't distinguish between good and bad officers," and that "Yes-sir men got promoted." Buz said he couldn't do that, had to speak up and be independent. "I can't see things slack and poorly run without saying something." He inherited more of his mother's brusqueness than his father's diplomacy.

From San Diego, Betty wrote newsy letters to her in-laws back in Lexington: "We have just invested in a set of Wear-Ever Aluminum Kitchen utensils which are supposed to cure all ills and make a new person of you. They are starting a new method of cooking in which food is cooked without water and at a low temperature which insures the preservation of minerals and vitamins. Buz and I are much impressed with the idea." She reports cooking thirty-one partridges that Buz shot, and that "Chickie [little Katie] fell at the zoo and scratched her nose, but came home and told me a monkey had bitten [it], a much better story, she thought."

Around 1940 letters between Greenlee and Buz began that, over time, outlined their different philosophies and their fears (on this they agreed) that Hitler would conquer the world if the United States were not vigilant, and that increased leisure time and higher wages would wreak havoc with the character of the country.[13]

Greenlee often wrote urgently and eloquently to legislators on these subjects; it is interesting that his vision outstripped theirs. Age had not dulled his acuity. On April 30, 1940, Greenlee wrote to the Honorable A. J. Ellender,[14] Senate Chamber, Washington, D.C., this letter, remarkable for several reasons: he was over seventy at the time yet still full of fight for the American way of life. He knew history; he knew military tactics. His energy was undiminished. America was overwhelmingly isolationist at the time, and Greenlee foresaw how disastrous it would be to continue on such a road. The letter, which seems visionary, especially coming two years before the Japanese bombed Pearl Harbor, follows in its entirety:

Dear Senator: Following our few minutes conversation Saturday evening concerning the policy the United States should take in the second World War, and feeling that this is of such deep importance, I take the liberty of restating the views I expressed to you and amplifying them. My opinion is that the world should know that the United States sympathizes with France and England, and if its help was necessary to save them from defeat by Germany, it would be given both in material help and becoming an ally. Of course, I understand that no congressional resolution should be passed to this effect at this time, but that our Congressmen and Senators should so express their personal views as to let Germany and the remaining neutrals of Europe know. My most earnest reason for this is that should Hitler win the war in Europe, he would of course take the military and naval resources of England and France, the colonies of France and England and Denmark, and although I have not at hand the exact date, I take it that this would give Hitler and Italy at least three times the naval power of America, and regardless of how brave our seamen might be, we would be swept off the ocean just as England has swept Germany off, and our thousands of miles of coastline would be under the guns of Germany. This would at once put us at war with Germany under our Monroe Doctrine as we could not and would not permit Germany to take Bermuda, the British West Indies, British Honduras, the Guianas, Falkland Island, etc., for if we did, we at once would subject ourselves to Germany and its fearful methods of peace and war. A victorious Germany would not for a moment acquiesce in our Monroe Doctrine and we would then have the entire burden of fighting Germany and Italy and perhaps Japan without the aid of France and England, and I cannot but think that such a contest would sweep us off the ocean and that the Panama Canal would fall to a blockade without the firing of a gun. With the possessions of Denmark in Iceland and Greenland and Newfoundland from England, Germany would have all of our rich northern section under her airplanes, and if she drove our navy off the sea, her first effort would be to destroy our shipyards such as Newport News so that we could never come back on the sea. This is no dream, but this is exactly what occurred in the Confederate War when the Federal Government had command of the ocean, although Lee and

Jackson could win great victories on land, as soon as they came under the range of the gun boats, they had to fall back helpless, and the life of the Southern Confederacy was famished and strangled. I have very little fear of Germany being able to land sufficient troops to come inland any distance, but I do fear that they would have our coastal areas and cities at their mercy, and the loss and destruction could be so vast as to be appalling. And knowing the methods of Germany, she would, for example, give notice to the United States that Boston would be destroyed unless twenty-five billions of dollars would be delivered. Some feel that by airplanes we could avert such disaster, but the lessons of the campaign in Norway now would seem to demonstrate that this is a fallacy. During the Confederate War, when the iron-clad Merrimac came out the first day and destroyed a number of the United States ships, the Memoirs of Mr. Welles in Mr. Lincoln's Cabinet show that had not the Monitor appeared the following day, it was the belief of Mr. Lincoln's Cabinet that the war was lost, and such would doubtless have been the case had the Merrimac remained invincible, but the Monitor appeared the following day, which was equal or superior to the Merrimac and reestablished Federal supremacy of the sea. . . . I feel that if England and France are destroyed by Germany, Germany under Hitler will become a power beyond the dream of Caesar or Napoleon, and America will have to fight for its economic existence and life at a cost of which present expenditures would only be a "drop in the bucket," and would be under a disadvantage so great as to perhaps set back liberty and democratic progress indefinitely. I was Captain of Battery F, 111 Field Artillery 29 Division in training in America and in France, and while I would regret beyond measure America being again at war, I feel that we may procrastinate and put this thing off and allow our natural allies to be whipped, and then find ourselves helpless to preserve our liberty and safety. Give your best thought to what I am writing as I feel that I can see it coming so plainly as to appall me. You gave expression to what I feel has been a propagandized fallacy since the first World War—that is, that that war was fought to make democracy safe and was a failure—while I feel that that war was the most beneficial war this country has ever fought since the Revolution or the Civil War, and that it did make democracy safe for twenty years and was absolutely a vital condition to keeping it safe in the result of this war. I am a great admirer of

Woodrow Wilson, and I think that his forethought and wisdom were almost inspired in taking us in and carrying us successfully through the first World War, and it behooves us to leave no stone unturned to continue to save democracy as he saved it then. I hope that I have not tired you in this long letter, but realizing the vantage position that you occupy for your country's good, I write you with all the urgency that I am able to muster. With hope and good wishes for the preservation of liberty and democracy. Sincerely, Greenlee D. Letcher.

Three letters he received in return must have discouraged him greatly. Harry Flood Byrd, powerful leader of the Democratic Party in Virginia, governor of Virginia, and U.S. senator, brushed him off: "My dear Captain: I have just received and noted with much interest your letter enclosing copy of letter you have written Senator Ellender. . . . I am always delighted to have your views about these matters and appreciate your kindness in writing me. With best wishes, I am Faithfully yours, Harry Flood Byrd."

He heard also from Virginia's Representative A. Willis Robertson,[15] a discouragingly frank note: "My dear Captain Letcher: Thanks for your nice letter of the 1st and copy of your letter of April 30 to Senator Ellender which I have read with interest. The developments in Norway must give lovers of a democratic form of government genuine concern, but the present sentiment of the Congress is overwhelmingly against any move by our Government that might actually involve us in that war. With best wishes, I am Cordially yours, A. Willis Robertson."

Ellender's response was the worst:

Dear Captain Letcher: I was glad to receive your favors of the 30th ultimo. Every man has a right to his own opinion. I believe that the English and French people know where our sympathies lie. Quite a few Senators have expressed themselves and I believe the President has aired his views on the subject. Sympathy is not what will win the war. What the Allies need is food and ammunition. If we should furnish either or both we would be taking sides in this controversy and the next thing that we would have to do would be to send some of our boys across the seas. I am unwilling to take such steps. I would much prefer to take care of our own people and let Europe take care of her own affairs. . . .

I expect to return to Lexington within the next few weeks and I shall be glad to play some more golf with you. With kindest personal regards, I am Sincerely yours, Allen J. Ellender.

Greenlee Letcher's graciousness was such that he responded to Ellender's short-sighted response:

> Dear Senator: Yours of the 6th received, and I will look forward to future golf games with you with the happy thought of the very pleasant one recently. . . .
>
> As to the World War I feel we will be obliged to fight Germany after the war if she wins now because she will unquestionably claim and endeavor to take the colonies of the Allies around us, and we will have it then to fight all by ourselves with Germany, having the combined resources and navies of the world, which will so outnumber us as to make us defenseless on the ocean; that we should go in and help the Allies while they are able to help us. Think over this terrible problem deeply. Sincerely, G. D. L.

Letters from John Paul at this time tell us that Charles, now ill, lived out his life at Ottobine with John and Alice. In 1941, Katie wrote on February 14 to Buz, her slanted scrawl now nearly two inches tall, "Of all the lovely Valentines—to hear you on long distance last night—you so pretty you so sweet—you that are my heart's delight. Mother."

Greenlee spoke in 1941 at a Blue Grass Trail meeting, introduced by Governor Colgate Darden. He gave the Memorial Day speech in Lexington. Introduced by Senator Willis Robertson, he had a portrait of his father presented to VMI and spoke once again of his father's accomplishments and how they were examples for today's men. On October 23, 1941, ever optimistic, although Jennie was dying of Bright's disease, he wrote to a cousin that he would visit, "as soon as my sister recovers from her present sickness."

In 1941, Greenlee urged a distant kinsman and one of his correspondents from Ann Arbor, Michigan, Henry E. Riggs, to retire in Lexington, where "you would receive a warm welcome. . . . [T]he libraries would be open for your use, . . . you would enjoy the distinguished lecturers and men who come here . . . and you would find the climate bracing and healthful, rarely too warm in summer, and with very little cold weather . . . the expense of living here less than cities or in the North." Greenlee, a one-man chamber of commerce, ended by noting that the elevation above sea level was a *perfect* 1,100 feet.

On December 7, 1941, Japan bombed Pearl Harbor, and two days later, Katie and Greenlee's second grandchild, John Seymour Letcher, Jr., was born.

In January of 1942 Buz got a promotion, and Katie wrote to him delightedly: "My precious old Buzz—This is just a line to give myself the pleasure of addressing a letter to Maj. Letcher U.S.M.C. and to tell you what a splendid looking fellow little Marse John is—you certainly have an out-fit to be proud of. Mis Lizzie told us about Chickie's [little Katie] shopping trip with 'a friend of the family.' She is certainly a delightful little person."[16] Seymour decided to go back to Panama by plane from somewhere in the Southwest to finally bring his family back to the United States to live, so he could spend more time with his dying brother, Charlie. Katie wrote to Buz that "Aunt Jennie is about the same. . . . Jane [Paul] and her mother have already taken an apartment in Harrisonburg. She is a lovely person. Mother."

Jennie died February 6, 1942. Later that month Greenlee wrote to another cousin, J. Hall Taylor: "It is a sad time to me, closing up the old home in which my people lived for fifty or more years, but such comes to all of us sooner or later, especially the younger members of a family who have outlived the others. I do not grieve so deeply as many do, feeling that when those near to me pass away, their spirits are still with me, and to a certain extent watch over and guide me." Charlie Paul also died that year.[17]

That month, February 1942, Greenlee had surgery for a bowel tumor discovered while the surgeon was repairing another hernia, on the opposite side from the one he'd had in 1918. He recovered completely, so the tumor must have been benign. In April of 1942 he wrote a friend: "I am very much afraid this war is going to last a long time and will sorely tax all our country's resources. But we have got to win it, if it takes everything we have, and I will not worry in the slightest about the burden to come, as I am ready to devote everything I have to it if necessary." He meant, of course, his only remaining son, who would soon be leaving for the Pacific theater. He suffered a heart attack later that month.

On March 14, 1942, Buz wrote from Camp Elliott, California, where he was training: "Dear Pop: I received mother's letter forwarded to me by Betty, dated 4th March and saying that you were getting along very well. I'm certainly glad to hear it and I hope you are soon able to leave the hospital. . . . Everything here goes well. It is pretty rugged living, hot in the day, cold at night and the wind whirls the sand and dust about incessantly, but I feel that we are getting a lot of good training. With love to all of you every minute."

As Greenlee recovered, in May of 1942 he sent cousin Henry Riggs advice about Riggs's ill wife: "Tell her to take things easy and rest. My wife has to do that, which causes her to be in bed a good deal of the time. The doctors say that when that advice is given, especially if it is given by reason of heart trouble, if the patient obeys, they live longer."

In September 1942 when Buz had to go fight the Japanese in the Pacific, Greenlee invited not only Betty Letcher and her two children but also Betty's mother, whose husband was also in the war, to come and live with them. That time Katie made no protest, presumably, perhaps because once again America was at war, and her patriotism was tapped.

Greenlee wrote to cousins that he planned to write a biography of his father, but he did not accomplish that task. On October 9, 1942, at a public meeting of the Rockbridge County Defense Forum, Greenlee posed to a large audience the question: "What would be done if Lexington were raided tonight in an air-raid that destroyed 1/3 of the town?" The discussion following, according to the *Lexington Gazette,* aroused an unusual amount of excitement. A month later, despite his advanced age, Greenlee was put in charge of distribution and sales of defense stamps to finance the war, speaking at his inauguration on "Nazi intolerance for Jews." He told the audience that Nazis were intolerant of Catholics, Protestants, and Free Masons as well, and in typical fashion called for "an end [to] religious persecution and prejudice, and an instilling of tolerance in all." He reminded listeners that Christ was a Jew so that "we owe Jews our greatest gratitude." He pled especially for help from the women of the town.

Mother, Johnny, and I arrived in Lexington in time for my fifth birthday, May 12, 1943, having crossed the continent in the 1939 Ford in eleven days. My grandmother Marston had declined Greenlee's kind invitation. Buz, bound for the South Pacific, fully expected that the West Coast would be the next Japanese bombing target. After several weeks, my mother moved us to a small apartment a half-mile away. I remained a resident of both house and apartment. That is when I came to know my grandparents well, and to adore them both.

On July 1, 1943, Greenlee wrote to Buz, who was now a Lieutenant Colonel in the Pacific,

> Dear Buzz: This letter has been delayed about a week as Miss Mae [Kincaid] who does my writing was off on a trip. I enclose you a copy of a letter that I wrote to Lt. W. C. Drewry, thinking it might interest you to read. His mother sent me his address in a very lovely letter which she wrote me. I also enclose you a copy of "The Boys' Appeal," Boys' Home Inc., Covington, Virginia, of April 1943, with a picture of

Greenlee, Johnnie, Betty, and little Katie, in the backyard of our apartment on Jefferson Street, November 1943

brother John and a complimentary column. I am trying to select and pay out to charities and churches the balance of the fund in his estate as I think it is important, in my advancing years and condition of health, to try to get everything in my hands completed without unnecessary delay. As I wrote you, I had an Angina attack on January 16th from which I hope I have measurably recovered with no immediate danger to my life but, at my age of life, there is no certainty about such matters.
. . .

I have never written you before about Teddy but just about the time you were going over seas, Teddy died. He ran off one morning somewhere and when he came back, he had a very severe dog bite in his left ear from which he was evidently suffering. We, at once, sent for the veterinarian who took him out to his dog hospital and reported to us that evidently some big dog had bitten him and his teeth had gone through the drum of his ear. He remained at the hospital for perhaps 10 days when the veterinarian brought him back, saying that he would eat nothing and that he had better be at home. He died the following day. I can't tell you how Katie and myself were grieved over it. The night before he died, as was my habit when taking him out, I called him to "Attention" and he made the best effort he could to arise to his feet but failing, I carried him out in my arms and brought him back the same way. I did not write to you at the time feeling that you had enough on your mind already and knowing what a grief it would be to you. We think of him every day and I so wish for him that he might be here with little Johnny and Katie as I think they would thoroughly enjoy him. . . .

I walked down to the V.M.I. this morning with little Johnny and he was in fine humor and health. Every Wednesday and Sunday Betty comes with the children for dinner and other days she generally comes for part of the day, knowing how much we enjoy the children. Katie comes whenever her mother lets her. Johnny is a great mother's boy and it's hard to get him to take a walk or leave the house when she is here but after he gets a little distance, he seems to take interest in everything; and, like you and Gee, I am trying to get him to come to "Attention" and "Forward March" and "Salute." He is a wonderfully smart child, especially for his age and has fine humor, and little Katie is one of the brightest children I ever saw. Everybody is fascinated by her. Dr. Murray, the Presbyterian Minister, told me she had called on him and he seemed wonderfully taken. Betty tells me the Presbyterian Minister from Falling Springs, who lives in the same house with her, is very much taken with Johnny. I held his hand and he wrote the enclosed, "Love, Jonnie Letcher. And daddy helped me write this," and I told him I was going to send it to you and it was strange how much his eyes would seem to indicate that he understood. Everybody who has met Betty seems charmed by her and I think that she is happy here. Mudder says to tell you that Katie is a lovely young lady and Johnny is the most courtly gentleman she has ever met at his age. He was much disturbed the other day when they were playing tea party because Mudder did not have a cup of tea. He lead her to the party and looked into her cup and anxiously inquired, "mo." Katie is now attending Bible School. With love from both of us . . . P.S. I copy from the letter of April 19,

1943, from Rt. Rev. John B. Bentley, the following sentence referring to you: "You have good reason to be proud of your son. It is characteristic of you that your first hope and prayer is that 'he may do his duty faithfully with honor.' I have every confidence that he will. I have not had the privilege of meeting him, but he could not be the son of his father and fail to do his duty with honor. I hope and pray that he may return safe to you and his loved ones."

In January of 1944, the *Lexington Gazette* headlines read: "Letcher's Unit Smashes Japs with Barrage," describing the siege of Bougainville. Lt. Colonel John S. Letcher, when asked to comment, stated, "The Japs won't use those guns again. The Marines blew them up with TNT."

In 1944, Greenlee wrote to another distant relative, "Cousin Nina Taylor": "Buz believes the Third Marines have not been given the credit they deserve, that the first Guadalcanal attack got all the publicity but in fact Tarawa and Saipan and subsequent attacks on Guam were much harder and bloodier." He added, hopefully, "Katie has been getting along nicely since she had her tooth taken out, and I think that was her real trouble all along." On November 1, 1944, he wrote a kinsman McElwee: "I believe that my shortness of breath is increasing, which of course is a danger signal but on the whole I am getting along about as well as I could expect. I still go to my office in the mornings, generally lying down during the evenings which is the only prescription the doctors have given me.

Much of what remained of Greenlee's last years comes from carbon copies of letters he sent to his many distant relatives all over the country. For instance, he wrote at the end of 1944 to Nina Taylor in Illinois: "I don't know whether I ever told you but Katie's eyes are very weak and she scarcely can read without a large magnifying glass and I read the newspapers, letters, etc. for her and write for her. This is quite a deprivation for her as in early life she was a great reader but she takes it philosophically. The unhappy effects of this have deprived her of almost entirely for sometime the pleasure of going out to social affairs as she does not recognize people which is very embarrassing as to her defective vision people are not generally conscious." To another cousin he wrote that

> Betty has just received word that Buz has been promoted to Colonel somewhere in the Pacific. So many thanks for the box of chocolates and the banana flowers for little Katie. We know she will delight in them. She is a lovely child as bright as she can be and little Johnnie is a wonderful little kid and I surely enjoy my walks with him, treating him as

a soldier all the time and once when someone said that he would one day be a soldier, he said, "I am a sojer now." I am looking for their mother to bring them down to my office in a little while for them to be taken care of while she has another engagement. They are splendidly behaved little ones and they are filling a big place in our lives. . . . Heaven is good to us in so many ways.

Buz, miraculously unscathed, came home in September 1945 and was stationed in Norfolk, and of course Betty, Katie, and Johnny went along.

In October of 1945, Greenlee wrote another kinsperson, Lizzie Blackwell Williams, that he was "just now past 78 and in the natural course of events I would be slowed but Heaven has been kind to me and still is, in the enjoyment of life and the attention to duties due to myself and others."

On May 9, 1946, Betty and Buz had boy and girl twins, the third and fourth grandchildren. Greenlee that month spoke against isolationism to the Virginia American League Convention in Richmond, stating "[t]hat our great rich country should be generous to the nations large and small, in so far as in us lies, to relieving their hunger, not only under the impulse of Christian charity, but under good policy, as satisfactory peace will never be assured to a starving world." His son continued to believe that America was giving itself away to the rest of the world, ought not to allow immigrants in, and should not help rebuild Europe.

In November 1946, to his cousin, Nina Taylor, who had written him, "When we toured down there, we were impressed with Virginia's fine roads," Greenlee replied: "Recently the Chamber of Commerce reappointed me Chairman of their Road Committee. I recently made a trip to West Virginia, looking over the development of a route, accompanied by an Engineer of the Virginia Highway Department. . . . [I]n the large sums of money the U.S Government is expected to expend on roads, it will again become very important. Our State Commissioner, General Anderson, will be gratified by your appreciation, which I will write him about."

Greenlee suffered a mild heart attack in 1946 and wrote some newly found "cousins" that he was retiring. But to another he wrote only a week later: "I attended one of our quarterly meetings of the Rockbridge Historical Society. It has gathered together a number of very old things—tools and books connected with our civilization and life in Rockbridge which were very interesting. I am on the Executive Committee of the Organization and take very considerable interest in it."

Of his sixtieth class reunion at VMI in 1946, Greenlee wrote to a cousin: "Our Class has been made up of men who have been doing the work of the world in a good way."[18] Also in 1946, he wrote to Nina Taylor: "I have, as Chairman of the Committee of the Bar Association, just presented a Resolution on it in our Circuit Court on the retirement of Mr. A.T. Shields, Clerk, after 61 years of service as deputy clerk and clerk of our court. He is a distant cousin of ours and had the longest record of service of any clerk in Virginia, and I expect in the United States."

Henry Foresman of Lexington, a retired lawyer whose early years as a lawyer overlapped Greenlee's last years, told a story about Greenlee's generosity: Henry was once, after World War II, head of the cancer drive for Rockbridge County. My grandfather called him up and wanted to know what the five largest gifts had been, explaining, "I never like to be the biggest giver, but I sure don't want to be the smallest." Henry remembers also that Greenlee once told the younger lawyer that he had lost many chances at wealth by unworthy investments, especially in the last years of the nineteenth century when there was a boom in Rockbridge County after iron and tin were discovered. Surely that is why Katie was so fierce in her demands that he not invest in other ventures later on. His enthusiasm, it appears, overcame his ability to judge the likelihood of success.[19]

In December of 1946 Greenlee wrote to another distant cousin in Missouri:

> My dear Cousin:—You are too good to us—many many thanks for the delicious box of candy—we are both fond of candy and are enjoying it, and appreciate your thought of us. Katie & I lead quiet lives and go out very little, she not at all. We both have some heart trouble but Heaven is kind to us. We have no physical suffering and I am keeping up some of my activities—Masonic and other national organizations, American Legion & Veterans of Foreign Wars, Church, W & L & V.M.I. Alumni, Historical etc.—but I can not give them the time I once did and am closing up some professional matters. One of which may call me to Missouri, & I have been invited if I go, to give a historical talk at Carrolton where one of our distinguished Letcher kinsman is buried—he was a noted lawyer. And in looking up the law of my Missouri Case, I ran across a case in the U. S. Supreme Court in which he appeared. Of the Letcher Family, the legend is, one Brother remained in Va., another went to Kentucky and a third settled in Missouri—and in the descendants of each were talented and distinguished

people—you and I have the right to be proud of them. My son and his lovely wife and his four glorious children, have as *you* can understand, brought into Katie's & my lives a delight beyond words; and in happy consonance with the myriad blessings a kind and good Heaven has bestowed upon us—May Heaven likewise be all good to you and yours is our prayer. Sincerely & affectionately.

In September of 1947, Buz brought his daughter to Lexington to live with Greenlee and Katie, preparatory to bringing the rest of the family, as Katie needed to be in school at age nine. On December 20, 1947, the day that Betty and the other three children arrived from Norfolk for Christmas, they were enjoying a reunion dinner when Katie collapsed at the dinner table, devastated by a stroke. She never regained consciousness, and a second stroke on December 23 killed her.

Buz, who had taken early retirement from the U.S. Marine Corps, moved his family into the house with Greenlee. Betty, never truly the mistress of Andaddy's house, wanted her own house, so Daddy built a small house in the backyard of the big house around 1951. Soon after, Andaddy moved into our little house with us.

Greenlee's later habit of answering letters with a carbon on the back of the original has preserved many of his responses. In 1949 he suffered a second heart attack, and an attack of what was called "heat prostration." That year he wrote to Charlotte, Seymour's daughter: "Katie loved and admired you. I am lonely without her but Heaven has wonderfully blessed me with the presence of Buz and his family. . . . Katie was stricken the day they came, and she lived only three days and their presence with me has been a blessing beyond words." Greenlee, after Katie's death, did not give up his correspondence and interest in local politics, but he slowed down dramatically.

The final battle of Greenlee's life exemplified his dogged determination in relation to things he felt strongly about. In 1949 he stepped up efforts to achieve a lifelong dream: he wanted Stonewall Jackson's classroom at VMI restored as a shrine, exactly as it had been when Jackson had taught there before the Civil War. Although severely hampered now by heart trouble, and eighty-two, he enlisted Julia Jackson Preston, Jackson's granddaughter, in the fight, pledged $1,000 himself, and sought similar funding from people he thought shared his opinion that this ought to be done. For his last five years he corresponded with state legislators, never taking no for an answer. He dogged VMI alumni and supporters, badgered the board of trustees, and gave newspaper interviews, keeping the matter alive. He secured at least one more $1,000 pledge, and in 1952 the Virginia General Assembly appropriated $10,000 to realize the project. But it was not to be.

VMI resisted, as the institute was crowded at the time, and Jackson's classroom now housed twelve cadets. Another room just below the real one was proposed, but Greenlee rejected that as a poor substitute for the real thing. During these years Lexington's new hospital was being constructed, freeing the house Stonewall Jackson had once owned, which had housed the hospital since the nineteenth century, to be made into a memorial. The governing powers of that project wrote Greenlee Letcher with what they called a "new and better plan." If he would donate his $1,000 to them, they would honor him as the first donor, and publish a picture of him in the newspaper handing his check to M. W. Paxton, chairman of the project. When it became clear that the VMI room shrine was not going to materialize, Greenlee turned his attention to the Stonewall Jackson House. A plaque was mounted outside the Jackson classroom as a compromise.

In his final years, he worked crossword puzzles daily to keep his mind alert, but complained mildly in letters that the heart attack had constrained him, that he had to rest in the evening, and was "being very careful." In 1949 he was honored, the *Roanoke Times,* September 18, 1949, reporting that

> *The Mary Custis Lee Chapter, United Daughters of the Confederacy, met Tuesday afternoon in the parlor of Jackson Memorial Hospital. . . . The Chapter voted to give one of the Virginia Division UDC prizes in honor of Captain G. D. Letcher. This cash award, donated by a Rockbridge County veteran of World War II, will be given annually in the name of the Mary Custis Lee Chapter to the winner of the best essay on the life of the famous John Letcher, father of Captain Letcher.*

Seymour Paul retired from his work in Panama, returning with his family to the Harrisonburg home where Kate Paul had taken her family several years after the death of her husband in 1901. Seymour lived until 1960, and I had the pleasure of knowing my Aunt Jane and my cousins, Seymour and Johnny, of visiting them for weeks at a time in the summers when we were teenagers. In 1950, Greenlee's nephew, John Letcher Harrison, died a pauper in New York, and his body and a few personal effects were shipped to Lexington. He had debts of over six thousand dollars outstanding. Greenlee spent the rest of his life tracking down and repaying those debts, though he was under no legal obligation to do so, only, in his mind, a moral obligation. Doing so diminished his own resources dramatically, but he insisted on it nevertheless.

The next letter, and the article enclosed with it from the Harrisonburg paper, is self-explanatory, and is dated June 16, 1953.

> Dear Greenlee:
>
> The enclosure will interest you. Mr. McCabe spoke also of your gift. John and Alice, Jane and I, were among the congregation. Miss Elizabeth Harris led the choir. Judge and Mrs. Haas were not at the church; they are still suffering from their accident of last fall. All of us are well, and so are Charlotte's people. Love to you all, Seymour

> TRINITY SUNDAY, MAY 31, 1953
>
> *Dedication of the "Katherine Paul Memorial":*
>
> *We dedicate today, immediately after the offertory, a memorial fund given by Capt. Greenlee D. Letcher in memory of his wife Katherine Paul Letcher, daughter of the late Judge John Paul, Sr. The late Mrs. Letcher was confirmed in Emmanuel Church. Born January 17, 1876, she was taken into God's care December 23, 1947. Capt. Letcher made this memorial gift as a perpetual gift, the income to be used at the direction of the vestry of this church. The vestry recently voted to use the income at present to establish a shelf in the library for the use of the layreaders of this parish who are serving the church so well; these books will be marked appropriately as a part of this memorial gift.*

In 1953, Greenlee received the DAR's First Award to Living Patriots, for being the "oldest American line officer serving in France in World War I." Sister Lilian died that year, and her body was returned for burial in Harrisonburg from the institution in Pittsburtgh where she had been incarcerated for about twenty years.

And on August 14, 1954, heart trouble and age caught up with Greenlee D. Letcher, and he died in our house, having lived with us for about three years.

The *Roanoke Times,* in an obituary editorial on August 15, 1954, remarked that Greenlee Letcher "combined to a rare degree a passionate devotion to the past with a civic leader's vision of the future."

Soon after his death, his friend, Willie Shields,[20] wrote this poem in tribute to him, which was published in the *Rockbridge County News* in 1956, and, for all its lack of literary sophistication, captures Greenlee's character quite remarkably:

Capt. Greenlee D. Letcher, '88, represented the oldest class here for Finals
and Hunter Lane, '53, the youngest.

*Greenlee Letcher, the
oldest alumnus at
Washington and Lee
reunion, 1953, taken in
front of Tucker Hall, the
law school*

Captain Greenlee Davidson Letcher;
July 19, 1867–August 12, 1954

Careful was he, wasted not,
Every cent he had he got
Honestly, was courteous,
Genial, zestful, generous,
Democratic, cultured quite,
Did what he considered right. . . .
Though he'd freely speak his mind,
Never was he curt, unkind,
Mean, malicious — no indeed —
Never swayed by selfish greed.
True he was — e'er, undisguised,

Shakespeare and the Bible prized;
Spoke well, wrote well, lore-immersed,
At the Institute stood first
(In his class) . . . No youngster, he
O'erseas with his battery
Bravely went in World War One,
Stopped not till his task was done
Thoroughly:—in Heaven I
Hope to hail him by-and-by.

Many a man marries a woman hoping she will stay the same forever, always as beautiful and adoring as in the beginning. Greenlee wanted nothing more and nothing less than Katie's complete love and adoration. His steady vision is evident in the use of the loving addresses to her through thick and thin. What was his he loved best: he chose to find his wife, his sons, his dogs, then at the end of his life, his grandchildren, the best of all.

Katie could not stay the same: time and tragedy took their tolls; childbirth damaged her body, chronic illness wore her down, and the deaths of her two precious boys hurt her in ways that most of us today can not even imagine. Aging has always been harder on women than on men. Yet Greenlee did not appear to notice the changes and never saw her as anything other than the Beautiful Angel he'd first spied that winter night of the lightning storm in 1895.

Katie married Greenlee hoping he'd change: this is evident in early references to his awful clothes, his uncut hair, his predilection for eating onions, and her dissatisfaction with his generous and easygoing nature. Greenlee, however, never changed.

Katie had legitimate complaints. Not only did she feel bad most of the time, but she lived with a man who protested his homesickness, yet would stay away from her. When the choice was to come home early or go on to another adventure, the adventure always won. In addition, Greenlee *was* visionary and impractical. As there was never enough money, very likely she resented all the time and energy he put into civic pursuits, which paid nothing, and in fact, it could be argued, took food out of their mouths. Katie had to cope daily with eked-out money, illness, school, homework and children's problems, with laundry, and the maddening succession of household help. Housebound, she had to face the ghosts more or less alone. Greenlee, however, could heal and return quickly and necessarily to his interesting and rewarding work and public service, his golf, his friends.

The cumulative effect of Katie's health problems, Greenlee's absences, concerns about money, and the deaths of their two children probably did not begin, but certainly entrenched, Katie's lifelong depression. After the baby's death, she was understandably overly cautious about Gee's health. And after Gee died, she was always uneasy about Buz. When she went reluctantly home to Lexington, it was only to be tempted back to Harrisonburg by her family, who appear never to have heard of "forsaking all others." It is impossible to say if she would have been different in different times and circumstances.

Although she was lucky in being white, relatively prosperous, and socially prominent, Katie was unable, or unwilling, to enjoy the privileges of her position. Greenlee's cheerful optimism, which was undoubtedly part of his charm, part of why she married him, grated on her sardonic nature, and she thought it naive of him to love and trust (and invite) everybody.

But when it came to spirit, to a sense of support no matter what, steadiness in the face of the cruel hand life had dealt them both, Greenlee gave Katie exactly what she needed. And at times she realized it. It's evident in the war letters, especially, that she appreciated him.

Meanwhile, he continued to tolerate her coldness, her selfishness, her moodiness, her piques, with that equanimity that was his core. And the evidence is that he didn't notice her failings all that much. Six weeks after her death, on February 15, 1948, he replied to a condolence letter written by their friend and cousin, Carter Hanes, then living in Chile. The letter is only partly readable, written in the palest blue marking pencil in an unsteady hand, but what can be deciphered is remarkable:

Katie had a stroke on December 20 from which she did not rally, and died on the 23rd, and you can imagine my shock and grief. But the happy years we were together, in their memory I accept the blow of Divine Will in grateful resignation. . . . Your letter touched my heart. She always admired you and Janey and felt near to you both. . . . Buz and his family have been a blessing to me and they are the very finest. . . . I have no fear of death. My heaven began the day I met Katie.

Final Note

This book completes an unintentional trilogy. Since 1982, I have taught, among other Elderhostel courses at several colleges and universities, a course entitled "Save Your Life," about how to write autobiographies to leave your descendants. Eventually, from that course, I embarked on my own childhood memoir about the years I lived with my grandparents, and about my lifelong interesting and difficult relationship with my father, *When the Fighting Is All Over* (Longstreet, 1997).

Finding among all the papers my father's weekly letters home to his parents, written while he and my mother were living an exotic life in China, I decided to edit those letters with Roger Jeans, a Chinese scholar at Washington and Lee University, for the book *Good-bye to Old Peking* (Ohio University Press, 1998), which reveals my father's thoughts and observations as a young Marine officer living in the Orient on the brink of World War II, with a wife and a baby and eleven servants. The book you now hold reveals another time, another place. The three books should be mutually enhancing.

Katie Letcher Lyle
Lexington, Va.
Nov. 3, 2001

Notes

1. Handwriting expert Dorothy Sara suggests that the writing of Greenlee Davidson Letcher (hereafter cited as GDL) (hasty, with hard pen strokes, and no slant) is produced by a quick mind interested in others, and one sure of being understood even though the ends of the words are often no more than a wave. It suggests no pretense in personality. See Dorothy Sara, *Hand-Writing Analysis* (Secaucus, N.J.: Castle Books, 1981). Of writing like Katie's (severely leaning words often over an inch tall), Sara asserts that the writer wanted to make few words look like many, suggesting she really *was* responding minimally, but also perhaps that she possessed a sense of grandeur, hoping for recognition and acclaim. "The more extreme [right] slant of writing shows an emotional person, one who may not be physically ardent, but who may be so in imagination" (58). The extreme slant suggests intensity, with all things expressed emotionally.

2. All his life, Andaddy kept notebooks which included anecdotes, jokes, quotes he fancied, aphorisms, passages from books he was reading, excerpts of speeches, and observations.

3. In 1839, J. T. L. Preston, founder of Virginia Military Institute, wrote to persuade F. H. Smith to become its first superintendent, "As a place of residence, I should hope you would find Lexington agreeable, as the population is intelligent, moral, and religious." (Letter of April 29, 1939, in VMI archives.)

4. In Mandarin, which I spoke as a baby, "Nainai" is one of several words for "Grandmother."

5. At the last minute, just as this book was going to press, I discovered information about Hashimoto's Disease, and for reasons mentioned elsewhere in the notes, I believe it could have been at the root of Katie's multiple maladies. See note 3 to chapter 5.

6. Carolyn G. Heilbrun, *Writing a Woman's Life* (New York: Ballantine, 1988), p. 27; also see chapter 5, pp. 95–108, passim.

7. In the 144 diaries of nineteenth-century Virginia women I had or skimmed, generally exemplary in their literary form, are many insights into religious sensibilities, all of them Christian, a lot about the weather, many observations about "servants" (slaves, then), one possible allusion to a lesbian relationship, one near-death experience, and one "secret vile sin" referred to by a young woman (probably nothing worse than self-pleasuring). I found some interesting and fairly gruesome medical procedures spoken of openly. There are many examples of uninstitutionalized, or private, charity; a great deal about miserable health problems, especially with teeth (abscesses); and one lurid description of a train wreck in which blood, limbs, and lives were lost. There is a diary of a nine-year-old relating day after day the chronicle of a yellow fever epidemic in Norfolk. I found curious conventions such as fainting, a lot of

self-recrimination and self-searching. These diaries gave me ideas for further study, and all of them intrigued me, but what these diaries omitted to mention was in the long run more interesting than what they chose to comment on. For instance, Lucy Rutherford, whose Civil War diary has been edited, is the only one of the 144 writers who expressed frustration that she had been born female. There is *no mention* of sex, sexuality, childbirth, or contraception—and rarely any admission of dislike of another person. Most of the diarists struck me as depressed, and, clearly, writing in the diaries relieved some of the stresses of repressive female roles which often offered nothing in the way of choices.

The diaries are, for the most part, about external events and people, as if introspection were an indulgence. Only rarely is a personal opinion ventured, although it was the personal glimpses, the dropped towels, so to speak, that interested me the most. The intention, as well as the convention, of these diaries, was private. They must have fulfilled a great need in an age that knew little of human psychology. I found no indication of an awareness of possible future readership, or any other public motive. Hardly ever in those diaries is there any mention of a need for privacy: as crowded as households were with relatives and visitors, a sense of the encroachment of others into one's private space is absent. Not one of the diarists ever mentions that she feels misunderstood, or expresses a need to be understood. Only one mentions a need for communication: a woman taken as a bride to New Mexico, where for six years she never spoke with another woman. Only one woman mentioned another person's physical appearance, which leads me to conclude that vanity, conformity, allegiance to some arbitrary standard of beauty, or the notion that someone falls short of it, may not have been nineteenth-century concerns. That world was without the influences forced upon us by mass advertising. In these diaries, scattered in archives throughout Virginia and in some cases North Carolina, some previously published in journals or as books, there is no sense whatever of that feeling so familiar to us today, of hassled impatience, of not enough time. Finally, all but two women were long-suffering; there is hardly a hint of a woman thinking that she had a right to happiness. There appears to have been no sense of entitlement among the diary-keeping women of Virginia in the nineteenth century.

CHAPTER 1

1. Every branch of the Letcher family is full of sons named after their kinsman, Sam Houston, from Rockbridge County—the hero of San Jacinto, member of Congress and the U.S. Senate for many years, the first president of Texas, and later governor of Tennessee. The kinship was as follows: the first Sam Houston's sister, Mary, married John Letcher, great-great-grandfather of Greenlee. Mary's brother, Sam, was the father of General Sam Houston. This made Sam Houston a first cousin of the Letchers, thrice removed by Greenlee's generation. Greenlee remembered from childhood Sam Houston's daughter frequently visiting his family.

2. A letter from John D., in Mobile, Alabama, to his mother, discussed this letter that Jennie was writing, describing ex-Governor Letcher's stroke, which John D. opined was "brought on by oysters—perhaps stale ones."

3. Born in 1846, Elizabeth Stuart Letcher would marry, at thirty-seven, James Albert Har-

rison, chair of the Modern Languages Department at Washington and Lee, later at the University of Virginia. They traveled in Europe each summer and kept travelogues. They had three sons, only one of whom, the third, survived infancy. He grew to adulthood, earned a Ph.D. in English, became a professor, served under Pershing as an ambulance driver in World War I, and later wrote for several New York papers. However, he died in debt and addicted to drugs on the streets of New York in January of 1950, having never married. Lizzie's husband, Professor Harrison, turned their travelogues into four moderately successful books: *History of Spain, Story of Greece, Greek Vignettes,* and *Spain in Profile.*

4. Sam Houston Letcher became a circuit judge in 1898. He never married, although he liked, according to his nephew (my father), women, whiskey, and cigars—ordering whiskey two barrels at a time, and cigars in lots of two hundred.

5. Maggie Letcher would marry Robert Showell in 1884 and move to Delaware to raise a family and become the lifelong postmistress of her small town, as well as an oft-published poet, returning to Lexington for visits. Maggie later wrote at least once for a Delaware newspaper about being a child invited to entertain three little Lee girls visiting Mrs. Robert E. Lee at the time of the death of Traveler. The warhorse had stepped on a nail in a plank and died several days later of lockjaw: "General G. W. C. Lee watched him until the last, and four little girls wept at the passing of a great horse of a great leader." The article is in a family scrapbook, but the newspaper name and date are cut off.

6. Jennie Letcher took most seriously her special place in the world as Robert E. Lee's only godchild, cultivating all her life her connections with the Lee family, mainly her godfather's children, and maintaining a lively correspondence with Mary Custis Lee until Miss Lee's death in 1918. Jennie is the member of the family most loved by all the others; there is frequent mention of her charm, her sweetness. She would marry Dr. Walter LeConte Stevens, a Washington and Lee physics professor from Louisiana, who arrived in 1898. The handsome Stevens was referred to as "Sissy" by the students; he wore tailor-made clothes and diamond rings and was regarded as a dandy, to the amusement of the rest of the family. Jennie and "Uncle Steve," as he was called by the family, were the most socially active members of the family, famous for hosting parties on Sunday afternoons to listen to operas on their Victrola as well as teas to welcome visitors to town, to introduce new folks to the social scene in Lexington, and to honor any visiting member of the Lee family. They had two stillborn children.

7. A graduate of VMI, class of 1873, John D. was an engineer who (according to family folklore) designed the first curved, wooden railroad trestle in the world in Lexington. He worked in a dozen states before marrying and settling down in 1908 in Norfolk with socialite Louise Taylor, who shared his singular religious fervor. The reason for his great religious faith, according to an unpublished biographical sketch that my grandfather wrote after John's death, was that at fifteen, he suffered a "severe attack of inflammation of the stomach brought on by playing ball and lying on the damp ground, from which he never recovered during life." He entered VMI at sixteen and later showed a "great gift for teaching." But malaria and diabetes threatened to end his life early. While in California, he prayed to be healed and was miraculously cured, at least for a while.

8. Sister Maggie, then aged twenty-seven, was married quietly at home a few days later to Rob Showell of Delaware, a Washington and Lee graduate.

9. William A. Anderson would in future become Virginia's attorney general. He and Green-lee remained lifelong friends.

10. Although only a light and occasional drinker himself, in 1885 Greenlee had promoted and backed a "wet" referendum for Rockbridge County, which carried, allowing liquor to be sold locally.

11. These records of the West End Glasgow Land Company are in the Rockbridge Histor-ical Society files, in the archives of Leyburn Library at Washington and Lee University.

12. William Jennings Bryan visited Lexington and spoke on July 8, 1896, and returned in 1908. A populist and a pacifist, he was secretary of state for Woodrow Wilson but resigned on June 8, 1915, upon Wilson's announcement, at the sinking of the *Lusitania,* that the United States would go to war. In the crucial 1925 Scopes "Monkey" trial, Bryan prosecuted Scopes for teaching evolution, won, then died of a stroke shortly thereafter, believed to have been brought on by the stress of the trial.

13. Katie refers to Margaret Freeland jokingly as Greenlee's "Sweetheart." Often in later years when Katie was out of town, Maggie invited Greenlee to dinner at her boardinghouse on Letcher Avenue. She aided him politically at least twice, and together they had conceived a plan to commemorate the cadets killed and wounded at New Market, which resulted in the now-famous mural at VMI, *The Charge of the V.M.I. Cadets at New Market.* Greenlee helped her through her final illness in 1908.

14. "Down the Valley" means in a northerly direction, as the Shenandoah River flows north.

15. Following the Civil War, passionate arguments raged in Virginia over whether it was more moral to pay the state's debts, leaving the state without funding for public schools and works, or whether the debt should be "readjusted," thus enabling public funds to continue to do their work in the state.

16. From an undated article in the *Clifton Forge Review* comes the story of how Judge Paul became federal judge for the western part of Virginia. He had served six months when he was offered a judgeship and was considering it when he learned a contest was pending. Democrats were in control of Congress and a debate ensued as to the party policy on the Morrison Tariff Act. The Democrats needed Charles T. O'Ferrall's vote to control the caucus and therefore de-cided to try to seat him. The Democratic leaders in Congress told Paul what they intended to do and urged him to take the judgeship. When Republican Paul learned of this, he resigned from Congress, and O'Ferrall was seated, and Paul accepted the judgeship.

17. Lilian Paul became a nurse, married Jack Flynn in 1917, was institutionalized for mental illness about a decade later, and died in 1953, childless.

18. A VMI graduate, John Paul fought in World War I, married Frances Dannenhower in 1914, was widowed in 1919, became a judge in his father's footsteps, married Alice Kelly in 1935, and died childless in 1964.

19. Charlie, also called Charles, was VMI class of '07, although he left without graduating. He worked as an engineer at various jobs until his health failed (he smoked heavily), was an

avid amateur photographer, once had a serious girlfriend (Miss Collins), but died single in 1943.

20. A newspaperman, VMI graduate, engineer and executive for the Panama Canal, Seymour Paul first married Kate Pittman, who bore Charlotte. Divorced, he married Jane Abbott and sired Seymour and John. He died in 1960.

21. Apparently the Paradise Club was an informal group of young people.

22. Carolyn G. Heilbrun, *Writing a Woman's Life* (New York: Ballantine, 1988), p. 92.

23. J. Hoge Tyler would be the next governor of Virginia, and he wanted Greenlee on his staff probably for his political connections as well as for his astonishing record. Both men were in favor of a silver standard instead of the gold. In 1900 when Congress passed the Gold Standard Act, the Virginia delegation in Congress voted against the silver standard.

24. Maggie and Housey Ott were Harrisonburg friends of Katie's.

25. As an illustration of the depth of ignorance about reproduction and sex, a friend of mine's mother reported that the only information she ever received about sex was at a girl's camp in 1913, where another teenage girl explained: "I will tell you what it's about: he takes his longest thing and puts it in your hairiest thing. So: he puts his nose under your arm."

CHAPTER 2

1. John Rockingham Paul and Susie were the parents of John Gray (and Peyton, who died in World War II).

2. Virginia was Katie's next sister, who in fact never married.

3. Susie Paul, married to Judge Paul's brother, Rock, was referred to as "difficult" and called "the Empress."

4. Bertha Howell was a Lexington character. The story goes that when she was a girl in Philadelphia, her mother told her: "You're not pretty so you'll have to achieve style to be noticed." Bertha was called Queen of Sheba by VMI cadets for her fussy skirts, voluminous curls, ruffled parasols, and outrageous hats.

5. The group would have been Lizzie and her husband, Dr. Harrison, and their son Letcher; and Maggie and Rob Showell and their four children.

6. At fifty-one, Kate Paul was probably suffering symptoms of menopause.

7. On February 15, 1898, the U.S. battleship *Maine* blew up at Havana, Cuba, killing more than two hundred sailors and officers, and precipitating a four-month war with reverberations as far away as Hong Kong and the Philippines. This war, every battle of which was won by the United States, left Cuba, the last Spanish holding in the New World, independent from Spain.

8. Presumably, the reference is to Benedict Arnold; Greenlee was a raging Democrat, and the Pauls were avid Republicans.

9. Collicello was the home place of the elegant Daingerfield cousins, who had removed to Kentucky in 1892.

10. Lewis Harvie Strother, VMI 1877, had taught mathematics and tactics at VMI.

11. These are two of Katie's fellow debutantes.

12. Admiral George Dewey (1837–1917) was the hero of the battle of Manila.

13. R. A. Marr, VMI 1877, was an engineering professor at VMI.

14. Quite likely this was Phil Nunn, a beloved character around town, freed in childhood by the Civil War. It was said that he was too large for any shoes, so he wrapped rags around his feet. Honest and hardworking, he saved his money in a sack. Once, after being jilted by a money-grubbing woman, he went to New York where he was accosted by the police and accused of stealing the $1,500 he carried. When the New York police called the Lexington police, they were assured that the man had earned every penny. Phil died in 1938.

15. Possibly it was considered *outré* to attend a social function so soon after his mother's death (five months). But it could also mean that Katie's mother, being Republican, did not approve of Tyler, a Democrat.

16. B. Estes Vaughan, a Lexington banker, was interested first in Virginia, then when that didn't work out, in Lilian. He later golfed daily with Greenlee. In a letter not quoted here, Lilian, while still single, found him "odd and funny," and he sent her a handwritten invitation to his induction as bank president.

17. Most likely tuberculosis is being referred to here.

18. In January 1901, Lillie Coles would marry George Catlett Marshall, revered today as the author of the Marshall Plan that revived postwar Europe in the forties and fifties of the twentieth century. A museum and research center in his memory are now located at VMI.

19. Mag's background may explain her life. When Susan and Maggie Holt were children, their father died, and their widowed mother married a Dr. Yount, and quickly produced three sons. But a typhoid epidemic swept away Dr. Yount and the three little boys, two of them on the same day, leaving the mother and two teenaged girls with nothing. So when the elder daughter married the young lawyer, John Letcher, shortly thereafter at the age of seventeen, the younger sister and mother came along as part of the package.

20. A Civil War veteran, General Roller was head of the Augusta Military Academy. At VMI he roomed with George Catlett Marshall.

21. W. W. Brannon was the Democratic candidate for the legislature.

22. Stevens had arrived the previous August from Louisiana to teach physics at Washington and Lee and took a room at the Letchers'. Family lore says that he and Jennie fell in love immediately.

23. "Refreshing the inner man" euphemistically referred to drinking whiskey or any strong alcohol; I heard it often as a child in Lexington.

24. Tin and iron were discovered near Lexington at the turn of the century, but the boom caused by the discovery soon fizzled out, another piece of bad luck for Greenlee, who of course invested in it. It turned out in this case that the tin ore, although plentiful, was difficult to mine, expensive to smelt, impossible at the time to transport, and ended up costing more than it cost to import refined tin from Bolivia.

25. After Judge Paul died, his friend, Botts Lewis, wrote to Katie: "No one knows and feels better than I how utterly helpless is human sympathy to even alleviate such a sorrow as yours. . . . During the last six or seven years I have traveled a great deal over your father's district and hundreds of people have inquired of him and I cannot recall ever hearing an unkind word spoken of him, while the affection felt for him by these men, many of whom had not seen him for years, could only have been inspired by a strong character and a good man."

26. Henry and Mrs. Dold owned a popular candy and soda shop in Lexington.

27. Hog killing, in the days before good refrigeration, had to wait until after the first hard frost.

CHAPTER 3

1. The reference to "the two little Johns and Papa" are to John Rockingham, Katie's next brother (who had died at age two), John Paul Letcher, and Judge Paul.

2. Hugh Wills was a mentally retarded man who did odd jobs around town, such as delivering ice and mail. Greenlee took charge of his affairs and may have been his guardian. Nell Owen Paxton related that someone once urged Hugh to get married, to have someone to take care of him. He shook his head no. The person then said:, "But Hugh, everyone gets married." His reply was famous for its simple wisdom: "Yessum, and a heap of 'em wish they wasn't."

3. Taz Hubard, VMI 1887, was a fellow lawyer.

4. Anderson was a Bath County judge in whose court GDL argued cases.

5. Jennie Bacon was from a poor but aristocratic Lexington family.

6. When I described my grandmother's symptoms to three physicians, one offered borderline personality disorder as a strong possibility, and a second, in discussion, agreed that such a diagnosis seemed reasonable. Sufferers sometimes shrink from people, things, and society in general, disliking people on only minor provocation, and are inflexible. My grandmother was not physically demonstrative, she clearly didn't care much for her husband's family, and there is evidence that she did not care for sex. For another possible explanation of my grandmother's symptoms, see note 3 to chapter 5.

7. By the time I married in 1963, the schools had so encroached on the street that the lot was the only privately owned one left between the colleges.

8. Frank Moore, another lawyer, who became the Lexington city attorney in 1928, would take over much of GDL's wartime affairs when he went to France in World War I.

9. She was the mother of Lily Coles, the wife of George Catlett Marshall.

10. Ernest and Frances Sale were my husband's grandparents.

11. Dr. Manley was a Lexington Baptist preacher.

12. Col. Will Moody was a wealthy Texas financier, VMI 1886.

13. This is a reference to the parents of Nell Paxton's husband.

14. When I lived with them, my grandfather used the front hall as a practice range, driving wadded up old socks its length, trying to hit a tin cup that he placed near the door. Nainai would not let him cut a hole in the hall carpeting so he could practice getting his balls into it.

15. General Scott Shipp was the beloved superintendent of the VMI.

16. Newspapers reported a powerful hurricane in the Atlantic that had delayed ships and caused great damage all along the middle Atlantic Coast.

17. This was near the anniversary of baby John's death.

18. The Fortnightly Club met (indeed, still does) in Lexington every second Friday, rotating hosts and speakers. Learned papers are delivered and discussed. Each member has to host the dinner-lecture every other year. My husband was also a longtime member.

19. GDL's office was down one hill, up another, a five-minute brisk walk from home; Gee, at age four, apparently went to meet him.

20. Lime was and is still used as a deodorant for water closets (toilets).

21. Buffalo Creek, beautiful and shallow, is five miles south of Lexington.

22. Florence Duval ran a Lexington boardinghouse.

23. Mark Hanna, capitalist and politician, Republican senator from Ohio, was William McKinley's wealthy campaign financer.

24. Col. Edward Nichols, VMI 1878, was a math professor who later became third superintendent of VMI in 1907. While a cadet he fell in love with a widow twice his age. But custom forbade her to respond to the young fellow's courtship. Nichols persisted, however, obtaining a teaching job there, and finally persuading her to marry him many years later, when he was around forty and she over sixty. They had a short but devoted marriage until she died and he became superintendent, in which capacity he served from 1907 until 1924, when he was hit by a rogue rock during blasting to lower the parade ground, an injury from which he died without recovering three years later.

25. VMI had beaten Virginia Polytechnic Institute.

26. Retired Lexington lawyer Henry Foresman recalled a time in the thirties when Greenlee took another Lexington lawyer along on a trip to Missouri, where he had some interest in lead and zinc mines. The friend was amazed when the first night they stayed with the governor of West Virginia, the second with the governor of Kentucky, and the third with the governor of Missouri, all of whom turned out to be Greenlee's personal friends.

27. It was during this month, May 1905, that Lilian graduated from Garfield Hospital Nursing School in Washington, D.C., and was evidently working and living there.

28. There is a well-known family story, not referred to in any letter, that Greenlee, seeing how they could become ensconced comfortably in his family home, now run by his unmarried sister, Fannie (Jennie had married Mr. Stevens and both Mrs. Letcher and Miss Holt had died), balked at doing anything beyond the digging of the cellar in 1905, feeling that in time Katie would come around and see the wisdom of such an arrangement, involving all of them (including Houty and Fannie), and forget about having her own house. But he did not reckon with Katie's determination, until Katie, without warning, after a year or more of shilly-shallying, took the babies one day and went to visit some Harrisonburg friends who had moved to Philadelphia and calmly wrote to Greenlee from Philadelphia of her intention to remain there until the house was ready. In this manner she finally got his attention, and the house went up in three months' time.

29. One of many such hazing customs at VMI was the beating of freshmen as they ran between rows of upperclassmen.

30. Ruth Floyd Anderson was the daughter of Greenlee's friend, William A. Anderson, and is the Ruth A. McCullough cited in the bibliography.

31. Although we cannot be sure of Mrs. Paul's malady, scarlet fever and measles both called for recuperation in darkened rooms.

32. The woodhouse was a wonderful rectangular, roofed edifice in the side yard. It was a sort of summerhouse, entered on a long side, with benches across each end, its latticed sides almost invisible under wisteria when I played in it as a child, the plank floor by then partially rotted through. It was torn down when my family and I came to live with Andaddy after Nainai's death, because it was considered dangerous and potentially snaky.

33. Peter Paul was a distant kinsman who, I mistakenly believed as a young child, must have invented Mounds and Almond Joy candy bars. Katie was always partial to those candies, coconut being another favorite of hers and Greenlee's.

34. Nephritis, kidney inflamation, was probably diagnosed vaguely from an anomalous urine sample.

35. "Sister" was Lizzie Harrison from Charlottesville, halfway home to Lexington. The abruptness of her reply hints that Katie did not care for her sister-in-law enough even to be gracious.

36. Letter from GDL to Dr. Glasgow, February 8, 1908, with reply on back.

37. Greenlee here referred to the infamous "Typhoid Mary."

38. This must have been an automobile.

39. Mr. Sheridan, GDL's friend, was a rare (if not the only) Catholic in Lexington. In addition to his livery stable, he built the Catholic Church. There will be more mention of him later, as Greenlee encounters reminders of Catholicism in Europe.

40. Here GDL refers to the ceremonies he and Miss Maggie Freeland instituted, including New Market Day, memorializing the brave boys of VMI who died there.

41. The letter, from John Paul in law school, read:

> Dear Kit
>
> I had wanted to come over Easter but I find I can't well spare the time. There are several girls coming up there, with Miss Duval, for the dances at Easter, getting to Lexington about the 20th or 21st—and one of them, I know very well; to be perfectly truthful, I might say I am extremely fond of her. They will be there right next to you and I want you to meet her and be nice to her. Her name is Frances Dannenhower and she is from Alexandria. You had just as well do all I ask of you, for you will probably have to be more civil to her than that in a few years when this looked-for legal practice of mine begins to come crowding in the door of my office. But anyhow I want you to meet her and see what you think of her—and tell me. But watch Mamma and don't let her hit the little girl with a brick-bat or a table leg or something. . . . I would like mightily to come over at Easter but I can't hardly do it. Give my love to Gee and Buzzy and tell them I want to see them a whole lot, but I guess I'll have to wait till Finals. Mrs. Renshaw spoke of seeing you in Lexington some days ago—in fact, she's been speaking of you and Gee ever since. That Gee boy is certainly "the devil with the women." Remember me to Greenlee and my love to Mamma; and always to yourself, dear sister, the best of love. *John* P.S. Sure enough, Kit, do what I ask, won't you, for this is no foolishness. *J.*

42. Seymour became an engineer with the Panama Canal, and edited a newspaper. He came home briefly every few years to visit. In Panama he married twice, in 1913 and again in 1930, and raised a family. In August of 1909 Lilian sent her trunk to Panama, intending to follow her brother there. She was delayed by various jobs, and did not sail until March of 1910, arriving in Panama in April. Virginia followed her there in August of 1911 but became ill with appendicitis soon after her arrival, then suffered from back problems. She stayed only one school year before returning to the United States. Lilian returned to America in November 1911.

43. Once every two years, each member took a turn entertaining the group, but, typically, it fell to his wife to plan and supervise dinner—thus "*your* Fortnightly."

44. Daddy used to tell the story: the horse one night got out of her stall, and attracted by the smell of food, stuck her head in a kitchen window and helped herself to whatever was on the counter or table under the window.

45. J. Cosby Bell was the rector of the Robert E. Lee Church from 1906 to 1911. Nancy, his wife, seems to have been Katie's only female friend beyond her family.

46. Under "Juvenile Court": "Seymore Letcher" was tried for "disturbing the peace, and for perjury."

47. Charlie had spells of being unable to work because of "nervousness" and unspecified illness.

48. Katie's friend Nancy Bell had met a woman just returned from Panama, who knew Lilian, "the very finest and most altogether charming person she ever saw—the whole isthmus concurs in that opinion." She thought Lilian would "finally yield to the determined besieging of Mr. Flynn, whose frantic devotion to her is recognized by the entire population of Panama." Of Mr. Flynn she reported that he "is in every way one of the best ever, delightfully clever" and "didn't see how any girl on earth could resist such ardent wooing from such a man." One letter actually referred to an engagement party for Lilian and Jack by a man identified only as "John O," whose last name seems to have been Collins. In a letter to Lilian, Jack called her his "wife-to-be." She did eventually marry Mr. Flynn but not for six more years. She left Panama in October of 1911 to return home. It is clear that they were not engaged all that time. Jack's letters to Lilian are at Ottobine.

49. Lizzie Graham ran a boardinghouse on Letcher Avenue. It may be that when Maggie Freeland died, Mrs. Graham replaced her.

50. This appears to be a reference to a party in honor of John's engagement to Frances Dannenhower.

51. One marvels at the inappropriateness of the evening bag, it, for Katie *never* went out. Perhaps it was Seymour's view that she ought to go out more at night. Perhaps it was chosen by a girl he was going with at the time, or perhaps he was merely helpless about choosing a gift for his sister. It was still in its gift box and tissue paper when I found it, with the letter, in 1994.

> Dear Kit:—I'm afraid that when this reaches you you will be all shot to pieces with the pre- and present hullabaloo of Christmas. At least you have the Christmas spirit, so sit down and enjoy it—till one of the kids blows you—or himself—up. Will even your patience agree with the dictum of the shopgirl—"Take it from me, kiddo, Christmas is a crime"? I hope you will have omitted me from those you packed and worried for. Not that I'm unappreciative. I appreciate you and your love just the same, and would rather you didn't bother. . . . Here's hoping all of you may have a very pleasant Christmas, and be well and hale on New Year's. *With greatest love, Seymour.*

52. Aunt Susie and Rock Paul's son, John Gray, graduated from VMI in 1916.

53. Lilian's own romance would follow a similar pattern.

54. Jack Mead, VMI class of 1923, was an overseas businessman.

55. Whistle Creek flows into the Maury, one-half mile west of Lexington.

56. Polk Miller was a white jazz musician who headed the "Old South Quartette."

57. My father remembered that show, starring Wild Bill Cody, all his life.

58. Surely Lilian is referring here to her beau, Mr. Flynn.

59. Aunt Sarah, who had been their baby nurse, was now hired to look after the children, ages fourteen and eleven. Fannie was Fannie Letcher.

60. Lilian writes "sad" because of baby John, and their own brother, John Rockingham, who had died.

61. Uncle Steve is Jennie's husband, Walter LeConte Stevens.

62. She was celebrating John's wedding to Frances Dannenhower.

63. Samuel Houston Letcher was a favorite of Katie's. "Houty" paid Gee and Buz a nickel an hour to pull up wild onions from his lawn: "Yankees brought 'em," he claimed, going on to say that there had never been any wild onions in Lexington before they came. "Brought it in the horse feed," he'd say, clamping his teeth down on his cigar, directing from the porch: "Pull em up! Pull em up, boys!" Uncle Houty, who favored good whiskey and good living, took it upon himself to teach Gee and Buzz to smoke cigars, and got them drunk at the same time, when they were about eight and eleven, apparently so that they would not be tempted to repeat either activity in later life.

64. Brannon's letter of March 29, 1915, read: "Dear Mr. Letcher: I intended to acknowledge receipt of your kind letter before, wherein you consent that, if I so wish, I may sell my interest in the property to which we have been making reference. I was about to close the deal at $15.00 per acre without any reservation, but my proposed purchaser flew the track on me, so that nothing will be done for the present. I would like awfully well to sell to you and Hugh and would be even willing to do a little better than that if I could sell to either or both of you. Let me hear from you on the subject. Very truly, W. W. Brannon."

65. Burbridge Daingerfield was a cousin a few years older than Gee and Buz.

66. It's hard to say what the Starcher reference means, but it sounds as if Katie may have been trying to avoid some social event.

67. Seymour and Kate's baby, Charlotte, was born two days later (died 1998).

68. A letter came to Katie from a Staunton friend, Mary Holt, on December 10, 1915, describing young Gee: "Greenlee came to see me Monday as all the younger Holts were at Stuart Hall, & I have been ever since meaning to write to you and say how really delighted I was with the dear young fellow. I don't know when I ever saw one of his age so nice & intelligent & altogether fine as he seemed to me, & I am so glad that you have just so promising a boy. . . . Henry & I send love to you & old Greenlee & Jennie. Sincerely yours, M. C. B. Holt." Governor Letcher's wife was Susan Holt, but obviously Mary and Henry Holt were known also to the Pauls, as Mrs. Holt wrote to Katie and not to Greenlee.

69. "Dear 'Gee' or O.B.," [Old Boy?] she wrote: "That book is perfectly ridiculous and sounds just like you had picked it out. Thank you for remembering me. We certainly have enjoyed it and had many a 'laff.' . . . I expect you had a fine time Christmas, tell me everything you did. I am recovering from an attack of grip so you can imagine I have had an unexciting time." It is signed "Katharine."

70. Letcher Harrison was charming and generous, but allegedly profligate. He owned the

first motor car (a Stutz-Bearcat) at the University of Virginia, according to my father; and when he came to visit his Lexington family, he brought boxes of Hershey Bars to Gee and Buz and took them riding in his auto at terrifically high speeds, sometimes in excess of fifteen miles an hour. Cousin Letcher also indulged Buz's preference for Sousa marches, and Gee's for Hawaiian ukulele music, and would bring each boy a new Victrola record when he visited. He died a broken drug addict in 1950.

71. My aunt, my mother's sister, who knew Katie and Greenlee, reads this letter far differently than I do. She interprets it as evidence of Katie's continued rejection of Buz in favor of Gee, even all those years later. Here was Buz, hoping for recognition by sending the roses, and Katie took them to Gee's grave—then told him she had done so. Aunt Polly avers, as do many old Lexington folk, that Gee was Katie's clear favorite. It is true that in the letter, Katie never thanked Buz, just used the roses to further recall Gee.

CHAPTER 4

1. Fannie Letcher's house had burned the previous winter, and was now repaired.

2. Quotation comes from the *Lexington Gazette*, October 25, 1916.

3. My father's fame as "Barefoot" Buz Letcher was alive and well in Lexington when we went to live there in 1943.

4. Fannie and Abe Paul were sister and brother of Kate Paul's late husband, who lived at Ottobine.

5. There was an epidemic of infantile paralysis that summer in the Valley.

6. Mary Custis Lee is Robert. E. Lee's second daughter (1835–1918).

7. Chambliss Keith, VMI 1895, was a lawyer in Selma, Alabama.

8. George Denny, chancellor of the University of Alabama, was a former president of Washington and Lee University.

9. Albert Howell, a lawyer and journalist, was VMI class of 1886.

10. John D. Letcher's sending her some religious material raised her hackles.

11. John Magruder, Lt. Col. AEF, was VMI class of 1909.

12. Thomas Pryor Gore (b. 1870) served in the Oklahoma territorial Senate from 1901, and as senator from 1907 until after World War I.

13. Disliking his name, Seymour added his dead brother John's name to the front of his; he thereafter called himself formally John S. Letcher and named his first son J.S.L., Jr.

14. "Leal" is a Scottish adjective meaning loyal, true, faultless. In a songbook the Letchers owned, *Heart Songs* (1909), there is a song that is clearly the source of Katie's remark. The first verse is:

I'm wearin' away, Jean, Like snaw-wreaths in thaw, Jean,
I'm wearin' away to the land o' the leal.
There's nae sorrow there, Jean, There's no cauld nor care, Jean,
The day is aye fair in the land o' the leal.
—Lady Nairne, "The Land o' the Leal"

15. Zimbro was the tenant on a farm Katie and Greenlee owned thirty miles northwest of Lexington.

16. The Letcher coat of arms shows, among other symbols, three crowns, because legend claimed that an ancient Welsh Letcher once entertained at his castle stronghold the kings of England, Ireland, and France—all at the same time. An undated news story indeed claims that the Letchers were one of forty American families who could walk in unannounced and gain audience with the British monarch.

17. The references here are to VMI argot: "keydet" is a variant of "cadet," a VMI student. Katie obviously enjoyed this argot, and later called Buz her "Big Dog."

18. He wrote in the same letter, "I will answer any telegram or letter I receive from Judge Brannon about the Wills land. I believe the land should bring more than $40 per acre, but if he insists on sale at that figure I will agree I guess."

19. Greenlee enclosed a note: "Mr. Geo. Zimbro, Craigsville, Va. Deliver Daisy my horse to my son Seymour Letcher, or to whomever he may in writing authorize. Greenlee D. Letcher."

20. Carolyn G. Heilbrun, *Writing a Woman's Life* (New York: Ballantine, 1988), p. 12.

21. This was the widow of Robert E. Lee's third child, "Rooney."

22. Hugh Wills had no regular job because of his mental disability, yet he knew enough to worry about being jailed if he did not join the service or have a full-time job.

23. At least some of the time, GDL was not allowed to say where he was.

24. In fact, GDL and Lily de Montaigu became fast friends. She died in 1928 in Lexington, where Greenlee had found her husband a job teaching French at VMI. She was buried in the Letcher family plot.

25. This is a rare reference to Greenlee's ever having read any fiction.

26. Eight days later, the armistice was signed.

27. Perhaps Buz's memory of this image—the "fine-looking Marines"—helped him decide to join the U.S. Marine Corps later instead of the army.

28. This was the widow of Fitzhugh Lee.

29. Although the story of the ring may be true, as a lifetime resident of Lexington, I've heard it on at least two other occasions—once connected with a West Virginia train wreck and once connected with a World War II plane crash. The survival of the ring, and *nothing else,* is the punch line of every story, suggesting the triumphal constancy of the VMI.

30. Greenlee, experiencing French country cuisine, remains as naïvely appreciative as ever. All was grist to his mill; no truer democrat ever lived.

31. Churchill Gibson served the Robert E. Lee Memorial Church for ten years, beginning in January 1918.

32. John alone, of all Katie's Republican family, came around eventually to a moderate view, and was one of the first judges in the 1950s to promote integration in Virginia public schools by several early rulings. He wrote from France to Katie, on January 4, 1919: "Everything is extremely high, food, drinks etc. and it must be admitted that our faithful allies have not overlooked the fact that Americans seem to have more money than they need." He was critical, in ways Greenlee would never have been, of the "efficiency" of the army, and of the French in general:

> Europe is in the devil of a mess and I am not at all certain that it isn't up to the allies, particularly England and America to practically control and settle the internal

problems of the Central powers, the Balkan states and Russia. . . . I don't believe
the future safety of the . . . world is secured by stopping now. Since we have an immense army, with unlimited equipment . . . the thing to do is to give Europe one
good policing and show them how to behave. Lord knows I don't want to go to
Russia. . . . [B]ut to pull out and leave that flaming anarchy to spread over the
world seems to me to be quitting the job. . . . It would be mighty costly to undertake the task of getting things straightened out and I know what a howl would go
up at home at the mention of it. . . . But if I've got the idea straight, this world is
facing about the biggest problems it ever saw and ones that are not matters of
months but of decades—problems so big that precedents don't count. . . .[I]f
there is anything in this "make the world safe for democracy" business, we had just
as well make it good and safe while we're at it. And the U.S. has as much at stake
as anyone else, and is better prepared to undertake the policeman's job than the
others. This war has cost France and England thousands where we have given up
only hundreds. How they stood four years of it, I cannot see. . . . I wonder what
T.R. [Roosevelt] would have to say of it all. I don't seem to get over the shock of
his death and my regret. It seems like a personal loss and I find myself thinking of
it a lot. The world never needed him as it needs him now.

33. My father was always an enthusiastic and inventive cook.

34. William Gibbs McAdoo managed the financing of the U.S. participation in World War
I and was the first chair of the Federal Reserve System while he was secretary of the treasury,
from 1913 to 1918. He was a contender for the Democratic presidential nomination in 1920.

35. This is a reference to the Spanish influenza that killed so many people in 1918–19.

36. The Lexington candy shop owner, Henry A Dold, was a recent widower, and Andaddy,
loving a joke, was apparently kidding Fannie about him.

37. From Mount Sinai Hospital in New York, Lilian wrote on March 26 to Kate Paul, who
was still in Lexington with Katie and Buz, "My dear Mamma— . . . We have been negotiating
with the First Nat'l through John Yancey to borrow a thousand dollars. . . . Frances thinks it is
lovely of you and Katherine to help her. . . . She is much touched by it. She says tell you she
wants you "to keep it for John, because he will need it"—to let him have it. . . . I don't want
Frances to have one worry over it, she will be too sick. I really think it would be better to de-
posit yours there to her credit, and if necessary I can draw on it by the signed checks she has
given me. . . . [W]e must first think of the present bills. If we get the thousand I will at once let
you know, but without it we are on pretty thin ice. . . . Dr. Lillienthal allows a year or maybe
more to pay his bill. . . . Thank God for the Pauls who stand by each other."

38. William Ruff and Aunt Sarah were evidently a servant couple.

39. Brig. Gen.l Samuel D. Rockenbach, VMI 1889.

40. This preference was short lived; my father signed his name John S. Letcher, but nobody
ever called him anything but "Buz."

41. Lexington young people fell into two factions: "Uptown" and "College Hill," thus "hillbillies."

42. This is the Nell Owen Paxton who told me about so many people in this book.

43. In a privately printed Lexington memoir covering this period, Grace Ecker mentions the Letchers' notoriously dreadful dog, slightly misremembering the name, but identifying him surely as "the only other airedale in Lexington than ours . . . Scamp, a big long rangy fellow of a rather different type [presumably from the Eckers' well-behaved Airedale] who . . . seemed to resent this newcomer." Ecker added: "These two dogs never met without a squabble. Fur flew, fast and furious." In Charles W. Turner, ed., *Mrs. Ecker's Lexington, 1918–1929* (Roanoke: Virginia Lithography and Graphics, 1990)

CHAPTER 5

1. My grandfather loved this story. It seems a local hotel got a watchdog after several break-ins involving liquor thefts from the bar. At first, there were no thefts, but they started up again, puzzling everyone, as the dog was still as fierce as ever. The thief, when finally caught, was wearing a bartender's uniform, so the watchdog apparently had decided he was all right.

2. It was announced at graduation that Buz would be a first cadet in the VMI Corps for the next (his senior) year, a great distinction.

3. Hashimoto's thyroiditis, an inflammation and swelling of the thyroid gland eventually causing goiter, may have been Katie's disease at this time, but also perhaps for many years before. This inherited, auto-immune disorder, which is responsible for 90 percent of hypothyroidism, causes nervousness, excessive menstruation, constipation, dry skin, brittle hair, weight gain, and extreme fatigue. Today, synthetic thyroid taken for life controls the disease easily. I have been on medication for hypothyroiditis since 1956, when I was eighteen. Katie's illness (she was, after all, my grandmother) could have had that early an onset too. Depression is often the first sign, and Hashimoto's is often mistaken for aging, menopause, and especially depression. Though too much speculation may be unwise, this disease may have been what plagued Charlie at various times in his life, and even poor Lilian, who was put away as "mad" for at least the final twenty years of her life.

4. Molly Laird, the DuPont "heiress," lived in Wilmington, Delaware.

5. Presumably, Lilian had gone fishing as part of the rest and recreation prescribed for her mental health.

6. This time, at least, Katie was probably suffering from sinus trouble. Dr. Miller was in Harrisonburg, and Dr. Mitchell practiced in Lexington.

7. Augusto Cesar Sandino (1895–1934) was a Nicaraguan revolutionary general fighting against U.S. military intervention on behalf of the United Fruit Company, an American business located there. Sandino and his followers, at odds with the national leadership in Nicaragua, conducted guerrilla campaigns against the U.S. Marines from 1927 to 1933. Sandino was eventually tricked into the open, and executed by Anastasio Somoza, longtime president of Nicaragua. My father in later life resented that he'd had to put his life on the line not in defense of his country but in defense of a big business conglomerate. He actually sided with Sandino.

8. Alice Roosevelt Longworth was the daughter of Theodore Roosevelt.

9. That any smear on the family name be cleansed, the Letchers collected articles about and testimonies to their members, including their cousin, Sam Houston (1793–1863), who had been *divorced*. In 1895, John Sayles of Texas, a well-known law compiler, wrote an account of Sam Houston's divorce: Houston, averred Sayles, while governor of Tennessee, fell in love with a Miss Allen, who, at her parents' insistence, married him. She was secretly engaged to another man (Dr. Douglass), but her parents forced her to break her engagement. On the night of the marriage, General Houston found her in tears in the bridal chamber. Upon her revelation that she loved another, he immediately left the house and headed west. True or not, it is epic cowboy lore.

10. In 1938 it was suggested by Congressman Flannagan of the Ninth District that the road be named the Greenlee Letcher Highway, although this did not occur.

11. Mildred Dunlap bested Buz in high school, earning the highest grades. In 1943 when we moved to Lexington, their daughter Susan became a close friend of mine.

12. Katie's brother, Seymour, died in 1960. After John Paul died in 1964, Jane moved into Ottobine. She then married her husband's cousin John Gray Paul, who was a widower. After John Gray Paul died, Jane Abbott Paul Paul lived on there alone until shortly before her death in 1999. Their oldest son, Seymour, and his wife, Barbara, have recently taken over that wonderful house, and it is currently undergoing another renovation and restoration. The fifth and sixth generations of new youngsters show up each year for reunions, many of them looking startlingly like their Paul ancestors. Those of us now in the older generation have trouble keeping the generations straight, for the babies we knew as young people are now older than their parents were when we were growing up and forming our familiar memories of them as young parents. Those babies I recall are now grandparents.

13. Buz wrote to his father in March 1940: "Equal distribution of wealth would not raise poor people but would reduce everyone to the level of the poor. 99 of 100 people cannot stand leisure or wealth without suffering moral and physical degeneration. It's better for 1% to get wealthy and go to pot than for everyone in the country to be leisurely and wealthy and all go all to pieces. 20 years ago, the poor worked hard and kept their characters up, and kept up the character of the country against a small rich class who debauched."

14. Ellender was from Louisiana, a senator for thirty-six years, from 1936 until 1972. He was a member of the Senate Naval Affairs Committee, overlooking marine and naval affairs.

15. A. W. Robertson was the father of evangelist Pat Robertson.

16. When someone in San Diego inquired who had taken me somewhere (it was my Marston grandmother, whom I did not care for), I replied haughtily, at age four: "Oh, it was just some friend of the family."

17. Charles Paul had been a lifelong heavy smoker and suffered from "nervous prostration" off and on his entire life. He died of "lung trouble."

18. Greenlee details some of them: "W. L Moody of Galveston, Texas, said to be one of the leading bankers and richest men of Texas. Another, W. H. Palmer is one of the leaders of thought and action in Richmond, Va. Another Albert Howell, whose father was head of the Constitution, was one of the leading lawyers of Atlanta. . . . There were other prominent engineers, teachers, business men, bankers, etc at their various homes, and Heaven has been kind indeed to us."

19. Only one venture, a Mutual Fire Insurance Company, was astoundingly successful, and today my family and I still reap the benefits of our grandfather's investment in it.

20. William Shields was devoted to Greenlee. Of a wealthy, eccentric Lexington family, Shields, a bachelor who had once lived in New York, had a propensity for showing up just at dinnertime at the Letchers', knowing he would be invited to stay. He did it so often that it was a point of irritation and comment with Katie—then later, with my mother, Betty, when my grandfather lived with us. I remember Willie Shields well, dramatically and spontaneously spouting quotations from Shakespeare as Andaddy and I would meet him walking home from uptown. A chapter of *When the Fighting Is All Over* is devoted to one such a meeting.

Selected Bibliography

Abbott, Shirley. *Womenfolks: Growing Up Down South.* New Haven: Ticknor and Fields, 1983.

Andeson, Joseph Reid. *VMI in the World War.* Compiled by the historiographer of the VMI, 1920.

Ball, Edward. *Slaves in the Family.* New York: Farrar, Straus and Giroux, 1998.

Bernhard, Betty, Elizabeth Fox-Genovese, and Theda Perdue, eds. *Southern Women: Histories and Identities.* Columbia and London: University of Missouri Press, 1992.

Boley, Henry. *Lexington in Old Virginia.* Richmond: Garrett and Massie, 1936.

Boney, F. Nash. *John Letcher of Virginia.* University, Ala.: University of Alabama Press, 1966.

Boorstin, Daniel J. *The Americans.* New York: Random House, 1973.

Brooke, George M., Jr. *General Lee's Church.* Lexington: News-Gazette, 1984.

Brownmiller, Susan. *Femininity.* New York: Linden Press of Simon and Schuster, 1984.

Cash, W. J. *The Mind of the South.* New York: A. A. Knopf, 1941.

Coulling, Mary P. *The Lee Girls.* Winston-Salem, N.C.: John F. Blair Publishing, 1987.

Couper, William. *One Hundred Years at VMI.* 4 vols. Richmond: Garrett & Massie, 1939.

D'Emilio, John, and Estelle B. Freedman. *Intimate Matters: A History of Sexuality in America.* New York: Harper and Row, 1988.

Goreau, Angela. *The Whole Duty of Women.* New York: Dial, 1985.

Grun, Bernard. *The Timetables of History.* 3d ed., rev. New York: Simon and Schuster, 1991.

Heilbrun, Carolyn G. *Writing a Woman's Life.* New York: Ballantine, 1988.

Jones, Anne Goodwyn, and Susan V. Donaldson. *Haunted Bodies.* Charlottesville: University Press of Virginia, 1997.

Kahn, Ada P., and Jan Fawcett. *The Encyclopedia of Mental Health.* New York: Facts on File Publishing, 1993.

Kerber, Linda K., and Jane De Hart Mathews. Women's America: Refocusing the Past. New York: Oxford University Press, 1982.

Lexington Gazette. Lexington, Va., 1895–1954.

Loughridge, Patricia R., and Edward D. C. Campbell, Jr. *Women in Mourning.* Richmond, 1985.

Miller, Nancy K. *Subject to Change: Reading Feminist Writing.* New York: Columbia University Press, 1988.

Ornstein, Robert. *The Roots of Self.* New York: Harper-Collins, 1995.

Register of Former Cadets. Memorial Edition. Virginia Military Institute. Lexington, Va., 1957.

Rockbridge County News. Lexington, VA, 1895–1955.

Sara, Dorothy. *Hand-Writing Analysis.* Secaucus, N.J.: Castle Books, 1981.

Scarf, Maggie. *Intimate Partners: Patterns in Love and Marriage.* New York: Random House, 1987.

Scott, Anne Firor. *The Southern Lady: From Pedestal to Politics, 1830–1930.* Chicago: University of Chicago Press, 1970.

Showalter, Elaine. *The Female Malady: Women, Madness, and English Culture, 1830–1980.* New York: Pantheon Books, 1985.

Trager, James. *The People's Chronology.* New York: Henry Holt, 1992.

Turner, Charles W., ed. *Mrs. McCulloch's Stories of Ole Lexington.* Verona, Va.: McClure Press, 1972.

———. *Mrs. Ecker's Lexington (1918–1929).* Roanoke, Va.: Roanoke Lithography and Graphics, 1990.

Wolfe, Margaret Ripley. *Daughters of Canaan.* Lexington: University Press of Kentucky, 1995.

Wyatt-Brown, Bertram. *Southern Honor: Ethics and Behavior in the Old South.* New York: Oxford University Press, 1982.

Index

Many of the individuals mentioned in the text are referred to by a single name, either first or last name. Whenever possible, these names have been completed for the index by consulting alumni directories or other biographical reference tools. Where no additional information was located, a qualifying statement has been added in parentheses.

The abbreviations KPL and GDL have been used for Katie Paul Letcher and Greenlee Davidson Letcher, respectively. Page references to illustrations are printed in italics.